FORTY YEARS
A
SALESMAN

A personal memoir of
40 years in the sale of
cranes and excavators
worldwide from
1958 to 1998

By Dick Lloyd

First published in 2005,
by Maygreen Publications.

ISBN No. 0 - 9550250 - 0 - 1

Printed in Great Britain

DEDICATION

This book is dedicated to my dear wife, Audrey, without whose unfailing support and love I could not have achieved what I did and enjoyed myself so much in doing it.

ACKNOWLEDGEMENTS

I started my researches to write these memoirs in 1999, soon after I retired, and I owe much to many of my old friends and colleagues for their contributions to my efforts.

First and foremost, the presentation of the work is entirely due to Bill Bromwich, former Publicity Manager at Priestman, who combines a truly artistic talent with an intimate knowledge of the latest publishing technology.   He is a perennial student, always willing to learn, which characteristic has made him an admirable partner in this enterprise.

David Steel's encouragement and the complimentary Foreword, tinged with dry humour, which he was kind enough to pen, have boosted my morale when it flagged, apart from the fact that I owe much to him for his opening up of opportunities for me throughout my chosen career.   To his cousin, Peter, I am indebted for anecdotes about his late father, Eric Steel, as also to Tunny Taft*. Bill Mowbray*, Frank Bacon, Vernon Leach, Bill Murray, Jeanine de Cock, Bobby Mazumdar and, above all, André Faes, all also made positive contributions to the Coles Section.   Bob Lester's widow, Tydfil, handed me a box of documents and old photos which have proved invaluable, for which I am very grateful. John Taylor provided the bulk of the historical information on R. H. Neal, and Fred Fusco helped with his own self-portrait.

Moving on to Hymac, Peter Hamilton* and Chris Wilson were both kind enough to read and comment on my draft, and Ron Walker and Don Hayes supplied valuable information on the history of Hymac after I had left the company. Tim Fisher, the man who shook hands in 1939 with Adolf Hitler, corrected my account of his inimitable experiences. Nick Johnson gave me Hymac brochures, invaluable advice on how to make the book appeal to a wider public, and then most kindly agreed to write a Postscript.

On my 14 years with Priestman, I was much assisted by Bill Bromwich, Stuart Anderson, Arthur Arundel, Charlie Hamshaw, Ron Draper*, Ken Deighton and Norman Taylor, and last, but by no means least, Kees Zeevenhooven. My source of information on Crown Cranes was Warwick Taylor.   Without Bill de Vigier* and his secretary, Lorna Powell, my account of the Acrow years would have been deficient and Norman Cunningham filled in some gaps.

I was most grateful to Eric Sennebogen Snr for telling me how he came to start his business, now a world-reknowned manufacturer, and Guy Alligand provided me with similar information on Manitou who are in the same category. Edelhart de Lille amended my historical notes on Sobemai, and finally my Polish colleague, Paweł Kędzierski, helped me to chronicle the changes from Communism to Capitalism in his country. My heart-felt thanks to all the above for their willing co-operation, some of whom (names marked with an asterisk*) are sadly no longer alive. If I have overlooked anyone else who assisted me, I offer my sincere apologies.

Dick Lloyd   June 2005

CONTENTS

FOREWORD

The reading public's appetite for memoirs is strong and will be sharpened further by this sparkling contribution from Dick Lloyd.

His is a picaresque journey through the bandit country of Communist Eastern Europe and elsewhere. Lloyd is the archetypal British exporter, "a man paid to go abroad and lie for his company". He and I were contemporaries in this field and I remember how, in the mid-sixties, some long-forgotten grandee in the Board of Trade urged us on with the slogan "Exporting is Fun".

Dick Lloyd always did his best to make it so.

Looking back on these adventures, it amazes me that he escaped death, imprisonment, serious injury , or legal process. Forever skating on thin ice, his appetite for risk and discomfort accelerates with age and we are invited to join him on every leg of his hair-raising progress towards retirement.

The value of these memoirs will increase as time goes by. I predict that in the future the "Lloyd Papers" will become an important source document for post-graduate theses on the origins of Export Marketing. Meanwhile, those of us lucky enough to discover them today will be well entertained.

David Steel,   Hillesden, June 2004
Former Managing Director, Coles Cranes Ltd.

PREFACE

How did I, a failed classical scholar from Felsted School in Essex, come to spend my whole career as a Crane and Excavator Salesman? My prep schooling had induced in me a strong interest in the Latin Language and with excellent teaching, this brought me a Minor Scholarship to Felsted, but to have accepted this was a mistake, only to be realised later. The teaching of Classics at Felsted was utterly boring. Halfway through I tried to switch to French, but it was not allowed, and the Senior French master was, in any case, an equally boring instructor, so it would probably have killed my enthusiasm for that language as well.

So, having, by some miracle, secured my place at Merton College, Oxford, for 1954, I left school with a very light heart in 1952 and joined the Royal Engineers as a National Service Sapper. It was only the magic of having been a CCF Cadet Sgt at Felsted which allowed me to choose the Arm of the Services which I wanted, and a retired RE Colonel friend of the family enthused me with the idea of becoming a sapper. It was a good choice. Although I struggled at the Officer Cadet SME at Gillingham with Bridge Classification, Mines and Demolitions etc (having not even done any basic Science at school), I scraped through and got my commission, and spent a very happy 12 months with RE Works Services at Port Said, where I had an independent job as a Liaison and Troop Welfare Officer, which did not demand any practical use of the training which I had received at Gillingham! It also gave me the chance to speak French and I started to teach myself Italian, but my bid to switch to Modern Languages at Oxford fell down because of lack of written and reading ability, and I ended up reading Jurisprudence, a general course of Law, which served me well in my chosen career, as did my hobby of learning to speak languages.

Three glorious years at Oxford came all too soon to an end and I had to get down seriously to considering a career. I attended the usual round of interviews with Shell, ICI, Unilever and the like, which these large firms provided for undergraduates in their final years, but they did not interest me. My RE experience told me that I must opt for an engineering firm. I had two opportunities, Rolls Royce and Coles Cranes.

Rolls Royce at Derby were looking for a Management Trainee. I was interviewed by a "Board" of grey-suited gentlemen with horn-rimmed spectacles. They tried to find out what sort of engineering background I might have, which was none. "I understand, Mr. Lloyd" said the 'Chairman of the Board', "that you run an old car."

This was true. I had a 1933 Morris Minor Tourer, which was maintained for me by an agricultural engineer (who also happened to be my namesake, Dick Lloyd) who operated his business from a Nissen Hut on a remote Welsh Border hillside near my home. However, I kept this information to myself at the interview.

"Suppose that you are driving with your girlfriend to a dance" the 'Chairman' continued, "and it starts to rain. Suddenly, your engine stops. What do you do next?" I could hardly reply: "Call the AA, sir", but really I had no other idea in my head, and in the end, I had to admit that I really did not know, and by that time I did not care either, because the last thing I wanted to do was to join a firm with such unfriendly oppressive people as my future bosses!

The interview with Robert Albon, Overseas Sales Director of Coles Cranes, at the Export Office at No 14 Berkeley Street in London's Mayfair, for the much more appealing post of "Export Trainee" went very differently.

"Well, Mr. Lloyd", he said, "suppose that you are calling on a Timber Yard with the intention of trying to sell them a crane, what would you look for?" This sort of question was much more to my liking, and I answered without hesitation that I would try to see what type of work was currently being done by hand which could much more easily be handled by a crane, and within minutes, Director Albon was telling me that he would like me to meet his Chairman, Mr. James Steel.

So, on September 1st, 1957, young Lloyd reported for his training at Crown Works, Sunderland, at that time the largest crane manufacturing plant in Europe, if not in the world. But not before I had had my first success as a salesman.

I had purchased my 1933 Morris Minor in 1955 for £45, and two years later I sold it for the same sum. In this I certainly had Beginner's Luck. I was in my last term at Oxford, swotting furiously for Finals, and I advertised it in the local Undergraduate Newspaper, which resulted in offers in the region of £20 to £25, with caustic comments about the amount of oil leaking from the rear brake hubs and other uncalled technical criticisms of my dear "Sue" (as the car was called after my first girlfriend). It was the Porter (bless him) who suggested that I advertise it instead in the local Oxford newspaper, and it was he who took the phone call from the widowed lady with the 17 year old daughter, who dwelt in a leafy suburb on the western side of the City.

Upon my arrival, this lady greeted me effusively with the words: "How kind of you to come", to which she added "we know nothing about cars - we are entirely in your hands". Technical knowledge about my old car was somewhat unnecessary - all that needed was some charm, coupled with hard business acumen.   After I had taken the young daughter for a short spin, carefully avoiding any crashing of the gears by the most practised double declutching, she told her mother that the car was wonderful and the sale was concluded on the spot.   I drove back to College with a cheque for £45 in my pocket, still in possession of the car for another two or three weeks (till after Finals), since, of course, as I took care to explain to the purchaser, there were formalities like arranging insurance which had to be completed for her before her daughter could be allowed to drive the car, for agreeing to do which I received more expressions of gratitude....   My father thought I ought to be ashamed of myself, but he was clearly so relieved that his son had actually landed himself a job, (followed, perhaps more surprisingly, by a Degree,) that he did not harp on the subject.

I do not think that I made any mistake in abandoning further pursuit of the Law instead of becoming a salesman.   In my last year my very academic Tutor, after reading my latest "Collection", as it was called, told me that it was "absolutely deplorable", and then added: "You are Lloyd, aren't you?"   He had been tuting me for a year, and still appeared not to know me....(Mind you, he was, if brilliant, somewhat odd, adopting the 18th Century habit of taking snuff whilst he conducted his Tutorial).   One of his written remarks on my paper went: "This the most amazing farrago of nonsense I have ever read!".

My first sale: My 1933 Morris Minor "Sue" standing outside Merton College, Oxford in 1957

Preface

Where it all began. The author at No. 14 Berkeley Street 45 years after he started life there as a Coles Cranes export trainee. The entrance to the offices remains totally unchanged

Coles 12 tonne S1210 Aeneas mobile on timber handling - answering the right question got me the job

COLES CRANES
CHAPTER ONE - STEELS

What sort of a Coles World did I enter upon in 1957? It is not the intention of this narrative to re-write the History of Coles, which was well documented in the Coles 100 Year Book published on the occasion of their centenary in 1979, but I think that a brief recap of the 20 years prior to my arrival on the scene is relevant.

The Derby days of Coles saw the innovation of the famous petrol-electric (soon afterwards diesel-electric) system, the brain-child of Arnold Hallsworth, a pupil apprentice who joined the company in 1918, and who took over as Chief Engineer and General Manager in 1927, and who was Managing Director when I joined in 1957.

Arnold Hallsworth was with Coles for 50 years, and really was the enduring symbol of the diesel electric era. Essentially a rather shy man, I found him quite approachable. He presided over some very difficult years in the early 1930s, when the company barely survived, and the big turning point came in 1937 with an order for 82 of the celebrated EMA cranes, which is the abbreviation for "Electro-Mobile-Aerodrome", with a capacity of 1.8 Tonnes at 2.7 metres radius, for the Air Ministry. This ensured the continued survival of Coles. It is interesting to note that Coles won this order in spite of the fact that their Tender did not meet the required spec, which was written around a non-slewing mobile crane which relied for its slew motion on a 3-wheel "castor" chassis. Coles had no experience with this type of product, so they decided to come up with a design incorporating a fully-slewing superstructure mounted on a separate self-propelled chassis and they won the Tender, and this order developed into a family of EMA cranes, with capacities increasing to 6 Tonnes.

The Takeover of Henry J. Coles of Derby by Steel & Co. Ltd. in 1939 was the beginning of the golden age for Coles. Steels were a family firm from Sunderland, which started life, by coincidence in the same year as Coles, 1879, founded by Lancelot Steel, as a Builders Merchants. He was succeeded by his son, Alfred, who died at any early age in 1920 after expanding the business to the extent that it already had a forge, foundry and assembly shops. His widow kept the business alive until his two sons, Eric and James were able to take it on. In 1937 Steels went public and in 1939 they acquired Coles for the princely sum of £26,000.

There are few still alive today who can recall the Derby era, but in 1999 I was fortunate in meeting Tunny Taft, then in his 87th year, who joined Coles in Derby in 1935, after serving his apprenticeship as a draughtsman with a Derby firm making corrugated steel pipes which expanded under heat and were much used in Power Stations. He started in the Drawing Office, and then graduated to preparing Instruction and Parts Manuals. He drew the images three-dimensionally by hand, and he went on to become the company's Publicity Manager, and he stayed with the Company up until his retirement in 1978. He remembers the sale of a diesel-electric mobile to Plymouth Dockyard in 1940, with a delivery date that was so urgent that it was decided to drive the crane all the way from Derby, which took several days, since stops had to be made after every hour or so to allow the electric travel motor to cool down!

Another very long served soldier for Coles was Bob Lester, who also started in the Drawing Office in 1935, and stayed with the firm until he retired in 1980 . When I joined Coles, Bob was already the Design Director, and he was the only director at that time who was known to everyone simply as "Bob". He always had a cheerful word for everyone. Bob was a great Team Leader and the men he assembled around him in the early fifties used their experience to establish a world-beating range of diesel-electric cranes, culminating in 1963 in the 100 Ton Centurion, but Bob knew by then that the future lay in hydraulics, and he hired specialists to get Coles really and truly in to the hydraulic era. I tried to get in touch with him again when I first started planning to write these Memoirs, but he was already too ill to receive me. After his death in January 2000, his widow handed over to me a host of documents about Coles, which have been very helpful to me. Amongst these were several of Bob's Notices to his Staff, from which it is very clear that he was a stickler for good Time-Keeping. Often the Notices were tinged with a dry humour, e.g. January 1950: "Drawing Office - Unwritten Law:"

"Noise - it is essential that the office is kept quiet. Whistling and singing is not permitted. We can buy a nightingale and a Vera Lynn if we require them."
"Tea Break: Anyone having sandwiches and cakes must be careful not to put crusts and crumbs in the wastepaper bins, as the place is over-run with rats, mice and cockroaches.

"In future, no cricket nor football is to be played within the Works, as too many windows are being broken. Anyone caught will be severely reprimanded. PS The Gestapo is on the prowl", and finally the moral code: "I have noticed lately a certain amount of undue familiarity between male and female members of the staff. This must cease immediately".

There is no doubt that Eric Steel was the driving force behind the company. Tunny Taft described him as a "human dynamo". He was also very much a man with the common touch - whoever knocked as his office, male or female, received the same greeting: "Come in, yer bastard". Eric was determined to bring some heavy industry to Sunderland, which was not concerned with ship-building, and this led to the acquisition of the Egis Shipyard on the banks of the River Wear, which was renamed "Crown Works" (in deference to the amount of Government work which the expanded group was undertaking) and to Crown Works the manufacture of Coles Cranes was progressively moved from Derby.

Crown Works suffered from problems with Unions, in common with many parts of British Industry, and I think that it has to be realised that almost all the original labour force were recruited from old shipyard workers. The cyclical nature of the shipbuilding industry made for strong Unions, and no Sunderland based employer at that time could avoid this problem.

Particularly strong were the Boilermakers, and inter-Union disputes were not uncommon. Eric Steel knew how to deal with militant shop stewards. His son, Peter, recalls that there was a particularly awkward shop steward called Charlie Black, who was extremely fat. Eric would give him a playful dig in the stomach in front of his mates, saying: "Charlie, if you are as fat as that, I am paying you too much", and all the others would laugh at him.

The division of responsibility between the two brothers was clear-cut. Eric ran the Works, and James did the selling. Eric was a workaholic (80 to 90 hours per week), but he was also a heavy smoker and rather overweight. According to Peter, he would see all the mail each day, divide it into piles for the attention of each departmental manager, who would then be called in, but not before Eric had picked out any problem areas and told the departmental manager to report back to him on them before the end of the day. Eric had a Company Airplane, a twin-engined De Havilland "Dragon Rapide", which was piloted by a clerk in the Purchasing Dept who was also an ex wartime Spitfire Pilot. Very often Eric would take over the controls himself in mid flight. I often heard it said of him that if he got to know of the illness (for instance) of the wife of one of the men in the Works, he would literally get out of his office and go expressly to see the individual to see whether there was anything which could be done to help.

Tragedy struck the Steel Group in 1956, when Eric suffered a severe heart attack whilst out hunting. He was carried home, still alive, and his son Peter told me that he is sure that, with modern medical techniques he would have survived, but the doctor who was called to his home decided to inject brandy directly into his heart and he died instantly.   I believe that this tragic event changed the course of history insofar as Coles Cranes are concerned.

James, far more reserved than his elder brother, had done a magnificent job in selling Coles world-wide.   From 1946, up until his brother's death, he travelled the world, setting up dealerships, but in 1956 suddenly he found himself having to accept also the tremendous responsibility carried by Eric.

I remember James Steel very well, " Mr. Jim", as he was affectionately known. Tunny Taft worked closely with him over many years.   Whilst Eric would make instant decisions, and very often mistakes, James was more cautious.   Tunny said: "He would have made a Good Vicar", but he added that he was an excellent boss, who took time to get to know, and who always stood by him in difficult situations.

Quoting from my own journal of the time:

"The trouble with Mr. Jim is that he can never relax, but is always on the go. Everyone is speaking of his brother Eric and what a very different man he was, who drove himself when he worked and played, but could forget everything when he chose and always had a cheery word for everyone".   This view of James is echoed by another ex Coles Employee, who started with the company in 1947, Vernon Leach. Vernon was one of the back-room stalwarts of the Coles Export Dept for nearly 40 years, and he recalled that James would ask questions about how a particular piece of business was going on when they were at the theatre entertaining distributors!

James's wife, Margaret, was a very warm and charming lady who made everyone instantly feel at ease.   I remember, when, as a young trainee, I danced with her at the 1958 Overseas Distributor Conference at Scarborough, that she said to me: "You are sure that you have not joined the wrong firm", to which I replied that I would go back to London and tell my pals who were working for Unilever or Shell that I would not swap with them for anything.   There was a great family feeling in Steels at that time.   The pride in the product at Crown Works was tremendous, and at that Dealer Conference several delegates got up and paid tribute to the Steel Family, expressing their strong gratitude and loyalty to the Company.

Eric Steel

C.B.E. FOR THE CHAIRMAN

For services to industry, the title of
Commander of the Order of the British
Empire was conferred upon the Chairman,
Mr. James Steel, by Her Majesty the
Queen in the New Year's Honours List.

Congratulations have been flowing in
and we would add our own – and reflect
those of our readers.

Mr. Steel was born in Sunderland in
1909, educated at Trent College and
trained in accountancy.   His whole
career has been spent with Steel and
Co. Ltd., originally a family business
which became a public company in 1936.

In 1936 Mr. Steel became sales director and subsequently assistant managing director.   He was appointed to
his present position on the death of
his brother, Mr. J. Eric Steel.

It has been during Mr. James Steel's time as chief executive that the
Group has expanded most rapidly to its present size and importance on
the international industrial scene.

In addition to his duties as active head of the Group, Mr. Steel finds
time to serve energetically on a wide variety of bodies governing various
aspects of British industry.   Amongst these are the Northern Regional
Board for Industry, the National Research Development Corporation, the
Wearside Productivity Association, the Federation of British Industries,
the River Wear Commissioners, the British Institute of Management, the
Institute of Directors and the Northern Gas Board.

CRANE MAKERS NEW CHAIRMAN

Mr. Arnold Hallsworth, Managing Director
of Steels Engineering Products Ltd., and a
member of the Board of Steel and Co.Ltd.,
has been appointed Chairman of the
Association of Crane Makers.

The appointment took effect from 13th May.
Mr. Hallsworth has been connected with the
Association continuously since 1929.

Coles Distributor Conference, 1959, held in Scarborough, where the Mayor, as guest of honour, was placed between James and Margaret Steel. A man of very small stature, he began his very witty speech with the words: "I am standing up, you know . . . "

COLES

MODERN CRANES.

Steam Cranes
Electric Cranes
Petrol Cranes
Diesel Cranes
Petrol-Electric Cranes
Diesel-Electric Cranes
Caterpillar Cranes
Mobile Cranes
Excavators.

HENRY J. COLES, LIMITED

Registered Office & Works:

LONDON CRANE WORKS

DERBY :: :: ENGLAND

ESTABLISHED 1879

Contractors to the British and Foreign Governments

Telephone No.	Telegrams:	Codes used
1266 Derby	"Coles, Derby."	A.B.C. (5th Edition) Bentley's

HENRY J. COLES Ltd. - LONDON CRANE WORKS, DERBY, ENGLAND

1929 Coles catalogue cover.

Coles 3 ton steam cranes for grabbing and hook duties

Coles Cranes

Two very early Coles petrol-electric lorry mounted cranes.

The first Coles petrol electric cranes came on self-propelled mobile chassis.

. . . and crawler mounted.

The crane which assured the survival of Coles in 1937, the famous "EMA" mounted on a Thorneycroft truck chassis of which hundreds were supplied to the R.A.F.

Coles helps the War effort. This picture shows a Coles crane in service with Royal Engineers preparing for the crossing of the Rhine by Montgomery's troops in 1944. The pontoon is being lowered into the water by bridging parties.

Diesel-electric rail cranes featured large in 1950's production line of
Crown Works, Sunderland.

Coles diesel-electric port tower version

Coles Cranes

The changing face of Coles

1879 Coles hydraulic crane

1879 Coles steam crane

1913 Coles direct petrol driven crane

1922 Coles petrol electric lorry crane

1924 Coles battery electric lorry crane

1928 Coles direct diesel mobile crane

1929 Coles petrol electric crawler mounted crane

1930 Coles direct diesel rail crane

Coles cranes have developed steadily and surely throughout the years, every advance in engineering knowledge has been adopted and adapted to improve their efficiency. As one of the earliest manufacturers to replace steam with internal combustion engines Coles progressively developed and subsequently discarded mechanical transmission, hydraulic transmission and different types of torque convertor before arriving at the ideal transmission for crane operation — the Coles Variable Voltage System.

1937 Coles all-pneumatic tyred petrol-electric crane.

1934 Coles diesel fluid drive crane

1935 Coles diesel electric mobile crane

1958 Coles modern diesel electric transmission crane

CHAPTER TWO - MY EARLY TRAINING

My own training commenced with a two month stint at Crown Works, where I came under the general direction of Bill Mowbray, who had just left the Drawing Office to act as Sales Liaison Manager, and there is no doubt that I owe a great deal to Bill for his guidance, coming, as I did, from a totally non-technical background.   I was indoctrinated with the benefits of the diesel-electric system as the perfect Power Transmission for cranes.   A general sales leaflet was put out by Coles in the late 50s in which it was stated that they had tried all systems, mechanical, hydraulic and electric and come to the firm conclusion that diesel-electric was the perfect answer.   In this brochure there was an illustration of a Coles hydraulic crane built in the 1880s, a rail-mounted crane, which was literally hydraulic - that is to say water-driven - and was designed to take its power from water stand-pipes at the side of the track.

This was hardly something to put in a Sales Promotion leaflet 50 years later as evidence that hydraulics were no good!   However there is no doubt that for precision handling, the diesel-electric principle was hard to beat.   Even official tests of modern day hydraulic cranes will allow for a certain amount of "creep", so that cranes for official testing are usually set up early in the morning when the hydraulic oil is cold.   On the Test Apron in Sunderland customers used to be invited to witness tests of 5 Tonne Loads cracking eggs without breaking them, or stopping alarm clocks without damaging them, and I doubt whether the most modern hydraulic crane could do that today.   The number of old Coles Diesel Electric cranes still in operation around the world is a tribute to their quality.   Having said that, there is no doubt that Arnold Hallsworth's passion for diesel-electric went overboard when he designed and built a prototype diesel-electric telescopic boom crane, named the S510, which, not surprisingly, never got beyond the prototype stage.   But if one sold a Coles Diesel Electric Crane for grabbing duties, as I did once to a customer in Greece, desperate to take the order against the much more suitable mechanical crane which was my competitor, then trouble soon broke out as electric motors overheated and burnt out in no time.

I got to know many of the Works Staff very well during my training period, and they would greet me whenever I went back with visitors, expressing strong interest and genuinely wishing me luck in my export venture.   One of the more colourful characters was Dave Edwards, the Assistant Service Manager, who had a large family of 12 children.   His conversation was liberally laced with the word "Fook", used either as a verb or in its adjectival version "Fooking".   He

had a rooted dislike for salesmen, whom he considered as an expensive super-
fluity to the crane business.

One evening he was working late on the Test Apron underneath a crane, trying
to fix a problem to the outriggers, just before an important Customer Day, when
a pair of smart patent leather shoes appeared at the side of the machine. "Fook
off" says Dave, taking a swipe at the shoes with his spanner, convinced that it
was just another layabout from the Sales Force. "Do you know who I am?", said
a cultured voice from above the shoes, and Dave was about to come out with
another expletive when warning bells rang in his head and he emerged from
underneath the crane and doffed his cap apologetically to Mr. James Steel! He
thought that he would get his "Fooking Cards", but the Chairman knew his true
worth and he didn't.

The company was not known at that time by the name of "Coles", but "Steels
Engineering Products", and indeed the early sales force were not just required
to sell Coles Cranes, but all other products produced at Crown Works, including EUK Catering Equipment. Because they were not very well designed, they
provided some entertaining stories. One such concerned a rep who appeared
in a Fish and Chip shop to investigate the problem with the Fryer. When he
enquired where the machine was located, the owner told him just to wait where
he was, and soon the machine, vibrating furiously, came in through the door of
its own accord! Another concerned a sales rep who spent all night trying to fix
a machine which heated water to the correct temperature for baking, and
appeared the next morning in the office covered from head to foot with flour.

However, the tale which caps all described the public launch of a Grain Dryer
patented by Steels, at the premises of a well-to-do Oxfordshire farmer. The unit
was installed in an old Tithe Barn on the farm and a week later the opening ceremony took place to which all the local bigwigs were invited.

On the appointed day, the guests were all assembled in front of the barn, champagne and canapés ready to be served. The tape cutting ceremony ensued and
the word given to the service engineer to start the drier up. There was a whin-
ing of electric motors and the drying trays started to clank round over the front
where the dried grain was supposed to appear. The machinery went on turning, but no grain appeared, and then there was the most terrible smell of burning bread and a load of blackened grain seeds resembling rabbit turds emerged
from the drying trays.

Frantic adjustments were made to no avail and suddenly the whole machine went up in flames. Unfortunately there was only one water point in the vicinity, used for filling the cattle trough about 10 yards away. The assembled males to a man did their best to quench the blaze from this inadequate source, but by the time that the Fire Brigade had arrived, the ancient tithe barn with the drier inside had been reduced to a heap of ashes.

However, by 1957 the UK Sales Force was organized on more professional lines, although training was confined to the periodic Home Sales Meetings held at Crown Works. I was an experiment, as the first ever "Export Sales Trainee". After two months "going through the Works", I was seconded to Home Sales for the remainder of my first year, to pick up what I could the hard way.

Home Sales was under the control of Reg Keates (Reginald Lionel Edward Keates, to give him his full name), who was also known as "El Supremo". Later on he acquired another nickname, "The Admiral", which referred to his War Service at Gravesend as a Chief Petty Officer. "Uncle Reg" was a character, albeit not a very pleasant one in many people's view. He ruled his Area Managers and reps with a rod of iron, and there was no love at all lost between him and my future boss, Robert Albon. Communication between the Home Sales Office in Sloane Street and the Overseas Sales Office in Berkeley Street was virtually non-existent.

Reg liked to spice his Sales Meetings with his own peculiar brand of sarcastic humour. We were all rather like the Victorian schoolboys in that passage in Oliver Goldsmith's poem, "The Deserted Village" about the village schoolmaster:

"Full well they laughed with counterfeited glee

At all his jokes, for many a joke had he..."

I remember when Reg, wanting to emphasise a point on administration procedures, passed the wastepaper basket around the class, and asked each rep in turn what it was.

After the last person had dutifully replied "A wastepaper basket, Mr. Keates", he suddenly screamed: " No, it ain't a bloody wastepaper basket - its the bloody filing system in all your area offices".

The other thing which he loved was the Demonstration Sale, where the hapless rep had to do his sales pitch in front of all his colleagues to either Reg himself, or an Area Manager. I recall one occasion when Frank Bacon, the rep for Birmingham, was trying to convince his Area Manager Ken Madin of the merits of the Coles diesel-electric system on a new rail crane as against his Smiths steamer. This was something which we were taught to do, by offering to go in a "do a survey". It was not too difficult to convince the owner of the economic savings which could be effected by the driver not having to spend two hours getting up steam in the morning before work, but when Reg, who had been acting as the customer's son, and interrupting the flow of Frank's discourse by offering him sweets, came up with the most important technical question: "Ere, Mr. Bacon, I suppose that on your newfangled diesel-electric crane, the driver can cook 'is bacon and eggs of a mornin' ", to which the luckless Frank, who, despite his surname, had to say "No", Reg told him that he'd gorn and lost the bloody sale...

There were pro- and anti-Keates factions within the Home Sales Force, and during a Sales Conference in Sunderland in January 1958, this produced a somewhat violent situation: An anti-Keates Newcastle rep started arguing with a pro-Keates rep from Sheffield after a serious drinking bout in the Roker Hotel. One was extremely drunk after downing a half bottle of whisky at one go, and the other was not far behind him, and the next thing that happened was that both men started a fight, and I was just too late to prevent a table full of glasses and bottles go crashing down on to the floor. With the aid of another rep I forced the two combatants apart and we held them down until they had cooled off, but moments later they were at each others' throats again and finally they repaired to the Seaburn Hotel to "have it out" with El Supremo himself.

I think that the Newcastle man was sacked, but then re-instated, because he was, in fact a very good salesman!

These Reps Evenings in the Roker Hotel were always very convivial. On another occasion (in the middle of the winter) we were all competing for the attentions of an attractive young lady travelling for "Phillishave", and finally, at about 10 pm she asked which of us was coming for a swim. Only I volunteered, and so won the day, but at some cost....

I spent my first few weeks in and around the Birmingham Area Office, where my mentor in the art of selling cranes was Frank Bacon. Frank joined Coles in 1949, as Office Manager to Robert Albon, who was later promoted to the position of Overseas Sales Director. Robert came from a military background, and after the War he was serving as Assistant Regional Commissioner of Police in Jerusalem. Frank recounted how Albon had witnessed a felon robbing a bank and as the man made his getaway with the swag, Albon drew his pistol and shot him dead. Within hours his photo was all over Jerusalem demanding his head in revenge, and the army had to rescue him to save his life, and so he arrived back in the UK with nothing. When Frank joined, he wanted him to look after the office so that he could get out and about amongst the customers and learn about selling cranes the hard way, and Frank said that they used to learn together, puzzling over spare parts and wondering which part of the crane they were intended for!

After a couple of weeks with Frank, I was anxious to go out on my own, and shortly after that I was sent down to South Wales to spy on the local rep, old John Wright Hamer, a Mancunian who had lived for years in Cardiff, and whom Reg wanted out. I had to report at what time he collected me from the hotel in the morning and how many calls we made in the day. Since old John did most of his business over the bar at the Glamorgan Wanderers Rugby Club, my reports had to be the figments of my imagination, but it had a marvellous spin-off in that during my two weeks down there there was a big rugby match at the Arms Park, Cardiff vs Australia, (which resulted in a victory for Cardiff by 14 pts to 11!) I wandered into the Club on the morning of the match and some kind soul enquired "Hullo, boyo, are you going to the Match", to which I replied that I hadn't got a ticket. " 'Aven't got a ticket - Ooh, that's bad" he replied, and then he shouted across the bar to one of his mates: "Dai Bach, got another Steward for you", and I had a first class view of the game!

The next stage in my training was to be sent out on my own into the wilds of West Wales to do some cold canvassing. They did not provide me with a car, so I used my own, a 1934 Austin 7, (which had replaced my 1933 Morris Minor), and was paid the princely sum of fourpence ha'penny per mile.

After doing my sales pitch one day in a run-down ironworks, where there was no more chance of selling a crane than a Bren-gun Carrier, I got my front wheel stuck in the railway lines which crossed the yard and had to return to the office for assistance to be winched out. After that most embarassing incident, I used to park the car out of sight round the corner before making my calls. After several weeks of this, I got bored and wrote to Ken Madin, the Birmingham Area Manager asking for a transfer to London. Ken agreed, but the reaction from Uncle Reg was rather different: "Oo the 'Ell does this young jackanapes think 'e is, telling us where to send 'im. London! Send the young pup to Manchester". This time I was provided with a real company car, made available by the summary dismissal of another Area Manager. One of my first assignments there was to be present at the delivery of an L3010 truckmounted crane to Frankie Marler of Dukinfield, an illiterate scrap metal-cum-crane hire merchant, who paid for his crane in dirty £1 notes. Young Lloyd duly turned up in his best suit, and picked his way across the filthy yard to the scruffy tin shack in the corner which was Frank's office.

"Good morning, Sir, Coles Cranes", I announced. The reply was unexpected, to say the least. "You from Fooking Coles! Well Fook Off outside my Fooking Yard this Fooking Minute!" When I enquired what was the problem, he replied: "Paintwork ont' crane is disgoosting. It'll have to be re-painted". I suggested that we take a look together and told him that I didn't think that it was too bad, which again landed me in trouble: "Listen, lad, I'm Fookin' Customer, and Fookin' Customer's always right". Since the situation was more than I could cope with I called up the local Service Supervisor, who promptly came to my rescue and said: "Thee won't worry about Paintwork, Frank, when thee starts earning brass wit' Crane", but Frank protested that "Young lad tried to argue with me, and I'm Customer . . . ". The Area Manager, a smoothie from London called Bernard Burden, who normally sipped gin and tonics, tried to solve the problem in the pub, but after 10 pints of bitter Frank still insisted that the crane be re-painted and finally, after he had got someone to write on his behalf to James Steel, he got it re-painted.

Reg. Keates and his team in 1950. He is third from right at back, with pipe in mouth. On extreme left is Vernon Leach and next but one to him at the back is Vic Canham. A true gentleman, Vic put up with Reg. until 1972 when, following the Acrow take-over, Vic assumed his mantle after he left the Company. Vic was held in very high esteem by the 1970s generation of Coles U.K. salesmen

STEELS
NEWS BULLETIN

Volume II, No. 22   Published by Steel & Co. Ltd., Sunderland, England   October, 1959

COLES TAKE OVER

and SAVE £1000 in six months

IT is common knowledge that a diesel-electric crane is more economical than a 'steamer' of equal lifting ability, but it is not so generally known by how much.

Figures sent to us recently however, by Jessop, Saville Ltd. of Sheffield, provide an answer to this problem and demonstrate how the cost of changeover to modern materials handling plant can literally be recovered in months.

For many years this company operated several locomotive type steam cranes, but with the continually increasing cost of coal fuel and the need for expensive maintenance and periodic boiler inspection coupled with waste steaming time, it was decided to invest in two COLES cranes.

The cranes were duly delivered—one, a model S710c and the other a model S1210c. After six months it was possible to compile a table of comparative performances which we reproduce below:

MONTH	FUEL USED GALLS.	PRICE PER GALL. s. d.	TOTAL £ s. d.	8 TON STEAM CRANE	£ s. d.
August	30	1 3	1 17 6	Average tons	
September	23	1 3	1 8 9	of coal fuel	
October	22	1 3	1 7 6	per month:	
November	34	1 3	2 2 6	11	
December	23	1 3	1 8 9	Cost per	
January 1959	29½	1 3	1 16 11	month	60 10 0
	Total for 6 months £	10 1 11		Total for 6 months £	363 0 0

From the above it will be seen that over a period of 6 months a saving was effected of no less than £350 on fuel costs alone. And this wasn't all! The cost of labour for 'getting up steam', 'damping' and 'watering' amounted to something like £25 per month. In the same period, therefore, an additional saving of £150 was effected in this direction.

Routine maintenance service costs on the S710c were assessed at £42. On the steam crane they amounted to £60.

No wonder Jessops are delighted!

In six months using only two COLES cranes they saved no less than £1,000.

ABOVE RIGHT:—
One of the cost-cutting COLES in action

Last minute plans are discussed by the Sparrow Brothers before taking their newly acquired, heavy lifting COLES Conqueror on its marathon journey to their headquarters in Bath.

The economic advantages of a Coles diesel-electric crane over a "steamer" are clearly illustrated here.

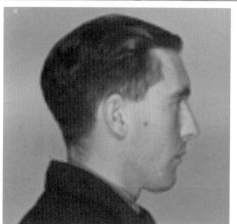

Bob Lester, Coles Design Director, served
in the R.A.F. in the second world war as a
navigator

Old colleagues from Coles get together in 1999. From the left, Dick Lloyd, with Bill Mowbray, Bill Scott and Allan Bent, all long serving Crown Works men

My first mentor in selling cranes, Frank Bacon

"Tunny" Taft at age 86 who joined Coles in 1935

CHAPTER THREE - MY EXPORT CAREER BEGINS

In September 1958, it was decided that my "Training" was complete, and after a fruitless attempt by Reg to keep me on Home Sales permanently, I was transferred to Export. Here the setup and the atmosphere was totally different. 14 Berkeley Street had the atmosphere of a respectable Gentlemen's London Club. Robert Albon was not really a dedicated Export man, but he was a highly respected figure, very direct, and the complete opposite to Reg Keates. He was certainly a man who could take decisions, unlike his predecessor, Basil Wakefield, who was reputed to believe that all problems would eventually go away if left unattended long enough. Vernon Leach told me that Basil Wakefield's typical response to any problem was to "put it on the side", and then it would go away of its own accord.

It is said that, on one occasion, a contract for several cranes arrived in the office from the Indian Government, and Wakefield tore it up without reading it, considering that it was of no importance, and, when the mistake was realised, he had all the staff searching the wastepaper baskets and putting the document back like a jigsaw puzzle!

Not long after I joined the Export Dept. I dropped a clanger which I thought might cost me my job, but here Albon's magnanimity really showed itself. I was commissioned to hand carry a Tender Document for ten cranes up to the City. Luckily for me, as it turned out, it was a lost cause, because the order had already been placed elsewhere, but the work had been done and it was decided still to submit the Tender. When I got out of the train at the Underground station nearest to my destination, I realised with horror that I had been so engrossed in a book that I had left the Tender Document on the bench of the station where I had boarded the train.

I rushed back on the next train, only to find that it had already been handed in and was on its way to the Lost Property Office from where it could not be recovered for at least three days, by which time the deadline for submission of the Tender would have passed. There was nothing for it but to return to the office and face the music, wondering if I would still have a job at the end of the day. Robert was a far-seeing man and his comment was short and to the point: "All I can say, young Dick, is that every Dog has his Day, and by God this is yours!"

Robert Albon's No 2 was Derrick Matthews, a gentle man in every sense of the word, whose politeness to colleagues was unfailing and he ran the administrative side of the business.   There were two other seasoned travellers, George Ricketts, who had been a Japanese prisoner of war, and Jack Trefusis, a rather superior individual who thought himself as good as the boss, and in fact George told me that they squared up to each other on one occasion and nearly came to blows! Trefusis left the company around the end of 1958, and in 1959 two more experienced guys came on board, John Isaacs, another ex Army Major, and Eric Drew, who came from the Lift Truck business.   John was a man of great charm and bonhomie, but, unfortunately, as I later learned, had a major drink problem. Eric was a rather crusty, but extremely good-hearted middle-aged bachelor.

Originally there had been a third traveller, one Major Botterill, who used to walk (or perhaps march, straight as a ramrod) from the Roker Hotel in Sunderland to the Works clad in a dark jacket and pin-stripe trousers, shirt with a winged collar, spats and bowler hat, carrying a rolled umbrella, but he had been fired because he was an extreme alcoholic.

I came to know the Major personally a bit later on because he introduced me to the Bulgarian and Rumanian markets, where he had started a representation business. He had stopped drinking by then, but I did not find him very easy to get on with, and I cannot say that he ever really taught me anything!   Naturally he always addressed me by my surname only.....

George Ricketts was the real character of the setup.   He used to go away for months on end, and it was said that his wife, whom I never met, had a great resentment against the company for this reason.   He had a huge map on the wall detailing all his travels, and he was an excellent mimic and raconteur.

In May 59 he was just completing a trip already several weeks long around SE Asia, when he received a cable instructing him to proceed to China to negotiate a Tender for 30 cranes.   The Chinese Communist bargaining technique was Third Degree, leaving him totally alone during the day, and then arriving at the hotel at 10 pm "to talk clane", until 3 am.   He said that it was like talking to masks, with no reaction whatever to his sales pitch, and whenever he stopped for breath, he was told to carry on.   I suppose that his experience as a PoW of the Japs must have stood him in good stead.

In the autumn of 1958, my very first trip was to Belgium.   I was so nervous at the check-in desk at West London Air Terminal that I left my passport, ticket and travellers cheques on the counter, and only realised it when they called my name over the Tannoy.   The Coles Dealer at the time was an aristocratic Walloon company run by Chevalier Guy Kraft de la Saulx and his smooth and rather wily son, Roland, and they just led me a dance with all kinds of technical problems, all discussions being deliberately carried out in French.

I think that Robert Albon realised that he had made an error by pitching me into such a situation, so the next trip was to a place where I could not do any damage and possibly some good, and that was Yugoslavia. It has to be remembered that few, if any, European Crane Manufacturers at that time had penetrated behind the Iron Curtain. Yugoslavia was quasi-Communist in that there were some State-run Agencies who were allowed to compete with each other, but they all had a plethora of franchises. Our main competition was from Jones, who had had the foresight to equip their Agent with a brand new Land Rover to get out and visit customers. Under pressure Coles had reluctantly sent out a clapped out old Ford Service van, and the Agent, Masinokomerc, was very disgruntled. This was the hostile scenario into which I was pitched, and after the first few very frustrating days of my visit, I was so depressed that I nearly took a plane back to London to throw in the towel. Hours of work were from 0700 to 1400. On my first morning I was kept waiting until about 1000 before the representative of Masinokomerc deigned to show up, and then only to complain about the bloody Ford van. Once work was finished, I was left on my own to wander desolately about Belgrade, not exactly a very interesting tourist spot.

My diary includes a number of programmes in Serbo-Croat for concerts, opera etc and I even found the odd cinema with English language films showing.

However this proved to be good training for my future career in selling cranes overseas. Firstly it made me very appreciative of hospitality as a lone traveller, and secondly it prepared me for what eventually became my speciality - Eastern Europe, which, 30 years later, stood me in good stead.

But back to Yugoslavia in 1958. It took me up to the middle of 1959 to secure my first order, and in the process I sacked Masinokomerc and appointed Jugohemija, who did sterling work for Coles over the next many years. Before leaving this chapter in my early career, let me relate one anecdote. During one of my negotiations, I invited the Port of Rijeka, a Coles user, to send a service engineer to Sunderland for training. The guy duly arrived by train and I met him at Victoria station in London, wined him and dined him and showed him the sights (including taking a photo of him standing next to Marshal Tito at Mme Tussaud's), and put him on the train at Kings Cross. Just before he left, he wrote a postcard to his wife, which I addressed for him. A few days later I was in Rijeka Port, to be given a very cool reception. The wife was waiting for me in the Chief Engineer's Office in tears with the postcard on which I had written the address, which told her that he had been arrested by the police on arrival in London and put in prison for three days! I just could not credit it, and it was not easy to convince the wife and the Chief Engineer that it was a complete figment of his imagination!!

At the beginning of 1959, Robert Albon decided to send me out to South America, which was a largely uncharted territory. Noting my interest in learning languages, he had arranged for me to take Spanish lessons during my training with Home Sales.

He was very well in with Shell in London, and he had just appointed an new dealer in Venezuela. In January 59 he accompanied me to Venezuela and I spent several weeks with the new dealer whom he had appointed. At that time the Venezuelan Bolivar was as hard a currency in Latin America as the US Dollar and the country was full of ex-Pats. These were a mixture of Americans, Brits, Dutchmen and East Europeans who had escaped the clutches of Communism. The new Coles Dealer was a company called ACO whose main business was selling American cars, Willys Jeeps and Hyster Forklift Trucks, and the company was owned and managed by Estonians. They had a very colourful salesman in Caracas named Bela Zeley, a Hungarian by birth, who had left his native land in 1944 just before the Communists took over, and had lived for a year or two in Germany and then arrived in Paris. At that time in France all foreigners had to do six months manual labour in order to get a permit to stay. He stuck at the pick and shovel work for two weeks, when one day he found himself labouring next to a railway line in the midday heat. A train stopped and he saw the first class passengers sipping cool drinks prior to luncheon in the Restaurant Car, and he threw down his pick and shovel there and then. When he was down to one shirt and trousers without the price of a meal, he purchased a pack of razor blades from Pringtemps with his last few francs, and sold them one by one at a large profit. From there he progressed to ties, job lots of old stock   Second hand typewriter sales eventually funded him a passage to Argentina, where he became a citizen (having learnt Spanish on the boat), and then he moved on to the more lucrative world of Venezuela. Zeley was a high pressure salesman who frightened the life out of me by the way in which he drove his jeep around Caracas, whose one ambition was to sell whatever he had available with a total disregard for the customer's actual needs.

"I VILL SELL AND HE VILL BUY" was his motto, and a customer needing a Lift

Truck to lift 2000 lbs would succumb to Zeley's salesmanship and buy one to lift 4000 lbs, because that was all that he had in stock.

Venezuela was a complete contrast to Yugoslavia, but, however exciting for a visit, it put me off any idea of spending time overseas just for the money. I could sense the falseness and the homesickness of the typical ex-pat's life. However, when I really got fed up with Coles a little later on, it did tempt me to apply for a job as a locally based Regional Manager for a Sheffield Steel Manufacturer, but by that time I was married and realised that it would be no life for a young English wife stuck on her own in a strange country, whilst I travelled the Sub Continent.

In November of that same year, 1959, Albon decided to send me on my own to Peru, Bolivia and Chile. It should be remembered that in those days nearly all overseas sales reps were ex Army officers in their 40s and 50s who had fought in World War II, not young men in their 20s. On a Sunday afternoon I flew to Amsterdam and stayed there overnight. On the Monday morning I boarded a KLM Super Constellation and after stops at Frankfurt, Zurich, Lisbon, Santa Maria, Curacao, Panama and Guyaquil, 42 hours later I fell out at Lima Airport. No one met me, and there was no message about an hotel booking. So I had to put my Spanish to the test by finding my own hotel, and the next morning I visited the Agent, Peruvian Trading Company. They were not in the least interested in me, my visit or my company, and after several frustrating days I had a Stand-Up row with the Managing Director and finally got some activity going, although I felt like firing them on the spot, but hesitated because of my inexperience. However I had the fascination of seeing Lima at a time when it was safe to walk about the city without being mugged and to record the clapped out 1920s vintage cars which thronged the streets on my cine camera.

I recall one trip outside Lima, to a steel works at Chimbote, further up the coast, which also boasted a fish factory, and when the wind changed in the middle of the night, the stink woke me up, and, despite the intense heat, I was forced to shut the window.

I finished my week with another day of broken promises and a further straight speaking session with the MD and when my handwritten report reached London, Robert Albon wrote a blistering letter to the Managing Director of Peruvian Trading protesting at the way I had been treated, to which came back the succinct reply: "Dear Sir, What do you expect if you send an immature young schoolboy out here?" I smarted for days over this unfair rebuke, but had to accept being teased about it.

There was one more unforgettable character in the Coles Export Office of that time, and that was Lindsay Watkins, the old Etonian Liaison Officer, whose job it was to keep in touch with the Commercial Departments of the High Commissions and Embassies, who were important for business in those post colonial days. Lindsay lived on a houseboat on the Thames during the summer and supplemented his income by renting his Esher home to wealthy American tourists. In the winter he returned to his more comfortable abode and let the houseboat out to impecunious students.

He was a man of the Old School, who was a member of the Devonshire Club, where his nickname of "Trade", presumably since all the other members were professional men. He would have been branded today as highly racist, with comments like: "I am just off to lunch with the Monkeys", when he had been invited to lunch at the Nigerian High Commission, but such remarks were always in the best of humour, and his manners towards African diplomats were always impeccable. He teased me unmercifully about the letter from Peru, and greeted me daily with the words "And how is my immature young friend?"

(When the Berkeley Street office was closed and the company moved to Steel House at Eastcote, Lindsay suggested to James Steel that he should provide him with a car to travel to the office, because he could not afford it out of his "minute honorarium", and a Ford Anglia was duly provided).

However, that late 1959 trip turned out to be one of the most interesting of my whole life, since instead of flying direct from Lima to La Paz, I flew in an unpressurized Dakota of Fawcett Aviation to Cuzco, and as we climbed to over 4000 metres, the passengers all had to don oxygen masks. Not only did I see Cuzco, but I also visited the lost city of the Incas at Macchu Picchu. This was before it had become a well-trodden part of the international tourist trail. We travelled on a narrow gauge railway up over the mountains, so steep in one part that the train had to switch back and forwards in a zig-zag fashion to overcome the incline, and then down the wild valley of the Urubamba River which tossed its way down the valley right next to the railway track. Then I continued my journey across the Andes by "main line" train, passing all day through some magnificent scenery, and riding most of the time on the platform outside the "First Class " compartment, to avoid the appalling smell of the lunch being cooked in the galley which adjoined it (of which I did not partake, needless to say). In the evening the train deposited me on the shores of Lake Titicaca, which I crossed overnight in an old paddle steamer named "Inca", which had been built in Hull in 1905, shipped in sections, and then brought up from the coast in parts on the backs of mules and assembled by the side of the Lake. Another train took us on to La Paz, winding for a full hour around the sides of the huge crater at the bottom of which the Bolivian capital is located. The agent proved to be much more co-operative, but the possibility of selling any cranes was somewhat remote. I was presented with a silver coin, one of the first ever minted by the Spanish conquistadores, and I decided to have this mounted on a silver ring as an amulet, and some 20 years later, when I was in Bogota, I had a very unpleasant experience connected with this ring. I was attacked and mugged in broad daylight whilst walking in a park near the city centre. I suppose that I had travelled so much in Latin America by then that I had not realised how dangerous it had become. With watch and wallet already gone I was being sat on by three young men with long knives threatening my chest, trying to stop them taking my ring, but in vain, and probably it was lucky for me that they did not have to cut my finger off to take it.

My last port of call on this most memorable 1959 trip was Chile, where Coles had a very professional dealer, and my visit was the first they had received after that of the drunken and arrogant Major Botterrill. The local Manager was an old Scotsman named Alexander Samson, to whom I put the question whether he ever became homesick for Scotland, to which he replied drily: "Och, aye, I used to. But I went home after the Warr and spent a whole winter in Scotland. It rained every day and it cured me of my homesickness".

During my trip I found an old Coles Steam Crane still in operation with Ferrocarriles del Estado, the State Railways. Its serial no was 347 and I estimated that it must have been built in about 1885. The crane driver had been operating it for over 30 years.

I came back from my trip really hoping that I would be given the chance of being the Coles Area Rep for South America, but that was not to be, since things were about to change radically..

In between trips abroad life in the Export Dept at 14 Berkeley Street was not very arduous. There was not much to do apart from reporting on the trip, doing any follow up work required and preparing for the next trip. We were supposed to devote time to calling on Consulting Engineers in the City, because all the day to day Admin Work was done by Derrick Matthews and his staff. The office did not open until 9.30 am, and most of us were off home soon after

5 pm. This was good for me, since in April 59 I became engaged to my Yorkshire girlfriend, Audrey, who had been the Light of my Life during my Home Sales Training in Manchester, and I was able to take time off looking for flats etc without too much difficulty, quite apart from cutting off early on a Friday to travel up to Manchester to spend the weekend with her, before she moved to London. Shortly after our engagement, I was sent to the Republic of Ireland, from which short visit I arrived at Heathrow Airport still in a very inebriated state, but I was quickly brought down to earth by my fiancée who had been flat-hunting. This was probably a warning to her of what it would be like for the next 40 years being married to a world-wide travelling crane salesman. Robert Albon and his wife were guests at our Wedding, and he thoughtfully arranged a trip to Italy for me in October, so that we could save one airfare on our belated honeymoon trip, which was a considerable bonus in the days before cheap air travel.

The beginning of 1960 was a time of great uncertainty and depression in the Coles Export Division, following the acquisition by the Steel Group of R.H. Neal of Ealing and Grantham, makers of mechanical, and F. Taylor & Sons of Manchester, of hydraulic cranes. The object of this amalgamation, according to the Financial Times in February 1959 was "to combat the bid of Continental crane manufacturers for world markets." It continued: "In anticipation of the European Common Market manufacturers in Germany and France have been closing their ranks and rationalising their production which puts them in a favourable position to compete with the larger but less integrated British industry". If one sees what is left of the British Crane Manufacturing Industry today, this comment has a certain historical interest!

Robert Albon was not involved in, nor was he consulted about the proposed amalglamation of the Export Division. The hierarchy were closeted in his office, leaving him to wander unhappily around the Admin Dept, totally excluded from what was being discussed and decided. Finally, when the news broke, it was like a bombshell.

The Export Division was to move temporarily to the offices of Neal in Ealing, whilst a completely new Sales HQ was being prepared in Middlesex, and the new Department, amalgamated with Neal Export Sales was to be designated "British Crane Company". A new sales organization under the even more grandiose title of "International Crane and Excavator Corporation" was to be set up in New York to handle Latin America, and another in Switzerland to look after the Common Market (even today Switzerland is still outside the EEC!).

Coles Cranes

The new Export Director in Ealing was to be the Neal Export Manager, Ron Cooke, with Albon relegated to a position of Regional Manager under him. We all felt sorry and angry for Robert Albon, at the shabby treatment which he had received, and I started to think seriously about going abroad for a few years, and decided to confide in him, because I was sure that he would leave the newly created British Crane Company.

However finally I decided that I must fight my own corner within it, partly because both sets of parents were very disturbed at the possibility of Audrey and me going overseas, and, indeed, I had doubts myself about the wisdom of such a move in career terms. So I sought a meeting with Ron Cooke. Although he seemed a likeable bloke, he lacked the presence and authority of Albon, and shocked me by telling me that I would be taken off "outside" duties and put "inside" because my Coles experience was needed to assist Dennis Mattingley, who was to be my new immediate boss, who was a Neal/ex Jones man. So I told Cooke that I wished to be considered for a position in the new Swiss setup, which was to be called "Steel AG", and the next day I discussed the whole problem with Albon, who totally agreed with me.

Furthermore he indicated that he himself had the prospect of a new job involving setting up a UK and Export Organization, and that there would be excellent opportunities for me, if I cared to join him. In the meantime, he advised me to write directly to James Steel, which I did, and Mr. Jim came down to London to see me, as a result of which he offered me the position of No.2 to the new Swiss boss, yet to be appointed. It is indicative of the estranged relationship between Robert Albon and James Steel that, when asked by me for his advice prior to the meeting, he replied tersely: "From that man, get something in writing, not just a verbal promise".

I still have the letter which contained phrases like: *"Your application for a position with our proposed European marketing company has been carefully noted......The salary will be fixed at the time commensurate with the duties involved and the cost of living in Switzerland. It is too early for me to say what this will be but I am sure that we will have no difficulty in coming to agreement on it".* In other words no real commitment was made.

On Friday, March 18, 1960. we had a party to mark the closing of the Overseas Sales Department at No. 14 Berkeley Street, when we presented Robert Albon with a tankard inscribed: "To the Guv'nor, with sincere appreciation from all at 14 Berkeley Street", and when he and Mrs. Albon left late in the evening, we cheered them off.

Robert Albon's three-and-a-half year association with Kato Cranes as marketing consultant has ended. He began his 30 year career in the crane industry In 1948 when he joined Steels Engineering Products (later to become Coles Cranes). For 17 years, until 1977, he held the position of sales director with John Allen (now Grove Cranes).

CRANES TODAY 1981

Robert Albon at our wedding in July 1959, and at the end of his career

Coles Cranes

Vol. II, No. 11   STEELS NEWS BULLETIN   April, 1955

BETTER CONTACT BETWEEN SALES ORGANISATION AND OUR U.K. PLANT

Appointment of three new Overseas Sales Executives to make regular visits

Every Distributor throughout the world is on our visiting list!

It is with great pleasure that we announce the appointment of three important new Executives to our staff:

Major R. Botterill
Mr. R. J. R. Trefusis
Mr. G. A. Ricketts

These men all combine three kinds of experience which will be invaluable to both you and us but which are difficult to find in any one man, they have their basic training in engineering, long experience in selling and a wide knowledge of countries overseas. For many months now they have been undergoing a course of intensive training at our Works and we are satisfied that they will be of great assistance to you in developing your market for COLES.

We shall be writing you separately to inform you how soon one of them will be visiting you.

Jack Trefusis

Major Botterill

George Ricketts

The original Coles Export Sales Team.

Venezuela in 1959. Maiquetia airport and downtown Caracas

Robert Albon relaxes
in the Hotel Tamanaco
pool and young Lloyd
inspects the garbage
people's houses

Bela Zeley: "I vill sell and he vill buy"

Coles in the interior

Coles Cranes

Left: Lima in 1959, and above, the Lost City of the Incas, Macchu Picchu.

The highest airport in the world

The Lake of Titicaca

BRITISH CRANE

CHAPTER ONE - PERSONALITIES AND POLITICS

The second phase in my career began with my first visit to the Neal Works at Grantham, just after the closure of the Coles Export Office in Berkeley Street in March 1960. We were met by the Works Manager, Bert Ward, who told us something of the Neal Company, how they had started in the 1920s at Ealing with agencies for cranes, expanding into manufacture under licence. There were three Neal brothers, Norman, Brian and Herbert. Dysart Works at Grantham began almost by accident. It had been built by Ruston & Hornsby, and when they transferred diesel engine production to Lincoln, one of the Neal brothers went up there to buy some machine tools, and ended up by purchasing the whole place outright in 1937. Ward was of the opinion that they could have expanded much more than they did, but that they never had a lot of money to invest and were always too cautious, and the fact was that none of them were businessmen. Norman, the boss, had a bad stammer, Brian was something of a playboy, who deserted his wife for a Belgian countess, and Herbert, responsible for finance, was reputed to have been so averse to paying expenses that, instead of paying out everything in £1 notes, he would opt for coins of lower and lower monetary value, because it gave him the impression that he was paying out less money! I was struck by the unhurried atmosphere of the place, and I realised that the Coles brain-washing which I had received on the total inefficiency of the diesel-mechanical as opposed to the diesel-electric system was a long way from fact.

The oldest surviving employee of R.H. Neal, John Taylor, started with them in 1946, as office boy. He told me that there were 35 applicants for the post. He had just come out of the RAF, where he had served during the War as a pilot in Coastal Command, in the UK, Algeria, Tunisia, Italy and France. He rose to be UK Sales Manager by the time of the Take-Over by Steels, but Reg Keates was not going allow any Neal executive into his Coles Empire (although I suspect that he had a lot to do with Robert Albon's demotion), and John was sent to Grantham to act as the Works Sales Liaison Manager.

The Neal crane was very robustly constructed. The NS 150, which could handle 15 tons free on wheels, weighed in at 28.5 tons and had no outriggers. It was destined especially for cycling work in steelworks. The NS 70 (7 tons free on wheels) had a very sophisticated precision hoist arrangement which could equal that of Coles. The problem was that each crane was designed by a different draughtsman, and there was absolutely no commonality of parts between models. Instead of harmonizing the design of all models using well-tried Neal technology, Coles arrogant production-orientated solution to this was to scrap the whole of the Neal Range and substitute it with a Coles mechanical system, utilizing Coles reduction gearboxes and Coles electro-mechanical brakes operated by air. The result was nothing less than a technological disaster. The "fail-safe" air-mechanical brakes on a grabbing crane sold to a Danish Port failed to danger instead and the grab went straight through the bottom of the boat's hull! All this change was too much for poor old Bert Ward, who had a complete nervous breakdown and sadly took his own life early in 1963.

In addition to their own home-designed products, Neal also manufactured two hydraulic machines under licence, the Hymax, a low capacity non-slewing crane designed for low headroom work and the Pelican, a small loader with an hydraulic grab. So, apart from continuing to build these two units, the Neal Works was turned over to the manufacture of Neal-Unit mechanical excavators, which was part of a deal for the Unit Crane and Shovel Corporation of Milwaukee to build Coles Cranes in the USA. The Neal-Unit was launched to the public at the Public Works Exhibition in November 1960, and attracted some derisory comments from the real excavator men from companies like RB and NCK. We Coles salesmen did not have a clue about selling earthmoving equipment, and, that apart, the Unit was essentially built as a crane, not as a navvy like the RB.

However, the Grantham Works tradition of high quality workmanship persisted, and it is interesting to note that in later years Grantham produced some of the very best Coles hydraulic cranes, the famous RT Husky Range. Grantham also never had the industrial relations problems which bedevilled Sunderland. Peter Steel, who ran the Grantham Plant from 1971 to 1976, told me that he only faced one major strike, when a large order for Libya prompted the militant Shop Convener to provoke a strike for higher wages. Peter sacked the Shop Convener and told the workforce that, if the strike did not end quickly, he would close the plant and put everyone out of a job including himself, and, after a week of meetings, when the men realised that he would not back down, they came back to work. Needless to say the militant was not re-instated.

Back in 1960 my first visit to Neal was soon followed by a visit to F. Taylor and Son of Manchester, the other crane manufacturer acquired by Steel and Co. The Taylor brothers had started business by buying up surplus War Department equipment and re-selling it at a profit. The crane business began when they mounted a home made hydraulic crane on an ex WD chassis, but this gradually expanded into a technically orientated business which was not what they were geared up for. One of the brothers died, leaving heavy death duties, and a smart cash offer of £350,000 from Steels was just what they were looking for. It so happened that during my training period on Home Sales in Manchester in 1958, I had had occasion to visit Taylors and to have a chat with the Sales Manager, who was very open and told me that he had been in very serious trouble with the Ministry of Transport over the Taylor Jumbo self-propelled crane travelling on the road at over 20 mph. The crane had rear wheel steering and had gone out of control, causing an accident in which 7 persons were killed. Somehow the matter was settled out of court (I doubt if that would have been possible today), but I think that this anecdote illustrates clearly that the Taylor Brothers were not really destined for a long-term future in the crane business, and the acquisition of this company by Coles marked perhaps the beginning of the end of the diesel-electric era.

Life in the "The British Crane Company", as the Ealing-based Export Sales Division was called, was very different from what we had got used to in Berkeley Street. The offices adjoined the main line railway from Paddington to the West, and when the express trains thundered by, all communication inside the offices had to be suspended until the train had passed. No more nipping off to the Linguists Club to practise his languages for young Lloyd, but, on the other hand, action for me in real exporting soon began from a totally unexpected quarter. Robert Albon had made a trip to Poland in 1959, and, with the aid of a strange Englishman called David Rutter who had made his home in Communist Poland, having married a Polish girl, had come back with an initial order for a 30 Tonne Truck Crane, the L3010 Ranger Truck.

Only days after we had moved to Ealing, at the beginning of April, 1960, a cable came from Poland saying that orders would be placed for three more of these cranes, provided that we could deliver the first one for the International Poznan Fair in June. Robert Albon had already planned for us to be at this event, but had decided that we ought to opt for the lower capacity 20 Tonner, the L2210 Endurance Truck, because of possible axle loading problems with the larger crane. Ealing were not used actually to sending salesmen out to secure orders, and Cooke at first prevaricated, leaving Rutter to deal with the matter. Rutter was an intellectual Communist, who was trying to supplement his meagre income as a University lecturer in Gdansk by unofficial representation of UK firms, but he was never taken very seriously, and in the end cooked his own goose by writing to the Ministry of Foreign Trade asking to be officially recognized, to which the answer was a flat negative and he lost the 1% commission which he had been paid through his own stupidity. Finally Cooke asked Albon for his advice, which was unequivocal: "Send young Dick Lloyd", and so I was rescued from the deskbound position to which I had been assigned.

Days later Robert Albon's letter of resignation landed on James Steel's desk, and he was required to leave immediately, because he was off to head up the Sales Division of John Allen of Oxford, maker of mechanical truck cranes, lawn mowers and ladder trenchers, and it was he who masterminded the approach to Grove to build their hydraulic tele-boom truck cranes under licence, leading eventually to the acquisition of the Oxford business by Grove. I still recall the devastating effect which his actual departure had on me. He had been my first boss, who had brought me up in the business world, and, as my journal recalls "The rock on which I had been leaning, even in the early days at Ealing, suddenly slipped and went". James Steel, whom Robert rather unkindly described as "The Fuehrer", was completely taken aback by the decision, and obliged him to serve his full three months notice at home before he could join John Allen. To give Ron Cooke his due, he fully realised the import of Albon's departure, and gathered together the old Coles staff to try and secure the loyalty which they had given to Albon to himself. He was never able to command the respect that Albon did, nor did he have the presence, and, as events proved, he had been promoted to a position of responsibility beyond his capabilities. Nevertheless he was basically a very decent guy, and when he died in March 1999, it was in fact I who gathered together a few of his old colleagues to see him off, whereas Robert Albon slipped away fifteen years earlier without any of his former colleagues to bid him farewell, because we had lost touch with him.

In 1960 Cooke's Empire comprised of three zones. George Ricketts took over from Robert Albon in the Middle East, Derrick Matthews handled the Far East, and the Neal man, Dennis Byron Mattingley oversaw Europe (and me) and it was he who gradually became my Bête Noir.

Dennis Mattingley was a thin, cadaverous dark-haired man, who exuded worry and angst. To start with, I trusted him, but by the time that we moved from Ealing to the new offices at Steel House in Eastcote, in the middle of 1961, I was beginning to have my doubts. We had had high words on the emotive subject of Robert Albon, when he tried to tell me that I had no call to continue to associate with him because he worked for a competitor. He even went so far as to say that if I walked into the office on a Monday morning and announced that I had spent the weekend at his house, he would ask me to find another job, to which I replied that this was business, not warfare! "Its War!" was the reply. By the end of that year I was having open rows and disagreements with him, after which he would call me in to make it all up, scared that he had gone too far with me and that I might throw in the towel.

He hardly ever travelled anywhere himself, and certainly did not expose himself to the tough sort of trips which I had to undertake, but he was very good at armchair criticism of what I should or should not have done in the field. The more I had to do with him, the more I realised that his supposed concern for the members of his staff, with his cosy confidential little chats, was just a façade, or pure hypocrisy.

He had a big chip on his shoulder, I believe, since one day he told me that his father had been an RFC pilot (as had mine), but he was turned down medically for service in the Forces in the Second World War, and had ended up in a Munitions Factory.

To be fair to him, he often came into the office looking like death warmed up, when I used to feel sorry for him. Whenever we had foreign visitors to entertain, he always insisted on our taking them to the Pigalle, a night club with an indifferent restaurant and floor-show in Picadilly, simply because he went there so often that all the waiters (and not a few of the show girls) would recognize him and greet him deferentially (or flirt with him), and this made up for the deficiencies in his own personal ability to get on with people at a normal level. I ended up by loathing the place, since, apart from anything else it always meant a very late night, and many of the foreign guests whom he took there would have much preferred a decent meal at a good restaurant.

Mattingley was determined to make me pay for having succeeded in getting myself promoted to be an outside man, rather than an admin guy, and was often telling me that I must be prepared to travel for six months in the year, to which I replied that I might not be able to tolerate that amount of travelling as a married man.

However there was one positive aspect which I learned from him and that was the importance of good administration, and it was to my benefit that I shared an office with Fred Fusco, the admin chap from Neal, rather than with the other OSEs (Overseas Sales Executives). Fred, born in Scotland, came from an Italian family who had established an Italian ice cream business in Dumfries, and he was, an still is, a bachelor who has occupied the same maisonette in Wembley since 1958. At work, Fred was a perfectionist, a stickler for detail, whose ethos, in his own words, was Quality rather than Quantity. Work apart, Fred's philosophy was to do as little as necessary to keep body and soul together. He owned a Ford Prefect car to which he did not do any maintenance whatsoever. He was even too lazy to wash it, content to let rust eat slowly and inexorably into the bodywork, until finally the carroserie parted company with the chassis as he was driving to the office one morning, and he had to pay £5 to have the wreck towed away, which highly incensed him!

Fred started life in the crane business with R.H. Neal in 1954, and in 1975 was presented with a gold watch for 20 years of service. His dry sense of humour, and his devotion to duty can be well illustrated by the following excerpt from his speech on that occasion, when he referred to his religious beliefs:

"During my cloistered years at Steel House - the Fuscos come from a long line of celibate monks - I had the following experience concerning one particular Works Order Acceptance. It suffered constant change. Amendment after Amendment was issued, and when No. 9 was reached I began to feel and look like Moses standing on Mt. Sinai, waiting for the omnipotent Central Order Dept to hand down the Tenth Commandment."

The Neal NS70 fitted either with strut or cantilever jib had a capacity of 7 tons free on wheels and a sophisticated hoist system.

CLEAN, SIMPLE TRANSMISSION LAYOUT

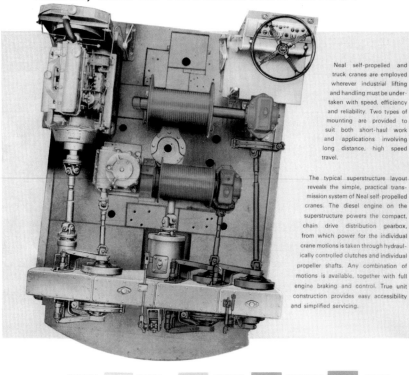

Neal self-propelled and truck cranes are employed wherever industrial lifting and handling must be undertaken with speed, efficiency and reliability. Two types of mounting are provided to suit both short-haul work and applications involving long distance, high speed travel.

The typical superstructure layout reveals the simple, practical transmission system of Neal self-propelled cranes. The diesel engine on the superstructure powers the compact, chain drive distribution gearbox, from which power for the individual crane motions is taken through hydraulically controlled clutches and individual propeller shafts. Any combination of motions is available, together with full engine braking and control. True unit construction provides easy accessibility and simplified servicing.

| POWER PACK | SLEW MOTION | TRAVEL MOTION | DERRICK MOTION | HOIST MOTION |

The truck crane superstructure deck is similar to the self-propelled machine, but has no travel motion take-off. Drive to the road wheels is provided by a separate, chassis-mounted diesel engine and transmission system.

Ref 10/4550

The production orientated "Coles Mechanical" system which was a technological disaster and effectively killed the Neal crane.

John Taylor just before he left the R.A.F. to join R.H.Neal in 1946, *and* in 1963 with Cliff Shore (on the right) and a visiting government minister at the Grantham works. Cliff Shore was the General Sales Manager of Neal, who retired soon after this picture was taken.

British Crane

STEELS
NEWS BULLETIN

Volume II, No. 23   Published by Steel & Co. Ltd., Sunderland, England   February, 1960

COLES INTERNATIONAL LINK-UP

New agreement spells further expansion for The Steel Group

AGREEMENT

An agreement signed on the 7th of January, 1960, at West Allis, Milwaukee by Mr. Arnold Hallsworth, director of Steel & Co. Ltd. and Mr. Arnold R. Corbett, vice-president of the Unit Crane and Shovel Corporation of Wisconsin, U.S.A., set the seal on a mutual manufacturing and marketing arrangement designed to increase the selling potential of both companies in world mechanical handling and excavating markets.

The agreement provides for Unit to manufacture COLES cranes in their Milwaukee plant for marketing throughout the U.S.A., Canada and Mexico under the name of UNIT-COLES. In return, R. H. Neal and Co. Ltd., a member of The Steel Group, will manufacture Unit cranes, excavators, draglines and back-hoes in their Grantham works for marketing throughout the world, with the exception of those countries covered by Unit, and subject to the existing Unit franchises in Australia, South Africa and the Benelux countries. These products will go out under the name of the NEAL-UNIT.

EXPANSION

Also, a Sales Company has been registered under the name of INTERNATIONAL CRANE & EXCAVATOR CORPORATION, with headquarters in New York, for marketing Coles, Neal and Taylor cranes and Unit cranes and excavators in South America and Central American republics.

This move, the latest in a series stemming directly from The Steel Group policy of "constant expansion", will further enhance the Groups' international status by enabling it to expand its crane sales in overseas markets besides adding to the wide range of products which it already produces.

An aerial view of the Grantham plant of R. H. Neal & Co. where NEAL-UNIT products will be manufactured.

'Clinching the deal'—the actual signing of the agreement linking COLES with Unit in the Milwaukee plant of the latter. Left to right: A. Hallsworth, Steels Engineering Products; A. R. Corbett, Unit Crane and Shovel Corporation; G. M. Bassnett, Coles Cranes Inc.; and H. R. Neal, R. H. Neal & Co.

Other signal steps in this expansion programme have been the incorporation within The Steel Group of the crane manufacturing firms of F. Taylor & Sons (Manchester) Ltd. and R. H. Neal & Co. Ltd. and the signing of an agreement between Steels Engineering Products Ltd. and Herbert Morris Ltd., crane manufacturers of Loughborough, to rationalise the production of each as an aid to greater sales.

One of the chief factors emerging from this series of transactions is that The Steel Group can now offer a range of excavators and the largest range of mobile cranes in the world, with lifting capacities ranging from 1 to 50 tons and incorporating all three accepted forms of transmission: diesel-electric, diesel-hydraulic and diesel-mechanical.

EFFECTS

It has been calculated that the existing Grantham plant is sufficient for the anticipated increase in work volume in the foreseeable future, but provision has been made to increase the labour force as and when this becomes necessary.

Although the terms of the agreement are being implemented at once, the nature and number of the problems involved will delay for a while the emergence of the many benefits which will accrue. It is confidently expected, however, that by the end of the year the scheme will have gathered full momentum and that the combined efforts of marketing and manufacturing forces will be instrumental in promoting peak production.

Production of Neal cranes including the handy one ton capacity GM model was superseded at Grantham by the licence for Unit excavators.

The aquisition of Neal and Taylor opened the eyes of Coles to the potential of hydraulic transmissions .

The Coles Husky Rough Terrain so successfully produced in the 1970s at the old Neal plant in Grantham.

THE STEEL GROUP

OF CRANE AND EXCAVATOR MANUFACTURERS

WORLD CONFERENCE

HARROGATE 1962

PROGRAMME

THE FACE
BEHIND THE

Signature

IN THE STEEL
GROUP MARKETING
COMPANIES

BRITISH CRANE COMPANY LTD.

C. C. BAILEY

P. T. BARTON

A. F. BROOKS

G. C. BULLOCK

R. COOKE

C. CURTIS

C. E. DREW

F. M. A. FUSCO

B. J. S. GREY

W. F. HARWOOD

R. J. LLOYD

D. J. MATTHEWS   D. B. MATTINGLEY   W. L. MURRAY   G. A. RICKETTS

J. WALLER   W. L. WATKINS   C. J. WRIGHT

INTERNATIONAL CRANE AND EXCAVATOR CORPORATION

C. ISKALIS   H. KING   H. P. STRACK

STEEL A.G.

H. HAAB   W. KIRCHHOFER   J. STEIGER

16

Fred Fusco, administrator par excellence, and I shared a room in the old offices of Neal Cranes at Plant House, Ealing in 1960. Here these two old timers in 1999.

CHAPTER TWO - POLAND

My first trip to Poland was unforgettable in many ways. To start with, I nearly missed the flight, (my first in a jet plane, a BEA Comet) because I confused the announcement to board with that to check-in, and when Audrey urged me to make some enquiries, I was told that the flight had departed! Had it not been for some technical hitch, I really would have missed it. I arrived late in the evening without an hotel reservation because someone had told me that it would not be necessary, illustrating what a naive East European traveller I was. The airport bus, which toured the main hotels dropping off passengers finally left me at a grey concrete block announcing itself as the Hotel Warszawa, where I pleaded to be allowed to sleep in a chair in the Reception Area, if need be, but luckily they had had a cancellation and I got a room. The next morning I could not get any breakfast there, nor change any money, but the kindly receptionist loaned me the taxi fare to the Grand Hotel, where these deficiencies could be remedied.

It was illustrative of the power of the End-User even at that time in Communist Poland that my first discussions took place with Mostostal, an organization of steel structure and bridge erectors, who had branches all over Poland. A young engineer called Tycka was the man who was going to be responsible for the use of the cranes and he was determined to get what he wanted, not what the State Trading Organization decided that he could have. However, we just could not alter the fact that the lower capacity crane was planned for the Poznan Fair, but it became clear that it was the shorter main boom length of the L2210 Endurance rather than the capacity which was the stumbling block, since the main boom only stretched to 100 feet (30 metres) as opposed to 120 feet (36 metres). I decided to go right to the top of the Coles tree to get an answer as to whether we could fit the longer boom on to the Endurance, and I put a call in to Arnold Hallsworth in Sunderland. I was not at all sure that it would be possible, because it has to be remembered that all Coles booms at that time were constructed of massively heavy mild steel. "Tell them that we will do it, Dick" came the answer "Get the order, lad", so I did, after a very tough two day battle over price and terms of payment with the Foreign Trade Organization responsible for all heavy machinery imports at that time, Centrozap in Katowice (one of the oldest established in the country, and still surviving in modern capitalist Poland). Ing. Tycka joined the discussions and warned me not to mention our previous meetings in Warsaw at all, but I made a terrible mistake in writing to him personally from the UK on my return, to thank him for all his help, as a matter of common courtesy, as I thought, but it landed him in a lot of trouble, for which I have always felt guilty, but it was due to my inexperience, and the inexperience of my superiors, which was illustrated time and again over the next few years.

I quote verbatim from my diary on the final round of the negotiations, after discount and terms of payment had been agreed:

"Finally I got them to cut something out of the spec, which saved us £250.   I then agreed to sign.   'Well', I thought to myself, 'I've got something out of the bastards.' But when they brought in the paper, I immediately spotted an extra, to which I had not agreed, priced at £400 which they had earlier said that they did not want, and finally they just slipped it in.   Again the battle raged, but I lost, and signed.   By then my mood was such that I could not have cared less if the whole place had gone up in smoke, and I travelled back to Warsaw highly disgruntled and depressed and muttering imprecations against the whole Communist system.   This mood was still with me when I woke the next morning, and I threw my slippers against the wall and was very pleased to see that they left a dirty mark".   Oh dear, what a lot I had still to learn!

As then so today, Polish people in the street were very friendly, even though I was usually taken for a German, since that was the lingua franca of the time in Eastern Europe (apart from Russian!)   One very friendly citizen took me all round the Stare Miasto, the Old Town, where volunteers were still at work restoring to their original state buildings which had been flattened in the War, and another, mistaking me for a German, said that Poles were even friendly toward their old enemies, but this was not always the case.

Although it was I who had negotiated the order for the cranes in Poland (and the management were, in fact, very pleased with the result) I was considered too junior to undertake the responsibility for the Stand at the Poznan Fair. This responsibility was given to John Isaacs with me as his assistant.   There is no doubt but that old John Isaacs taught me a lot about the way to establish a good rapport with the customer, which is always, to my way of thinking, the basis of good salesmanship.   When he was sober, John was a superb salesman. He could charm the birds off the trees and everyone loved him.   I was "Adj", he acting as "CO", and, to begin with, this relationship worked well. But he left me to do all the negotiations.

John and I set out for Poznan much later than we should have done, and we stopped in East Germany to picnic and bathe, and were lucky not to have

British Crane

landed ourselves in trouble with the Volkspolitzei ("Vopos" as they were called), because Transit Visas were issued strictly on the basis of "Ohne Aufenhalt" - *No Stopping.* There had been no time to assemble and test the extra long boom on the L2210 Endurance Truck before it left the Works in Sunderland, so this was undertaken for the very first time on the Fairground, the day before the Show opened to the public, under the direction of a stocky cool-headed Geordie Service Engineer named Bill Meddis. The 120 foot (36 metre) Coles mild steel boom was laid out across the Fairground over the rear of the carrier, and an ancient Fiorentini self-propelled mobile crane hired from the Fair Authority to assist in the erection. Unfortunately this crane was only equipped with a very short jib, and it could not lift the Coles boom high enough for the L2210 to take over itself. So the old crane was moved to a position lower down on the Coles boom, and the lift was re-attempted. As the operator slewed round to improve his position, disaster struck. There was a report as if a cannon had been fired, and one of the old crane's three hook rollers shot out into the crowd of onlookers, many of whom leapt to safety and fortunately no-one was injured! One of the slings supporting the Coles boom snapped, the operator jumped out of the cab and legged it away from the crane as fast as he could, and the Coles boom was left swaying perilously in mid-air, suspended by the one remaining sling, which, by some miracle, did not snap too.

Old John's personal connections now came to the fore, and we had no alternative but to go cap in hand to our competitor, United Construction Machinery, who were the Jones Agent for Eastern Europe. They agreed to loan us their KL66 (6 Ton Mobile) to complete the erection of our boom, and, with the Jones taking the weight at the top end of the boom, up she went until the point of balance was just reached, enhanced by the hookblock being hung over the cab at the rear of the crane to give extra counterweight. Then a further problem arose, because the Jones hookblock was entangled in the pendant ropes of the Coles, and the only remedy was for someone to climb up the boom to free them. The extra weight of this person could easily have tipped the crane, but old John certainly did not lack courage, and he insisted that only he should make this attempt. It was typical army officer reaction of "leading from the front", and fortunately his mission was accomplished without mishap, and the first Coles crane ever to be exhibited in Eastern Europe was finally erected. John then descended into his first really serious drinking bout and I began to realise the size of the problem on my young shoulders of having him as my senior colleague.

The crane survived the Fair in its erect position, but the problem re-appeared when it reached the operating site at Turow, in the extreme southeast corner of Poland, where it was to work on the construction of a new Power Station. This time, again with the assistance of a local crane with much too short a jib, Bill Meddis commandeered every worker on the site to sit on the cab as extra ballast, and remarked philosophically as he screwed additional jacks under the rear of the chassis: "I'll get me bloody cards if this lot comes down".   It didn't, but the front wheels were about a metre off the ground before the point of balance was reached!

After our return from this first Poznan Fair, I became recognized as an outside man, and my salary was adjusted accordingly.   In December a large delegation came over from Centrozap and placed orders for 7 or 8 more cranes, after long discussions on price and credit terms, which came to a successful conclusion by my typing out a Letter of Intent at about 8 pm in a fairly inebriated state, on the final evening of their visit, after several days of wining and dining.   So I decided that it was in my better interests to forget about joining the new EEC Marketing Company based in Switzerland.

But I was inevitably questioned by Cooke and Mattingley about John's drinking habits, and, after he had been threatened with the sack, our relationship became rather strained.   Although I did most of the East European travelling, we both teamed up again for the Poznan Fair in 1961, but during this second trip he was worse and on several occasions I had to have a stand-up row with him, and frequently to look after his passport and travellers' cheques.   On one occasion he attempted to drive the Land Rover when he was totally drunk and I seized the keys from him to be greeted by the angry words: "You young pup, who is in charge of this ship?" Although the Polish customers continued to be very tolerant, many of them getting often as drunk as he was, it was clear that some of the more experienced men amongst our fellow British exhibitors began to be disgusted at his behaviour, and when the inevitable post-mortem was made after the trip, I was assisted by the fact that Fred Fusco had been out to Poznan for part of the time as well and really there was nothing to say but "Never again".

In March 1962, two new colleagues joined the European section, Bill Murray, a Scotsman with a very dry humour a few years my senior, and Stephen Grey, two years my junior, an ex-pilot, who had crash landed a Hunter in which one member of the crew had died, which had given him migraine and caused him to be invalided out of the RAF.   I took to Bill immediately and we have remained lifelong friends, but I was much less comfortable with Stephen, of whom I wrote at the time: "He has a superior air about him - slight elevation of the nose. However, this is only a first impression, and maybe because his temperament is nearer to mine. He drove us to the pub like a madman in his Mini Cooper. I hope that he doesn't drive the Land Rover like that." This last comment was prophetic. It had been planned to keep old John Isaacs out of the Poznan Fair, which was to be run by me, but, at the last minute, Fate intervened - there was an accident with a crane and suddenly it was he, the confirmed alcoholic, who was the only man able to sort it out. The "new boys", Bill and Steve were given the difficult task of following him out and, on the way, Stephen jack-knifed the Land-Rover towing the exhibition caravan on the autobahn in Germany and the whole lot tipped over and was wrecked. Poor Bill had just handed over the driving to him, and was very badly bruised in the accident, and I don't think that that incident endeared him to Stephen very much either.

Mattingley himself finally also went out to Poznan and that was the end of John's career with Coles. John thought (and indeed the weak management had led him to this self-delusion) that he was indispensable in Poland, and was abusive and arrogant to Mattingley, so that the latter came back in tatters, and it was I who was told to summon John back to UK - he had not dared to do this to his face himself.

My "summons" in the name of Director Ron Cooke was just laughed at by John and in the end they had to leave him there until such time as he ran out of money and had to come home to be fired. He eventually got a job with the dealer in Finland, where they were tolerant to heavy drinkers, for a year, but that came to its inevitable end. I met him again in 1966 at the Plovdiv Fair in Bulgaria, for the last time as it proved, when I was myself no longer with Coles. Jones Cranes had given him one last chance, but he blew that and ended his life in the gutter. The example of John Isaacs certainly was a life-long lesson to me.

Leaving aside this particular problem, those early Poznan Fairs were tremen-dous fun. The trips were of long duration. The Fair itself lasted 15 days, and in 1961 I actually did not go out until half way through, but still did not manage to get back home until 4 weeks later. We used to drive all over Poland having innumerable meetings with end-users and Centrozap, and we had to tow our exhibition caravan to Gdansk to have it shipped back to the UK, so that the strain of carrying an alcoholic colleague during all these peregrinations was hardly surprising.   Polish roads, with pavé surfaces and curved cambers, often tree-lined with long stretches reminiscent of roads in northern France, were almost deserted of motor traffic.   Ox-carts were a much more familiar sight and often when we stopped in villages, we would be immediately surrounded by a crowd of curious children admiring the car. On the old German autobahn which had once connected Berlin with Breslau, hens scratched for a living, because in Communist Poland the road no longer went anywhere.   At times John's humour really came to the fore.   On one occasion when we had driven straight over a narrow gauge rail crossing, where the rails were rusty with disuse and no train had travelled on them for years, we ignored the Stop Sign and drove straight over it.   A policeman was hiding in a wood about 100 metres past the crossing and he jumped out at us and waved his truncheon for us to stop.   John got out of the car and with a charming smile saluted the policeman with the words: "Good morning, Admiral" and the situation was immediately defused, and we were let off with a warning by the officer with a large grin on his face.

The length of the Fair inevitably gave rise to periods of boredom, but, on the other hand there was a great camaraderie amongst the British Exhibitors, with riotous parties in the local restaurants in the evenings.   The most unforgettable character on the East European Construction Equipment circuit was the boss of UCMC, perhaps the pioneer of Construction Equipment Sales into that region, who helped us out in 1960, Walter Husser.   Walter was a large man who resembled, in looks, President Nasser of Egypt, who had been born on a small island off the coast of Yugoslavia. He spoke fluent German and Russian, in addition to his perfect English, and what he did not know about selling in East Europe in those days was not worth knowing.

One of the biggest pieces of business which Walter pulled off at about the time that I met him was the sale of 300 Priestman "Cub" mechanical excavators to the Polish excavator manufacturer, Warynski, with manufacturing rights thrown in. My future career was to have close involvement with these two manufacturers, so there was a remarkable thread of co-incidence here.   He was a born raconteur, and he had a table reserved every single night of the Fair at a particular restaurant, where he would hold court like some foreign potentate.   We all had access to Black Market Złotys, so that we could wine and dine to extreme extravagance without anyone querying the level of our expenses, and I fell out with John because he proposed that we line our own pockets with the profits which we made, but, since we had such a good time at the Company's expense, including the odd weekend in the mountains, I felt that this would be dishonest. Our own source of funds came from our Mr. Fixit Stand Manager, Alfred Gorniok, known to generations of Coles men as Alfski, whom we inherited with the small hut which was our first Pavilion, from AEC, who had decided to pull out after 1959. He took part of his holiday from his normal occupation to assist us at Poznan Fair. Alfred could work the system in Communist Poland, and organize or obtain practically anything, so long as he could arm himself with the necessary bottle of cheap brandy or whisky from Baltona, the ship chandlers who made a fortune on the appetite of both exhibitors and Polish customers for alcohol. He used to arrange for our "funny money", which were złotys at about three times the official exchange rate. This was not done by direct exchange, but through a mysterious character in West Berlin, whom we never met, and who was known only as "The Professor". Alfred advanced us the złotys, and then, once over the border into West Germany, we would remit the agreed amount of Deutschmark to him by postal order. He always trusted us, and I was particularly incensed to find out, after John's departure, that he had failed to repay "The Professor" after his last trip for Coles, so that I made good the debt myself. Not only that, but old John also wrote a letter to Centrozap implicating Alfred in doing these deals, which could have landed him in a lot of trouble, but fortunately no investigation took place. I never really forgave John for that, but Alfred never bore him any grudge.

Following the departure of John Isaacs, I handled the market once more and during the bitter winter of 1962/3 made no less than three visits to Poland in connection with the requirement for an 80 tonne Valiant Truck Crane which was urgently required for the building of the Refinery at Płock. The Poles were insisting that the crane be exhibited at the Poznan Fair, but the Coles Management would not agree to do this unless we had something in writing to confirm that the crane would be ordered beforehand, and I was the being put in the hot spot to accept responsibility if it were not sold.

Even after the first visit we had verbal assurances that the crane would be purchased, but no-one could give any firm commitment because of money being tight, aggravated by the severe weather. In January the temperature outside was minus 25 degrees C, and inside the Grand Hotel, where the Head of Reception sat muffled in his overcoat and fur hat, the temperature struggled to get above 8 or 9 degrees. Hot water was only available for about one hour in the evenings and getting into bed with a bottle of whisky was the only way of keeping warm. Alfred came to Warsaw to act as my interpreter on the first of the three visits, and when we boarded the train to Katowice, it gave a severe lurch just as the hapless Alfski was putting my bag on the rack, and he was thrown against the window. The heavy suitcase smashed the window and Alfred bravely held on to my case, nearly precipitating himself out with it. The compartment, which had been full, rapidly emptied. Katowice was always a grim dirty town, where trams weaved their way crazily along uneven tracks, but in that intense cold, with poor street lighting, it was decidedly grimmer than usual. The Hotel Monopol remains in my memory as one of the darkest, gloomiest establishments which I ever stayed in, but, in contrast, I have always found the Silesians to be the most hospitable and friendly people in Poland.

In the train from Katowice to Poznan, which we boarded on the Saturday morning at 6 am, the train stopped outside the station in Katowice for an hour and the heating subsided, and never came back for the whole of the six hour journey. I was frozen to the marrow. Fortunately there was a hot bath waiting for me at the Hotel Bazar in Poznan and when I ventured out in the evening by taxi to join my friends at a restaurant, where the lively music and convivial atmosphere was a very welcome contrast to the cold and dark outside, I was commenting to the taxi driver on the freezing weather, to which he replied that it was nothing compared to the bloody Communist Government, who took everything and gave nothing. It was not uncommon, even in those dark days to hear Poles openly critical of the regime in public. I never heard anyone use the word "Comrade" or "Tovarich" in Poland.

However, on that trip, I really became ill with the cold and decided to pull out and fly home, since I really could do no more in any case. I was already checked in and through Immigration, when a huge snowstorm arrived, and the pilot of the KLM Flight coming in from Moscow decided to overfly Warsaw. KLM negotiated all afternoon with LOT and finally succeeded in hiring an Iluyshin 14, the Russian equivalent of a Convair Metropolitan, to get all the passengers out. An arrogant German businessman, clad in an expensive fur coat, drank too much in the Departure Lounge and became very loud-mouthed and objectionable. I had to intervene to prevent a Mancunian who announced his intention to thump "that bloody Kraut" if he did not shut up, from carrying out his threat, but when we finally boarded the plane he started again, shouting down the aisle to the Polish hostess that he wanted a drink. She was right at the back of the plane and literally marched right up to his seat with the words: "I only speak English. Nichts verstehen!", which deflated him completely. This was a clear indication of the anti-German feeling which still existed in Poland then, which has, fortunately, long since disappeared.

Dealing with East Europeans in those days often impinged on one's personal life. Because they were deprived of modern consumer luxuries, and even more essential commodities like sophisticated medicinal drugs, one often travelled burdened with a lot of shopping. The recipients often did not realise the amount of trouble which one had to go to meet their requests, particularly with medicines which were only available on prescription. On one occasion we had to put up with a very unwelcome house guest in our own home when Mostostal sent over their first representative for technical training to the UK in April 1963, a very smooth ex-Cavalry officer named Edward Juffy, who spoke flawless English. He was a complete contrast to the friendly down-to-earth and totally undemanding Technical Director, Stefan Kosminski, who spoke no more than pidgin German, and who was very pro-Coles. Sadly Kosminski was tragically killed in a road accident a few years later, when his driver was completely drunk. Juffy came to the UK earlier than the date planned for his appearance in Sunderland, "for private reasons", and I felt that I could not expect the company to put him up in an hotel when he was not officially on business, but I should not have been allowed to put my wife to this additional strain, especially when she was looking after a four month old baby. Juffy expected to be waited on hand and foot, and he would suddenly appear in a room without any warning like some Deus ex Machina, because he always opened the door so noiselessly, which we found really impeded on our privacy in our own house. I even provisionally agreed to lend him £50 from my own pocket, (about one twentieth of my annual salary at the time) to be repaid later in Warsaw, but fortunately I backed down on this and pretended that I thought that he wanted me to ask the Company for this loan, whereupon he said that it was of no importance. However he brought it up again later and this time I raised it officially and he ended up with an expensive imitation fur coat instead, supposedly for his wife. I shall never forget how his eyes lit up with greedy pleasure at the trinkets on display in Woolworths, which were so different from the bare counters in the Warsaw Department Stores. All in all, it was with a sigh of relief that we saw him on to the train at Kings Cross for Sunderland after having him to stay for a week.

Stephen Grey and I, inevitably, became rivals, although we got along together personally quite well and even exchanged visits to our families. We did have one thing finally in common, and that was our antipathy to Mattingley, although, to start with, the latter played upon our rivalry.

A crisis point in my relationship with Dennis came in May 1963, when after the frequent trips to Poland to assure the successful outcome of the decision to send the 80 Tonne Valiant Crane to the Fair, the Poles told us that it must be shipped in two sections and assembled on site, due to road regulations. This meant that the Poznan Fair trip would be 7 weeks in duration and Mattingley put pressure on me to undertake the whole trip on my own, which was totally unfair, telling me that he was sure than Stephen Grey would be ready to do it, if I did not. I had already agreed to release the Czech and East German markets to Steve, where I had done the groundwork, and we accepted trips of four weeks, or even five, but seven was just too much to expect a young married man to put up with. When I broke the news to Audrey, she was naturally very very upset, and we had a sleepless night. When I was shaving in the morning, I suddenly broke down and dissolved into uncontrollable weeping - I was on the edge of a nervous breakdown and I can honestly say that such a thing has never happened to me before or since, even though I have had my moments of depression.

I went in to the office ready to throw in the towel, and then Mattingley, realising that he had pushed me too far, completely backed down, and Bill Murray immediately stepped in and volunteered to help me out by undertaking the first part of the trip.

I was very grateful to Bill for that favour. A few days later I witnessed the crane being loaded in two parts in the Pool of London just opposite the Tower by an ancient steam floating crane, and shortly after my arrival in Poznan to take over from Bill, Kosminski and Juffy and colleagues from Mostostal came on the Stand with news that the purchase had finally been approved. It turned out to be the only piece of heavy equipment purchased from the Fair that year, which resulted in the most enormous Piss-Up which began in the morning, and continued through lunch on the Stand until mid-afternoon, when they disappeared for a couple of hours. I went back to the digs and stuck my head in a bucket of cold water to sober up in time for the British Reception which began at 6 pm. The Mostostal boys had continued to drink elsewhere in the interval, and we ended up taking them out to dinner and letting some of them share our digs because they had nowhere to stay for the night. It was incredible how much booze these guys could put away and still stand upright.... However it was not until two weeks later that we finally signed the contract with Centrozap in Katowice. The Head of the Import

Dept was a charming old gentleman named Godula and he it was who had taken the brunt of the pressure exerted by me since January for a decision on the crane and in the inevitable final discussion on price, he said to me: "Herr Lloyd, Sie glauben dass wir machen Theater. Wir machen kein Theater und ich bin krank mit diese Sache" (*Mr. Lloyd, you think that we are making a Charade out of this - I can assure you that this is no Charade and this business has made me ill*). I do not think that I ever felt sorry for any official in one of the Communist Import Organizations, because, generally speaking, I regarded them as my opponents, but for dear old Godula, I certainly did!

Mattingley himself spent two or three days at the Fair and he brought with him the Service Manager, Bernard Dawes. Two more diverse characters would be hard to imagine, except that they both were equally nervous about being in Poland, and "doing the right thing". Bernard was a down to earth Derbyshire man with a heart of gold, to whom everything was a novelty, like a child with new toys. He kept telling jokes which depended for their humour on a play on words and expected me to translate them into German! He gave away more warranty claims than had ever been given before, since he just could not bear to upset the customers, and Bill Meddis, our stalwart service engineer, who arrived just after he had gone home, said that many eyebrows were raised in the Service Dept in Sunderland as the telexes from Bernard flowed in! So whilst Bernard really added spice and humour to the party, Dennis was just the opposite, constantly worrying and flapping about this and that, interfering in the running of the Stand, and whilst I did my best to treat him as "The Boss", finally I had flaming row with him when he overstepped the mark in meddling.

I was feeling on top of the world, my self-confidence which he had undermined had totally returned and I was just not going to dance to his tune any longer and it was a great relief to see him off to Warsaw to catch his plane back to London, fretting whether he would need a DDR visa when the plane touched down in East Berlin.

Accompanying first Bill Murray to Poland for that Poznan Fair and then working under my direction was a young language graduate called Colin Wright. To start with I found him difficult to get on with, partly because of Mattingley's policy of "Divide and Rule" in which there was no seniority under him, so Colin thought that he was my equal. However his attitude changed during the Fair and he started to respect me for my greater experience. When he got emotionally involved with a girl named Christina, whom we all knew to be in the service of the Secret Police, I warned him not to let the fun he was having with this girl ever get to a stage of helping her to leave the country. Actually I rather liked her, dark-haired, pretty and vivacious as she was, but when I found out that she was to accompany us to Katowice after the Fair, I was not pleased, and told him that she would have to pay for herself in the hotel. He said that she had persuaded him to take her with us to visit her sick mother...... We did have a very convivial evening in a "Kneipe" when she, cavorting with me around the floor, pleaded with me to tell him how much she loved him. I deliberately avoided adding fuel to an already dangerous flame, but all in vain. He returned to Poland in August for a holiday and married her!

Within a matter of weeks she had got permission to leave Poland and join him in UK, and Ron Cooke had a visit from two gentlemen from MI5, which confirmed that she was definitely in the employ of the Polish Secret Police. But the marriage did not prosper very well, since she expected a life-style in Capitalist England which was beyond his means. Mattingley did not want to repeat the experience of Dick Lloyd with him at the Poznan Fair any more so in 1964 he sent Bill Murray with Colin to do the initial stint. Colin had only just passed his driving test, and he insisted on taking Christina with him to see her family. She was already expecting a baby. Mattingley had to agree, but gave him strict instructions just to take her to Poznan and not to travel around Poland with him, which he ignored and then Fate stepped in. He was travelling up to Gdynia on a wet pavé tree-lined road clearly at too high a speed for the conditions. He was overtaking a truck when a motor-cyclist came out of a side road straight in front of him. He braked violently and the car skidded into a tree. Christina and the motor-cyclist were killed instantly and Colin himself very badly injured. I had expressed doubts to Dennis about his lack of driving experience but to no avail. This was an avoidable tragedy.

British Crane

A clear indication of the weight of the tubular mild steel boom which caused us such problems of erection of a boom of this construction 36 metres long at the 1960 Poznan Fair.

The old Fiorentini crane, hired from the Fair Authority, which collapsed in its attempt to lift the Coles boom

The Coles boom is finally erected.

Poznan Fair 1960.

Left:
Alfred and Renia
Gorniok

Right:
John Isaacs rides on"Adj"

Below:
Relaxing at Zakopane
Left to Right
Dick Lloyd, Bill Meddis,
David Rutter and
"Uncle" John Isaacs

Coles Ranger Truck , L3010, sold in 1962 to Mostostal Warszawa, still in operation with a private company in Poznan in 1992.

British Crane

BRNO Fair 1964.
seated, left to right: Dennis Mattingley, Ron Cooke, Stephen Grey
standing (left) Ron Walker, the experienced Coles service engineer whom I stole for HYMAC, and
(right) Peter Allison, the last Export Sales Director of Coles, 1979 - 84

Poznan Fair, 1963.The 80 tonne Coles Valiant Truck sold, after much hard work and hassle, to Centrozap for Mostostal Warszawa.

Walter Husser with some of the Priestman Cubs shipped to Poland.

CHAPTER THREE - THE BALKANS

It was in 1960 that I made my first visit to Bulgaria, during a trip which took me away from home for the usual month. When one considers the problems of phoning back to the UK, waiting hours sometimes for connections, slow and totally unreliable postal systems, the strain on married and family life for wives and children of export salesmen is not difficult to imagine. That particular trip took in the Brno Fair in Czechoslovakia, Poland, where I was nearly arrested for taking pictures of a Coles crane operating in a steelworks, the Plovidv Fair in Bulgaria and finally Yugoslavia, and, as a small compensation to my long-suffering wife, I met her in Paris for a weekend on the way home.

A London-based company called Lamet Trading, which Major Botterill had by that time joined, was organizing a British Stand at Plovdiv. I arrived by plane at Sofia from Budapest, only to see the last flight that day departing to Plovdiv as I was queueing up to change money, so the only way to reach Plovdiv was by train.

The first class carriage was completely full, but a friendly Bulgarian who resembled Nikita Kruschev made room for me with the words: "You are a foreigner and our guest". We arrived at Plovdiv Station at 1 a.m., and, with no sign of any taxis, my helpful friend secured me the service of an ancient horse-drawn vehicle, so I clip-clopped my way through deserted cobbled streets to the Hotel Ko-Op where a room had been reserved for me by Lamet. The "hotel" was a very scruffy looking place and I had great difficulty in making myself heard. Finally an old woman came to the door and shook her head to indicate that there was no room free. (In Bulgaria, the positive headshake known to us Westerners, in fact indicates negatively, and vice versa).

However I was insistent and I actually found and pointed to my name in the booking register, my acquaintance with ancient Greek giving me some insight into the Cyrillic script. The old lady then disappeared up in the lift and returned to announce, with suitable signs, "Zwei Bulgarische Maenner schlafen", so clearly my late appearance had resulted in my room being re-let. Further insistence on some form of accomodation, followed by another disappearance into the lift by the old bird resulted in my being shown into the attic room, which clearly normally did duty as a broom cupboard for the cleaners. The floor was thick with dust, and the wash basin was filthy, but she had laid out sheets and blankets on the couch and I was so tired that I was ready to sleep anywhere. Just as I was settling down, I heard a scratching and scuffling noise, and something ran across my hand.   My first thought was cock-roaches, but I could see nothing, and then, when the scuffling resumed I saw a mouse quite clearly sitting on the bedside table, regarding the strange visitor into his sanctum with some surprise.

I switched on the light and hunted him round the room with my slipper for five minutes without success, but I must have frightened the life out of him, since he disturbed me no more.   In the morning two large buxom chamber-maids entered the room to collect their overalls and brooms.   They made several exits and entries and seemed quite unperturbed by my presence, and one of them procured me a cup of luke-warm water for shaving.   I breakfasted in a dirty café from a cup of black Turkish coffee, not daring to touch any food there, and then found my way to the Fairground to recount my adventures to Lamet Trading, where my luck turned when a very pleasant middle aged guy selling musical instruments offered me the spare bed in his room at the Hotel Trimontium, the best in town, and I gratefully accepted.

Really the whole Lamet Stand, which was purely a pictorial display of a multitude of different products, was a waste of time and money.   The Bulgarians were only interested in purchasing equipment actually exhibited, and the only exhibit in our line was a large German excavator and even that was not bought. Appointments with officials were very difficult to arrange, and it was recommended that I return to give a film show, but over a year passed before it happened in early 1962 when it took me three days in Sofia to fix up a film show, and I had to operate the old 16 mm Projector myself, cine photography being fortunately one of my hobbies

We decided to have another go at the Plovdiv Fair again in 1962, and although promises to purchase finally disappeared because of lack of funds, we did get to the stage of quoting and having discussions!   However the Fair was certainly a livelier affair than the previous year.   The Board of Trade still did not rate Bulgaria worth any official participation and Lamet gave up, to be replaced by a motley crew who called themselves Pan-European Consultants, consisting of three part-timers:

Ronnie Thompson was a Cockney who normally exported paper, Norbert Schlang a small dark-haired Jewish businessman from Vienna who specialised in Bulgaria, and Andy Mulligan a wandering freelancer who had played Rugby for Ireland and the British Lions, and who also played the banjo. Ronnie was regarded by the Bulgarians as the "Director of the British

Pavilion", and got him into some difficulties when it was found that one or two visiting businessmen participating in the venture were found to have comforted themselves by entertaining local Bulgarian girls in their hotel rooms and he was held responsible, and resorted to banging on the doors of the alleged offenders and telling them to "get that woman out of there"! Andy and I got involved with a group of musicians who performed at the only "Night Club" in Plovdiv.   It was just after Cuba had gone over to Communism and Latin American songs had come into vogue, and this group, with no knowledge whatever of the Spanish language, gave a very fair imitation of their Latin American counterparts.

This gave rise to an incident which has stuck in my mind ever since and was a grim reminder of the horrors of World War II.   Just before the show opened one evening, I was looking for a place amongst the small round tables which made up the "auditorium", already full, and found just one seat free.   "Ist dieses Platz frei?" *(Is this seat free)* I asked one of the men already sitting there. "Nuer der Stuhl ist frei" *(Only the stool is free)* was the strange retort, upon which he turned his back on me.   I duly sat down and then invited him to have a drink with me, to which he replied: "Sie koennen dort Platz nehmen, ich will aber mit Ihnen nicht drinken und nicht sprechen" *(You can sit there, but I will neither drink with you nor speak to you).*

I then realised that he naturally took me for a German and when I explained that I was English, his attitude completely changed.   He was a Pole who had spent two years in a Concentration Camp, and we ended up by getting pretty drunk together.

Another unforgettable character whom I first met at that Plovdiv Fair, and many times later on the Circuit was Guy Checketts, "Director" of Hawker Siddeley International.   Guy admitted that his title was simply to impress, and in Communist countries this was no bad idea, because practically everyone with whom we had to deal was a Director.

Guy was the caricature of an English Gentleman who walked around the streets of Plovdiv clad in bowler hat and pin-striped suit.   One evening we had a party in his room in the hotel and he recounted how fed up he had been on first arrival with the habit of not making up the bed properly, but simply folding the blankets over at the end, so that when he got into bed late at night after a skinful, his legs would shoot out at the end, and he would say in a loud voice: "Why cannot these bloody Communists make up a bed properly?"

After a few nights the bed was miraculously made up in the way in which we are accustomed, so we shouted rude things about the Communist system into what we assumed was the hidden microphone in the wall - a "Ventilator" to the bathroom which only had one vent!

Tito's Yugosalvia at that epoch was always a very pleasant place to arrive at after experiencing the frustrations of Bulgaria and Rumania, which is a contrast to events of the 1990s.   Hotels were well-appointed and comfortable, travel easy to arrange and one had an agent to rely on.   Probably the fact that I had already had my Baptism of Fire in that market in 1958/9 also helped. My main problem in 1960 was juggling between the Coles and Neal Agents, both of whom wanted the total "British Crane" franchise, and Neal had already become involved in a manufacturing licence in Slovenia, where a very urbane "gentleman" called Ing. Birsa, whose excellent command of English endeared him to the aristocratic Brian Neal, was busy conducting a campaign to cut out the Neal Agent in Belgrade from any commission.   I cannot say that I was so acutely aware of the rivalries between the different nationalities who made up the Yugoslav Federation at that time, which is a tribute to the power and political guile of Tito.

If someone had predicted the break-up of Yugoslavia into civil war by the end of the century in the early 1960s, I would not have given it any credence.   I became close friends with the Director of Jugohemija (the Coles Agent, whom I had appointed), a charming man named Bob Maletić, who had once been a priest.   He was an avidly pro-British, having lost three brothers in the War, and I recall how moved he was at the death of Churchill early in 1965, saying that in Yugoslavia his death was felt very keenly.   Bob loved nothing more than a glass of whisky and my visits to his flat were always accompanied by a bottle - his eyes would light up as he pronounced the words "Scotch Whisky" as if it were Holy Water.   Bob half talked me into buying a piece of land on the Yugoslav Coast, which was going very cheaply at the time, and building a small holiday house there. Fortunately the idea never really took root, but it shows the confidence at that period in the future of Yugoslavia.

One of the compensations of this East European travelling was the characters whom one met in the hotels who were also "on the circuit".   On one of my visits to Sofia I spent an evening with a "West Country farmer" type by the name of Cauldwell, whose outward appearance belied a very astute business acumen and who dealt in agricultural machinery and livestock.   He related one particular story about a whole lot of tractors from the Soviet Union with which he was landed after agreeing to take them in part payment. The price was extremely low and he found a gullible purchaser in the USA who did not enquire where they had been manufactured. After he had been satisfied technically, he signed a Contract of Purchase. He even heard Cauldwell ask the telephone exchange for a Moscow number to issue the shipping instructions. "Your representative now in Moscow?" he queried. "Yes" was the laconic reply, and it was only when the consignment arrived that they discovered the country of origin, and then the buyer sent Cauldwell urgent cables saying that the contract must be cancelled. The wily Cauldwell simply presented the cables to the bank who issued the Letter of Credit as proof that the goods had been delivered, and there was nothing which the US purchaser could do about it, but he was apparently forced to melt the tractors down for scrap!

Major Botterill also introduced me to the Roumanian market, but there was really no reason to pay commission to Lamet on business which we could do as well directly.

However there is no doubt that Roumania proved to be the most difficult of all the Communist markets at that time. The bureaucracy was very heavy, and each organization had a Protocol Office through which one had to make all one's appointments. Upon arrival one would telephone for an appointment with a particular individual, and have to wait for the Protocol Office to come back with an agreed date and time, and having spent sometimes the first two days of any visit simply trying to make appointments, very often one found they clashed. Even when I reached the stage after some years of knowing an individual sufficiently well to call him on his direct number and arrange a meeting with him directly, he still would ask me to put an official request through the Protocol Office.

My home from home in Bucharest was the Athenée Palace Hotel, where nearly all visiting businessmen put up. Although old-fashioned it was very comfortable, and a packet of Rothmans to the Manager on every trip assured one always of securing a room. The Head Waiter, known as "Monsieur George", a large bald-headed character with a suitably deferential air, would attend to our needs from the supposedly French cuisine offered in the restaurant, and the bar was the meeting place where one could nearly always count on running in to someone else "on the circuit". Within a few minutes' walking distance were the old Concert Hall, which always seemed to me like a miniature edition of the Albert Hall in London, and the new Concert Hall modelled on the Festival Hall. I was privileged to attend a concert here given by the

French singer, Gilbert Bécaud, to a very appreciative audience to whom French was a second language.

On my first visit early in 1961 I made the acquaintance of Eugene Schental, known to his friends as "Genie", who proved in fact to live up to that appellation.   He was the Commercial Officer at the British Legation and had been previously employed by Masinimport for about eight years, until they suddenly discovered that he had previously worked for the British not long after the War, and so they shot him out as not being politically acceptable. . . They lost the services of a very talented and intelligent man, who spoke fluent English, German, Russian and French in addition to his own native language. I soon became good friends with him and his charming wife, Jessie, and was frequently a guest at his flat, which was a particular pleasure in a country where no-one with whom one associated in business ever dared to invite you to their home.   Genie used to make appointments for me in advance of my arrival and this saved me a great deal of time and helped to beat the bureaucracy, although some State Organizations were even reluctant to deal with the Commercial Office of the Legation.   Genie became known to most British businessmen visiting Bucharest, and to newcomers he was much more informative about the actual situation than the English Commercial Secretaries who only spent two or three years at their posts, and when they had spent sufficient time there to become useful, they would be posted elsewhere.   I can only suppose that this was Foreign Office policy to avoid them become tainted with or sympathetic to the Communist System, but it certainly did not help lonely businessmen like me out there trying to sell Britain...... Some visitors claimed that Genie was "also working for the other side", but I discounted such rumours as being of no importance, even supposing that they was any truth in them.   Very likely he did have to make reports about his contacts with Western businessmen, but I do not suppose for one moment that he would have passed on any sensitive information and to me he was always a very helpful friend with whom I kept in touch every Christmas until in 1999 I did not hear from him and I learned later that he had died suddenly of a heart attack.

Over dinner one evening in the Bucuresti Restaurant, Genie related a most interesting story.   The Bucuresti was the top restaurant in Bucharest, complete with chandeliers and plush velvet curtains unchanged since the heady days of the 1930s.   The manager was a Greek known as "Papa Costa", a distinguished white-haired old gentleman who had owned the place before the War and the

Government had allowed him to continue to manage it, and I suppose that the top Party officials often dined there. The food was superb, provided that one took the recommendation of Papa Costa, who was also partial to Rothmans cigarettes, a 200 pack of which I gave him on each visit to Bucharest. The tale which Genie unfolded to me in these comfortable surroundings concerned a pilot of TAROM, the Roumanian State Airline, personally known to him, who had landed an Iluyshin 18 Airliner with 70 passengers on board in 1962 on a beach in Cyprus on only one engine, all three others having cut out as he came in to land. (The Il 18 was the Russian equivalent to the British Britannia, a large four-engined turbo-prop aircraft which was my favourite means of transport in Eastern Europe). At the time there were some NATO exercises and some French pilots came up and wanted to see the plane, but the pilot had received strict instructions not to let anyone go near it, pending the arrival of experts from Moscow. Nevertheless the Frenchmen managed to get the Roumanian talking on what actually occurred and they were able to tell him that they had had a similar experience with a similar aircraft and had solved the problem. It was something to do with specific atmospheric conditions causing the engines to fail and it could be remedied simply by fitting a filter in a certain place. From this the conversation moved on to how much reward the pilot could expect for having saved 70 lives and a valuable aircraft, and the estimates ran into thousands of dollars....

When the pilot returned to Bucharest, he was given a hero's welcome, and sent off to rest in the mountains with his family, but five days later he was recalled because Iluyshin himself wanted to see him in Moscow. It seems that, at that time, the Iluyshin Aircraft Works was run by father and son themselves, even though it was, of course, a State Organization. The reception accorded him in Moscow was tremendous, and the elder Iluyshin was delighted that he had proved that his aircraft could still fly on only one engine, something which no test pilot had ever achieved. He wanted to reward him, and since he could do nothing official, he proposed to present him with a motor car from his own pocket. The Roumanian was very pleased and arranged to collect the vehicle the next day, but he was called to the Roumanian Embassy, the officials of which had not been invited to the party. They had heard the news and questioned him about it, and then, to his intense chagrin they told him that he could not possibly accept the car, because it was a Roumanian plane and it would not be right for him to accept a present from the Russians, since it would be the Roumanian Govt who would reward him, so he was sent back to Bucharest without even being able to bid farewell to his Russian hosts. He returned to his family in the mountains to complete his vacation, at the end of which a special ceremony was arranged at Baneasa Airport when he was decorated by a high-ranking Minister and given a "Cash Reward" as a special gesture amounting to 500 lei (£12 at the official rate of exchange at the time). Apart from the incredible meanness evinced in this story, I think that it also illustrates very well that official relationships between the two hardline Communist Governments were not very good, as evidenced by later events.

Strangely the other Commercial Attaché who also proved to be a helpful friend was none other than Nicolae Cocos, based at the Roumanian Commercial Office in London. Nicolae always seemed to be extremely busy with several telephones in his office constantly ringing. Whilst engaged in one conversation, he would pick up another telephone which started to ring and, without bothering to find out who it was, he would almost shout into it: "I am in another line, pleez to ring back in five minutes" and then slam it down. James Steel's son, David, joined the company at about that time and part of his initiation was to spend time with me on my rounds, and when I took him to meet Nicolae, the imitation which I had so frequently given of this telephone performance was apparently so accurate that David had great difficulty in keeping a straight face when it happened! Cocos was almost an essential in procuring visas to visit Roumania, and there was one particular occasion when he tried very hard to save some important business for us, which was one of the bitterest experiences of my early selling career.

In the Spring of 1962, I was outwitted by a wily Swede, who was my competitor. I had negotiated for two weeks to sell a clutch of five truck cranes to the Ministry of the Chemical Industry, and I established a very good personal rapport with the Technical Director, whose name was Molnar. I thought that I had found an End-User like Mostostal in Poland who would dictate to the State Importer, Masinimport, what they had to buy. During the technical discussions I even commented in my journal on the professionalism shown by the technical engineers, but it was an illusion. However I left Bucharest after the initial visit with a Letter of Intent for one 80 Tonne Valiant Truck and four 50 Tonne Conqueror Trucks, but the confirmation did not materialise. We exerted pressure through the Roumanian Legation in London without success and finally I returned to Bucharest just before Easter to try and sort matters out. I found that four "50 Ton" Koehring Cranes had been offered at prices 30% below that of Coles, through a Swede named Kaminski (who was in league with Walter Husser.) He knew nothing about the cranes, but he had a masterly appreciation of how to secure a contract for goods in Rumania - by simply quoting the lowest price. Masinimport refused to let me see a copy of his offer, but assured me that technically it was equivalent to ours. When I pointed out to my friend Director Molnar and his colleagues that they had specified diesel-electric cranes, and that the Koehring cranes were diesel-mechanical, they assured me that I was wrong, and, on producing the spec sheet in English (which they could not understand) they pointed the to word "electric" which was followed by the word "lighting"!

They then acknowledged their error, but could do nothing about it because all had now been approved by the Ministry of Foreign Trade to buy the Koehrings. However, they promised to insist on Coles, provided that we could accept the 30% reduction in price. I informed Mattingley and Cooke back at base and assured them that I still thought that we could get the order. The company was desperate for big truck crane orders at the time, even at cost to cover Works Overheads and finally James Steel himself gave the OK. I went back to Masinimport with a 30% price reduction, only to be asked for an additional 5%, at which point I blew my top and left. My superiors should have been experienced enough to tell me to walk away from the deal instead of making a fool of myself. The Roumanians found that they had contracted to buy four basic machines without any booms or hooks (even a layman must understand that a crane without a boom or hook cannot lift anything....) for a price 30% lower than we had quoted for four complete units, and not only did they have to reduce the number of cranes to three in order to equip the cranes with booms etc, but they also had to de-rate them, because the capacities were in US Short Tons based on 85% of Tipping Load instead of Metric Tonnes at 66%. Cocos realised what a stupid mistake Masinimport had made and tried hard from London to get the decision reversed, but Masinimport just did not believe that we had not loaded the price in the first place. Masinimport even tried to get us to reduce the price on the firm order for the 80 Tonne Valiant by 30%, threatening cancellation if we did not agree, but Cocos and his boss Radulescu helped us to resist this and this stood us in good stead later on when the customer really began to appreciate the difference in quality between Coles and Koehring. A year later I had established an excellent rapport with a senior Vice-Minister in the Petro-Chemical Industry, Cioroiu, and we sold several more cranes.

But even now that we began to be successful, every single order was a tremendous price battle - Masinimport never recognized that Western manufacturers sometimes had to increase prices, and there is no doubt that Roumania was the toughest market with which I had to deal. I had a Russian-speaking friend who assured me that he found it easier to deal with the Soviets than with the Roumanians. This was also confirmed by a high official in the Board of Trade at the time, who described the Roumanians as "commercial blackmailers and the worst people to deal with in Eastern Europe".

But April 1962, with the loss of the order to Koehring, was definitely one of the low points in my life, because, added to this business disappointment was the fact that my dear wife, Audrey, (as it proved to be, in the early stages of pregnancy with our first child) was getting very fed up with being left alone in a small Chiltern village, where we had purchased and renovated a Victorian cottage, whilst I travelled for such long periods, and, after my return on Easter Sunday having lost this important order, we were faced with the decision of selling the cottage after only 18 months and moving nearer to London. For me, it was a question of chucking in the job, or acknowledging that the purchase of a country cottage had been a mistake. Fortunately we made the right decision, and moved to Uxbridge, which remained our home up until I retired, and I stayed in the business of exporting cranes.

Two of the characters with whom I had my regular dealings at Masinimport remain indelibly inscribed in my memory. The Head of Department was Mr. Trailescu, a small dark-haired individual with one of the meanest looking faces I can ever remember. It was necessary, but difficult, to butter him up, and the only time which I can ever recall cracking some sort of a smile from his twisted countenance was when he suddenly came out with one or two words in English and I quickly paid him an unctuous compliment: "Mr. Trailescu, I had no idea that you spoke such good English", to which he writhed in "umble" pleasure rather like Uriah Heep and replied: "One leetle". His assistant, Nenetu, was much more open with me, but scared of becoming too friendly. He spoke good French, in which language all negotiations were conducted and all contracts written. He was always, however, scruffily dressed, to give the impression that he was a good comrade, and sometimes, to add effect, he came to the office unshaven.

The Chief of the Protocol Office, who was a very important man to cultivate, since it was he who controlled the allocation of appointments, was a man named Rentz, with whom I established a good rapport. It was in the Spring of 1963, when we were beginning to get over the debacle of the lost order, that he asked me one day if I would do him a favour, which both surprised and pleased me.   He spoke very good English, but his request was if I would agree to his recording my voice by reading some passages from his English textbook, so that he could perfect his accent.   I duly turned up at the office in the late afternoon after the close of business, and I started reading out long vocabularies and passages about going shopping etc.   I really was concentrating on voice production, as if I were competing for the School Reading Prize, and I did not pay too much attention to the text, until I suddenly woke up to the fact that I was starting to churn out political propaganda. The text went like this: "England is the oldest of the Capitalist Countries and depends upon her livelihood by the ruthless exploitation of her Colonies".   I managed to omit the words "ruthless exploitation", so I did not completely fall into the trap, but I refused to continue by reading out that "all land was still in the hands of the landed gentry".   So I stopped reading and protested angrily at the wording of the text.   Rentz was visibly embarassed and apologised, and then we went on to some passages which were totally innocuous. Interestingly enough, the only piece of genuine literature quoted was from Pickwick Papers, one of my favourite novels!   When we had finished, I went back to the disputed passage, and found myself in heated argument with a totally convinced Communist (or one who appeared to be such), and we continued the discussion out in the street, which struck me as being highly incongruous.   I challenged him that he would never agree to invite me to his flat, to which he gave a very half-hearted assent, but explained that the reason why visiting businessmen like myself were not usually invited into people's homes was because there was always the danger that this would lead to bribery and corruption.   He considered the Roumanian system of doing business to be perfect.   However, I think that he somehow respected me for standing up to his arguments, and in fact from that time on he was always extremely friendly and helpful in such matters as getting me an appointment with one of the top Directors, and often referred to the fact that he had been listening to my voice on the tape.   One day he suddenly disappeared, and I have no idea what became of him.   Perhaps he overstepped the mark..........

As a great contrast to the scruffy officials at Masinimport was a director of the Ministry of Construction, Dinu Giurcaneanu, the son of a pre-War Banker, who was hospitable and friendly on a personal level to an amazing extent. He had adjusted to life under Communism, concentrating on his technical job and keeping his nose out of politics.   He took me out one Sunday to see the old Palace of the Kings at Mogosoia, which had been built in the 1930s by the Hohenzollens, Roumania's foreign princes, and he was a particularly good guide because he had been in charge of the re-construction. Each room was designed and furnished in a very lavish style representing different cultures, all done at a time when the peasants were starving. Giurcaneanu, who was very informative about Roumania's past history of Turkish and Hungarian domination, clearly felt that Communism was a better option than the pre-War Kingdom.

He told me, for instance, that poor people could obtain State loans to build their own cottages, but this was at a time when Gheorghe Gheorghiu-Dej was still President, before the policies of destroying old villages and herding peasants into concrete blocks initiated by Ceausescu. I was actually in Bucharest in March 1965 when Gheorghiu-Dej died and there is no doubt that there was a genuine feeling of national mourning at that time. This was on the occasion of my last trip for Coles, just before I handed in my notice, and whilst I was sitting at dinner in the Athenée Palace Hotel with my half Russian friend, he pointed out to me a rather unattractive greasy hook-nosed Arab and told me that he knew that he would be on the same plane as I to Sofia the next day and to avoid him at all costs. My friend proved right about my travelling companion, but he caught me as I showed my passport at the Check-In with the words: "Oh, you are Briteesh, too, I see" and promptly introduced himself and started to ask all about me in an inquisitive and persistent manner to which it was very difficult to reply without being actually rude. He sat next to me on the plane and it was then I discovered that his religion prevented him from taking alcohol (a Muslim, I supposed). At Sofia, where I was in transit to Athens, there were interminable delays, because of bad weather and a party was started amongst the stranded passengers, some Italians, Frenchmen and a Jordanian, which was noticed by some Soviet officers who were carousing with their Bulgarian counterparts on the other side of the restaurant.

An extremely inebriated Russian colonel came over with a bottle of cognac and greeted me warmly, referring to our having been allies in the War ("Churchill - Stalin...."), and insisted that we all drink with him. When he came to the greasy Arab, who refused, he became very upset and said in a loud voice: "You vill not drink ze health of ze Soviet Union!" and I forestalled an international incident by saying to him in a loud whisper; "Take it, you fool, you don't have to drink it!" and steering the drunken Colonel away with the excuse that my Arab friend was not feeling well. Useless to explain to a Soviet officer about possible religious scruples.

British Crane

Dinner in Belgrade in the early 1960s with Bob Maletić and his wife.

Guy Checketts (left) of Hawker Siddeley International, who walked around Plovdiv in remote Bulgaria wearing a bowler hat and carrying a rolled umbrella, pictured here with David Steel at a trade fair .

CHAPTER FOUR - THE MEDITERRANEAN

Away from Eastern Europe, my responsibilities also encompassed Spain, Portugal and Greece, which countries I first visited at the beginning of 1961. Coles were represented in Lisbon by a very aristocratic company called Guedes y Almeida, and the Guedes Family ran the show. They were very charming and extremely hospitable people, and I soon got on very well with the youngest member of the family who spoke impeccable English and had been educated at Cambridge, and I know that this had been one of Robert Albon's favourite stamping grounds, referring to the Portuguese as "our oldest ally", but I have to admit that I felt rather uncomfortable in the Portugal of Dictator Salazar, where the extremes of wealth and poverty were so obvious. I used to be entertained in expensive restaurants where there were more waiters than diners, and this I found embarassing to a degree, and even more so when Angola was seeking her independence from Portugal and everywhere there were signs announcing that Angola was part of Portugal. But in those days Guedes and Almeida did a very professional job for Coles, and really my visits were not very arduous, although satisfying in that one had a very full programme organized for one's trip.

Franco's Spain was very different. I felt that there was definitely a middle class which did not seem to exist in Portugal, and one could wander about Madrid feeling perfectly safe, which is certainly not possible today as we found out from a recent visit.

The Coles Dealer, or Agent, I should say, was a very reputable company called Gumersindo Garcia, headed by Don Gumersindo himself. "I recognized the old gentleman" I wrote in January 1961, "from the 1958 Conference, and he claimed to recognize me, but I think that it was just politeness. He is 72, enormously tall and very fat, with a head as bald as a coot and about three necks, but a very kindly old boy." Our conversation was frequently interrupted by phone calls, coming, it seems from different parts of the world, and he had just been presented with some award from the Belgian Ambassador, so I was careful to offer my congratulations. I was shown the great books wherein were inscribed tributes from General Franco, from the Ministry of This and the Ministry of That, and the signatures of the Big White Chiefs of the Companies he represented.... Coles was a minor account compared to such names as Bucyrus-Eyrie and Le Tourneau Westinghouse. Every machine was sold direct to end-users, nothing was held in stock and I do not think that they even carried many spare parts. High tariffs protected local crane manufacturers, so there was not much market for Coles at that time. I did eventually persuade them to take a crane for stock, but, in practice, it was already on-sold, and only after interminable discussions about terms and risk-taking, with my being squeezed in between the demands of the desk-bound Sales Management in the U.K. and Spanish pride in not being trusted to confirm a promise to order. "What happens if the customer lets us down?" Coles, at that time, were entirely unfamiliar with the idea of taking any risks in the market. However in 1962 Gumersindo Garcia took on an excellent Sales Engineer, a rotund cheerful character called Salvador Salvador, who became a lifelong friend, and together we did some deals direct with important customers like Dragados y Construcciones. I think that the number of friendships which I made during my selling career was one of its greatest pleasures and I just could not bring myself to do business with people whom I did not like or could not trust, however expedient this might have been at times.

Lunch as a guest of Don Gumersindo was indeed an occasion. On that particular day in January 1961, there were nine of us, including a number of foreign visitors like myself. The meal started at 2 pm and finished at 5 pm, when we went back to the office to work! "You like lamb?" the old gentleman enquired of me, to which I replied enthusiastically that we ate a lot of lamb in England. He corrected me: "In England you eat mutton" and I soon found out why, because, after two courses of hors d'oeuvres, mountains of fresh seafood and then smoked ham, the main dish was placed on the table on a huge silver salver - a complete roast lamb, and I do not think that there was much left at the end of the meal, since the waiters piled each plate high with the meat, which was washed down by some excellent red wine.

Prior to my first visit to the Gumersindo Garcia organization, in 1959 the Home Sales Jamboree took place in Madrid. This was a reward to all the salesmen for meeting their targets, and they would be fêted at some attractive place abroad, together with their wives, and, of course, all the senior managers and directors. The Jamboree included a visit to a bull farm just outside Madrid, which had a small ring used to train would-be youthful bullfighters. This is the account of what happened, as recounted by Frank Bacon, who was one of the party:

"The head man ordered the gate to be opened, and in lolloped a small bull, a poor specimen whose every movement was a real effort. The potential matador, aged about 20, predictably performed well, to the applause of the onlookers. A second bull was then summoned, and matador number two gave an equally satisfactory display.   At this point the entire audience had been conditioned to believe that learning the art of bullfighting was a simple process, starting with a docile creature, and progressing from there.   Accordingly the head man suggested that someone in the audience might wish to try their hand, and so, keen to obtain the approval of his peers (and to demonstrate his undoubted nerve) up jumped smoothie Bernard Burden, (the Area Manager from Manchester, who had unsuccessfully tried to persuade Frankie Marler of Dukinfield to drop his insistence on having his crane repainted, as I have recounted earlier.)   The third bull was then summoned, and in charged a very sprightly animal, intent on dire trouble to anyone standing in its way.   Poor Bernard could not believe his eyes.   He just stood there protecting himself with his cape, and as the bull was about to deal a severe blow to the satisfactory continuation of his love life, someone shouted that a sideways stance might be more effective, which was followed by frantic shouts from his wife, Lulu, to get him out.   To his credit, Bernard pulled off a couple of passes from the bull, but the horn injured his thigh in the process, and then, to the intense relief of the Coles Party, and the raucous laughter of the Spanish onlookers, the officials stepped in and rescued the luckless Burden."

Perhaps Greece was the most fascinating place of all three of these countries on my patch, because the Coles Agent there, much frequented by George Ricketts, were a pair of quite unforgettable characters called Dracopoulos and Petratos.   Old Draco, as he was affectionately known, was the Senior Partner, who made all the decisions. Their premises resembled a small warehouse, filled with a jumble of dusty parts and pieces of machinery, which gave straight on to the street.   On one side of the interior was a gallery accessed by a steep staircase, and from this eyrie old Draco looked down on and regularly shouted, or rather screamed, down at the diminutive Petratos who occupied a much humbler position on the floor.   Draco was filled with his own self-importance, and on one occasion he said to me in the slow pompous manner which he adopted when speaking English (as opposed to screeching at Petratos in Greek): "I remember the occasion when Meestair Eric Steel visited us here in Athens. 'Meestair Dracopoulos', he said, 'you are the Very Man to represent us here in Greece.' "   He was particularly proud of his connections with the Port of Piraeus, who had a large fleet of Coles Cranes, all purchased by Public Tenders carefully written around the diesel-electric system in such a way as to exclude the majority of competitors.   George Ricketts used to recount how Draco visited the Port with a bag of gold coins which were discreetly distributed to the important decision-makers.

However, when I first visited Greece for Coles in April 1961, old Draco was a crumpled figure. He had invested more money than he could afford in some disastrous ill-advised projects in Italy, and had been declared bankrupt, so it was my task to look for another agent. In this I was very ably assisted by the Federation of British Industries local representative, Henry Malcolm. Henry was an ex-patriate Scot from a military family background, which he had rebelled against. He was forced into the Regular Army by his father, and was put into a unit where his brother was the RSM and picked on him unmercifully, but Henry approached his CO, explained the circumstances and got himself transferred. His father even tried to stop him leaving the Regular Army after the War, but Henry, who had fought with the forces who liberated Greece from the Nazis in 1944, had other ideas. He had been so enchanted with the country that he returned after the War and married a Greek girl, Haroulla, who was related by marriage to old Draco. He recounted how marriage was still based on the Dowry System, and the first engagement party to which he was invited turned out to be a haggling session between the prospective bride and bridegroom's family, with better offers from some other party being put on the table! When Henry himself went to his prospective Father-in-Law to ask for the hand of his daughter, the old boy started to enumerate what she had to offer and he was cut short with words to the effect that if she only came with the shoes that she stood up in, he wanted to marry her. The old gent was much taken aback, but when he saw that he was serious, he reached for a bottle and said: "Well, let's celebrate!" Henry had his own business, and did not really want to get involved with Dracopoulos and Petratos, but, after seeing several other candidates for the agency, I decided that it would be best to stick with them, provided Henry baled them out, and this, in effect, is what finally happened, with some pressure to do so in order to retain family pride. However, before this old Draco was like a broken reed, almost dissolving into tears, whereas Petratos, who had been opposed to these deals (but had given in to keep the peace) was much more resilient.

Then Draco would suddenly become convinced that someone would wave a magic wand and all would be OK again, and, when Henry had finally baled him out and saved the business, his old pompousness and bounce returned, as he convinced himself that really the rescuing of the business was all his own work. "He has a hide like a rhinoceros" was Henry's dry comment, but I know that, at times, he drove Henry mad, particularly when he did things behind his back, which was not infrequent.

British Crane

I learned more about modern Greece from Henry Malcolm than years of Classical Education had taught me. There are, or were, two spoken languages, Demotic Greek and Pure Greek. One of the reasons why the Communists gained so much support after the War was that they published newspapers in demotic Greek, as a result of which it was later forbidden. One tends to forget that Greece was almost sucked into the Communist bloc, and indeed Haroulla had been kidnapped by them from her home in Athens and marched toward the Bulgarian border for 14 days with very little food or water. She was helped by some friends in a village through which she was passing, who bartered for her release with tobacco and then hid her until the danger had passed.

Henry and his family became close friends of ours. He went on working until the end of his life, cut short by his refusal to give up smoking, even after he had had extensive surgery to replace main arteries furred up by the dreaded weed, despite the repeated warnings from Haroulla, who, to this day, has never quite forgiven him for shuffling this mortal coil before his time..... Henry's very dry sense of humour, very necessary for existence in the cacophonous Greek world, was unforgettable. When the screams and shouts of the females of the Malcolm clan became too much, he would beckon significantly to me and propose that we "slip out for a beer". He used to drive around Athens in a somewhat clapped out Austin Cambridge, and, being small of stature, his nose would only just appear above the bottom of the windscreen.

He used frequently to get reprimanded by Haroulla for eyeing the figures of the young Greek girls from this low vantage point as he drove along, to which he would make the excuse "But they change shape very quickly". That old car made several trips all the way to London, because, I believe, Haroulla preferred that method of transport at that time to flying, and when I took Audrey on a visit to the Salonika Fair in September 1963, Haroulla insisted on buying some chickens to take back to Athens. It was a two day journey, and by the time we reached their home, the stench in the car was almost intolerable.

But Henry could be very sensitive and, on one occasion, the director of a potential customer whom we had visited in Greece, Halkis Cement, and whom we had quoted for a crane, turned up in London to finalise the deal, and told me that, whereas several agents representing our competitors had visited him since we last met in Athens, there had been no visit from Henry Malcolm. I thought "Friendship or no friendship, I cannot let him get away with that" and I wrote what I thought was a tactful, but clearly critical, letter.

The response was a written tirade directed to Ron Cooke against the insolent young upstart who had presumed to criticise a man of his experience, comparing me to a subaltern presuming to tell his CO what to do etc etc. I have to give Ron full credit that he immediately discussed it with me and I told him the background, and he left it to me to reply, which I did promptly and apologetically. A week or two later, Henry himself arrived at the office and immediately asked for me, and when I broached the subject he laughed and said that he was feeling a bit off-colour that day! Although a true blue Scot, Henry had certainly absorbed some Greek into his make-up....

On one of his last visits to London, in the mid 1980s, Henry arrived carrying a piece of polished wood and asked me if I could take him to a particular address in south London in connection with this artefact. When I enquired the purpose of this visit, he told me with a chuckle that he had to obtain an exact replica of his mother-in-law's wooden leg!

The Home Sales Jamboree in Madrid 1959.
Left to Right: Reg. Keates, Don Gumersindo and James Steel.

Bernard Burden the Bull-fighter.

Greece: Henry Malcolm (2nd from left) with Petratos (centre) and Dracopoulos (right).

Reception at the Salonika Fair with both our wives, Haroulla (centre) and Audrey on the right

CHAPTER FIVE - B.C.E.C

In July 1963 James Steel announced to all staff that he had finally succeeded in obtaining permission to use the grandiose and currently popular title for the Group of "Corporation", and "British Crane Company" became "British Crane and Excavator Corporation", to equate with British Motor Corporation which Donald Stokes of Leyland had acquired for his company.

BCEC was to take in all the three manufacturing plants, and the off-shore marketing organization of Incranex in New York and Steel AG in Switzerland were to come under Ron Cooke.   I recall that Reg Keates was not very happy about this at the time, and doubtless started laying plans for his own aggrandisement at some future date.   Soon afterwards it was decided to close the two off-shore marketing organisations, since dealers in Europe and Latin America now had a chance to explain directly how much they resented the attentions of a stolid German Swiss and a brash Yankee. Robert Albon's firm opposition to these two ventures was now totally justified.

Early in 1964 I was called in and asked to take over the Latin American market for BCEC, after the decision to close down Incranex, so I was not too put out by being snubbed over the Poznan Fair.   I found out later that Herb Strack had insisted with James Steel that I was the only person to whom he would agree to do this Hand-Over, since he knew that I was still well remembered by some of the dealers from my trips in 1959.   I was careful to exact a promise from Mattingley that, if I so decided, I would be given the position of Regional Sales Executive for the area.   Audrey was backing me, hoping that my itineraries would be better planned in advance, rather than the instant demands for travel dictated by direct selling into Eastern Europe.

The trip, which took place in July / August (and started shortly before my fifth Wedding Anniversary) was a very tough one indeed and involved five weeks of continuous travel, starting with a week in Red Bank, New Jersey, where the office was located, going through all the files.   The first leg of the trip took in Trinidad, Jamaica, Venezuela and Colombia, and this I did in the company of Herb's Strack's colleague, Herman King, who spent the whole 10 days telling me how much he hated Strack and how he had made up his mind to leave anyway.   From Peru through to Chile, Paraguay, Uruguay and Argentina I travelled with the bombastic Herb for two weeks, and not only did I have to contend with some embarrassing meetings with dealers who had become totally fed up with his Yankee approach, and were very pleased to see an

British Crane

English face again (especially the old Scotsman in Chile, Alexander Samson, who remembered me very clearly from my trip in 1959), but at times I had to make it very clear to Herb that I was taking over the market and things would be done my way and not his.   The only place where he seemed to have any friends was Buenos Aires, but the bragadaccio mentality of some Argentines probably found a soulmate in him.   The Brazilians would not agree to see him at all, so at least the last leg of the trip was more peaceful, but by that time I was getting extremely tired, and I had to route myself back through New York for a final session.   The last straw on that least of enjoyable trips was the Bolshie attitude of the cab drivers at Heathrow Airport, when I arrived, in a state of complete and utter exhaustion, late on a Sunday evening.   This was at the time that cab drivers could charge what they liked outside an area within a radius of six miles from Central London (which dated from the days of horse-drawn cabs) and it was a question of negotiation.   Uxbridge always was (and still is) an unpopular run, and the "going rate" at that time was £1. 10s. If the meter had applied it would have chalked up about 5s, so the fare was already exorbitant for distance.

No driver would take me at all, so the porter called a policeman over who instructed the first cab driver on the rank to take me.   I carefully agreed the fare at 30 shillings, and then, as soon as the copper had walked away the driver leered at me and said:"Two quid (£2) to you, Guv".   I was so infuriated that I all but landed my fist in his face, but instead wisely recalled the policeman, who promptly threw him off the rank and another driver took me for the agreed amount.   As if this was not all, when I returned to the office, Mattingley was away, and Ron Cooke, after receiving my verbal report, said briefly: "Well thanks very much, Dick.   Just hand it all over to Eric Drew". Not a word of discussion even about the promise that I should handle the market if I so desired.   I liked old Eric as a colleague very much - he and I shared a strong admiration for Robert Albon, but he was not of my calibre, and if he was to handle the market why had he not been asked to do the Hand-Over Trip.   When I think back today, my mind just boggles at the appalling management technique of Coles Export at the time.

CHAPTER SIX - FAREWELL TO COLES

The final straw in my relationship with Mattingley came at the beginning of November.

In actual fact, as my hard work in Eastern Europe was really starting to bear fruit -- even Bulgaria was about to produce its first order, and I was starting to get really interested in the possibilities of counter-purchase, I was not unhappy about "losing" South America, but just incensed at the manner in which it had been done. With pressure from Stephen Grey, Bill Murray and me, Mattingley finally had to come off the "Divide and Rule" fence and make some decisions about splitting Europe into zones.

A moustachioed ex RAF goon who happened to speak Spanish called Ted Scoones (known to the Spaniards as "Sco hones") had joined the firm and I was abruptly informed that he would be taking over Spain and Portugal from me. Ted never sent cables but "signals" and turned out to be another alcoholic.... Be that as it may, I was left with Poland, the Balkans and Greece, and Colin Wright was to work with me. Colin had recovered from his injuries and was back in harness, but I did not think that he would be prepared to accept me as his immediate superior, and I was right. I had told Dennis that, with my greater experience (and indeed maturity!) I expected to run the "zone" and he agreed, but he presented a different picture to Colin, evidenced by the latter saying to me that we must decide which territories each of us should handle.

We both decided to tackle Mattingley together, who squirmed and prevaricated in an attempt to keep us both happy. The interview did make me happy, in the sense that it brought me to a decision to leave Coles (I should say BCEC, but I could never accustom myself to that, as I was always Dick Lloyd, Firmy Coles).

It must be appreciated that this was a momentous decision for me. One did not change one's job easily in those days. I loved the product, I was finally successful, I was well thought of at high level by the Senior Directors in the Steel Group up to the Chairman himself, but I just had to get away from Dennis Mattingley.

As soon as I had made my decision, I felt a great sense of relief. I did a trip all over Yugoslavia shortly afterwards, when I actually hired a car and covered potential cranes users in the Forestry Industry, discussing also the possibility of doing business by barter, in which I was just getting interested, despite Mattingley's opposition.

This trip, which took in Poland as well gave me a couple of most hair-raising air journeys I have ever had, both in succession.   I had to fly to Orly Airport in Paris to pick up a Yugoslav Airlines Caravelle to Zagreb.   The take-off was delayed from 1515 to 1930 hours and the plane, full to capacity, started pitching about in a most abnormal manner as soon as we had taken off, and the engines never settled down to their usual hum.   There were very tense faces all round as the Captain announced that we would have to return to Orly Airport.   I really felt that my number was up and I had a mental picture of the morning newspapers showing the wreckage of the aircraft.   I tried to pray but couldn't and just sat there clasping my amulet on my little finger.   The plane, still tossing and weaving, came down safely and the sighs of relief as we touched the runway were quite audible.   We were told that there would be further delays and then were invited to have dinner at JAT's (Jugoslovenski Aerotransport) expense. I split a bottle of Beaujolais with a Frenchman booked on the same flight, and then we decided to have another, so that by the time that we took off at midnight, I didn't care what happened!   There were very few passengers left - most had decided that enough was enough and made other arrangements.   We finally reached Zagreb at 3 am and I got to bed at 4.30 am....   During my trip, I was also nearly written off by a bloody fool overtaking a bus on a blind corner on a winding mountain road, and I finally had to abandon the hire car because the clutch packed in and I finished my journey by taxi and train.   It was a fascinating trip, in which I came very much to appreciate the differences in the various states which made up the Yugoslav Federation.   In Slovenia, even under Communism, one might have felt that one was in Austria.   The hotels were clean and comfortable, the service in the restaurants excellent, and they even had night clubs with strip-tease artistes. The reader might raise an eyebrow in surprise that such a thing was worth commenting on, but socialist morality normally completely forbade anything like that in those days.

As a contrast, Bosnia was primitive.   Although there were modern blocks alongside the old Turkish houses built round wooden frames, the streets were normally still of mud with great piles of rubble littering the pavements.   My companion, a young Serb called George Hranisavljević, who was quite partial to a drop or two - and sometimes too many - suggested one day as we were travelling that we take a look inside a farmhouse, he hoping that we would be regaled with a glass of slivervića (he was disappointed), but we were permitted by complete strangers to look inside.   The drive up to the farmhouse consisted of cattle track about a foot deep in mud and wet slime and around the dwelling hens were scratching right on to the verandah and possibly inside, and the only difference there was that the mud was hard packed and dry. Everything appeared to be very dirty and a couple of ragged children clung to their mother's skirts in a dwelling where the lifestyle did not seem to have changed much for several hundred years.   Our trip included a visit to Sarajevo, where I made my first ever visit to a mosque, and explored the old streets with their rows of tiny shops where the coppersmiths were working and selling their wares.   At the time it struck me as most unusual in that Socialist land of State Organizations to find these rows of ancient private shops, gleaming with hand-beaten copper articles, each with his little charcoal-burner used for the dual purpose of heating the copper and the room.

My flight, this time in a Convair Metropolitan, on to Warsaw began uneventfully enough on a beautiful sunny morning, but it soon clouded over and the plane started to descend through dense cloud as we prepared to land.   But, when we did finally break through the cloud, we found ourselves only what seemed to be 200 or 300 metres high above thick forest, and the pilot immediately climbed back into the cloud again, which produced some uncomfortable feelings in my stomach once again.

I asked the Steward if we were lost and he assured me not, and he was correct in that when we did come out of the cloud a second time, we were right over the runway, and the pilot then had to put the nose down sharply in order to land.   We hit the tarmac about half way along the runway and he just managed to pull up before the end.

I was thankful that I was in a propeller-driven aircraft and not a jet!   After my battles with the Roumanians, I found the Poles a soft touch on that trip and tied up a contract for further cranes within two or three days.

It took me several weeks to find a new job and during that time I avoided confidential chats with Mattingley, and had to invent imaginary meetings out of the office, in order to attend interviews, because I knew that if Dennis suspected my intentions, he would talk me round.   Business on my "patch" was starting to roll in, and the Roumanians were now going for Coles in a big way, despite the fact that a 70 Tonne Gargantua tipped over during installation with the maximum length of boom on it.   I suspected that it was the Service

Engineer's fault, because, instead of making a proper square wooden block by clamping pieces of solid timber together to be placed under the outrigger jacks, he had relied on a couple of railway sleepers, but I argued that the ground had given way, and whilst I knew that we would have to replace the smashed boom, I fought like a tiger with Masinimport to get them to "take this into consideration on the next round of negotiations". All the thanks I got from Mattingley was criticism that I had tried to fool him about it, when my sole concern was to protect the company's interests. He did sense my coolness, and called me in "for a quiet little chat", enquiring "solicitously" what the matter was. "Nothing", I replied, "Why do you ask? Am I not doing my job properly?" He had no reply to this, and said that he was relieved to hear it, to which I answered coolly: "Thank you for your interest", to which came the answer: "It's not interest, it's affection"! I felt like replying to the effect that I had not yet turned homosexual....

Robert Albon offered me a position as an "Export Specialist" for John Allen of Oxford, but he insisted on a minimum of six months' travel a year and, much as I liked and respected him, I also felt that it would be a retrograde step to go back to him.

Peter Hamilton of Hymac bent over backwards to create a new position into which I could fit, and since this involved several meetings with him and his colleagues, I began to run out of subterfuges for skipping out of the office. In the evening of the day in May 1965 when I actually got the job over a breakfast meeting, Mattingley again started to probe, so, knowing that the letter was in the post, I finally agreed to talk and suggested that we go into his office. "I am leaving the company" I stated coldly and with great satisfaction, and you would have thought that I had shot him with a pistol as he slumped in his chair and his pale face went ghastly white. I had been totally successful in concealing my intentions from him - I think that he must have thought that I was about to confide some marital problem to him. All the protestations about how I should have consulted him etc etc just washed straight over my head.

At last I was free.

Personal sadness then intervened when my Father had a severe stroke from which he never recovered, so that I was able to absent myself from the office on compassionate grounds, because, although I was asked not to tell any of my colleagues, I was grounded during my three month period of notice. Towards the end of that period, David Steel invited me to dinner and I spilled all the beans to him.   Although he had no involvement at that time with Export, he predicted changes, and Reg Keates became unusually warm and friendly, indicating his anticipated rise to greater heights in the Steel Group hierarchy.   David asked me to stay in touch, which I did, and this proved to be fundamental in the shape which my future career was to take.

COLES OVERSEAS

Coles did come back later into my life, but indirectly, and before I leave it as my main theme, I would like to record something of their manufacturing and sales subsidiaries outside the UK, because it does illustrate what an international organization they were.

In the 1950s, assembly plants for Coles diesel-electric cranes existed in Australia, the USA (which supplied cranes to Boeing for handling aircraft engines) and in India, where a manufacturing licence was set up in 1960 with the CAT dealer, Tractors India. The Indian Factory went on producing diesel-electrics long after production had ceased in the UK, and this company still exists today as "TIL Ltd" (originally Tractors India). More than 3000 diesel electric cranes have been manufactured in India, production of which was gradually switched to hydraulic machines in the late 1980s. Today the company builds mainly Grove RT Cranes, following an agreement made in 1996, but there is still one survivor from the old Coles days, the Hydra 830M, a 30 Tonne Truck Crane based on the old Coles Hydra Truck. They currently sell between 500 and 700 cranes a year into India, which represents 80% to 90% of the market, and they also export to neighbouring countries like Bangladesh.

However first in the field was Coles Krane in Duisburg, Germany, which was founded as early as 1946/7, soon after the War. Heinz Heyer was the eccentric, but brilliant Managing Director, who had been in the Hitler Youth and fought with the Wehrmacht at the age of 16 in Russia. He was a law unto himself in the Coles Organization, since he reported directly to Arnold Hallsworth, and Coles Export had no jurisdiction over him at all. A very hard worker himself, he was a paranoid taskmaster who drove his staff unmercifully.

Jeanine de Cock, Belgian by birth, who gave Coles and Grove many very loyal years of service as a District Manager began her career in the crane business as his secretary in 1968. She told me that he was a very moody man, whose temper tended to improve as the week progressed, after Monday, which was always for him "Waschtag", or "Washing Day", devoted to clearing up the "mess" from the previous week.

Heinz regarded Coles Krane as his own private company. He adopted a completely independent line from Sunderland on development of crane models - he built what he considered saleable in the German market, and sometimes he designed cranes specifically for individual customers, including a Crawler

Crane with outriggers to give it extra stability, and a very special Container-Handling Crane, Model BL30, of which only one was ever built. The LH 1000, which started life as a 100 Tonne capacity Truck Crane, built in 1973, and ended up as a 140 Tonner, was certainly the largest fully hydraulic crane in the world at that time. Those apart, he was one of the innovators of the now very modern All-Terrain Crane (which, for the uninitiated, combines the advantages of the off-highway Rough Terrain Crane and the road-based Truck Crane), producing a prototype in 1973, the LH 400S, which was a Truck Crane with four axles, all of which were steered and driven. It started life as a 40 Tonne Crane, but was quickly up-graded to 50/55 Tonnes and re-named 500S.

It was way ahead of its time, but it was nine years later, in 1982, that the first four-axle AT Cranes were produced by Liebherr which bore a remarkable resemblance to the LH 500. (Some wag spoiled the only photo I have with the words: "Gott im Himmel, wir sind in der Scheisse, Herr Heyer"- *"My God, we are in the shit"*). Heyer's prototype was produced specifically for potential sales to "Braunkohlminen" *(Open-cast Coal Mines)* in East Germany, but only a few were actually sold.

According to Jeanine, Heinz sometimes used to conceal his prototypes from the prying eyes of the Steel Group Directors when they visited, and often the first time that they were made aware of the new model was when it appeared on the Coles Krane Stand at the Hannover Messe. Heinz used to refer to the anticipated arrival of the UK bosses as "The Tommies are coming...." He maintained a very close personal rapport with his customers and lost some because he refused to deal with the sons after the father had retired! In the early 1970s, increasing attempts were made by the UK Management to bring him into line, and, whenever baulked in his chosen path, Heinz would resign, confident that his resignation would be refused. It was, to start with, but came the day in 1976 when it was accepted. His world was shattered.

For a year, he worked independently, and then, just as he was about to be taken on by Liebherr, he drove his car into a wood, and with the engine still running he piped the exhaust fumes into the interior and so ended his life.

Coles Krane closed its doors in 1984 after nearly 30 years of crane production, probably never more than about 50 units per year, but it was a pioneer in crane design.

One of Heinz Heyer's only friends on the sales side was André Faes. Sales of Coles Cranes in France up to 1964 had been minimal, so James Steel decided that the answer was to form Coles own sales company and to head up this operation he selected André Faes, who had had 12 years of experience in the sale of US earthmoving equipment in France and in Morocco. André, to my way of thinking, is not a typical Frenchman. His family originated from Flanders, and his father, who fought in the trenches in the First World War, and wrote a fascinating account of his experiences in later life, only learned French when he became an adult. When André started from small premises at Argenteuil, in the outskirts of Paris, the Coles Order Book was full, with deliveries running at one year. He was offered four diesel-electric mobiles of varying capacities and a Neal-Unit excavator. He sold them all. A man of immense Gallic charm with a lively sense of humour, he welded together a first class team of salesmen, service engineers and technicians. Sales went so well that in 1972, they moved to a purpose-built avant-garde Sales Office and Repair Workshop at Cergy Pontoise. The design of this edifice was André's and he had some difficulty in convincing the Steel Group Board that he wanted a sales-orientated building and not another "Works".

He had a special rapport with Heinz Heyer. I suppose that the fact that they were both unique as the only senior European managers in a British company brought them together. André recognized that he had been luckier than Heinz to have been born a Frenchman rather than a German in the inter-War period, and he had a lot of sympathy with what Heinz had had to endure as a teenage soldier on the Russian front.

André sold quite a number of cranes produced in Duisburg, and Heinz even designed and built a special prototype off-road crane for the French market, but it had a number of faults like lack of synchronisation in the operation of the hydraulic outriggers, (when one went up, its opposite number went down!), and it was never really a success.

But the important thing was that both recognized that the needs of the French and German Markets were markedly different from that of the UK, around whose needs the Sunderland Design Team tended to orientate themselves, especially in the development of very large capacity fully hydraulic cranes.

The happy relationship between these two Continentals came to an end when André was promoted to the position of General Export Director for Coles, based in the UK, in 1974. This followed the departure from Coles and Acrow of Stephen Grey, after he had realised that further promotion within the Group for him would not be likely. André then realised that Heyer's sales in the German domestic market were very limited, with a potential twice that of France, and he put pressure on him to professionalise his sales team and sell the UK built product as well, and Heyer refused.   He believes that, in some ways, he contributed to the downfall of his old ally.

André Faes remains a legend in the annals of Coles Export.   During his five years as Export Director in the 1970s, he gained the respect and affection of seasoned Export Sales Executives, even though his attractive (sometimes exaggerated) French accent caused hilarious mirth.   On one occasion he had to dismiss a rather pedantic, but nonetheless worthy Sales Administrator and his constant repetition of "You are sack-ed" failed to register understanding of the reality of the situation in the unfortunate individual's brain, so that he kept re-appearing in the office!

André was well known throughout the Acrow Group for his sense of fun, and during a Group visit to Kuwait in the 1970s, attended by several Senior Executives, André purchased a "Dish-Dash" (Arab costume) in the Souk, and, disguising himself as a member of the Religious Police, he knocked on the doors in the hotel of his colleagues, whom he knew to be consuming forbidden alcohol, and chuckled as they emptied whole bottles of Scotch down the toilet before they dared to admit him!

André's absence from Coles France, despite the fact that he still remained in command and kept a close eye on it, was, in my opinion, not in its best interests. However he returned permanently to the country of his birth in 1979, after five years of managing Coles Export, and he paid tribute to the high professionalism, adaptability and effectiveness of the Coles Export Team, which, he said, "I inherited - I did not build it myself".   Always a modest man, André Faes was a master of Sales Promotion, with the Open Days which he organized at Cergy Pontoise.

At Expomat in 1982, when Coles France were also representing Priestman (and hence my personal involvement), he produced "Un Cahier de Coles" (*an exercise book in Coles*) for students with "lessons" for each day of the week".   "A l'Ecole de Coles", is a magnificent play on words which is completely lost in translation, *("At the Coles School")*.   He is still not retired today and runs a company which is the Publicity Agent for dealers of leading Construction Equipment Manufacturers in France.

When Acrow collapsed in 1984, Coles France went on trading.   It had a healthy bank balance and was far from being bankrupt.   Fortunately the Grove management were dissuaded from closing their French subsidiary down and today Grove France is the sole remnant of the Coles Empire which has survived under the Grove banner.

When André retired in 1988, having received, as a French citizen, the unusual and distinctive honour of being awarded an OBE for his long service to Franco-British trade, Gilles Marchand took over. André was a hard man to follow, but Gilles has proved a worthy successor.

André Faes and Gilles Marchand at the Batimat Exhibition 2003.

Coles diesel electric mobile crane handling aircraft engines for Boeing in the U.S.A.

Coles Overseas

Coles Krane works at Duisburg.

Coles Krane customers included some big names.

Coles Overseas

The L 125 diesel-electric crane with a capacity of 125 tonnes.

One of Heinz Heyer's most inventive cranes.

COLES CONTAINER - MOBILKRAN TYP BL 30

Auf dem Lagerplatz oder am Container-Zug kann ein Container über einen zweiten im Fahrzeug mitgeführten hinweg umgeladen werden. Ein fahrender Sortierplatz, der die Umschlagsleistung des Gerätes zusätzlich erhöht und die Fahrwege verkürzt.

COLES KRANE GMBH, 41 Duisburg, Krabbenkamp 13
Telefon 44 60 51, Telex 08 55691, Postfach 234

Coles Overseas

Jeanine De Cock, originally secretary to Heinz Heyer, pictured in 2004.

The LH500S, built in 1973, was possibly the first all-terrain crane ever built.

COLES FRANCE IN 1982.

André Faes, President Directeur General.

The modern premises at Cergy Pontoise
(Grove France today) and the original
offices in 1974 at Argenteuil.

Eric Freake takes the teacher's role whilst David Steel and Jeanette de Vigier (the "Old Man's" daughter, who often added her personal touch of colour to overseas exhibitions) look on. (Eric, originally a Service Engineer, was brought over by me to Priestman Export, valued for his technical knowledge.)

allez coles:
la brillante réussite d'Expomat

HYMAC

Britain's First All-Hydraulic Excavator Comes Out

"Hy-Mac 480 crawler-tractor to be manufactured in Monmouth by Rhymney Engineering Co.,Ltd. Power for all motions, including travel, is transmitted hydraulically" *Contractors Record and Municipal Engineering* *7th February 1962.*

Hymac

The HYMAC 1080, weighing 22.5 tonnes, in 1965 possibly the largest hydraulic excavator in the world.

CHAPTER ONE - THE ORIGINS OF HYMAC AND MY ROLE

Hymac was the brain-child of Peter Hamilton, who, after War Service in the RNVR, when he travelled all over the world in Ocean Going Rescue Tugs, started his career in the sale of earth-moving equipment with Blackwood Hodge (for many years a household name as an international dealer in muck-shifting) in 1948. He stayed there for 10 years, and then, after a brief spell with Michigan Wheeled Loaders, he became MD of Fred Myers, at that time the CAT Dealer for Southern England. However he always wanted to do something which would give him greater independence, and in 1960 he saw an advertisement for a fully hydraulic excavator called Hy-Hoe, built in the USA. There was only one model, which had a nominal bucket capacity of 1/2 (4/8) cu yd (400 litres in modern parlance), but all slewing tracked excavators built in the UK at that time were mechanical. The original Hymac 480, which had a limited swing function, was rapidly succeeded by the first UK designed machine with full circle slew, the 580, (5/8 cu. yd or 500 litres), which was the foundation stone of the whole Hymac range and certainly the most well-known machine they ever produced.

Peter knew Sandy Shand, Chairman of Lehane, McKenzie and Shand, a medium-sized Civil Engineering Contractor operating from Matlock in Derbyshire, and together they negotiated a licence to build the Hy-Hoe in the UK under the name of Hymac. Peter was to organize the sales and Ken Dabell, the Plant Director of Shands, was to act as Technical and Service Director, using the Shand service facilities. The big Welsh coalmine owner, Powell Duffryn, provided a suitable manufacturing facility at Rhymney in one of the mining valleys of South Wales, where they had joint ownership of an engineering company with International Combustion.

Rhymney Engineering had started life in the 19th Century as an ironworks, which had closed in 1890, and it was re-opened in 1942 to make shell cases for the war effort, and after the War it continued to act as a general engineering sub-supplier to the steel and mining industries. This work had fallen away by the end of the 1950s, and the opportunity to build the Hymac was a godsend. However there was no long tradition of manufacturing construction equipment, and this did not help Hymac as it began to expand.

My first visit to Hymac Works at Rhymney was on a Saturday in February 1965, when the Managing Director, Geoff Taylor, took the trouble to come in personally to meet me and show me round. This very courteous gesture impressed me enormously after the way in which I had been treated at Coles, and it was certainly what decided me to go for Hymac, subject to a satisfactory position being created for me.   For this is exactly what Peter Hamilton did. I had originally applied for the position of Assistant Export Manager, based in Matlock, and turned it down because I was not willing to move.   That apart, I felt that I had as much experience and ability as the Export Manager himself, although I both liked and got on well with Chris Wilson, who occupied that position.   I found his UK sales colleague, who seemed also to be PH's right hand man, rather reserved and somewhat difficult to sum up, but the position which was finally created for me was that of a split responsibility between Home and Export, reporting directly to PH himself, and based at the London Office in Berkeley Street, just a few doors away from where I had started my career with Coles.

Peter's own out-going personality and bonhomie (strengthened by his bubbly wife, Susie) permeated every nook and cranny in the company, which was a unique conglomerate, but there was a tremendous open-ness and team spirit. We were the pioneers of the crawler hydraulic excavator, and we acted like that.   Even JCB was slow to follow Hymac in that particular field, and the main competition in the UK market at that time was the French Poclain, who really were the originators of the European machine.   I was called "Projects Manager" and my projects were many and various, from top level contacts with large   Civil Engineering contractors like Wimpey,   managing various other UK franchises which PH had collected (he was a great agency collector), and finally Eastern Europe on the export side.

My daily association was with the other members of the London Office staff, who were a colourful and varied lot.   Dominating the scene as Chief Administrator was the admirable Miss Priscilla Chase, a single lady of great charm and very good looks, who had worked with PH for many years and was his faithful and loyal servant to the end, keeping a Scrap Book with every newspaper report and cutting about Hymac, which Peter still had.   My attempts to introduce myself at top level into the Wimpey organization, who bought their Hymacs five or ten at a time, came to an abrupt end even before they had started.   They didn't want me interfering in a well-oiled purchasing system between their Buying Office and Priscilla Chase!   Priscilla had served as a First Officer in the WRNS in the War, and I think that her fiancé had been killed in action, because it was indeed surprising that as a very attractive young lady she had never married.

Another somewhat bombastic character, was the Southern Region Sales Manager, Douglas Hancock, who always signed himself as "Squadron Leader".   He used to make me cringe at the way in which he would introduce himself to new customers on the phone by blaring at them: "My name is Hancock, Douglas Hancock, and I am the Sales Manager, Peter Hamilton Equipment". On one occasion, he made an appointment to see a contractor called Biggs Wall, who were loyal users of Priestman and his visit only served to re-inforce their existing purchasing policy. The MD , Gordon Brown, was a very religious man, who neither smoked nor drank alcohol, and certainly disapproved of strong language. He was also very punctilious and Hancock's first mistake was to arrive late for his appointment. This was then compounded by his opening remarks: "Sorry I'm late, Mr. Brown, - God, the Fucking Traffic..... Let's nip off to the local boozer and I'll make it up with a pint". Gordon Brown brought the interview to an abrupt conclusion and then rang PH and told him in plain words: "Never send that man to my office again". His opposite number in the North, Bob Sheavyn, was a man more to my taste and our paths were to cross again the future.

The London Team was completed by the Irishman who sold the used machines and was always about to put the phone down as it was his very last offer, and a part time lady, Pip Boath, who was always accompanied by her large Labrador dog. She helped me to look after the Pettibone Crane Franchise, which just involved us in handling piles of literature, all in US norms only, because we never did anything serious to promote the machines, and another US product, the Cleveland Trencher. There were only about five Pipeline Contractors in the UK at the time, who all bought their Clevelands direct from the manufacturer, and knew far more about the machines than anyone in the Peter Hamilton setup. However, I had Beginner's Luck in selling my first Cleveland to Turriff Construction only a couple of months after taking on the new job (and even finding a home for their trade-in, which clinched the deal), and I certainly enjoyed learning about one of the most fascinating pieces of earthmoving equipment with which I ever had to deal. I had to be patient when ferrying the large mid-Western American rep around the customers, who just never stopped talking, but he certainly knew everything there was to know about trenchers, so I just sat on the side, whilst he and the Plant Managers talked pipeline jargon.

CHAPTER TWO - BACK TO EASTERN EUROPE

Inevitably, I was drawn far more back into my one Export role. In fact I began looking into the possibilities of export into Eastern Europe as soon as I started, and found that the Polish excavator manufacturer, Warynski, who had been building Priestman Cubs under licence for a number of years, was looking for a licence for a hydraulic machine, and I postponed my planned holiday in France with the family and my newly widowed mother very soon after I had started in order to meet the Polish delegation and show them the Works at Rhymney. I then started planning an East European trip and decided to do it by road, which rather surprised PH, but he immediately backed my decision, and when I pointed my company Ford Corsair at the end of October down the Dutch autobahn after flying it over to Rotterdam on "Channel Air Bridge" in a converted Bristol freighter, I felt like a bird which has been locked up in a cage and suddenly been let out! I had not done a trip outside the UK for over six months....

From Warsaw I drove all the way to Bucharest, a cross-country trip which took me two or three days. The car was well stocked with small tins of cold meat, baked beans etc and beer, so that lunch was never any problem, and I was invited by some young lads to whom I gave a lift in Hungary to stay the night at their home. I had no Hungarian money, because it was just too complicated to change currency at the border just for a transit run, and so it suited me to accept. The family had clearly formerly been well-to-do, and the house in which they now had two rooms had once been their property. The living rooms were well furnished in an old-fashioned way, with couches by day being converted into beds at night, but they shared kitchen, toilet and washing facilities, which were primitive to a degree, with no running water. They were extremely welcoming and hospitable to me as a complete stranger, and I was able to repay them with a bottle of Scotch, and food from my travelling larder.

On the way down to Bucharest I nearly ran into the back of an ox cart in the dark. The only lighting which they had was an oil lamp swinging between the shafts, and, when one dipped one's lights to avoid blinding an oncoming car, any ox cart in the road became quite invisible. Later I met another English wayfarer who had collided with and completely destroyed an unlit gypsy caravan in the middle of the road. Fortunately for him it was a car with right hand drive, since the gypsies attacked what they thought was the driver's side with axes, and he got out on the other side and legged it up the road to safety

- he was a good runner and he out-distanced them.   His car, when I saw it, was covered in small indentations made by a hammer as they had beaten out the dents.

Despite my previous contacts, I found the Roumanians still very frustrating and difficult to deal with, but one proved exceptionally valuable, and this was Dinu Giurcaneanu, who had moved from the Ministry of Construction to Agriculture, where they were looking for excavators for land reclamation, so that my week in Bucharest was not wasted.   I then started on the return journey, calling in for a few days at Budapest, where I found the Hungarians very co-operative and easy to meet, but it was clear that there was no money for excavators.   A welcome weekend in Vienna broke into the darkness of East European travel in winter, and I made my first acquaintance with the Hymac dealer, a dynamic young company under the ownership and direction of Alfred Stambach, with whom I was to work closely in the future.   Vienna, with its lights, music, comfortable hotels and restaurants, was like an oasis in a dark sea.

From Vienna I went on to Prague, where I had some difficulty in getting an hotel room . I had cabled the No.1 hotel, the Alcron, a week before, but they simply told me that they were already fully booked, so I managed to get a room "for one night" at another rather more old-fashioned establishment, the Yalta, and charmed the Reception Girl with a bottle of scent so as to prolong my stay.   When I paid the bill, I said to the clerk on duty that accomodation seemed very difficult and what length of notice was required, to which he replied: "At least a week".   I murmured that that was not always possible and, thanking him for his help, I put a 100 crown note on the counter.   The clerk immediately scribbled his name on a piece of paper and pushed it across to me with the words: "There you are, sir, mention my name and you will always have a room".   This was the only way in Communist countries.

In April 1961, I had made my first visit to Prague, but I did not make much headway here.   It was difficult to get past Strojimport, the State Trading Organization, although an elderly official there named Kunze was most helpful.   He was a tired looking overworked man whose hands had a perpetual shake, and I was given to understand that his former Jewish wife had been murdered by the Nazis in front of his eyes before he was himself flung into a concentration camp.   During this visit I had plenty of time for sightseeing in one of the loveliest cities in Europe, and, although many of the old buildings were at that time sadly in need of repair, at least one of the benefits of

Hymac

Communism was that the place had not been defaced by excessive tourism. On the day of my departure, before leaving for the airport, I had time for a last look over the city from the immense statue of Stalin, who towered over the north bank of the Vltava.

It was Stephen Grey who had really developed the market for Coles, and I have to say that he handed on to me one very good contact, which led to another long friendship, as well as giving me some very limited success in Czechoslovakia for Hymac. Prokop Maxa was a senior engineer in a Construction Company, and he was an exceptionally cultured and erudite man, whose father had been the Czech ambassador to Poland in the Inter-War years. Like so many of his background, he and his wife occupied a few rooms in a house which they had previously owned. Prokop spoke flawless English and German, and I still have many of the letters which he wrote me in a clear scripted hand. He told me that the Communists had in fact been voted in quite legitimately after the end of the War, because they were the only party who had a clear policy, the others being weak and divided, and that, at first, they were moderate, but in the early 1950s they started purges. Prokop himself had come under investigation because he had been involved in the supply of some essential equipment just at the end of the War which was contrary to regulations later introduced, and several times he had to go to the police for interrogation. He told me that each time he would take his toothbrush and pyjamas, because he never knew whether he would be allowed home. In the end he was put on trial, but fortunately the case was heard in Slovakia, where they were less Stalinistic, and the judge dismissed the case being brought against him. Even so he was under suspicion for some years and unable to leave the country etc, until the regime softened.

As it happened, it was in Slovakia where Prokop found a market for the few Hymacs that I did succeed in selling to Czechoslovakia, and the hospitality which I used to receive in Brno was overwhelming. It always involved a nocturnal visit to some wine cellars, not far from the Austrian border. The entrance to these cellars was through a door in the hillside, which led into an ante-chamber, where large amounts of cold meats and salads would be laid out. Steps then led further down into the bowels of the earth into the cellar proper, lined with barrels on either side. The Master of Ceremonies would dispense the wine from a long glass tube, letting it spurt into the glasses by simply lifting his thumb to release the suction which held the liquid in, and, although the glasses were small, they were re-filled constantly. We used to arrive at about 8pm and sally forth at one o'clock in the morning, and I shall never forget the effect of the rush of cold air on to my befuddled head. The great feature of these evening was the singing - they all seemed to have very musical voices.

I completed that five week trip in November 1965 with a return visit to Warsaw, by which time winter was closing in, the roads were very perilous and the cans of beer and juice in my car boot froze. I had arranged for the senior technical man from Rhymney, Des Young, to join me in discussions for the potential sale of the manufacturing licence to Warynski. Des was a Welshman who made decisions and did not like hanging about, and he was very frustrated at first at the bureaucratic delays to which I was totally accustomed, and he asked me whether there was any particular financial incentive for working in Eastern Europe, and could not understand why I put up with it without! But he certainly knew the technical side of Hymac very well and was of invaluable assistance. Chris Wilson often used to say that he did not know what the company would do without Des Young, the most positive man of action at the Works. A year or two later we found out, when he was struck in the eye by a golf ball which caused a brain tumour and in six months he was dead. It was a great blow for Hymac. We did eventually sign up the Licence Deal, which involved a payment to Hymac of £180,000, no small fee in those days, carrying only rights to export to the Communist bloc, but it was never ratified, and later I found out why. Hymac had naievely exhibited a 580 in Moscow in 1964. The Russians had tested it and dissected it, and rejected it as being not tough enough, and when the Poles announced that they were going to build it under licence, with the Soviet Union as their main export market, the Russians dis-illusioned them. I was unable to emulate my old friend, Walter Husser with his deal for 300 Priestman Cubs.

By this time, Peter Hamilton was insisting that I should get more involved in Export than simply handling Eastern Europe as a special project, but Chris Wilson was resisting this in view of my refusal to move to Matlock and act as his Assistant.

PH won the day and after my next long foray by road into Eastern Europe early in 1966, I ended up in Italy looking for a dealer. On my way home, driving through the Austrian Alps towards Munich, I had an unusual experience when I had the misfortune to hit a deer on a winding road through forest at dusk. It was following its mate who ran out of the wood straight in front of the car, and, although I managed to brake sharply and miss the first animal, I hit the second.   Another motorist stopped and helped me to carry it, bleeding profusely, to the roadside and at the next village I stopped at a Gasthaus and asked the way to the Police Station to seek help.

"You need a hunter, not a policeman" was the reply, and in a quarter of an hour one appeared, a little old man resplendent in green costume and breeches, smoking a long curly pipe, accompanied by a young lad.   Together we set off in their Land Rover, the hunter armed only with a pistol, but as soon as we reached the stricken animal, the deer suddenly leapt up a high bank and bolted off into the forest, closely pursued by the hunter's dog.   The lad was despatched back to the village to fetch a rifle, but after half an hour the dog came back alone.   It was too late to do more, so I arranged to stay the night at the Gasthaus and accompany the hunter again in the morning, but, although we found traces of blood for a kilometre or so, there was so sign of the deer.   I presume that I had only struck it a glancing blow, and it had only been badly shocked, and in fact I was very relieved that I had not injured it severely so that it would have to be shot.

All the preparation work which I had carried out in Eastern Europe culminated in a Grand Tour in the autumn of 1966, when I ran three exhibitions, assisted, because of the close timing, by Robin Adams, the future long-served Export Manager for Thwaites, who had joined Hymac Export on the same day as I had.   I set out at the beginning of September with a truck-mounted Hymac called the "Polester", because it had a post-hole auger attachment.   I think that it was a prototype, but I had found an interest in Roumania, and it gave me a machine to demonstrate, which was an un-heard of activity in those days at an East European Trade Fair.   We were not allowed to dig on the actual Exhibition, and had to arrange a site nearby and transport potential clients to and from it.   The demonstrator, who had hardly been out of Matlock in his life, drove the machine all the way to Brno, with me escorting him in my Corsair.

We were not allowed to drive on Sunday so I broadened his outlook by taking him to a Bavarian Bierfest.   Peter Hamilton himself came out to Brno and was delighted by the fact that we were awarded a Gold Medal for the Hymac 380, the baby brother of the 580 of which very few were ever produced, but which the Czech agriculturists had preferred.   This visit by PH was a turning point, because I had been approached by Hydrocon Cranes for the post of Export Manager, but I really did not want to leave Hymac after such a short period, so Peter proposed that I be promoted to the position of European Sales

Manager, and take over all of West Europe, apart from Scandinavia where Hymac were already well established, which was being very competently handled in any case by Robin. I had to accept reporting to Chris Wilson, but I remained based in London, and I think that Chris realised that I would not be a subordinate who would toe any lines.

Robin accompanied the Polester from Brno down to Plovdiv, until such time as I could catch up in my car after winding up Brno, and once again we were awarded another Gold Medal. I did succeed in selling both machines exhibited, as I had in Brno, but the contract was not finalised until just before Christmas. The condition of the contract proposed by the Bulgarians was that the Hymac 580 (with its 500 litre bucket) should be able to guarantee a continuous production rate of 150 cubic metres per hour, in all conditions including blasted rocks. Chris Wilson nearly had a nervous breakdown when he read the terms and I was obliged to return to Bucharest and Sofia in the week before Christmas, because all East European purchases had to be tied up by the end of the Calendar Year to fit in with the exigencies of the Five Year Plans.

On that occasion I reached Sofia on the morning of the 23rd of December by an overnight steam train from Bucharest, with the sole objective of getting this totally unreasonable condition removed from the contract. I certainly found out how they had arrived at this calculation. Hymac used to put out Field Reports on particular applications, and one had stated that with a large swamp bucket for handling very easy drainage soil, "the output, at times, reached as much as 2.5 cubic metres per minute".

The Bulgarians had multiplied this figure by 60 and added in the further stipulation about blasted rocks for good measure! I got the condition removed, and the contract finally signed, but only by giving some more extra discount!

Then the fun began. With signed contracts in my hand from both Bucharest and Sofia, I was due to fly out on Christmas Eve to Vienna, through to London and then up to Yeadon in Yorkshire, where Audrey was waiting with the children for me to join her for Christmas at her parents' home. There had been a heavy fall of snow during the night, but the Bulgarians had no equipment for clearing the runway, so Austrian Airlines refused to land at Sofia and at 1100 hours I realised that all chance of getting home for Christmas was lost.

Hymac

All the passengers, already checked through Customs and Immigration, with passports stamped as having left the country, were taken by bus to the Air Terminal and eventually to the Railway Station.

Here we were not allowed to get on the train without first surrendering our passports, at which several of the passengers protested loudly, but the Airline hostesses, who were doing their best for us, insisted that that was the only condition under which the Railway authorities would allow us on board, so we had to accept.   Half of the passengers were on board and the other half were still queueing up to get aboard, when the whistle blew, the steam engine puffed into action and the train started to move.   It had travelled about a hundred metres, and was gathering speed as the stranded passengers ran after it in a vain attempt still to get on, when a Frenchman, already safely aboard, shouted: "Où est mon passeport?" and promptly pulled the Emergency Stop handle and the train came to a halt, enabling the remainder of the panting passsengers to climb on board.   After a short pause, the train set off again, and when we reached the Yugoslav frontier station, the Railway and Customs Officials, on discovering that we had neither tickets nor passports, instructed us to get off the train.   But we were united in our determination to stay on board and we all flatly refused to budge.   Whilst the argument was still raging, a cheer suddenly went up as a taxi pulled up at the station in a flurry of snow and from it emerged the Airline hostesses with all our passports!

It was not a very cheerful way to spend Christmas Eve travelling through the snow with no refreshments on offer at all, but we sang a few carols to keep our spirits up, and somebody produced a bottle of slivova.   Belgrade, where Christmas was not celebrated at all at that time, was cold and unwelcoming and some passengers decided to stay on the train through to Vienna, but I got off the train to take my chance on getting a flight in the morning, and was lucky to find a flight leaving to Zurich.   Landing there in mid morning on Christmas Day, as I got off the plane, I saw a United Arab Airlines aircraft loading passengers, and I just had a feeling that it was bound for London, which it was.   Told that the flight was closed, I pleaded with the Swiss Transit Desk official and was allowed back on to the tarmac with no guarantee that my luggage would accompany me.   By the time that I reached the aircraft, the steps had been retracted and the pilot was about to taxi to the runway, but he stopped when he saw me, lowered the steps, and, as I started to climb up, by some miracle a luggage truck appeared with my suitcase and I was at Heathrow by midday.

My neighbours were surprised at their Christmas dinner by my appearing at the door asking for the key to my house in Uxbridge, in order to get my car out of the garage and drive up to Yorkshire. It was no use trying to communicate with Audrey, because her parents were not on the phone Halfway up the M1 I realised that I needed petrol. Every service station on the motorway was closed and finally I pulled off into Liecester, where I found a fire station manned by a sympathetic fire officer who broke all the rules and sold me some petrol. Arrived in Yeadon 24 hours late, after such heroic attempts to get home for Christmas, I was greeted by my mother-in-law who responded to my salutation of "Merry Christmas, Mum", with the words: "Christmas is over - you should have been here before"......

The only market which really produced any substantial business for Hymac in Eastern Europe was Roumania, mainly for the Minstry of Agriculture. Through the good offices of my friend, Dinu Giurcaneanu, I established an excellent personal rapport with the First Deputy Minister, a dynamic character named Barbu Popescu.

Following the Plovdiv Fair in September 1966, I went on to a British Exhibition in Bucharest, where I met President Ceausescu himself. Here a Hymac 580 on wide undercarriage, with wooden swamp pads 1000 mm wide and equipped with a trapezoidal bucket, caught the Minister Barbu Popescu's attention and after demonstration he promptly decided to order four units. With such a powerful figure backing me, Masinimport could only haggle about the price, although they beat me down again in December on an order for three more. I was infuriated by this tactic, occasioned by a cheaper offer from Italy, and stormed into the Technical Director's office with the words: "I hope that you will be pleased with the Italian excavators you are going to receive". "I am certainly not buying Italian excavators" he retorted, and seized the phone to speak to Masinimport, and a furious discussion ensued. "Go back to the hotel" he told me, "and you will be called back to Masinimport", which is exactly what happened, but I had to give a few more percent nonetheless. As price bargainers, Masinimport officials were unbeatable.

In April 1967, the Minister decided to come to the UK to visit the Hymac Works personally, and he brought with him a delegation of about 7 or 8 persons. He was afraid of flying, so they all had to come with him by train, and we met them at Victoria Station in London. I laid on a tour to take in some sightseeing as well as machines in action, and we stayed one night in

Hymac

Glastonbury. At dinner, the Minister was very abstemious with the drink and no one else dared to accept my invitation to another glass of wine after the Minister had refused, but when the tyrant had gone to bed, one by one the others slunk back from their rooms into the bar. It was the same when he went round the Works - if the Minister was interested in a particular aspect of manufacture, everyone had to show interest. If he wasn't interested, the whole party moved on! I think that he liked me because I had learned some basic Roumanian (not a difficult language for me with its Latin background) and I was able to joke with him.

As we came up to the toll booth on the Severn Bridge, he expressed some alarm at the barrier, and asked what it was. "Its the Welsh border crossing, Minister", I replied, "I hope that you have a visa to enter Wales", and, momentarily, he was taken in!

Whenever I went to Bucharest, I always got a meeting with the Minister, and, on one occasion, I was told that he was in hospital with a broken leg, following a road accident, so I just accepted that I would not see him. However, one of the engineers advised me to ring up the Protocol Office and simply inform them that I was in Bucharest, but, he added, please do not tell anyone that I have suggested this.

I duly did so, and the next day a car was sent to the Athenée Palace Hotel to collect me and convey me to the hospital, a special one for Members of the Communist Party only. Foreign visitors were strictly forbidden to enter this edifice, but an exception was made for me, and I was dressed up in a white coat and made to appear like a member of the hospital staff. The Minister was in a private ward (as was only to be expected), with his leg encased in a heavy plaster, and he was holding a meeting with several senior members of this staff. As soon as I entered, he exclaimed: "Domnu Lloyd, che fac?" ("Mr. Lloyd, how are you?") and he immediately brought the meeting to a rapid conclusion and dismissed his aides to talk to me. I was extremely flattered! I often wonder what became of him and if he survived the collapse of Communism.

The Ministry of Agriculture ended up with a fleet of about 20 Hymacs, but this loyalty to the brand was only supported, as it was in the UK, by exceptional back-up service. The Hymac Service Manager was a died-in-the-wool plant man, with many years of service in the Construction Industry behind him. Lew Dunster was an old Sapper from the Second World War, who called a spade a spade, and carried out his duties with military precision. When we got drunk together, we could give a hearty rendering of the Sapper Song, which used to be sung by inebriated Sapper Officers charging round the Mess in a crocodile:

"Good morning , Mr. Stephens, its a lovely day today - Hoorah for the CRE...

We've been working very hard, down on Upton Hard - Hoorah for the CRE...

You make fast, I make fast, make fast the dinghy, make fast the dinghy pontoon,

For we are marching on to Latham's Plain, to Latham's Plain, to Latham's Plain

Where they don't know sugar from tissue paper, tissue paper, marmalade or jam.

I saw a nigger boy sitting by the fire, I saw a nigger boy pulling at his wire,

Hold him down till I get at him, Hold him down till I get there,

I cum a zeemar zeemar rinkum, I cum a zeemar zeemar zee..."

and then it ends in a great shout! All complete nonsense, of course....

(I am aware that there are various versions of "The CRE", but this is the particular one which I remember. I am given to understand that the song dates from the Boer War).

As service engineer on the territory I had Ron Walker, whom I had persuaded to desert Coles for Hymac. Ron, a Scotsman who eventually settled in South Wales, (where he still lives and organizes Scots Festivals like St. Andrew's Nights, for the benefit of the local Celts), was a good linguist and he spoke quite a lot of Roumanian, and was ready to spend months away from home travelling in Eastern Europe. He stayed with Hymac until 1979 and was very much involved in the later history of the company.

Another stalwart who gave me enormous support was Hymac's No. 1 Machine Demonstrator, "Dickie" Bird. His real name was Tony, but he was always known in Hymac as "Dickie". He hailed from Norfolk and spoke with the local burr, and he had an attractive habit of mispronunciation: "That ain't the properly way to do it" was one of his favourite expressions, and, on one occasion, when he found our Exhibition Caravan, which had been laid up for the winter somewhere, in a very damp state, he graphically described what he found as "Frons and Sattelites" growing inside!

Hymac

Apart from the fact that he could make a machine do double somersaults, he also had a great deal of practical "First Aid" service knowledge, and he never gave up on a problem. He inherited, as a service car, my old Company Car , the Ford Corsair, and was driving this vehicle back to the UK when he narrowly escaped death on the single track "Autoput" or motorway which ran from Belgrade to Zagreb. He was suddenly confronted by a truck on the wrong side of the road, dangerously overtaking another, and, to avoid a head-on collision, he simply drove right off the road and landed in a field. Most people would have given up at this stage, abandoned the car and flown home, but not Dickie Bird. Somehow he managed to get the car towed back on to the road and continued his journey back to the UK in the battered remains of the vehicle.

It was in this Ford Corsair that I had the following experience. It was after the Exhibition in October 1966, towards the end of my 10 week trip, and I was getting very tired! We had a wheeled excavator, the Hymac 610, on demonstration at a site some way outside Bucharest, and I had taken an engineer from the Peoples Town Council who were interested in buying it (and eventually did so). On our way back in the dark, we came up to a rail level crossing. As usual, the gates were always closed at least half an hour before the train was due, and already in front of me waiting to cross was an ox cart, and a motor cycle. I drew up behind them and switched my engine off to wait. Then without warning from behind a black Mercedes, with headlamps glaring, came up on the left hand side of the road to the top of the queue, followed by another, and I could see a line of them, one behind the other.

My patience suddenly snapped, and I started my engine and blocked the passage of the third Mercedes. My Roumanian passenger started visibly to tremble at this point at my audacity. An officious looking man got out of one of the cars and I could understand his verbal warning that this was a Ministerial delegation, to which I replied, in plain English, that I didn't care a tuppeny tinker's cuss if it was the King of Ruritania, he could bloody well take his place in the queue! Fortunately the man simply explained to his superior that I was some kind of deranged foreigner, and, before there could be further discussion on the matter, the train passed, the crossing gates opened and we were on our way. Travelling through the night on a rough pavé road at 120 to 130 kph, which was the absolute top speed of the Corsair, I kept my place in the line of black Mercedes until we reached the outskirts of Bucharest, and then discretion returned and I turned off down a side street to let the cortege flash by, much to the relief of my passenger!

Whereas my early trips to Roumania for Coles had been tough and lonely, by the time that I returned for Hymac, I had a lot of experience in the market place, I could speak passable Roumanian and understand a great deal more, and very often I was accompanied on my visits by Ron Walker or Dickie Bird. The other great bonus was that I had a completely free hand, and did not have Mattingley clinging on to my back like the Old Man of the Sea.   I was a frequent guest at Genie Schental's flat and I had another "friend", with whom I always made contact.   He was a well qualified and able engineer in one of the Ministries, who had helped me in the latter days of my time with Coles, by insisting that Coles was specified.   However, he had a long term axe to grind and his "friendship" proved not to be as genuine as I had imagined.   Martin Kiczales was a Jew, and had declared his open intention of getting out of Roumania to Israel, with the result that he was refused all promotion, which he otherwise certainly would have received.   His wife, Simona, always seemed to know when I would be coming, saying, when I rang up out of the blue from the Athenée Palace "I knew it was you", and I used to call her "the witch"   I have to say that when I went down with a very bad dose of 'flu during one winter visit, her ministrations and potions were extremely welcome! On one occasion only, they invited me to see their flat, in a house which had previously belonged to their family before being appropriated by the State, a usual situation in Communist Europe, and I was appalled at how dingy and depressing it was, with dark brown walls which had not seen a paint brush for years, to the extent that I actually offered to help them re-decorate over a weekend.   "No", they said firmly, "if we re-decorate this place, or attempt to make it more comfortable, it could detract from our absolute determination to get out of this bloody country".

Well, in the end they did get out, although I never seriously thought that they would. A deal was done, sometime in the early 70s, whereby the West German Government agreed to a War Reparation Payment to Israel in the form of buses manufactured in Roumania, and paid for in hard currency to the Roumanians by Germany, provided that the Roumanians allowed a certain number of Jews to leave. I had always agreed to help the Kiczales with a loan, should they ever get out, and, immediately that they did, they started to demand that I keep my promise. I could not afford it, but my dear Mother agreed to a loan of £500, which was a considerable sum at that time.   Despite promises, it was never repaid and gradually the promises and the excuses smalled and died away.   When I heard from Lew Dunster, several years later, that Martin Kiczales had been over in England, looking very prosperous, and had never contacted me, I realised how much his "friendship" had been worth.

My efforts in Eastern Europe culminated in my being awarded a Certificate of Merit under the National Provincial Bank's "Young Exporter Award"in May 1968, and I have to admit that I was quite proud of this. Peter Hamilton was delighted, and Priscilla Chase almost embarassed me with her compliments. There was one other Construction Equipment recipient of the Award and that was Richard Smalley, who went on to make a much bigger name for himself in the design and manufacture of Smalley Excavators. He was always a very modest unassuming guy, and I always called on him at Exhibitions and Trade Fairs. I was really sorry when his business finally folded, because he was the epitome of inventiveness and enterprise, bringing out machines which were different and special.

In the Spring of 1968 I was in Prague shortly after Alexander Dubćek became First Secretary of the Communist Party and started to put a human face on Communism. The atmosphere was incredible - one could sense the people's joy as one walked about the streets. Then came August and the terrible retribution brought on the hapless Czechs by the Russian Bear. We were at our Devon cottage at the time and were glued to the radio to hear the reports (we did not boast a TV then at our second home). However the Brno Fair took place as usual in September and off I went by road to Slovakia to attend it. The atmosphere now had completely changed. Russian tanks ringed the old city of Brno, not very well hidden in the woods surrounding the city. I was scheduled to go on to Bucharest, and during the Fair there was a strong rumour that the Russians were on the point of invading Roumania to punish Nicolae Ceausescu for supporting the Czech independence. The border between Roumania and Yugoslavia had been opened and Tito was co-operating with Ceausescu. I had an exciting journey, but nothing untoward happened. When I reached Bucharest, Genie Schental informed me that the Roumanians were prepared to fight if the Russians invaded, but I do not think that they would have stood much chance against the Soviet might. Fortunately it did not come to that, but they were stirring times. In fact the Observer revealed some very interesting secret papers on events of the period in January 2000, when it was stated in an article that Prime Minister Harold Wilson had made detailed contingency plans for military intervention in Eastern Europe, had the Russians invaded Roumania, and that on September 6th, 1968, when I was in the region, secret plans were discussed at high level between Harold Wilson, Michael Stewart and Denis Healey to send crack British troops to the Balkans to arm and aid Yugoslav guerrilla fighters.

On the business front, I started seriously to look into the possibility of Compensation Trading, or Barter. Hymac produced a small access platform at that time, which was designed to be mounted on the back of a Land Rover and I found a serious interest in this product with the Ministry of Electric Power for maintenance work on power lines.

They wanted to mount the platform on a Roumanian Four Wheel drive equivalent, which seemed to be a practical approach, but the project did not have any priority, and the only way to solve the problem was to accept payment in Roumanian goods.

I tried carpets and got involved with an Arabian Nights character, a white-haired old Greek called Athanassoglou, who looked as if he travelled about on a magic carpet himself, but nothing came of these negotiations, so I discovered a charming businessman in the City of London called John Little who was prepared to purchase agricultural products. He sent a humourous Scotsman to Bucharest who was interested in buying tinned pears. This gentleman told me that the quality was terrible, and averred that when a sample was offered him, he put his fork into the pear and it was so hard "that it jumped up to the ceiling, and I said to the wee lassie that she wouldna' offer it to her husband for breakfast, but," he continued, "the price is gude, and we'll put luvly wee label on the tin, so the housewife willna ken".... Anyway the final result of all this was that I succeeded in getting an order for 50 Hymac Platforms under the Compensation Trading arrangement. The funds from the sale of the produce went into a blocked account in a City Bank and Hymac were paid Cash against Shipping Documents without any risk at all, but I believe that John Little's company lost money on the deal!

When John Little retired, he was succeeded by a most interesting character, Tim Fisher. Tim was a retired regular Army officer, but a very unusual one. Born in the UK in 1920, he had been brought up in Italy and in Swtizerland from the age of three, and witnessed the coming to power of Mussolini at a time when large sections of the Italian population were starving. He admitted to me that his place at Cambridge in 1938 to "read Modern Languages" was somewhat of a sinecure, since they were, in fact, his native tongues. In April 1939 he went to Germany during the Easter vacation to improve his German, and stayed with a family in a lakeside village near Munich. At a luncheon party to which he was invited was a high-ranking guest, none other than Adolf Hitler. Tim was advised to be diplomatic, even if he disagreed with Hitler's views, on what he said at the luncheon table. This was just after the re-absorption of Memel (modern-day Lithuania) into the German Reich, and Hitler was feeling very pleased with himself. He then addressed Tim directly with these words: "And what would our young English friend think of England being taken into the Reich?" He replied that for an 18-year old Englishman, it would be difficult to reply.......with courtesy. He told me that his impression of Hitler on that occasion was that he was very presentable and exuded charm, although he also commented on his piercing and penetrating eyes, but that when he saw him on other occasions in uniform at public meetings, he looked a rather unimpressive and slightly comical figure, in his bumfreezer jacket.

In August, Tim returned to Munich to attend a summer term at Munich University. At a rather wild party, when he and most of his fellow students were pretty drunk, he took on a wager with one of them that he could join and stay in the German army for at least 14 days, and he joined up immediately. It seems that they were so desperate for recruits that not too many questions were asked. He styled himself "Anton Fischer, in Muenchen geboren". All went OK for the first seven days - while waiting to be kitted out and undergoing drill like any other recruit, but on the seventh day, his squad were all lined up and two volunteers were asked for to join the SS.

This actually meant that two men were selected as "volunteers" and, to his intense chagrin, he was one of them. He refused, of course, despite pressure being put on him that it would be a great privilege. Nothing was said for 2 or 3 days more and then he was hauled up in front of a junior officer and asked to confirm that he really was "Anton Fischer, in Muenchen geboren". He stuck to his story, wanting to win his wager, but to no avail. They had identified him as a registered student at Munich University, and he was discharged, but they seemed to accept that it was a huge prank, and no disciplinary action was taken, much to his relief. They even paid him for his 10 days of service! He went on to Budapest via Vienna with another English student. In Vienna they got involved in trying to prevent some Jews from being evicted from their homes and was rifle-butted in the mouth by an SS guard, and he then returned to Munich in late August in time to sit his exams. But on September 1st, when Poland was invaded, he decided it was time to head for home. He crossed the German/Belgian border at Aachen on the morning of

September 3rd, to discover that Britain had already been at War with Germany for about half an hour. When he got back to England, the first thing he read was a newspaper headline which announced: "ENGLAND DOOMED", but it had nothing to do with the outbreak of war - it referred to our performance in the Test Match against Australia....

Tim then joined the British Army, where he served in the Western Desert and in Italy, during which time he was selected for the Regular Army, from which he retired in 1958. In civilian life, he was immediately valuable for Export because of his linguistic abilities, but he grew tired of working for manufacturers who denied him freedom of operation, and finally went in to the Import/Export business. He told me that Compensation Trading was the activity which interested him most and he concentrated on that, becoming involved in some very large projects between Eastern Europe and the West. Margins to be made were high, but the success rate in bringing deals off was very low, in proportion to the number of negotiations undertaken. On one occasion, his guns were spiked when the director of a Canadian firm on whose behalf he was negotiating a very big deal with Roumania, being himself of Roumanian origin, betrayed the level of his fees to the buyer. Tim agrees with me that the Roumanians were some of the most difficult people to do business with.

I have met a lot of interesting characters in my career, but Tim Fisher tops the list.

Hymac

HY-MAC
H-E POLESTER
Hole borer and pole erector

This was the demonstration HYMAC which travelled to BRNO in Czechoslovakia, to Plovdiv in Bulgaria and ended up in Roumania.

PRAGUE 1970.

Prokop Maxa with his wife, Eva, and son Honza in Prague in 1979, with Audrey and our oldest daughter, Lucy-Jean on the left.

Peter Hamilton receives the gold medal for HYMAC at the 1966 BRNO Fair.

Hymac's stalwart Service Manager, Lew Dunster

BUCUREŞTI — Sala Palatului R.P.R.

Bucharest in the 1960s. The "Festival" concert hall

The main Boulevard.

Typical Communist high-rise buildings.

Genie Schental "The Genie" of the British Legation in Bucharest.

Hymac

dacă nu este HY-MAC

el sapă în rocă

el sapă în mlaştini

el sapă în colţuri strîmte

HYMAC versatility as publicized in Roumania.

el sapă în zăpadă

el sapă în
jos pînă la 9 metri

el sapă în argilă

şi gheaţă

...el sapă oriunde pe teren

Hymac

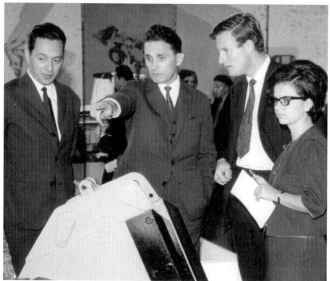

I meet President Nicolae Ceausescu with Genie Schental looking on wth a smile.

First Deputy Minister of Agriculture, Barbu Popescu, points a dynamic finger at the HYMAC 580, with Dinu Giurcaneanu at his side.

Another gold medal for HYMAC at Plovdiv in 1967. On my right is my stalwart colleague, Dickie Bird

Hymac

MY PROUD MOMENT.

National Provincial Bank Limited

Young Exporter Award

This is to certify that
Richard John Lloyd
has been selected to receive

This Certificate of Merit

in recognition of his outstanding contribution to

British Exports in the year 1967

May 14th 1968   Chairman.

Adjudicating Panel:

P. F. D. TENNANT, CMG, OBE,
    Director General, British National Export Council
A. J. TOWNSEND, CBE, MC,
    Director and General Secretary, Institute of Export
J. D. imTHURN,
    Deputy Overseas Director, Confederation of British Industry
E. W. READ,
    Assistant General Manager, National Provincial Bank Ltd.

The HYMAC Lift Platform of which I sold 50 to Roumania, for mounting on a locally-built chassis, totally paid for by counter purchase. The picture shows the larger version. Inset: Tim Fisher, the man who shook hands with Hitler and joined the German Wehrmacht for a few days in August 1939 for a wager, pictured with the author in 2002.

CHAPTER THREE - EUROPEAN SALES MANAGER

From the beginning of 1967, I started to get involved in Western Europe, in my new position of European Sales Manager.   This took me to France, to Spain and Portugal, to Austria and Switzerland, to Italy and Greece, but not to West Germany.   Oh No!   Here Hymac had established their own Direct Selling Organization, Hymac Baumaschinen GMBH, located in Duesseldorf.   "You concentrate on motivating the Dealers, Dick, because in Germany the MD will report directly to us" said the Management.   So I did, and I thoroughly enjoyed it.

I have always loved France, where Audrey and I have spent holidays nearly every year since we first met, so the opportunity actually to visit la belle France at the Company's expense was a godsend.   However to try to sell British excavators of questionable technical quality into the home of Poclain was, frankly, a lost cause from the start.

We were represented by the Aveling Barford French subsidiary, located just north of Paris.   Chris Wilson was an ex Aveling Barford man, and hence the connection.

The MD of Aveling Barford France was a charming, well educated Parisian called Jean Legrand, and because I could speak his language with reasonable fluency, he invited me into the intimate circle of his friends, which I recognized as a great privilege, but, unfortunately, it did not help to sell Hymacs. Because of all the technical problems, Jean Legrand finally decided to come over to London and have a personal "face to face" with Peter Hamilton.   Peter invited him, with me, to lunch at the Coq d'Or, and the conversation ranged on polite generalities, Jean clearly embarassed and not knowing how to intro-duce the unpleasant subject of the unreliability of the Hymac excavator, and, finally, it was I who forced both of them to face the facts.   I don't think that much came out of it, except promises on the part of PH, but it was an excellent luncheon!

I flatter myself that I held the European dealers together by the force of my own personality, by my linguistic ability and the fact that I made friends of business associates.   In France, Aveling Barford engaged the services of a rather wild Corsican of whom my main recollection is of his description of the proprietress of an hotel where we stayed when she tried to cheat him on his bill: "La Vache!" was his succinct comment.   Calling a woman a cow is one of the rudest descriptions in the French language!   In Switzerland we were represented by an extremely difficult old Schweizer-Deutscher called Aeberhardt, who used to argue over every small point of principle, but he had a flamboyant sub-dealer for la Suisse Romande, Louis Morand, who hailed from a small village called La Tour-de-Trême, near to the well-known little town of Gruyère, famous for the cheese of its name. Louis spoke not a word of German and used deliberately to drive down One-Way Streets in Zurich and shout at the policeman in French: "Je ne comprends pas" ("*I don't under-stand*") when he was pulled up. Louis sold many more machines than old Aeberhardt, and in the end we sacked the latter, extricating ourselves with much difficulty from the Dealer Agreement and appointed Morand direct. The new Zurich dealer was a lot easier to deal with and used to entertain us to riotous evenings at the famous Kindli Restaurant where they specialized in playing Alpine horns several feet in length.

On one August night I nearly came to an untimely early death at the hands of Louis Morand's salesman. I had actually started my journey that Monday morning from my holiday cottage in Devon at 4 am and driven straight to Heathrow to catch a plane to Geneva. By midday I was sitting in front of the potential customer, but the owner of the business who made the decisions was not present, so Louis proposed to beard this gentleman in the evening in his summer chalet retreat at the top of some mountain to which the final access was by funicular railway from the carpark, which was reached by a steep winding mountain road. I was not only tired by this time, but rather embarassed at our audacity in arriving unannounced at this complete stranger's private domain at about supper time, but his wife was extremely co-operative and offered us refreshment both liquid and solid. I restrained myself on the vino and schnapps, but not so Louis and his salesman, and at about 2 o'clock in the morning I persuaded them that we really ought to take our leave, especially as we were due to make a very early start the same morning to see another customer in a Canton over the mountain at 8 am which could only be reached after a two hour drive, and this new potential customer was, apparently, a stickler for punctuality. Both Louis and the salesman were as drunk as owls, and swayed conspicuously as we descended the steps to the carpark, the funicular being, by this time, closed. Louis had a powerful low-slung racing car, and this is where I made my near fatal error. Since I knew that he would drive very fast indeed down the winding mountain road, I elected to travel with the salesman in his Peugeot 404. As I had expected, Louis set off at the rate of knots in his "Rennwagen", but, what I had not expected, the salesman tried to keep up with him. There was no safety belt and I just braced my feet on to the floor as we screamed round sharp corners almost on two wheels and narrowly missed the rocky mountainside, which loomed up ominously on each bend. I was petrified, and when he finally deposited me at 4 am at the door of the hotel, I abused him roundly for nearly having killed me and he seemed completely taken aback!

I soaked in a hot bath and went to bed and set my alarm for 5.30 am. After only one hour's sleep I dragged myself from my bed, showered and shaved and at 6 am I was waiting in the Reception for the expected pick-up by Louis, feeling like death warmed up. Quarter of an hour elapsed, half an hour, and then three-quarters of an hour and still no sign of him. I knew that the Works opened at 7 o'clock, and I phoned at that time to find out where he was. He had not showed up, so they gave me his phone number at home. Clearly my call was a Wake-up Call. "Oh, Mon Dieu", he cried, "Richard (he always called me by my proper Christian Name) j'arrive", and, twenty minutes later, he did just that. When I queried just how we were going to be able to keep our 8 am appointment in the next valley, he smiled confidently: "Pas de problême. Tu vas voir" ("No problem. You'll see"), and we drove straight to the local aviation club where his mechanic was already warming up the engine of a small single-engined four-seater plane. It was a beautiful summer morning, and the view as we climbed up over the mountain and dropped down into the next valley was breath-taking, not to mention the fact that I felt far safer in the air than on the road. We were at the customer's premises promptly at 8 o'clock, and after the meeting was over, back at the local airstrip, we were having breakfast in the cafeteria when Louis announced that it was his birthday and ordered champagne! We took off mid morning for Geneva and re-visited the offices of the customer from the previous evening, which ended up in an alcoholic lunch and an order for some Hymacs. I had to be back in Zurich that evening to continue my planned itinerary for the week, but nothing could prevent Louis dragging me and the pilot into the bar of Geneva Airport before we took off, to celebrate the order. Light aircraft have to take off before dusk, and we only just made it, the pilot and I propelling the totally inebriated Louis across the tarmac and into the plane. He sat in one of the rear seats and I next to the pilot, resisting Louis' provocative suggestions for me to pull this or that lever to see what would happen! But the story does not end there. We landed safely back at La Tour de Trême, and it was agreed that Louis would drive me to Berne to catch a train to Zurich. We had just set off from the airstrip and were driving down the main street, when three women brandishing umbrellas appeared out of the shadows and, with a sigh,

Louis brought the Rennwagen to a halt.   "Pourquoi on s'arrête?" I enquired. "Mon Dieu " was the reply, "C'est ma femme, ma mère et ma belle-mère". *("What are we stopping for?- My wife, my mother and my mother-in-law").*   I feel that I rose to the occasion.   I got out of the car, greeted all three ladies effusively and apologized for having kept Louis away from home on his birthday, telling them that it was all my fault, and inviting them all to dinner.   This took the wind out of the sails of their brollies, and we all drove to the nearest restaurant.   The hors d'oeuvres had barely been put on the table, when Louis announced in an unaccustomed feeble voice: "Pardon, je suis malade", and promptly disappeared to the toilet to be sick.   He never re-appeared, and I, drooping with exhaustion by this time, was obliged to entertain the ladies on my own.   Finally, after settling the bill, I persuaded his wife to drive me to an hotel near the railway station, so that I could get an early train to Zurich and catch my morning flight, but, before leaving, I wanted to bid my friend farewell.   I found him carousing with his mates in another room.   He kissed me on both cheeks and declared that I was his lifelong friend.   Although I was not very pleased with him, I just had to forgive him and I had to recognise that, as a salesman, he was superb.....

A year later, that friendship reached breaking point.   Hymac had launched a bigger brother to the well-established 580 even before I joined them, the 1080, with a one cubic metre bucket capacity.   This machine had its problems (tumbler-type track running gear and track drive motors exactly the same as on the 580 being two of them) but the Hymac 880 with its tractor-type running gear and 800 litre capacity bucket was hailed as the Hymac of the Future.   Louis sold one of the first to an important customer, who put it to work in a quarry up a mountain-side.   It broke down with such regularity that, when I arrived at his Works with an offer to accompany him to the site to attempt to pacify the irate customer, he told me to bloody well go by myself. I did. Before I reached the inoperative machine, I passed a long line of empty dump trucks queueing up the mountain road, waiting to be loaded.   Not even the most persuasive salesman in the world could find words to combat that situation.

It was a similar picture in Austria.   The 580 was fairly well established and its small pecadilloes could be tolerated, but any other model seemed to me to spell disaster, not least its wheeled equivalent, the Hymac 610.   Alfred Stambach was a dedicated and enthusiastic Hymac dealer, but the 610 nearly broke him.   In September 1967 I was due to call on him en route to the Brno Fair in Czechoslovakia.   My plan was to set off at crack of dawn by car to

Hymac

Southend Airport on the Monday morning, and be in Vienna in time for dinner on Tuesday evening. Heavy rain and floods on the Sunday night made the road to Southend impassable, and I called him to try and postpone the meeting until Wednesday. He was so upset with Hymac's technical problems that he refused and insisted that I keep my appointment for the Tuesday evening. During Monday, the floods subsided and I arrived in Rotterdam at about 8 pm and drove to the Dutch/German border where I stopped for the night. The next day I set off at 6 o'clock in the morning and reached my hotel in Vienna by 8 pm, totally exhausted after driving 1400 km non-stop. Stambach was waiting for me in the hotel reception flanked by his two aides-de-camp and the meeting was frosty. It could equally have been held the next day, and after I had called back to base and got some action going to sort out the problems, I went in to the office and ate such humble pie on behalf of the company that the atmosphere thawed and we were again friends. But this was the beginning of the end for me in my five year career with Hymac.

My overall responsibilities for Europe took me back to Spain, Portugal and Greece. John Chryssafis did not really resemble Dracopoulos and Petratos from the Coles Era, since he ran a very professional Construction Equipment Dealership which stocked machines and offered parts and service to the customers, but he had the same excitable Greek temperament. On one occasion I arrived at his offices and waited patiently outside his office door whilst a furious altercation ensued within. Suddenly the door flew open and John emerged, red in the face and addressed the whole office in Greek in a high-pitched scream. He looked at me, but appeared so entranced in his rantings that he closed the door without seeming to notice my presence, but something must have registered and the door was immediately re-opened and he said in a quiet voice: "Oh, you here, Dick, please come in".

John dealt exclusively through a London City financier called BOECC (British Overseas Export Credit Organization). These guys lived on the backs of the UK Government Credit Underwriter, ECGD (Export Credit Guarantee Department), with whom they insured all their business. Larger manufacturers like Coles had their own expert to deal with ECGD, but for smaller organizations who liked to have cash payment, it was preferable to pay BOECC a commission to do the credit business for them. Not only that, but BOECC were expert at getting better terms than the manufacturers direct, because, instead of dealing with ECGD through a desk-bound administrator, they employed high-flying executives who wined and dined the

Hymac

Underwriters, and also threw the net wider by seeking finance through other channels.   I was a great believer in using BOECC and always found myself, as an Export Manager, at loggerheads with the company's financial gnomes who could not see the point of paying anyone else a commission to do what they thought they could do as well themselves.   BOECC enabled many a small or medium-sized Construction Equipment Dealer who handled British products to build up a substantial business, and a visit to their offices in the shadow of St Paul's nearly always brought the promise of an excellent luncheon with guys whom I found to be of an outlook and attitude very similar to my own.

In Italy, I came near to landing a big fish for Hymac, none other than the Caterpillar Dealer, CGT (Compania Generale Trattore).   These were long before the days when CAT started their own production of hydraulic excavators, and with the increase in sales of these machines, CAT dealers took on separate franchises for them.   I had already found a dealer for Hymac in Italy, at that time a small company in Bologna called Cerioli.   They do not exist today, but before they collapsed in the late 1990s they had grown into one of Italy's leading construction equipment dealers.   When I set them up for Hymac in 1967 I negotiated the Dealer Agreement with old Cavaliere Tonino Cerioli himself in Italian.   Even the Agreement had to be in that language, as he understood not a word of English.   My Italian was limited and I kept on using Spanish words which were much more familiar to me, but he clearly regarded me as a man who might do him down, and often wagged his finger at me: "Lei Avocato, Signor Lloyd", based upon my having read Law at Oxford. Cerioli only sold a couple of Hymacs - even at that time there were plenty of local manufacturers of hydraulic excavators which were probably just as good as Hymac and certainly very much cheaper.   When CGT approached us out of the blue, I realised that I must go after them for all that I was worth.   They had been offered Atlas, but the Managing Director, a charming man called Segre, was a Jew and very anti-German, and so Hymac were given a chance. The executive who was to head up the new department, Armando Rossetti, came over to the UK to prepare the ground.   He was no fool.

Hymac had opened a new flow-line assembly for the 580 at the Rhymney Works which was proudly shown to Signor Rossetti.   "Which way do you put the tracks on your excavators?" he blandly enquired.   The answer to this question was beyond my technical capability as a salesman, so I summoned the Chief Engineer.   Had it been Des Young, all would have been well, but poor Des was dead and his successor much less competent. His reply did not inspire confidence. "Well," he said, "It doesn't really matter, as an excavator goes backwards and forwards", to which Rossetti replied by pointing to a machine where each track had been mounted in a different direction with the dry comment: "Well, at least you should be consistent". All in all the visit had not been a great success, but Rossetti was still prepared take matters further and Segre himself arrived with his wife and senior colleagues. He wanted to spend a weekend with his wife in a typical English village, so I found a small Cotswold hotel and booked them in, but courtesies like this could not make up for hard commercial dealings. They were prepared to take the franchise and place a substantial stock order, subject only to agreement on price. Rossetti warned me that the meeting was crucial, and agreement must be reached there and then. I passed this information on to the management, but it fell on deaf ears, and they clearly felt that they could play for time in negotiation, and a counter-proposal was made.

The Italians returned to Milan promising to give it consideration. Rossetti visited the customer who was operating one of the two machines which we had sold and was not impressed. I urged him to let me take him to Sweden, which was Hymac's biggest export market. Bergman Borr had represented Hymac from the inception of Hymac in 1962. Every machine was taken into their workshops to be adapted to Swedish Regulations (more comfortable driver's seat, better heater etc) with the digging arm strengthened to cope with the tough excavating conditions in Sweden. This was the key to their success and Rossetti did not fail to notice it. At the end of the visit, I asked him what was now his impression of Hymac, to which he replied with a twinkle in his eye: "I think that you have a very good Dealer in Sweden". End of Story!

CHAPTER FOUR - HYMAC EXPORT EXPANDS

After I had been about two years with Hymac, I pressed Peter Hamilton to let me engage an assistant.   In order to short-circuit the process, I placed a suitable advertisement and invited potential candidates to phone me up and then I conducted a series of interviews in the offices in Berkeley Street.   We were not able to offer a very munificent remuneration and the well-qualified candidates turned us down, so that I ended up with a man of little or no experience, but with an out-going and enthusiastic personality.   He certainly got along well with people, and was a highly entertaining character, but he proved to be the most irresponsible confidence trickster whom I ever had the misfortune to employ.   His expenses were outrageous, and I eventually discovered that he was changing all his travellers cheques in Vienna into Black Market East European currency, and then charging the company with huge bills at the official rate.   On one occasion he had found it necessary to charter a private aircraft in Czechoslovakia with the excuse that it had been the only way to combine two (as he claimed "very important") appointments in geographically distant areas in one day.   We all did a modest amount in Black Market currency, to cover wild parties etc as I have already recounted earlier in these Memoirs, but this guy engaged in profiteering in it, sailing extremely close to the wind in so doing.   The final straw came when I followed him in to Bucharest where he had been responsible for setting up an Exhibition, not just for Hymac, but for the whole Powell Duffryn Group.   After I had taken over from him and he had left, I dutifully got up very early one morning to drive a senior executive from one of the other companies in the Group to Baneasa Airport, and narrowly prevented him from trying to change Black Market Lei (which my colleague had sold him with a substantial profit for himself) back into pounds at the official Exchange Office in the Airport.   It might have meant that they man would have been arrested!   I returned to London demanding permission from Peter Hamilton to sack him on the spot, his guilt being proved by the fact that his expenses included an exchange voucher for an enormous amount of Roumanian Lei from a bank in Vienna, for which he was at a total loss to account.   However he had, in the meantime, conned PH into sponsoring him in a European Motor Rally, (in which JCB were already involved), where he had persuaded him that a Hymac rally car would bring enormous benefits, so the sacking had to be postponed until after the rally had taken place.   I think that the Hymac Car, driven by one of his mates, went off the road early on in the rally and did Hymac no good whatsoever!

Hymac

In 1968, Powell Duffryn bought the shares owned by Lehane, Mackenzie and Shand, and formed Hymac Ltd, as their wholly-owned subsidiary. The Sales and Service Headquarters then moved from Matlock to Newbury. Audrey and I seriously considered moving from Uxbridge to Newbury at that time, and even went and looked for a suitable house in the area, but some Sixth Sense prevented us, and I continued to operate partly from the London Office. The Sales Department in Newbury was a joke - a huge open-plan layout with desks situated cheek by jowl one with another and no sound-proofing whatsoever. I recall the occasion when I was starting to get involved in Counter-Trade and was talking, or rather shouting because of the bad line, down the phone to Bucharest, to establish a list of agricultural products which the potential customer was prepared to offer. All other activity in the whole office ceased as everyone was forced to listen to my conversation, which was further disturbed by the cackles of mirth from my colleagues in the background.

Regional Managers had, by now, been engaged for the overseas markets, and the company decided that an overall Export Manager should be appointed. Why this was necessary when we had Peter Hamilton himself as "Managing Director, Sales", under-studied by Chris Wilson as Export Director, was beyond my comprehension, but these were the days when it was fashionable to build up hierarchies. All of us Regional Managers were invited to apply for the post, and everyone assumed that I, as by now the longest-served Regional Manager, would get the job. Even before any information was passed to me I knew that I would not.

I was returning from a long road trip to the Balkans at the end of November 1968, when my life on this planet nearly came to swift end. I had left Salzburg in my Ford Zephyr at 6 am on a foggy morning with the temperature slighlty below zero and was travelling up the autobahn towards Munich at what I thought was a reasonable speed for the conditions (but was clearly too fast), when suddenly someone appeared out of the fog at the roadside frantically indicating me to slow down. I saw the shape of a large vehicle just ahead of me and calculated that I could get past as I slammed on the brakes and the car went into a huge slide. I do not remember any more, until I came to standing at the side of my car with blood cascading down my face, regarding with horror the wreck of the Ford crashed into a bus and pointing in the reverse direction. In my semi-conscious state I thought that I had caused the accident, but what had actually happened was that I was the last vehicle to plough into a huge pile-up -"Massenverkehrsunfall" - on a viaduct which had iced up.   The car turned 180 degrees and crashed into a bus.   If I had not been wearing a safety-belt and driving a car with right-hand steering, I could hardly have survived.   As it was, I was thrown upwards with the impact, split my head open on the roof of the car and was knocked unconscious, and, in this state, I unhooked the belt and got out.   Two policemen escorted me firmly to a police car, despite my protests of: "Ich bin OK - bitte nehmen Sie die Menschen vom Autobus heraus".   *(I am OK - please get the people out of the bus)*. The screams from the injured in that vehicle still remain with me today.   As it was, I was incredibly lucky.   Sixteen stitches in my head is my excuse for the bald patch in the same area today.   I enjoyed my two or three days in a Bavarian hospital, particularly at lunch-time when the beer trolley came round, and, when I had returned home a new Ford Zephyr was ordered for me, which is how I knew that I had not got the job, the size and model of the Company Car being a clear indicator of one's place in the pecking order!

When I had recovered, I was summoned to Newbury for an interview with Chris Wilson.   After offering me commiserations on my misfortune, he went on to explain that the Management had decided that I would be more use to the Company if I continued in my position as European Manager, with promises of two new assistants.   I was not unhappy - I did not really want to swap my travelling role for a desk-bound job.   "But", he continued, "You do know the man whom we are going to appoint - he used to be with Coles".   I racked my brains to think who it might be, and when he told me, it was like a bombshell: "Dennis Mattingley".   Without hesitation, I replied: "Chris, you are making the most terrible mistake.   That man will destroy the wonderful team spirit and comradeship which we have at Hymac, and the moment that he walks in through the front door of these offices, I will walk out at the back, job or no job!"   He was flabbergasted and protested that Mattingley had spoken very highly of me, to which I repied; "Of course he bloody did!".   I insisted that he persuade Peter Hamilton to speak to David Steel, and I immediately drove back to Uxbridge and informed Audrey of this terrible turn of events. I rang David Steel, to whom PH had already spoken, and he replied: "Dick, I would like to help, but Mattingley left here under a cloud and there is not much more than I can say".   (The fact was that Coles had had to promote others around him so that he ended up as Manager without Portfolio and then he resigned).   I asked David if he would agree to meet PH personally and he immediately acquiesced but when I reached Berkeley Street, my discussion with PH was the stickiest in our relationship.   "You've burnt your boats, young Dick" were the words with which he greeted me, but he listened to my

Hymac

pleadings, met David Steel and Mattingley was never appointed.   The let-out for Hymac was that he had not admitted to the series of jobs which he had been through after he left Coles.   That was the last which I heard of Dennis Byron Mattingley.

What happened next was that Hymac appointed a man, similar to Mattingley in his deviousness, but much less clever and with a drink problem.   It did not take me long to realise this, and I fought him from Day One.   Chris Wilson had kept his promise and I poached the fluent German-speaker Terry Dracup from Coles to back me up in Eastern Europe and the German-speaking territories and found a Spanish speaker for the Iberian Peninsula.   Both proved to be very loyal and competent colleagues and Terry, with whom I was to cross paths many times again, still retains his Puckish sense of humour combined with an exceptional gift for mimicry.   He, as everyone else in the Export Team, soon saw through the new Export Manager, Sydney Burton.   The Area Manager for the Middle East opined that his knowledge of hydraulic excavators could be written on the back of a postage stamp, but I don't think that anyone fought him like I did.   In the middle of a trip to Eastern Europe I received a cable from him: "Don't sign any contracts - Burton".   The Board of Powell Duffryn had, for some reason, become worried about their executives committing the company to important contractual obligations without formal approval from the Board, but whoever dreamed up this new regulation had no knowledge of Eastern Europe, where every sale was a Contract.   I was in Belgrade at the time about to sign a contract for two Hymac 1080s.   I attempted to contact Burton by phone, but he was "not available".   So I signed the contract and confirmed it by telex.   Burton asked Terry Dracup whether I had received his cable and Terry replied that he had just received my reply.   "Please make me a copy" smiled Burton, and I came back to the office to receive a reprimand for disobeying Company Rules, instead of being congratulated on securing an important order.   Unbelievable!

In March 1969 I organized a German speaking Dealer Convention in Zurich. Burton attended as "Obergruppenfuehrer".   Several of the dealers knew him. He was drunk for most of the time and it was extremely embarassing, but it enabled me, finally, to convince the Management to sack him.   This time there were too many witnesses.

The wreck of my Company FORD Zephyr on the German autobahn near Munich in November 1968. How I emerged from this appalling accident alive is amazing.

CHAPTER FIVE - HYMAC BAUMASCHINEN AND FAREWELL

Shortly after this the Steel Group bought out Priestman, and it was not long before David Steel invited me to dinner and offered me the position of Export Manager (Worldwide) for Priestman, alongside my old rival Stephen Grey, who was to occupy the same position for Coles under the new organization. Of course I wanted to accept, but Hymac refused to let me go.   In April 1968 they had offered me a Powell Duffryn Contract, with three years duration, which brought with it a Top Hat Pension Scheme and was, in fact, a privilege. But I now argued that, as they had passed me over three times for the Export Manager position (after Burton, the job was offered to one of the other Regional Managers junior to me in length of service), they should release me. They refused. They wanted me to go to Germany for 12 months to sort out the problems of their German subsidiary, Hymac Baumaschinen in Duesseldorf. This was ironic, to say the least, since, as earlier recorded, upon appointment as European Sales Manager, I had been told firmly to keep my nose out of Germany.

What had happened was that a man had been appointed as Geschaeftsfuehrer, (MD), who turned out to be a crook.   He was a man whom no German manufacturer or dealer would touch, so he conned Hymac into giving him the job. He recorded, as sales, hire contracts to mates of his and when the hire period was over, the machines were secreted away from the prying eyes of the visiting directors from the UK in a stockyard away from the main centre of operations.   Eventually he was found out, of course, but he had ensured that his contract of employment was so well tied up that it cost them a lot of money to get rid of him.   He was at least a salesman, even if a crooked one, but the man whom Hymac found to succeed him, Dr. Dahmen, was a bureaucrat, and Hymac judged that it would be a good idea to send Dick Lloyd out as his Sales Manager.   PH tried to persuade me that it would be a big feather in my cap with Powell Duffryn if I succeeded in turning the situation round, but I knew that the Hymac excavator could not begin to compete technically with the German manufacturers, Liebherr, Atlas and O & K, and that the task was a hopeless one.   General engineering quality apart, Hymacs were all built with simple gear pumps manufactured by another Powell Duffryn subsidiary, Hamworthy Hydraulics, which did not provide such digging power as the more sophisticated variable displacement hydraulics adopted by the German producers.   So I refused to change my decision to break my contract and go back to the Steel Group. Impasse!

It was Reg Keates, now elevated to the position of Marketing Director with the Steel Group, who made the suggestion that I should compromise and agree to go for six months only. He assured me that the job at Priestman would be kept open for me - "You are the man we want, Dick, and we will wait for you". It worked.

I insisted on taking the family and proposed a living allowance equivalent to what it would cost Hymac to accomodate me in an hotel, which was £50 per week. It was only just enough - in those days the cost of living in Germany was much higher than in the UK. We found lodgings with a family called Schubert in a Duesseldorf suburb, and the two elder daughters, Lucy-Jean aged 7, and Josephine aged 5, were sent to the local school, where the teaching methods were still "learning by rote". It was very hard for them, with no knowledge of the German language. It was harder still for Audrey, with the youngest, Fay, aged only 3, and no car to help with the shopping.

I still recall Fay's wonderment at a dockside crane as we got off the ferry at Rotterdam: "That crane's got big eyes -That crane's got big eyes - THAT CRANE'S GOT BIG EYES"......

As "Englaender", we were not totally welcome in 1970 in Duesseldorf, which had been blasted by the RAF 25 years earlier and occasionally stones were thrown at the car.

However, our landlords, the Schuberts, were charming and most hospitable, but not so their daughter. On the only night which I spent away on business during our entire stay, Lucy-Jean became very ill and her temperature rose alarmingly, as often happens with young children. The old Schuberts were away on holiday and Audrey asked the daughter if she could use the phone to call a doctor. "There is a phone box at the bottom of the street" was the callous reply. Not only that, but Audrey was attacked by a potential rapist whilst with the children in a Spiel-Platz in the neighbouring wood. She screamed and the kids came to her rescue, and the attacker fortunately panicked and made off. In a state of terrible shock, she tried to explain to some locals who arrived on the scene shortly afterwards what had happened. They led her out of the wood, but left her on a totally unknown roadside without any further attempt to help. She tried to explain what had happened to a traffic policeman, but in the end it was not until I got home in the evening that we were able to report the incident, and then the police took it very seriously, but it cast a nasty slur over our sojourn in Germany.

Hymac

But, that apart, for me personally, our short stay in Germany was an experience which was to stand me in very good stead 15 years later. As a family, we had strong German connections. When I arrived in Duesseldorf in March 1970, I spoke only very limited German picked up during my trips to Eastern Europe, backed by conversation sessions with an old lady living in London who was a Jewish refugee from Nazism, a colleague of an aunt of mine who had married a distinguished German Jewish writer, himself a pre-War escapee from Nazi Germany. As a widow, this aunt lived for many years in Munich, involved in promoting her late husband's writings, and when I had my accident on the autobahn, I was on my way to have breakfast with her. My father had been a First World War RFC Pilot, who had been shot down in his SE5 biplane in 1917, and, badly injured, was very well cared for in hospital, as a PoW.

He had met my mother in a German police court in 1923, when they were both on holiday independently (he with his brother and my mother with a female friend) and were in trouble for not having reported to the police. My parents employed German maids right up to the outbreak of the Second World War, after which they often had holidays in West Germany during the 1950s. Although my father spoke only very limited German, he often played German Volkslieder at Family Sing-Songs around the piano, a Victorian custom which continued in my family until his death in 1965.

During my own sojourn in Duesseldorf, my knowledge of German increased by leaps and bounds. I would dictate memos to the salesmen in Pidgin Deutsch, and then would learn from the Hoch Deutsch into which the secretary translated my words.

I got the impression that Dr. Dahmen suspected me as a spy from Head Office and maintained his distance, although he did have the courtesy to invite Audrey and me to a soirée at his home on one occasion. The only time when he ever accompanied me on a visit to an existing customer was when he had concluded a sale of a Hymac 880 which had lain in stock for months (if not years) on terms which were certainly not divulged to me. But in the meantime I got on with my job, appointing and training salesmen, visiting customers and organizing demonstrations. The British Army of the Rhine were using Hymac excavators, so I concentrated on that to try and obtain sales from civilian customers. I held an Open Day for Hymac at RAF Bielefeld, and had the interesting experience of lunching in Hermann Goering's former Officers Mess, but the result was negative and after three months I grew impatient to start my new job.   Finally I bearded Peter Hamilton as he stepped off a plane at Duesseldorf Airport, and he agreed to let me go.

In my agreement to stay I had insisted that my company Ford Zephyr should remain at my disposal for a family holiday in Eastern Europe.   Hymac paid for the car to have a complete overhaul prior to this trip, (which infuriated some of my colleagues who were still with the company), and off we set.   We visited friends in Poland and Czechoslovakia, but underwent the most difficult border crossing in the Tatra Mountains between the two countries which I had ever experienced.   Once on the Roumanian/Hungarian border they had strip-searched my car and found a bunch of keys under the back seat which had been missing for a long time, but that was all done with great good humour.   Not this time.   Clearly, with my passport full of stamps showing me to be a frequent traveller in Communist Europe and the fact that I had my family with me gave rise for suspicion.   Probably, also, I had been spotted taking a picture with my cine camera in Krakow of an old steam train crossing a viaduct - photographing railways was tantamount to spying.   I knew that, but just could not resist this souvenir from the past, and I certainly did not imagine that I would be seen.   After the Polish Customs had spent two hours searching the car for incriminating evidence (and fortunately not finding some Czech crowns purchased from a West German Bank), they demanded to see all our cameras and confiscated all the undeveloped film.   At this point, Lucy-Jean, whose camera they had also taken, started to weep, and I lost my temper. I banged my fist on the table in front of the Customs Officer and shouted at him in German that he had no right whatsoever to treat me, a British subject, in this way.   His face went white and he gripped his revolver, and Audrey besought me to calm down.   The cameras were returned, empty of film, and the Czechs, most embarassed at what had occurred, waved us through and we continued on our way, but I fumed over this for days.   I lodged furious complaints with the British Embassies in Prague and Warsaw and the Polish Embassy in London, and eventually the films were returned to me, with scenes like that of the steam engine cut out and all the colour washed out.   There was no apology and no explanation.

It made me feel anti-Polish for some time, but this soon wore off in the excitement of my new assignment.

Hymac

March 1970. The Lloyd family leave for Germany for three months.

Jo, Fay and Lucy-Jean on the banks of the Rhine.

We lived in the attic of this house in the suburbs of Dusseldorf.

CHAPTER SIX - THOUGHTS ON HYMAC

I feel that perhaps in these writings I may not have not been entirely fair to Hymac. Looking back, these five short years were perhaps the most colourful of my whole career. There was tremendous Team Spirit in the Hymac Organization, emanating from Peter Hamilton himself. There were no politics which affected me personally, which was the reason why I opposed the appointment of Mattingley so vehemently.

On the UK Sales side, Hymac were very successful - the 580 being its flagship. The main problem with it initially, apart from the usual hydraulic leaks which probably most hydraulically driven construction equipment machines suffered in the 1960s, were the tumbler type track running gear, where a combination of grease and dirt formed a grinding paste which chewed up the rollers in a short time. So out came the 580B, with some improvements. The Dutch representative (Geveke, the CAT dealer) fitted their own tractor-type crawler, and eventually Hymac followed suit with the 580BT, and the final version, the 580C was a pretty reliable machine, and sold in quantity. But, as I have already indicated, other models were less successful. However it should not be forgotten that Hymac produced some of the UK's earliest hydraulic cranes, based on the 580 design.

When I say that there were no politics which affected me, there was certainly some dirty work at the cross-roads going on above my head, as Powell Duffryn became disillusioned with this expensive baby which started to lose money, and in January 1971, only six months after my departure, Peter Hamilton was forced to resign.

I was very upset at this news, and I am sure that after that, the Hymac Spirit started to deteriorate. I was not privy, of course, to the circumstances surrounding his forced resignation, but I did hear the word "Judas" from one very loyal person's lips.

Peter Hamilton was invited to join forces with Joe Bamford, and a company called "Hamilton-JCB" was formed. Peter told me recently that Joe Bamford was very kind to him in his misfortune, but I am sure that Mr. JCB also knew the value of Peter Hamilton's name and personal reputation in the marketplace. "Hamilton-JCB" was formed as a top echelon sales unit, but it only lasted a year or two, mainly because PH himself really found that he could not "sell JCB" after so many years with Hymac, the company of which he was the Founding Father.

Hymac continued to exist for about another 25 years, changing from one owner to another. Powell Duffryn finally sold out to IBH in January 1980. IBH was a fast growing conglomerate founded in 1975 by Horst Dieter-Esch, a young German entrepreneur, who had been successful as a sales manager for the big UK international dealer, Blackwood Hodge (from which he coined the name for his new enterprise, the "I" standing for International). He began with a significant equity base of £250,000 which he had made by trading Blackwood Hodge shares and his policy was to buy up ailing, loss-making companies. He started off with three German small family firms, Zettlemeyer, Hamm and Duomat, all manufacturing compaction machines, followed in 1978 by the acquisition of three French companies of similar size, making loaders, excavators and compressors, Derruppe, Maco-Meudon and Manubat-Pingon. His aim was to rival Caterpillar in size, by creating a European Giant of similar proportions, and after swallowing Hanomag, a German manufacturer of much greater size for which he had to pay Massey Ferguson in cash, he approached Powell Duffryn for Hymac, which he cunningly purchased in exchange for a PD equity stake in IBH. He followed this with a similar deal for Wibau in Germany, taking in the very old-established British paving equipment manufacturers of Blaw Knox and Winget, and finally, the biggest fish of all, Terex, the construction equipment subsidiary of the US giant, General Motors.

Dieter Esch was the talk of the industry and I recall that I sat next to him at a CECE dinner at the BAUMA in 1980, when the IBH empire occupied an entire pavilion. He left the dinner, having partaken of no alcohol, after the second course, after which I took the opportunity of asking my fellow guests (all old hands in the game) what they thought about his meteoric rise. "He is a gambler" said one grey-haired German sales director, "Either he will continue to be very successful, or else he will crash". Three years later crash he did, and was charged with breach of trust and violating German company law, for which he spent a few years in gaol.

Under IBH the 580 was continued with a "D" version, which lasted into the next period when NEI (Northern Engineering Industries) took over Hymac after the collapse of IBH in 1983, and transferred production from Rhymney in South Wales to Wolverhampton. A 590 and 890 replaced the old 880 and 1080, and technical reliability improved. NEI brought out an entirely new range, replacing the the old model nos. which had been based on cubic capacity, by the weight classification nomenclature, and the Model Range started at 12

Tonnes (121), progressing up to 30 Tonnes (301). The 580 was produced up to 1987, by which time over 10,000 units had been produced, so there is no doubt but that this is the model by which Hymac will always be remembered, particularly since this represented well over half of the total output of hydraulic excavators bearing the Hymac name. The new Model Range also finally saw the introduction of variable displacement piston pumps and motors to replace the simple gear pumps to which Hymac had been wedded from its beginning.

At the end of 1988 Hymac acquired yet another owner, the Brown Group, but they went into Receivership less than two years later, and Hymac's final resting place was with a large dealer in Northern Ireland, John Kennedy, but production declined rapidly, especially after 1993, when the Wolverhampton Works was closed. However, Hymac have the distinction of being the very first and the very last UK company to produce fully hydraulic excavators of a totally British design, over a period of 40 years.

Hymac

HYMAC Cranes. The Hylift had some success and I found some still in operation in the mid 1990s

Peter Hamilton handing over HYMAC 580s to the Army

Peter Hamilton, the founder of HYMAC, with his wife, Susie in 1999.
He died on 7th January 2005, at the age of 83.

PRIESTMAN

PRIESTMAN BROTHERS,
HULL & LONDON.

THE PATENT DREDGER,
AS SUPPLIED TO THE HULL DOCK COMPANY.

TESTIMONIAL FOR THE ABOVE.

Dear Sirs,   Dock Office, Hull, 5th December, 1878.
          I have pleasure in informing you that the Patent Bucket Crane which
you supplied to us, and which we have had at work nearly four months employed in
dredging mud from our Docks, continues to work in a satisfactory manner. * * * *
During six days, whilst at work in about 19 feet of water, it raised $52\frac{1}{2}$ tons per hour on
an average : and a maximum during one day of nearly $68\frac{1}{2}$ tons per hour.
          The cost per ton of mud raised amounted to 1·63d., which includes all
labor, coals, and stores, but is exclusive of interest on cost of crane and lighters. * * *
          Yours faithfully, R. A. MARILLIER, *(Engineer in Chief.)*

[P.T.O.]

A survivng postcard from 1878 used to publicise the new product

CHAPTER ONE - PRIESTMAN HISTORY

I shall never forget my first visit to Priestman in March 1970. The contrast from Hymac could scarcely have been greater. Coming from a vibrant young company which had only been in existence for 8 years, I found myself looking in at a justly proud but hierarchical family business, which had remained in the same family for 100 years, steeped in tradition, which had just suffered the indignity of losing its independence. In this, it was unique. No other manufacturer of Construction Equipment can, to my knowledge, lay claim to have survived a century as a family business, but there are those who started after the Second World War, Liebherr, JCB, Sennebogen and Manitou who may well be able to make the same claim in 50 years' time.

David Steel took me up to Marfleet Works in Hull in March 1970, for my introduction as the potential Export Manager whom he proposed to impose on this company which had been very successful in the 1950s and early 60s, but had started to decline.

We were entertained to luncheon in the Directors Dining Room. At Priestman, there were three classes of Dining-Room, for Directors, for Managers, and for the Shop Floor Workers, which was not unusual for old-established UK manufacturers.

At the head of the table sat the white-haired patriarch, Philip Priestman, Life President. Next to him, his son James, who, until the Take-Over, had occupied the position of Chairman and Managing Director. One more Priestman, Will, who was responsible for Taperex, completed the members of the family, and then came Norman Brocklebank, Technical Director, Ray North, Works Director, and Neville Moody, Company Secretary. Deferential, with impeccable manners like a well-trained butler, Neville Moody proved to be a very good friend to me in later years.

The reception which I received, as the man chosen by the Steel Group to take on the task of running the company's export department, (and, as I was soon to discover, sorting out the mess which it had got in to) was nothing less than royal.

Maybe they had no choice, but after that initial interview, where sweet sherry was served before an excellent meal, washed down, according to tradition, by lime juice (the Priestmans were Quakers, and it was old Philip's favourite beverage), I was sold completely and absolutely on joining the Company, and I formed an attachment to Priestman which went far beyond the normal loyalty of an employee - it got into my blood. Norman Brocklebank conducted me personally round the Works, and the contrast of this engineering operation, with its quality and varied machine tools, where it was clear that excavators and cranes were manufactured and not assembled, impressed me very much. He had served under Philip on the on the sales side for many years, and at the age of 60, he was still an enthusiastic salesman. As I later found out, he was also an astute politician, but he and I established a personal rapport at that first meeting, which, despite the ups and downs of our relationship over the next 14 years, developed into an enduring friendship.

William Dent Priestman had founded the company in 1870 primarily to manufacture parts for the flour, oil, paint and sugar mills, powered by wind or water, which were dotted around the Hull area. An 1873 Directory described Priestmans as "Smiths, Engineers, Iron and Brassfounders", and in 1875 the first steam-powered Grab Dredger was designed and built to try and recover sunken treasure lost from a Spanish galleon 200 years earlier in Vigo Bay. No treasure was ever recovered, but the next dredger was supplied to Hull Docks in 1878 and the Priestman Grab Dredger started to make its way into docks and harbours all over the world. The modern rope-operated grab was first designed by Priestman and patented in 1875, and Priestman's reputation for grabs was world-wide. In 1970, the Grab and the Grab Dredger Departments were still isolated from the main business of the manufacture and sale of Cranes and Excavators. The man chiefly responsible for developing this specialist side of the business had been Sydney Herbert Priestman, nephew of the founder, who joined the firm in 1897, to be followed by his cousin, Philip (the patriarch described above) who came on board as an apprentice in 1909. Sydney was, as far as I can ascertain, a retiring modest figure, despite being the technical genius of the family.

In 1946 he published a book on the whole history of Grabs, on which he must have been the best authority in the world. But in the Works he was, perhaps, hardly known by sight to junior employees, and the young girl for whom he opened the swing door and stood politely by whilst she hurried through, was probably totally unaware of the privilege which she had enjoyed.

Priestman remained in their first location in Holderness Foundry in Williamson Street until the end of the Second World War, but their success in the war years, when over 500 excavators were supplied to the Ministry of Agriculture for food production, called for expansion and between 1950 and 1956 brand new Works and Offices were built at Marfleet, on the eastern side of Hull, which were specifically conceived to build mechanical excavators in quantity with as high as possible a content being produced "in-house". The 1950s and the 1960s really were the boom time for British manufacturers of Construction Equipment, and I quote from "The Priestman Story" published in 1968: "In 1950, it was still impossible to meet all overseas demands for excavators, and a quota system was introduced to attempt to apportion machines as fairly as possible.

The order book was full for four years ahead. The Sales Team found overseas marketing opportunities in the Caribbean, Belgium, France, Holland, Italy, Spain, Portugal, Scandinavia, Malaya, Switzerland and Yugoslavia. Sales soared in 1959/60 and outstripped production facilities, and the Williamson Street Works, which had been offered for sale, was partially re-occupied."

Priestman launched into setting up subsidiary companies overseas to distribute and service their products, Canada in 1950, Australia in 1961, and Sweden in 1965, and back at home in Marfleet, a new subsidiary was formed, Taperex Ltd., in 1956 to manufacture and sell cross-roll slewing rings, patented at the time of its design. This was first intended for their own production, before becoming a business in its own right. It was in advance of its time in Britain, since traditional "Navvy" manufacturers like RB were still using the old centre post and hook roller method of slewing, and Coles an open "Live Roller " ring which still required a centre-post, and when they changed to a ball ring, it was through a licence from the German manufacturer Rothe Erde.

There is no doubt but that Philip Priestman, autocrat that he was, was a very highly respected man. I could not approve of the way in which he had purposely designed the layout of the Directors' offices at Marfleet, whereby they were all secreted behind a closed corridor, so that one director could move from his office to that of another without being seen by the ordinary mortals outside, although, strangely enough, after the old man died in 1974, I used his old office whenever I was in Hull. Old Priestman employees have argued with me that this was no different from many other companies of a similar era, and one Director regarded it as a positive advantage in that negotiations could be held with senior Union officials without even their presence being noted by prying eyes within the company. But certainly there was an air of secrecy at Priestmans, when, even if an unpleasant fact was known to certain members of the Board, it might "not be known" by an individual who deemed it more politic that he did not know it. Rumour has it that a staff employee once left the office of a senior executive muttering: "He's got more faces than the Town Hall Clock" . . .

But to return to the character of the patriarch. Philip Priestman was certainly very shrewd, and it is he who must take the full credit for building up the business during the 20 years after the end of the War. He did not do this by sitting behind his desk in Hull - in the 1930s, late 40s and 50s he travelled the world selling his company's products. In my own travels for Priestman, many years after his, I always found that he was still regarded with great respect, as a man of decision who kept his word.

He was benevolent towards the shop floor workers, and quick with personal sympathy to anyone in distress and was able to inspire exceptional efforts from the workforce in difficult times. During the depression in the 1930s, the Company was at one point in deep financial trouble, but they had an order for 12 machines for the Soviet Union. Philip is reported to have addressed the workforce and painted a true picture of the position, which was that there was no money for wages, but that if they agreed to work for nothing, the order could be completed and better times might lie ahead.

He got the full support of the employees and the company did indeed survive.

The history of Morris Cranes embodied in a book entitled "Cranes and Craftsmen", published in 1974, tells a similar story of how they also survived the depression of the 1930s by accepting a very large order for dockside cranes for Estonia, which was a brave decision in view of the political antipathy of the time to the first Communist Government, with the risk that they might not be paid, although, from my own experience, the latter was something they did not need to worry about.

After the move from Williamson Street to Marfleet had been accomplished without any hitches during the two week Works Holiday in the mid-50s, Philip Priestman rewarded the two senior executives involved with a £50 bonus, a considerable sum in those days.

However, managers may have been financially well looked after with a pension scheme to which the Company contributed to look forward to, but the workforce only began to participate in this benefit after the merger with the Steel Group. He was certainly a man who was careful in the way he spent money. In the 1950s a number of Priestman executives visited the Hannover Fair, and Philip, as a British Railways director, obtained a specially discounted rate for them on the Hull to Rotterdam Ferry, and then asked the Dutch dealer to transport them by road to Hannover (at his expense!) Norman Brocklebank used to re-count how, when he was on sales in the Birmingham Area, he secured an important order, but was obliged to give 2% discount to obtain it, on which the Old Man drily commented: "A sharp piece of buying".

Another old employee who knew the Patriarch well was Ron Draper, one of Priestman's longest served and most successful salesmen. He started life as an apprentice with Ruston and Hornsby and then worked for a number of years with RB. On the outbreak of War in 1939, Ron was made liaison officer to the Royal Engineers, responsible for the supply of all excavators required for fortifications and works, starting off with those sent over to France with the BEF. After the evacuation from Dunkirk, he was transferred to Lincoln to the secret Design and Construction Team of Naval Landing Equipment. This was a huge earthmoving machine especially designed to construct sunken approach roads enabling large numbers of tanks to lead British invasion forces right up to the old German Hindenberg Line without being detected at ground level. The machine travelled along the bottom of the wide trench, excavating the soil and discharging it on to either bank by means of two elevating conveyor belts. A prototype was built by Ruston and Hornsby, and tested secretly at an RAF station near Lincoln, but it was abandoned after the Germans overran France in 1940. Ron ended up as a senior Plant Adviser to the War Ministry from which post he was not released until 1949. He then joined Priestman to head up the excavator sales division, but at first he did not have a particular title, since it was not Philip's wont to be too specific about responsibilities. Ron was, however, the first Priestman Export Manager in fact, if not in title, and amongst other markets to which he was sent was Canada where he succeeded in setting up the Priestman subsidiary, first of all travelling by ocean liner and then in a converted Lancaster bomber, where first class passengers were provided with a bed to sleep in.

Philip Priestman left him there without specific instructions as to how long he would be expected to remain, which the Old Man chose to communicate first to Ron's wife back in Hull - it was three months! As my own career has showed, considerations for the wife and family of travelling executives in lengths of trips were not the same as today, where most people now engaged in that sort of role expect to have their weekends at home. Ron also pioneered Priestman sales in Europe, South America and the Caribbean, where his name still rang bells 20 years later. Family considerations finally caused him to revert to the Home Market, with a London base, where he was invaluable, being highly respected by and totally introduced at all levels into the large Civil Engineering Contractors like Wimpey, Taylor Woodrow and Costain. He retired after 25 years' service in 1974, and died at the grand old age of 94 on December 11th, 2002. I had a lively lunch with this unforgettable old soldier only three months before his death.

Charlie Hamshaw is another long-served Priestman executive who knew Philip well. He joined the Company in 1947 after serving his apprentice-ship at Herbert Morris, the Overhead Crane Manufacturer at Loughborough. Charlie had left school at 16, but he went to Night School and was made a foreman at 21. At Priestmans he started at the bottom, on the shopfloor, but Philip recognized his potential and sent him off to a number of other manufacturers within and without the Construction Equipment Industry to learn the art of Production Control. However, in 1960, he decided to emigrate to Australia, which was encouraging UK citizens to go out by offering passage for themselves and their families for only £10, provided that they stayed for a minimum period of time. Priestmans then asked him to carry out a market survey, which led to the establishment of their Australian subsidiary, and, when that was completed, he was invited to come back to Hull to take over as Works Manager, to assist Ray North, who was getting out of his depth. He was continually passed over, by subsequent regimes, for the position which he richly deserved, Works Director, with various outsiders being brought in, leaving of their own accord or being fired for incompetence, until 1978, when he finally made it to the top. Apart from his talents in running production lines, Charlie also had a lively sense of humour. He came upon one of the Demonstrators, whose duties also involved driving machines on the Test Apron, sitting in the office reading a novel one day. This individual was a superb machine operator, but of an idle disposition, and, during the testing of the travel transmission of the wheeled hydraulic excavator, Mustang 90, he had been caught sitting in the cab asleep with the machine jacked up on the outriggers and its wheels spinning round furiously to put the required "Test Hours" on the hourmeter. On this occasion, in response to Charlie's sharp question as to what exactly did he think he was doing, he replied: "Educating meself, Mr. Hamshaw, by reading the dictionary", to which came the swift rejoinder: "Well, look up the word 'Work' and get back to it sharpish".

James did not inherit the shrewdness of, nor was he respected like his father. He was "Il figlio di Papa", as the Italians have it, and was propelled into the business by his father against his own will - he himself wanted to become an actor. My own impression of him was that he was rather arrogant and self-opinionated, and it was certainly clear to me that Norman Brocklebank, who had a very high regard for old Philip, shared my view. During the discussions with the Steel Group, James was the one who conducted the negotiations, but they did not retain his services for long.

It was only a few months after I joined that I was unexpectedly asked by Reg Keates, by then promoted to the position of Steel Group Marketing Director, to accompany him to Hull, after informing me that the Steel Board had sacked James Priestman.

I was aghast at the possible repercussions in Hull, not being privy, at that time, to the situation. In the Boardroom awaiting us were Don Hassall, the Steel Group Managing Director, and Norman Brocklebank. Discussion went on as to who should take James Priestman's place at the Head of the Table, and finally the chair was turned, in a dramatic gesture, empty, to face the wall. In questioning old Priestman employees about James Priestman, I have, despite my own views about him from a very short acquaintance, found that there was a lot of sympathy for his predicament in having reluctantly to follow in the footsteps of his illustrious father. But at the time of the Steel Group Takeover, he was Chairman and Managing Director, he was the current head of the family business which had survived for a century, and when he was suddenly thrown out by the new masters (with, I suspect, a fair amount of inside collaboration), the shock to him was tremendous. One of Priestman's longest served and most successful sales reps told me how he met JDP (as he was known) a year or two later quite by chance on a railway station en route to Hull with important customers, and James, holding only a second class ticket, joined them uninvited in the first class carriage, to give them the impression that he was still "The Boss".

For me, the true successor to Philip Priestman was Norman Brocklebank. He started his career as a draughtsman in 1926 from where he rapidly graduated on to Sales, and was sent to Birmingham, where he was eventually appointed Sales Manager.

One of the original Cubs, with a wooden cab, which, dating from 1934 and rebuilt by the apprentices, used to stand outside Marfleet Works, was an excavator first sold by Brock, and this machine can still be seen in the hands of a contractor in Warrington.

It may be that it was this particular Cub which provoked a complaint from the customer that the muckshifting output was considerably less than he had been led to expect. Brock wisely carried out a site investigation, and established that the driver loaded his horse and cart with the excavator, and then the horse pulled the cart to the end of the field to discharge the load and returned for the next load. To convince the customer that his output estimates could be reached, Brock hired ten horses and carts and lined them up, one behind the other, so that the Cub was kept continually in productive work and his point was proved. In 1952, Brock was taken off sales and appointed to the position of Technical Director, on the very same day that James Priestman was appointed as Sales Director, but the latter was senior. This explains much.

Norman Brocklebank was a survivor. He coped with the Steel Group hierarchy and maintained as independent a stance for Priestmans within the Group as possible, but later he used to refer to those "terrible Board Meetings in Sunderland" where he only had the support of Neville Moody as Company Secretary as a true Priestman man.

All the other directors were from Steels and co-opted on to the Priestman Board.

So the arrival of Acrow on the scene must have been a tremendous relief for him, because the first thing that he told Bill de Vigier was that he wanted Priestman separated totally from Coles and he got his way on this. He rapidly turned his sails into the prevailing wind and became an Acrow Group enthusiast, and he survived as Managing Director until he had almost completed half a century of service with the company. Then de Vigier appointed the ex-JCB firebrand, Alan Cooper, in his place, but Alan, who had joined the company as Deputy MD in April 1975, always respected and often deferred to him. "What do you think, Norman", he would ask after everyone around the Boardroom table had expressed their opinion on a particular matter. I can hear his educated Yorkshire voice reply, slowly and deliberately: "Well, I - er - I don't know.....I've been listening to what you've all been saying and er - it seems to me that - er - there's one aspect of the matter which you've all missed" and then out would come some shrewd comment from the depths of his long experience. He never used a calculator, but always had his pocket slide-rule ready to hand, and he continued in office as an executive director until 1984, the year when the Acrow Group collapsed. Even then, at the age of 74, he could not stop working and in the last few years of his life he was retained as a Consultant by JCB.

He died very suddenly at the age of 80 in November 1990, and my last meeting with him was only just over a year before his death, when I stayed the night at his home, and we reminisced over old times, in particular the countless number of times when he had said to me: "You are swimming in shark-infested waters, lad", which never deflected me from my chosen path, nor did he, I think, ever seriously think that it would. That unforgettable last evening together ended by our watching together and chuckling over "Yes, Minister", one of his (and my) favourite programmes.

At the time of my arrival on the scene, Fred Ingram (known to his colleagues as "Fred the Dredge") was the sole and undisputed King of the Grab Dredger Department. A stout, friendly, helpful man, he was a Law unto Himself. He was the only man in the Company who knew how to build up a quotation and carry out the technical sale of a Dredger, and he travelled the world doing just this, never taking any other currency with him other than £ notes in various denominations. There was no such document in my day as a Dredger Price List, the only one which I know of having been published in 1896. One could give him the name of a potential customer, but, beyond that, the Export Department could have no further involvement in the sale. Fred played his cards very close to his chest and was very careful to ensure that nobody else gained any insight into the secrets of his trade. After Fred's untimely death, a very competent design engineer carried on his work, and dredgers were still occasionally sold, but the magic of the character that was Fred The Dredge had disappeared for ever. Fred never owned nor drove a motor car - he travelled everywhere by public transport, and the numbers of Grab Dredgers still in operation today around the world is a tribute to him and his forbears.

Next to his office was the Grab Sales Department, where three highly skilled specialists also ensured that few others penetrated what to outsiders was regarded as the "Black Art" of specifying and selling Grabs, of which a 1958 promotional publication claimed that the company could offer over 2500 different types and sizes. I tried very hard to get some understanding of the Grab Business, and at least I succeeded in forming a very good working relationship with the "Three". Mike Read, Tony Davies and David Millington worked in the same office and had individual areas of responsibility, with Mike carrying the title of "Grab Sales Controller", but not really being regarded by the other two as any better or more knowledgeable than themselves, which made life difficult for him, as he carried the can for the department. There was a fourth, Mike Dale, who had gone to Australia to add strength to the local production of grabs out there. He returned to Hull in the late 70s, but had trained his Australian deputy, Alan Fairlie, so well that Alan still carries on producing grabs near Sydney today, originally based on Priestman designs. Despite their undoubted technical and engineering skills, the "Three" were not a very harmonious team, each individual engrossed in his own responsibility, but they all certainly knew their onions and repeat orders from large and important users formed the bread and butter of grab sales. After the Steel Group Takeover, Grab Sales was never individually represented at Board level, and my impression was that they were, in my time, always the "poor relation" in the company, regarded by some as a bunch of cranks whose turnover was insignificant in comparison to the crane and excavator division. This was not a fair assessment of their high skills in keeping the Priestman name to the forefront in a very specialized business, and in fact, on a world-wide basis Priestman's reputation for grabs was probably much greater than for any of its other products. A separate Grab Shop was finally built for them, and they were undoubtedly one of the most profitable sections in the business but I do not think that much of it ever went into the pockets of the "Three".

The development of the Grab Dredger had led into more general crane development, and a very early steam-driven, chain-operated grabbing crane required a very big strong man to drive it, since the lifting function was engaged by pushing a mechanism sideways with one leg, whilst standing on the other! In 1917 a special crane was mounted on a tank track, designed to clear minefields, but the War came to an end before it ever reached the battlefront. Was this the original crawler crane? I think that it might have been, since up to that time nearly every crane was mounted on rails.

The breakthrough was in 1920, when Sydney Priestman designed the "Priestman Ditcher", the initial sketch for which was drawn on the back of an envelope. The original machine was driven by a primitive form of Power-Take-Off from a crawler tractor, and from this was developed the famous Priestman "Cub", a crawler-mounted, diesel-, petrol- or paraffin-driven excavator with a capacity of 8 cu.ft. (225 litres). It is said that the name was coined by Philip Priestman when he was searching for one of the first of these machines with its green wooden cab in the East Anglian Fens, and he commented that it was like looking for a cub in the undergrowth. However that may be, the tradition of christening machines with animal names began, (with bucket capacities originally designated in cubic feet) Panther, 12 cu.ft. (340 litres), Tiger 14 cu. ft.(400 litres), Lion 27 cu.ft (800 litres), with a Wolf somewhere in the middle of this lot, Caribou, a truck-mount originally aimed at the Canadian market, and Bison, a larger crane version of the Lion. The animal names continued on into the hydraulic excavator era with Beaver and Mustang. Land Drainage was the speciality in which the Company excelled. The Side Dragline, whereby irrigation canals could be cleaned alongside the crawler tracks, enabling a continuous travel motion to be engaged was a purely Priestman innovation in the mechanical excavator era.

In 1960 the most famous of the Priestman menagerie was re-born - the Lion. This new version was undoubtedly one of the most sophisticated and highly engineered mechanical cranes ever built, the prototypes, after involving 100,000 hours of design time, being tested to destruction. Air controls to the clutches and brakes, gearing enclosed in oilbaths, piped lubrication system, all units being mounted on a totally machined superstructure base - these were the features of the Lion. It had a special sealing system on the crawler tracks which was far more maintenance free than the standard tumbler-type undercarriage. Over 2000 units were produced in various versions and sold all over the world, and the Lion was a by-word for reliability and versatility (as a Liftcrane, Grabcrane or Dragline) Nearly ten years after I had left Priestman, I sold a reconditioned Lion to Zimbabwe, and as far as I know it is still in satisfactory operation in that strife-torn country. In Britain, in Holland, and in many other countries there are countless Lions still in operation today.

In my view, its entry into the hydraulic era spelled the end of the golden days for Priestman excavators and cranes, even though a strong recovery was made after the initial problems. Nevertheless they prepared the ground well. As early as 1960 a "Think Tank" was set up in the Drawing Office to consider all the aspects and problems of entering the hydraulic field, and they started talking to manufacturers of components. One senior Design Engineer involved in the project avers that the Sales Force at that time were not interested, and that the change was led by the designers, with the sales force being in opposition. As with all other traditional manufacturers of mechanical excavators, the transition to hydraulics was not easy to fit in to a Works totally geared up (in a literal sense) for the production of machines where, traditionally, all components were built "in-house". There was the problem of cleanliness required for hydraulic components, and the fact that reliance had now to be placed as much with outside suppliers, rather than with sub-assemblies under the direct control of the producer. Hydraulic components were not then as reliable or sophisticated as today. Priestman can claim to have been one of the most successful of the traditional mechanical excavator manufacturers to produce a quality hydraulic digger. They were also not far behind Hymac, who started manufacture in 1962, and JCB, who produced their first fully slewing excavator, the JCB7, in 1964. The change was cautious and began with the "Hydro-Cub", which was simply an hydraulic bucket ram fitted to the old dragshovel, which grew into the "Beaver", launched in 1964, which had a fully hydraulic front end equipment, with mechanical slew and travel, and then came the fully hydraulic "Mustang". If Priestman had stuck to what they knew best and concentrated on crawler machines, there might well have been a different story, but they did not. Instead they took a leap into the dark and produced the Mustang 90 on wheels. Why did they do this? They were clearly strongly influenced by the success of the Europeans such as Poclain and Atlas who pioneered the wheeled excavator. But the UK market remained, for many years, wedded to the crawler, partially, at least, due to the dominance of Plant Hire companies supplying small earthmoving contractors with machines as and when required by transporting them to site on a low-loader, whereas the European market was developed around small earthmoving contractors owning their own machines. In the largest potential wheeled excavator markets of the day, Germany and France, Priestman was hardly represented at all, and in one of its main export markets, Sweden, it had its own subsidiary company which was running into financial difficulties.

I do not think that James Priestman would have been aware of these considerations, and he moved the Company away from what they knew and from where they had experience. It could be argued that the decision to go for a very technologically advanced wheelmount was a very courageous one, which might have come off had it not been for the vulnerability of the highly sophisticated automated transmission for the undercarriage. The Lucas transmission was manufactured within a very large and reputable group, English Electric, and was technically far ahead of its competitors, but it proved to be extremely susceptible to misuse, and soon gained a reputation for unreliability, as well as being very expensive to repair. Its crawler-mounted brother, the Mustang 120, was much more successful, but suffered from the fact that the front end equipment was the same as had been designed for the Mustang 90. The wheelmount certainly could dig, but I suppose that the stresses on the boom and arm were less on a wheeled than on a crawler machine. Just as I joined, Priestman had gained an important order for 16 Mustang 120s for the Office of Public Works in the Republic of Ireland. Every boom and arm cracked and had to be plated and strengthened. Priestman learnt from this experience and the Mk II and Mk III versions became very reliable machines. In 1975 the Ministry for Water Resources in Indonesia purchased 31 Mustang 120s, in addition to numbers of Hymacs, Poclains and Japanese excavators. The Mustangs were scattered all over the country on individual sites and swamps, and, despite very little proper maintenance, outlasted all their competitors. This is also, in my opinion, a shining example of where the simple gear pump, with its fixed displacement system, triumphed over the more sophisticated high pressure variable displacement hydraulics which are the hallmark of all modern machines. The story of how this order was obtained will be recounted later, but it serves to illustrate my contention that this was one of the most reliable, durable hydraulic excavators produced anywhere in the 1970s.

I suppose that there were a number of factors which led Priestmans being forced to look for a new master. With the advent of hydraulics, the market for mechanical machines declined rapidly. Despite the brilliance of its technical innovation, the Mustang 90 cost the company dearly. The subsidiary companies in Canada and in Sweden had incurred heavy losses and had to be closed and sales and service handed over to dealers. Philip needed a competent and forward thinking successor to take the Company into the second half of the 20th century, but his son, James, failed to live up to this role, and the autocratic system put in place by Philip gave James total and unlimited power, which he was not competent to use wisely. The Take-Over by the Steel Group was to some extent motivated by the IRC, the Industrial Re-Organization Corporation set up by the Labour Government, and headed up by a banker named Charles Villiers, whose brief was to "rationalise" British manufacturing industries, which resulted in the formation of British Leyland, into which two manufacturers of Construction Equipment, Coventry Climax and Aveling Barford, were incorporated. British Leyland also looked seriously into acquiring Priestman, but, after examining the books, they declined. IRC encouraged the Steel Group to buy Stothert and Pitt, the very old established dockside crane manufacturer from Bath, but it was turned down. They then proposed Priestman, and came up with a generous financing package and the deal was soon done.

I count myself very fortunate that this decision resulted in such a rewarding and interesting position for myself, but I wonder whether it was a wise decision on the part of the Steel Group, who were forced to seek merger terms themselves only two years later.

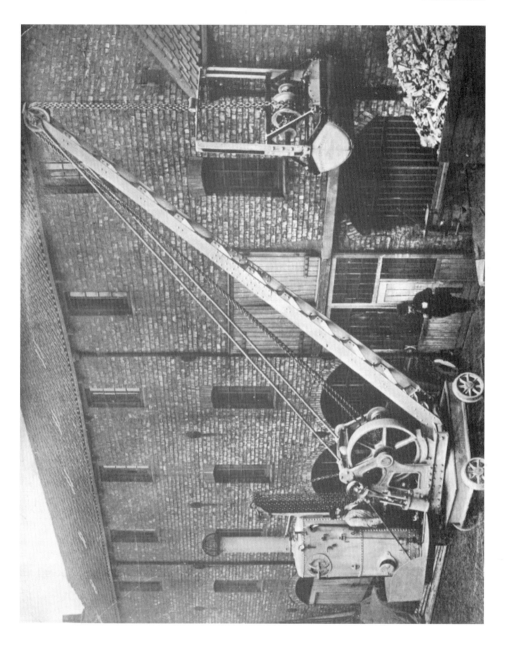

An early Priestman steam-driven grab crane with chain operation

1917 prototype of a Priestman steam-operated grab crane mounted on a tank track, designed to fill shell holes on the Western Front in World War I

THE PRIESTMAN DITCHER—Model No. 1

ENQUIRIES.—The preparation of tenders will be facilitated by information on the following points—

1. Type of Ditcher—Self-contained with internal combustion engine or tractor driven.
2. Material—Earth, clay, mud, etc., wet, dry, hard, or soft.

3. Variety of materials encountered.
4. Sketch of cross-section of drain.
5. Contour and condition of banks.
6. Distance spoil to be placed from drain.

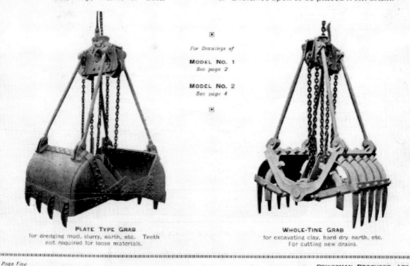

For Drawings of

MODEL No. 1
See page 2

MODEL No. 2
See page 4

PLATE TYPE GRAB
for dredging mud, slurry, earth, etc. Teeth not required for loose materials.

WHOLE-TINE GRAB
for excavating clay, hard dry earth, etc. For cutting new drains.

PRIESTMAN BROTHERS, LTD.

The 1921 field drain ditcher, designed by Sydney H. Priestman in conjunction with the Ministry of Agriculture, to recover poor land for agriculture

Priestman Cub with skimmer equipment, clearing bomb damage in Hull during the second world war

The patented side dragline equipment, used for cutting/cleaning ditches which are close to hedges or other obstructions

A Priestman Cub with a wooden cab built in 1934 and first sold by Norman Brocklebank. It was restored by apprentices and can still be seen today in the hands of a contractor and collector in Warrington

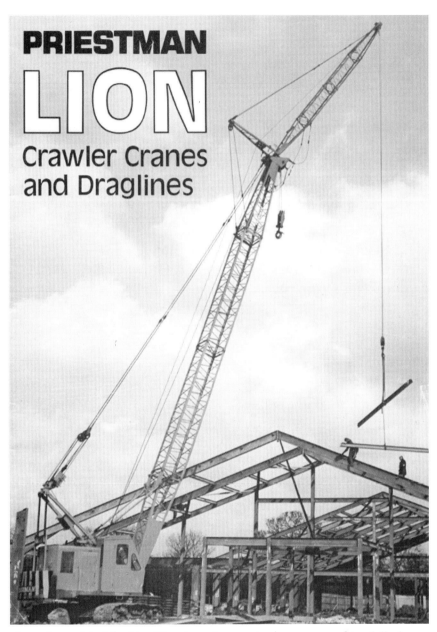

PRIESTMAN
LION
Crawler Cranes
and Draglines

An early model of the Lion III universal excavator/crane, a machine full of original design features, that was to prove immensely successful, and developed into a wide range of specialist cranes.

Swing and Travel Plate Clutches

Large diameter plate clutches give smooth operation of swing or travel, the function being selected by the driver and air operated. The whole clutch assembly and pedestal housing can be removed from the machine as a unit if this should ever be necessary. The design consists of two half shafts each carrying a plate clutch and bevel gear, connected by a central muff coupling; the drive is applied to the left hand shaft. To engage a clutch, air is applied to the pair of pneumatic cylinders operating the clutch fingers, and engaging the pressure plate with the friction lining. Segmented friction linings are easily replaced and can be adjusted by transferring a packer under each clutch finger. Where a low swing speed is required, but maintaining high rope speed, a split flow transmission can be fitted.

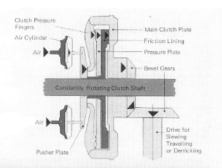

Independent Boom Hoist

The ability of Lion to operate swing and boom hoist, whilst lifting a load, is a valuable time saving feature contributing to smooth working cycles and high output. Independent boom hoist is powered from the clutch shaft through an internal expanding clutch and gear/chain drive down to the rope drum. To lift the boom, the central air control lever is pulled rearwards, and power is applied through the clutch to rotate the drum and lift the boom. Immediately the control is released the automatic spring brake is applied arresting boom movement. Pushing the control forward lowers the boom, by releasing the clutch and brake, allowing rope to be paid off the drum at a speed governed by clutch shaft rotation and engine throttle setting. This is effected by allowing the rope pull to drive a chain connection with the clutch shaft, through a sprag clutch which locks boom lowering speed to that of the clutch shaft.

The sophisticated transmission of the Lion.

The Hydrocub. A ram-operated bucket was fitted to an otherwise standard Cub VI excavator, to prove the increased output achievable with hydraulic power

MUSTANG
from
Priestman
introduces
stepless transmission
on a digger

90

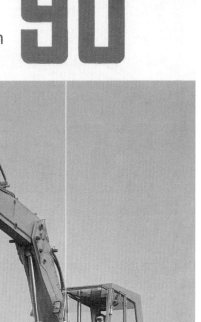

Mustang 90 was the first fully hydraulic excavator launched by Priestman.
This wheel-mounted version was to meet the demands of contractors overseas who particularly needed a machine that could travel between sites under
its own power

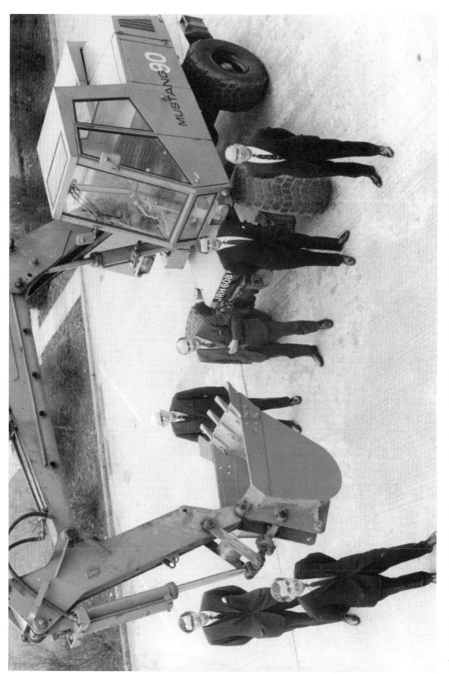

The Priestman Board of Directors proudly show off their new Mustang 90. *From the left*: James D. Priestman,(*rear*) John Martin (*foreground*). Philip D. Priestman, E.R.North, N. Brocklebank, and A. Wilkins.

Priestman

A Mustang 120 MK I working in appalling conditions in the West Indies, reclaiming a swamp. Numerous snakes presented the driver with a serious threat if he left his cab, and extra fuel tanks were fitted to the machine which was working a considerable distance from any roads

Mustang 120 in its Mk III version

One of the MUSTANG 120 Mk III excavators supplied to the Ministry of Water Resources, Indonesia

The new Priestman works to the east of Hull, occupied a 63 acre site, and was completed in 1958. It was built for the production of excavators, cranes, grabs, Taperex slewing rings and dredgers *Inset*: Philip D. Priestman.

Ron Draper, the veteran salesman, and (above) with the author at the age of 90

Charles Hamshaw (second from left) with a group of customers examining a Taperex slew ring

Two of the very large Priestman grabs supplied to Hong Kong for the underwater excavation of a trench, to form the base of a new dam, with a reservoir to increase the supply of fresh water

A tiny grab used to remove core samples from a bore hole, (standing in the foreground) and a large rivetted construction grab, with some of the men who built it

Mike Read with a delegate from Egypt, and (below) the rest of the grab sales team: Tony Davies, Mike Dale and David Millington

13th September 1976, Norman Brocklebank celebrates 50 years of service with Priestman. *Left to right:* Tony Bodimeade, Kees Zeevenhooven, Alan Cooper, Norman Brocklebank, and his wife, Enid, Dick Lloyd, Brian Wildsmith, Bill Bromwich.

The author (left) with Bert Richardson and his wife in Sydney in January 2003

Norman F. Taylor,
Service Manager
(see Chapter Four).

Fred. V. Ingram,
Chief Dredging Engineer, known
to all as "Fred the Dredge."

CHAPTER TWO - PRIESTMAN IN THE STEEL GROUP

Steels did not make the same mistake as they had when they took over R.H.Neal in 1960, in that they made no attempt to integrate the Priestman product line into Coles. But then the product was totally different, so it would not have been practicable.

What they did do was to amalgamate Sales and Marketing, but this had its disadvantages. Reg Keates, as Group Marketing Director, responsible for all sales, was fortunately kept from any involvement on the Priestman Export Side because David Steel had been appointed Export Director. When I re-joined Steels, and was greeted by him with the words "So, you've come back, Dick" I replied firmly: "At your invitation, Mr. Keates". I was careful, however, to keep closely in touch with Norman Brocklebank. I may have been a Steel Group import, but I was determined to become a Priestman man.

On the UK Coles side, Vic Canham, who had worked under Keates for over 20 years, also knew how to handle and contain him. When he had achieved his long-term ambition to become the Steel Group Marketing Director, Reg had acquired a brand new black Mercedes, and was travelling with Vic and one of the reps one day, when he overtook an extremely battered old car in order to beat it to a traffic lights. However the lights were against him, and the overtaken car managed to pull up alongside the Merc, and the driver tapped on his window, indicating that he wanted to speak to him. "You drive like a young man, sir" said the driver of the battered vehicle, and Reg beamed with pleasure, and then, just as the lights changed and he let in his clutch, he added: "Not like the silly old Fart which you are". It is said that Vic Canham had great difficulty in keeping a straight face!

But for the Priestman boys, there was no such shield. Prior to the merger with the Steel Group, they had suffered from very poor top management, under a toffee-nosed "English" South African, who had been brought in by James Priestman to replace the far more experienced and competent Ron Draper, who was relegated back to his position in the South. The South African had moved the centre of sales from Hull Works to Birmingham, which added confusion to chaos, but he was so incompetent that he only lasted a few years and then came John Martin, about whom everyone spoke very highly. Whether he would have wanted to serve under Steels is not known, because he died suddenly of a heart attack on the same day as the merger took place, and so began the reign of Reg Keates, again with the sales centre in the South and not at the Works. Reg dominated their UK Sales through an extremely gentlemanly, but rather weak Home Sales Manager, who had previously been on export and whom I had replaced, and who eventually resigned and left to buy a newsagent's business. Norman Brocklebank had little confidence in the new set-up, whereby the crawler cranes were sold by the Coles Sales Force and the excavators by the old Priestman Sales Force.   Forecasts for excavator sales were not met, and I can remember attending a typical Reg Keates session when the pressure was on him to dispose of a large stock of Mustangs which had built up.   He had all the Area Managers sitting round the table, listing their prospects, with reps standing by at the end of telephones.   One reported that a particular order had been agreed at local level, but that it required Head Office Approval.   "'Ow long will that take?" demanded Reg, and after hearing that it would be three or four days, he retorted:

"Four days!   Is it being sent to 'Ead Office by 'Orse and Cart?   In this electronic age, 'asn't anybody 'eard of the bleedin' telex?"   Reg may have been a bully, but he certainly did not lack a sense of humour, and he could certainly achieve sales himself, even if the clientele who would accept him were rather limited.   He had a saying which sticks in my memory, about attitudes to selling:

"Two men looked through prison bars,
One saw mud and the other saw stars!"

Priestman Export Sales were also moved from Hull to Steel House in Eastcote, and amongst those who moved with it was a bright young man named Stuart Anderson, who had been started life in the Hull Export Department at the age of 17.   Art School trained, he came from a working class background, and never had the chance of a university education.   He was put on probation for no less than seven months before he was given a permanent position, and he spent his nights absorbing technical information from brochures and catalogues to perfect his product knowledge, which made him an ideal person for creating and implementing some Sales Training methods for dealers, which was sadly lacking.   When we appointed a new dealer in Norway, Stuart did such an excellent job on the training that I decided to give him his head and make him the Scandinavian Sales Executive, and he tells me that this was one of the milestones in his career development.   I purloined an experienced administrator from Hymac, John Davies, and then brought in a deputy, so that I could free myself from the day to day running of the department to go out and sell.   Peter Purves was a retired Army Major, who had been involved in Secret Service work in the war, and been one of Winston Churchill's bodyguards at the Yalta Conference, and we had got to know each other at East European Trade Fairs, when he had been Export Manager for Chaseside, the wheeled loader manufacturer, before they were swallowed up by JCB. He was a great friend and colleague, but, when in his cups, he had an annoying habit of telling me, sometimes in front of dealers, how to run the department, and, after he had sobered up, I would take him to task on this, which caused him to hang his head in utter shame and his profuse apologies were almost more embarassing than the original offending behaviour!

I also inherited a couple of travelling men, one of whom specialized in Latin America. One was a highly emotional man, whose business acumen was limited, and he had got himself into a terrible mess in Brazil (he spoke Brazilian Portuguese fluently), involving a court case with a previous agency run by a couple of particularly unpleasant ex-Nazis, and one of my first tasks was to resolve this problem. I did a whirlwind trip around the sub-continent with him, being introduced to all the dealers, in which we were wined and dined to an extent that he ended up with a severe attack of hepatitis, which made him unfit to carry on the job, and I was able to ease him out.

However I could see that Latin America and the Carribean was a good potential market for Priestman, and I was to spend a lot of time on this, my original stamping ground.

But, mainly I turned my attention to Europe. There were two major problem areas here, Sweden and Spain, two of the "successful markets" mentioned in the 1950-60 era. In both, the problem was the Mustang 90, where in both dealers' yards there were quantities of broken-down machines returned from dissatisfied customers.

In Sweden, Priestman had managed to sell their subsidiary company to a finance company, so at least they were not continuing to bear the losses. The Managing Director was an amiable Swede called Lennart Anderson, and he took on a Sales Manager of the same name. Stuart Anderson and I still recall with mirth the advertisement which they put out to customers to sell the huge stock, not only of Mustangs, but Lions in various stages of disintegration: "Anderson och Anderson - Grafiskmaskiner" with pictures of themselves, convinced that the customers would be queueing up to buy from two such clearly well-known personalities. Lennart would always preface his business telephone conversations with "Hallo, hallo, Good Morning, how is the weather over there?" However dire the situation, nothing seemed to perturb him and although his employers eventually put in a more dynamic guy over him, he seemed always to be around, and, in later years, used to turn up on occasions apparently successfully making some kind of living selling used machines on his own account. He was a delightful man, but how he survived remains still a mystery to me.

However, at least Sweden did not cost me as dearly as sorting the problems in Spain. This was where the Mustang 90 had sold well, but every machine was returned to the dealer's yard with problems, and eventually he threw in the towel, or possibly went bust - I do not recall which, and I had to set to and find a new one. I knew to whom I should talk. The company who had actually managed to sell a few Neal-Units was the one I targeted. It was an interesting set-up, the owner of the Spanish dealership, Hermenegildo Mugica, relying totally on his English partner to deal with the principals and arrange the payments. Gordon Poole, who described himself as a "Commercial Truck Concessionaire" was an eccentric smoothie, who drove an ancient Bentley, but he was no fool. After I had done my sales pitch on him and on Herme, it was agreed that their Spanish Sales Manager would visit Priestmans to make an assessment.

The guy was going to be in the UK for a full week at the end of November 1970, and I was to make arrangements directly with him. He proved hard to get, and told me that he had a full programme for the whole week, but could be available only on Saturday morning. Here I have to pay full tribute to my new colleagues, who all turned out on the Saturday morning in Hull, so that I could show him the Works, and machines on demonstration.

The visit was a complete success, and I drove him back to London in the afternoon and issued an invitation to dinner in the evening. We went to one of my favourite restaurants, the Dolce Vita in Frith St., Soho, where excellent Italian food was accompanied by guitar music and song (sadly it has long disappeared). At that time, minicabs were only just beginning to make their appearance on the streets of London, and I had not "driven up" to their existence. So I took my car, knowing that, after 11 pm, there would be no taxis available and the Underground Stations would be closed. The breathanalyser had also only just come in. I had reckoned that a good dinner with wine was all that would be required. I was wrong. The Spaniard wanted to go to a Night Club, and here lay my undoing. As I drove up the Finchley Road at about 3 am, after depositing my guest at his hotel in Hampstead, I had but one thought - to get home and face the anxiety and the wrath of Audrey, to whom I had promised that I would be home by midnight. Every traffic light was against me, but between them I drove my company Triumph 2.5 petrol-injectioned car (of which I was very proud) to its maximum speed. Suddenly I became aware that I was being closely tailed by a Police Car, who overtook me and signalled me to pull in.

"My God, I've been drinking" was my immediate thought, so I got out of the driving seat and met the police officers (there were, unfortunately, two of them) halfway between my car and theirs. "Officers", I began, "I know that I have been speeding. I am an Export Manager, and I have been out all night with an important overseas customer, and I am desperate to get home to my wife and family." The two policemen exchanged meaningful glances. Had there been only one, I am sure that I would have got away with it, but came the inevitable question: "Have you been drinking, sir?" Out came the breathanalyser and my car was locked up and I was taken to the nearest Police Station to await the arrival of a Police Surgeon to take a blood test and the two policemen were busy trying to re-assure me that the blood test would not necessarily confirm the reading of the breathanalyser. I felt like a criminal and, unhappily for me, it showed that I was marginally over the limit, and I was sent home in a minicab (why did I not order one in advance?), where I arrived home at 6 am to be greeted with great relief by Audrey, who was convinced that I had been killed.....

For Priestmans, I walked for 12 months - even though the magistrates were so impressed by my impassioned defence (Export or Die was the cry at that time of British manufacturing industry) that they "retired for 20 minutes to consider the verdict". They had no choice. An order for two Mustang 90s was placed by Gordon Poole, "subject to a 48 hour continuous satisfactory test" in the Quarry at South Cave, the Priestman "Test Ground". During the test, the transmissions failed. Here ended the First Lesson.....

But there is a sequel to this story. I took the Driving Ban sentence on the chin and accepted that my Driving Licence be immediately suspended, (at least I kept my job) so that, 12 months later, before Christmas, I got it back. As I was driving down to Devon to join my family at our cottage for the New Year at the beginning of 1972, I attempted to overtake a Humber Snipe on the A303, at that time a single track winding road. The vehicle swerved to the right and I pulled back. At a second attempt, the same thing happened, and I realised that the driver was totally drunk, so I kept behind, awaiting events. As we approached a small Dorset village, the Humber weaved out again and hit an oncoming car a glancing blow, and continued. I stopped and the other car stopped and I explained the circumstances. He turned round and we gave chase, and I allowed him to overtake and force the Humber to stop. The driver was a woman. "Wassa matter?" she said, thickly. We explained that she had hit an oncoming car and not stopped, which she denied, so at that point I offered to phone the Police from a nearby pub, whilst he immobilised her vehicle by removing the Rotor-Arm (can you do this on a modern car?) She cursed, whilst we exchanged addresses and eventually the Arm of the Law arrived in the form of a sole policeman on a motorcycle. "Oh Aarh, Oi'll 'ave to get the Breathalyser to 'er" he pronounced, and here I made my mistake. I drove off, having given him my address, hearing her say, in an imperious voice, "You can't touch me, I am a Police Officer". She proved to be right - when I was summoned to court as a witness, I was unable to attend because it coincided with the Hannover Fair, where Priestman were exhibiting, and, upon my return I was politely informed that the "Defendant pleaded guilty to driving without due care and attention - fined £10 and licence endorsed". My reaction to this news is not printable!

However there was one bright spot in the Priestman European Sales picture. The family firm of Zeevenhooven had represented Priestman in Holland since 1935, when the founder, Kees Zevenhooven, persuaded Philip Priestman to change the Dutch dealership. Tragically he was killed on the very first day of the German invasion of Holland in May, 1940, by a German paratrooper. His widow had continued to manage the business after his death, and it survived the wartime period by selling the consignment stock of another of their pre-war principals, Consolidated Pneumatic Tool Company, which kept their employees from being forced to work for the Nazis in Germany. The contract with Priestman was renewed after the War, and Zeevenhooven managed to sell about 4 Wolf Draglines per year. The eldest son had joined the family firm after the end of the war, but unfortunately suffered brain damage following a very severe road accident, and in 1950 the next son, Kees, came on board. One of the first problems that he had to deal with was the re-payment to CPT of the consignment stock, which would have bankrupted the company, but he managed to conceal the fact because the book-keeping was running behind.

In February 1953, there were disastrous floods in Holland. I remember these also all too well, since I was at that time an RE Officer Cadet at Chatham who was put on flood relief work on the East Coast, humping sandbags up to all hours, and attempting to drag cows, very reluctant to be forced to swim, behind lightweight folding boats, with hilarious consequences. After the first cow had almost overturned the boat with her thrashings in the water, and then ended the journey belly up until she touched dry ground, we resorted to driving the beasts from "island" to "island", ferrying farmers between the land gaps who beat the water with their sticks, accompanied by wild shouts to drive the swimming cows. Back in Holland, Kees was persuading Ron Draper to send a Panther on consignment for a Trade Show in Utrecht, and this led to the sale that year of about 30 of these draglines, and sales then really took off.

A clock with a silver plate commemorating 1955 and 1956 as "World Record Sales Years" for Priestman was presented to Kees by Philip Priestman. This success was achieved despite the fact that the nett price to them as a dealer was the same as the nett price to the UK customer, on top of which they had to add a decent margin to cover sales promotional and after-sales service costs, which, as customers became more internationally orientated, became a major problem. His younger brother, Frans, joined the company in 1966 and David Steel advised me to make early contact with the Zeevenhooven brothers, and it was probably only a month or two after I took on the job that I went over to Holland and was introduced, not only to them, but to the relaxation of cruising on the canals in a Dutch river barge. We established an immediate rapport, which has developed into a lifelong friendship.

I felt that Priestman were not sufficiently appreciative of what Zeevenhooven had done for them over the years in the Dutch market. There were Priestman Lions (Leeuw), and numbers of earlier mechanical machines, on every water-side, and Mustang 120 hydraulic excavators were also well introduced into a country where competition from Germany was very fierce. When I told Kees and Frans that it was my intention to tackle the German market, they welcomed this idea warmly, saying that the lack of Priestman presence there was a con-stant disadvantage in their efforts to sell in Holland. One of the reasons why they were "taken for granted" in Hull, and their regular and substantial orders regarded as a production inconvenience, was the fact that, by 1970, they gener-ally only ordered Lion engine-less superstructures, and the final assembly of every machine was completed in their own workshops with a Dutch diesel engine and a fully tractor type crawler. This adaptation to local market condi-tions was the secret of their continuing success.

Many would have said that to try and sell British hydraulic excavators in the highly competitive German market, where there were at least half a dozen indigenous manufacturers, all much larger and more powerful than Priestman, was mad. But it was a very large market, and Priestman had started to develop new models with a high pressure variable displacement hydraulic system, akin to that developed by the Germans. The first of these, the Mustang 320, was, frankly, a joke. It was very ponderous, weighing over 30 tonnes, had a massive superstructure much more akin to a mechanical excavator, and used hydraulic equipment from a little known UK supplier. I think that they only built four, and I certainly was outspoken in my criticism. The next development, the Mustang 220, a 25 tonner, was much more interesting. This was a machine which could compete in Germany, but it hardly constituted a range of machines! But Caterpillar, at that time developing their plans to get into the excavator business, paid Priestman the compliment of adopting many of the features designed into the Mustang 220 in their prototype, the CAT 225, which was in the same weight and capacity class.

My first approach was to Heinz Heyer, of Coles Krane. He refused, point blank, to have any involvement whatsoever in selling Priestman excavators in Germany. He was right, of course, and no pressure from higher level in the Steel Group could make him change his mind. So I persuaded David Steel that the only way in was to appoint a German Sales Manager, with the mission of setting up a network of regional dealers.

I selected one of the best salesmen from Hymac Baumaschinen. He did not succeed in the task to which he had been appointed in a strict sense, and he was rather expensive, but he found us a rather unlikely dealer for the whole of Germany, Aporta Baumaschinen, from Wallau, a small village near to Wiesbaden. Arnold Aporta, as his name suggested, was of Corsican origin, and he claimed that his great-great-grandfather had fought with Napoleon's army in Russia, and had stopped off in the Rhineland on his way back from Moscow, and settled there. He was certainly not a typical German, small of stature, very flamboyant, and speaking with a very strong local "Hunsrueck" dialect, of which I was much reminded when I saw the Epic German film "Heimat" years later. I had great difficulty in understanding him, but we got along very well together. He needed Priestman, as a manufacturer, to gain respectability in the market, because he had built up a very successful business with used Caterpillars. He had been the Used Equipment Manager for the powerful Caterpillar Dealer, Zeppelin Metalwerke, and had set up on his own as a competitor.

One of his publicity stunts was to produce small plastic Zeppelins with "Aporta" written on them. He produced the only scale model ever of a Priestman hydraulic excavator. He spent money like water, and because he represented Priestman, he was allowed to participate in the Hannover Fair and the BAUMA, which otherwise would not have been possible, since entry to this world-famous Construction Equipment Exhibition was barred to dealers in used equipment. He built a huge multi-storey office and workshops outside a small village called Wallau, not far from Wiesbaden, near to an autobahnkreuz, so that it could be clearly seen from two autobahns. He employed administrators, service engineers and salesmen, each of whom was equipped with a car-phone in his Mercedes, not so usual in the early 1970s. My first experience of using a car phone, was when Aporta, piloting me round the night-clubs of Munich during the BAUMA of 1973, insisted on demonstrating his new toy by ringing my wife from his car at about midnight, causing me the most acute personal embarassment.

The Mustang 220 had its teething troubles, as the Zevenhoovens learned to their cost, but their sojourn in Germany was sufficiently short-lived that it did not really affect their minute effect on the market. Probably many of the customers were old mates of Aporta - I recall one who boasted about being stopped by the police on the autobahn for driving at 260 kph. "Bin ich zu schnell gefahren?" he asked. "Nein, zu tief geflogen". *(Was I driving too fast? - No, flying too low).*

But the highlight of the Aporta period was the German-speaking Sales Conference which I organized at his premises, to which came the Dutch and the Swiss dealers, the latter, Ulrich Rohrer Marti, being also a very long-served Priestman distributor, who were curious at the rapid success of this newcomer. It was only for two days, with a dinner at the end in a local restaurant perched on a hillside above the Rhine. The bus was due to take us back to the hotel at midnight, but we were all so drunk that it was at least half an hour later before we were all on board, and the driver was very upset.

He was known to be an awkward fellow, and matters came to a head when, amidst riotous singing on the way back, I was doing acrobatics in the aisle using the hanging straps to put my inebriated body through a complete circle, when the driver pulled the coach into the side of the autobahn, jumped out of his seat, opened the door and shouted: "Aussteigen! Aussteigen!" *(Get out!).* The effect was electric. Frans Zeevenhooven, without thinking, leapt to his feet, gave a Nazi salute and said in a very loud voice: "Jawohl! Heil Hitler!", to the great embarassment of our German colleagues, who persuaded the driver to get back in and continue to drive the coach, and I promised to behave in a more gentlemanly manner. However, the driver simply took us to another village where his boss lived, and stopping the coach outside his house, began knocking on the door loudly at about two o'clock in the morning.

Eventually a light went on in an upper window, and a voice enquired as to what was the problem. In the meantime, we were all sitting waiting on the coach, so I decided that a couple of toots on the horn to remind the driver that he was paid to drive the coach would not come amiss, and I got up from my seat and made for the driver's seat to do this. But he clearly misunderstood my intentions, and thought that I was trying to drive the bus myself, so he leapt back into the vehicle and grabbed my coat lapels.

I would have left it at that and sat down again, but suddenly at my side appeared old Peter Purves, ex-bodyguard to Churchill, with the light of battle in his eyes, and without a word he delivered a powerful punch to the unfortunate driver's chin and knocked him head over heels clean out of the bus. There is no doubt that Peter would have been a very good companion to have in a tight spot! The boss then drove us back to the hotel himself, but the whole incident gave us considerable kudos, since it was not the first time that the driver had proved to be difficult, and left his passengers stranded just because they were slightly late. Peter was often asked on subsequent visits: "Ah, Herr Purves, haben Sie einigen busfahrer noch geklopft?" (*Have you knocked any bus drivers out again?*)

There is no doubt that Aporta had a good team under him, with enthusiastic and experienced personnel, but unfortunately the whole edifice was constructed like a House of Cards, on the backs of a local bank, the Bornheimer Volksbank, who financed the Aporta enterprise. ECGD insisted that for every machine purchased by Aporta on credit, secured by Bills of Exchange, payment should be guaranteed by this bank, and when the crash came in 1972, we, as a company did not suffer.

The Bornheimer Volksbank crashed with Aporta, and Deutsche Bank had to stand surety for the creditors. Thus my efforts to establish a Priestman dealership in Germany came to a very sticky end, but we sold machines and had a lot of fun.

After I had been in the job for about a year, David Steel invited me out to dinner and said that we had to make some radical changes, because I had too uphill a struggle and the only economic solution was to merge the Priestman Export Dept with Coles. I would be given a senior position, that of Regional Manager for the Middle East and Africa. I was totally shocked and refused point-blank. David had clearly not expected such a reaction, and I told him the reasons:

Priestman

"First of all, you will kill Priestman Export, and secondly, I will never accept to work under Stephen Grey."

He was my old rival and had been elevated to the position of General Export Manager under David, when they had acquired Priestman, and so we were equal, at least in name. I also knew that Coles Export Salesmen, good though they were, did not have the "fight of the underdog" problem that we struggled with, and it used to irritate me to have some of my Coles colleagues drop in to my office announcing that they had "just done another million pounds worth of sales", when I had fought like hell to sell a couple of machines. So I proposed to David that we reduce the department to handle Europe directly, and rely on Coles for the overseas markets, and he agreed, and young Stuart Anderson crossed over to Coles and began his rise to greater things.

But the storm clouds were gathering for the Steel Group. James Steel had retired from the position of Chairman and handed over to Alf Howe, a brilliant accountant, but with a somewhat withdrawn personality, who did not, in my estimation, command the same respect that James Steel did. Sunderland was over-manned and union-dominated, and Coles could not compete on price in their own home market with Grove, who had stolen an early march on them in the hydraulic tele-boom market through their Oxford plant, formerly John Allen. Ron Cooke, in his new capacity of Marketing Manager, went to Pennsylvania and told me that he found that Grove were producing 1500 cranes per year with 800 employees and Coles only 1000 with 3000 employees, although it has to be said, in fairness, that Coles produced a greater number of components themselves than did Grove. In addition to the former Neal Works at Grantham, and Glazebury, formerly Taylor Jumbo, they had opened a new place at Darlington in 1969 to build heavy cranes. Slater Walker made a bid for the Steel Group and, frightened by this well-known predator and asset stripper, they looked around for someone else in the business with whom they could merge, and they made an approach to Bill de Vigier of Acrow. This was the beginning of a new chapter for both Coles and Priestman.

Stuart Anderson at the controls of the Mustang 90 at the age of 21.

The Zeevenhooven brothers from Holland, with Kees on the left, and Frans on the right, with Edelhart de Lille from Belgium (see Chapter five) with his wife in the centre. They operated in very different ways, from one another, but, in very diverse ways, their contribution to Priestman prosperity was considerable

March 1973, Priestman at BAUMA
with Aporta Baumaschinen.
Arnold Aporta is in the centre

CHAPTER THREE - THE ACROW TAKE-OVER

The history of Acrow did not bear much similarity to that of Steels / Coles and Priestman, who stretched back into the 19th century. Acrow had been created in 1936 by a young Swiss entrepreneur, named William de Vigier, who decided that there was more to be gained in the UK than in his native country, and who built up his business by first developing the famous Acrow adjustable prop, which revolutionised scaffolding methods at the time, and then continued to expand into all varieties of formwork for use on construction sites. The name "Acrow" was derived from the name of the solicitor, Arthur Crow, who formed the original company, so that it would be top of the alphabetical list in any directory of industrial firms. "Grow with Acrow" was the catch-word.

By 1972 Acrow was a public company with a turnover of £16 million in the UK, yielding a £1 million annual profit, having absorbed a number of other companies manufacturing products as diverse as racking and storage systems, water purifiers for use in the desert, grain dryers, pressure boilers and containers, not to mention emergency, quick-assembly bridging, which came from the acquisition of Thomas Storey, manufacturers of the Bailey Bridge, made famous by its use in the Second World War. Overseas companies had been established, some manufacturing and some simply selling, in the USA, Canada, Spain, Peru, Argentina, Rhodesia, South Africa, India, Hong Kong, New Zealand and Australia. In most of these overseas organizations, Acrow PLC had only a minority shareholding, with Joint Venture Capital shared by local partners, a strong financial interest remaining in the hands of William de Vigier himself. They had also ventured into the overhead crane business, designing their own small overhead crane and hoist in 1958, and nearly succeeding in a bid for George W.King, the overhead crane manufacturer, in 1967. But nearly all of the products which were in their portfolio did not involve after-sales service, and the merger with the Steel Group was certainly the largest and most ambitious acquisition which they had ever undertaken.

Bill de Vigier was the undisputed master of Acrow. Although it was a public company, the only shares available to members of the public were non-voting "A" shares. The Group was controlled by de Vigier and his family, who held the vast majority of the voting shares. Throughout the Acrow Empire, his word was law.

He himself was a superb salesman, with a business eye for the big chance, even

ACROW
The success story of achievement through team spirit

1936　　1975

		1936	1975	
3 employees		10,000 employees		
	Owned by the group			
	Factories	sq ft 3.228,000	sq m 296,000	
	Offices	370,000	34,000	
	Total owned	**3,598,000**	**330,000**	
	Rented by the group			
Works (rented) sq ft **3,250**	Factories	371,000	34,000	
Offices (rented) sq ft **150**	Offices	134,000	12,000	
	Total rented	**505,000**	**46,000**	
	Total sites world-wide	**544 acres**	**220 hectares**	
Issued capital	£150	Issued capital		**£7,482,544**

Group headquarters, Paddington, London

The ACROW headquarters at South Wharf, Paddington, London

The ACROW Chairman, William de Vigier

if it meant taking large risks.   Up to the time when he was approached by the Steel Group, he had never failed to expand and improve upon the performances of the companies which he acquired.   When he took over Thomas Storey in 1960, it was losing money.   Under Acrow it flourished and became one of the most profitable companies in the Group.   Like most dynamic entrepreneurs, he was surrounded by quite a number of yes-men, but he liked people who stood up to him.   One of the many stories related about him concerned a luncheon which followed an Acrow Board Meeting.   He had a fleet of Cadillacs, all with registration plates numbered DV1, DV2 etc   Two of these had been put at the disposal of the directors to convey them from the offices to the restaurant. None of the assembled directors wanted to get too close to the Chairman, and so they all crowded into one of the two limousines, seeing which, de Vigier asked: "Gentlemen, is nobody willing to travel wiz me?   Vot is wrong wiz me - do I stink or somezing?"   Even after many years in the UK, he never lost his Swiss accent.

Bill de Vigier admitted to me recently that with hindsight, perhaps he had made a mistake in taking over the Steel Group, but at the time he was extremely flattered, and he bought it for £24 million without even visiting one of it manufacturing plants - the deal was done from his Swiss home.   Construction News reported at the time that the Acrow Financial Director, an old Scot named Ron Gourdie, commented that the first reaction to the Steel Group approach was: "Steels?   What do they make?"   However, it must be said that de Vigier had been looking round for further acquisitions.   In 1969, he had battled with Glynwed for the purchase of Allied Ironfounders, makers of cast-iron baths and similar products.   Glynwed had out-bidden him, and they were also after the Steel Group.   He was determined not to be beaten a second time, and it was not, in fact, the first time that Acrow had been involved in the mobile crane business. In the 1960s he had obtained the Liebherr franchise for the UK, through having set up a country-wide network of depots for Acrow, but after three years, in which he had invested £750,000, Hans Liebherr himself came to see him, and announced that he was setting up his own subsidiary in the UK and gave Acrow three months' notice.   Mr. de Vigier told me that this was a big lesson to him.

There are some old Sunderland employees of Steels who hold the firm opinion that the Acrow merger was a disaster for Coles Cranes and that the enthusiasm for the product and the company which was so prevalent when I joined them in 1957, died.

The merger was rapidly followed early in 1973 by a major strike at Crown Works in Sunderland, which lasted for 13 weeks and set up a lot of bitterness towards the new owners, but de Vigier was not too concerned, as the Acrow Group profits soared to nearly £3 million. Acrow also brought into Sunderland what were described to me as "Hatchet men" from British Leyland, particularly on the personnel side, who were not popular.

Bill de Vigier himself admitted to me that he had not realised how strong the Unions were in the North-East, and he felt that he personally did his best to meet the shop floor workers by lunching in the Men's Canteen and talking personally to the Union Conveners. There were no less than 11 different unions, with particular animosity existing between the Amalglamated Engineering Union and the Boilermakers, each of whom had 1000 members.

Mr. de Vigier knew Martin Benchoff, the President of Grove Cranes in Pennsylvania, personally, and, shortly after the Takeover of the Steel Group, he went over there and visited the Grove Works. He told me that he was particularly impressed by the automatic welding methods he saw, in contrast to the hand welding still being used in Sunderland and he tried to introduce this, but there was strong resistance on the part of the workers for fear of redundancies.

In fact he went on to invest a lot of money in Coles, certainly far more than he put into Priestman. Coles always retained a certain independence within the Acrow Group. They, as still one of the leading crane manufacturers in the world, had a prestigious name which added much to the standing of Acrow in the Construction Equipment business. Following the merger, several of the Steel Group directors resigned. Alf Howe, as Chairman, departed, and James Steel was offered a seat on the Acrow Board. Reg Keates was never going to accept a new boss like Bill de Vigier, and my own view is that his departure was no loss, but the very sad consequence was that he took the Coles Managing Director, Don Hassall with him, and his deputy, Bill Mowbray, another key man at Sunderland Works, as well. Hassall knew how to talk to, and was highly respected by, the Unions, and the loss of his long experience in production engineering and methods must have been a sad blow to Crown Works.

Hassall and Keates set up a crane manufacturing company to rival Coles. It was called Crown Cranes, and later changed its name to Cosmos. It was financed by the big crane hire company, Richards and Wallington, Reg Keates having a very strong personal connection with Roy Richards, and, of course, there was a ready-made customer for the new enterprise as well. R & W were also involved in a Joint Venture to establish production of the Rothe Erde slewing rings at

Peterlee, not far from Sunderland, and Bill Mowbray left Coles to manage that, which turned out to be a very successful enterprise. Cosmos was purely an assembly operation, concentrating on the production of a 25/30 Ton Truck Crane for the hire business, employing about 100 persons, including some top Design Staff from Coles.

Warwick Taylor, who, following a distinguished career as an RNAS Observer in the war, spent his formative years in the crane business with Jones, joined Coles in 1963 to take over the military sales function, also jumped on the Cosmos Cranes bandwagon. He felt that they should also have developed a 15 tonner, which would have appealed to the military as well. However that may be, the enterprise only lasted about 5 years, from 1975 to 1980, and Warwick Taylor returned to Coles, and it was the swan-song for Messrs Hassall and Keates in the crane business. With hindsight, the whole venture was crazy, and, had Don Hassall stayed with Coles under Acrow, Sunderland would have retained a very experienced and key man at the helm, who certainly would have stood up to Bill de Vigier.

For Priestman, the Acrow merger brought happier times, but with mixed blessings. Norman Brocklebank was delighted by the Acrow Takeover, since he was fed up with kow-towing to the Steel Group Board, although I suspect, never having been privy to any of the meetings between them, that he was not as crushed as he made out - he was too wily for that. He wanted a complete separation of Priestman from Coles, with their own independent Sales and Marketing Organization once more. In this he was absolutely right, and, despite the fact that I was a "Steel Group" man, old Brock recommended that I should be promoted to the position of Priestman's Export Sales Director. David Steel advised me that de Vigier would summon me to his presence, and that this was in the wind. It was "one in the eye" for my old rival, Stephen Grey, who had to wait a little while before a similar position was offered to him in Coles!

However, I was more ambitious, because at the same time it was announced that a new position of Sales and Marketing Director for Priestman, based in Hull, would shortly be filled. The Priestman UK Sales Force was demoralized and leaderless, and I knew that it was useless to try and increase exports unless there were a solid home sales base. So my reaction to being offered a directorship was to tell my new Chairman that I was also interested in the top job, and the reasons why. He eventually agreed that I should take over responsibility for Home Sales as well until such time as the new Supremo be appointed, and that I was free to apply for that position. But everything depended on old Brock, who, despite the fact that I had up-staged him temporarily by obtaining the Chairman's agreement to UK Sales as well, was determined that this young upstart would not be allowed to get too big for his boots, and impinge on an area which he really wanted to control himself.   So he agreed to the temporary arrangement, and, upon my request as to how I should be styled, he craftily suggested: "Director and General Sales Manager", which I naively thought must lead to the top job.

The next six months were challenging and exciting.   I found that the Priestman Home Sales Force were a loyal and dedicated bunch, but demoralized and frustrated. I brought in an experienced man from Hymac, whom I had got to know as one of their best salesmen, to take over Southern Area, Rodney Akester.   I think that there was probably a bit of resentment amongst the old guard at this appointment, but he brought in experience from Hymac which was badly needed to boost the sales of Mustangs.

He had particularly good contacts in Plant Hire, where Priestman had made little impact, the Mustangs being sold mainly to River Boards and Contractors. Coles had been selling Lion cranes, which had temporarily lost their identity in being renamed "MC" (mechanical crawler) followed by a model number showing the capacity, which was sad, and now the Priestman boys could once more sell the whole range, which was another morale booster for them.   I organized a system so that we could accept trade-in machines, something which Priestman had always shied away from, having, of course to inflate the list prices to allow for unrealistic trade-in values, which was a simple con trick, but it worked.   Later Priestman engaged their own specialist for this purpose, another ex-Hymac man called John Wishart, an engaging character who certainly knew about selling Used Equipment.   On one occasion he was trying to sell a used Mustang 90, about which he assured the potential customer (an existing user) that it had "been through the Works", which meant, in a literal sense that someone had driven the machine in through one door and out through another.   He wasn't lying!   Shortly before the arrival of the buyer, it was found that the outriggers were not functioning, so he asked Service to put them right, but was informed that there was not time, and that all that they could do was to take them off.   This was duly done, and John applied a coat of orange paint to the ends of the machine to disguise the fact. The demonstration of the excavator went successfully and the customer decided to purchase it, but, at the last moment, he recalled that his other machine had been fitted with outriggers. "No problem" said artful John, "I happen to have some in stock.   They will cost you extra, of course". But the customer was not such a fool as all that and detected the wet paint, so that he got his outriggers fitted and working within the agreed price.

I did not need to know much about the Home Market, as there was plenty of knowledge in Priestman Home Sales, and all that they needed was motivation and support. That apart, my chief aide-de-camp in the office was old Ron Draper, with years of valuable experience. He occupied the outer office, and anyone wanting to see me had to negotiate their way past this doughty old soldier. For me, he proved to be a tower of strength. In October 1972, we organized a Works Visit in Hull and flew customers in from all over the UK, and, as always on these occasions, the Works staff put on an excellent show. But the honeymoon was not to last. At the beginning of 1973, I was very pointedly pushed back into the Export field, to allow for the appointment of a new Home Sales Director in Hull, Brian Wildsmith, a "down to earth" Yorkshireman whom Norman Brocklebank thought was the right man for the job. Brian may have been a good salesman himself in Yorkshire, but, in mine and most others' views, the UK Sales Director's position was completely beyond him. Later, after he had departed, old Brock admitted to me that he had made a bad mistake. Wildsmith and I just did not get on, especially when he did things like selling machines to UK contractors at rock bottom prices for work in overseas markets without telling me, expecting local service back-up for nothing. Tony Bodimeade, a long-served Acrow man, who had been brought on to the Priestman Board by de Vigier as Director of Purchasing, but who, in some respects, acted as deputy to Norman Brocklebank, had to intervene sometimes between us, as he put it, "like Dr. Kissinger".

With hindsight, my failure to get the top sales and marketing position in Hull, which would have meant moving up there, was a blessing in disguise. All my talents and interest were in export, and old Brock gave me a totally free hand, apart from keeping a tight rein on pricing, of course. The man who suffered most by the decision was my friend Rodney Akester, who had joined on the clear understanding that he would be working for me, and he, every inch a Southerner, clashed seriously with the new Home Sales Director, whom he nicknamed "Cockalorum". After a year or so, Rodney crossed the floor and joined my export team.

When I was shunted back to Export, I insisted on being allowed to hold a Priestman Dealer Conference, to which Bill de Vigier immediately agreed. As I was later to find out, Dealer Conventions were one of his pet hobby-horses, but this first conference was very much my own show. We had about 30 delegates from Europe, Latin America, South-East Asia and New Zealand, and we chartered a special rail coach from Kings Cross to Hull, serving dinner and drinks on board, so that it was a very convivial party who arrived in Hull and poured themselves off the platform into the Royal Station Hotel, a rather old-fashioned but very comfortable establishment where I have spent many nights and eaten excellent dinners. When the delegates returned to London, Mr. de Vigier insisted that we all went to the Opera and we were obliged to sit through four hours of a very heavy performance of Simon Boccanegra. One long-served Priestman executive said that he had taken his very first girlfriend to this opera, after which she had promptly ditched him, and, after we had all seen it, I could well understand why.

At that first conference I asked the question about what new products should we develop and the unanimous answer from the delegates was that we should build bigger crawler cranes. There is no doubt but that they were right, but we never got beyond one or two prototypes, and the reason was that this development was stymied by the decision to enter the offshore crane market. In my opinion, this was totally wrong, although some of my colleagues in Hull have pointed out that it was influenced by the fact that we, on the sales side, were not selling the other products in sufficient quantities, and so it was justified, but I cannot agree with this viewpoint. I was certainly never involved in this decision, nor was my opposite number, Brian Wildsmith, and I believe that it was imposed upon us by the Acrow Group Chairman, Bill de Vigier, to take advantage of the North Sea Oil Bonanza, with pressure from the Government for a UK manufacturer to design and build a special crane for work on oil rigs, and some attractive funding from the Department for Trade and Industry. Coles were first asked to develop it, but they refused, and so it came to Priestman. There is, however, no doubt but that the result was probably one of the finest engineering achievements of the company, the Sealion. The first unit was built in 1976, with a capacity of 60 Tonnes at 9 metres operating radius, and supplied to Conoco. The crane's special feature was that it had no projecting counterweight like a conventional crane, so that it could take up much less space on the oil rig, and the lack of counter-balance was only made possible by the strength of the Taperex slew ring. Altogether 19 units were built, with capacities up to 100 tonnes, but almost every crane was different, and the profit margins built in to initial pricing were whittled away by the endless modifications demanded by the customers. The crane was also particularly designed to withstand the tough operating conditions in the North Sea, so that sales were confined to that area - it was too expensive to be sold in the Middle East. It was therefore limited in market appeal, and the effort put into Sealion certainly should have been channelled into larger crawler cranes, with a much higher sales potential. As can be seen from the display board behind the delegates at that 1973 Conference, Priestman already had five different product lines, and now there was sixth. Instead of reducing the diversity of what we produced, we were proliferating it.

Warwick Taylor, seasoned technical sales expert, who started life with Jones cranes, then to Coles, Cosmos, and finally back to Coles, at the age of nearly 80 in 1999.

Priestman International Conference 1973, in the Conference Room, at the Hull works.

The Priestman Sealion 60 working on the Conoco platform in the southern North Sea

Sealion 100D working in Abu Dhabi from a maintenance ship, handling pipework

CHAPTER FOUR - PRIESTMAN UNDER ACROW
LLOYD THE GLOBE-TROTTER

The Acrow Group Headquarters was situated in old-fashioned premises, adjoining and owned by St. Mary's Hospital, Paddington, at South Wharf, overlooking the Grand Union Canal.   Here the Chairman held court, and this was the Sales HQ of all companies in the Group, except, of course, for Coles.   But the knell soon sounded for the "London HQ" of the Steel Group in Eastcote, the first sign of which was the movement of my small operation to South Wharf.   I knew that this was "in the wind", and old Brock told me, in response to my enquiry, that he thought that the decision had probably already been made, but he had no official information.   I secured his promise that, should it be so, I would be granted a meeting with de Vigier himself, because I was determined to do all in my power to resist it.   We now had an excellent working rapport with Coles Export, I had good local staff, and it was very convenient for me personally at Eastcote.   I was not even in the office when the Movement Order came in the open mail and the secretaries threatened to resign, so I simply informed old Brock that I was suspending all further overseas travel until I had the opportunity to discuss the matter with the Chairman.   My appointment with de V came swiftly, and he was very charming, but it was clear that there was no moving him on the decision, one of his main reasons advanced by him being that he wanted me in closer proximity to himself. This certainly added colour to my daily life.

So, having been forced to accede on the main question, I then proceeded to stipulate a number of other conditions, to which I received his immediate assent.   The first was more space, the second was better furnishings, the third was to pay all rail fares for staff to compensate for greater travel costs (which caused some problems with the Inland Revenue later on), and the final and most important, was to maintain our own Imprest Account.   I did not fancy having to go cap in hand to the Acrow Gnomes to have every expense claim paid, as I knew that everyone else at South Wharf had to do.   When the cheque came from Hull to open the account, I had to quote the Chairman's authority to winkle the Letter of Authority to the bank away from the Gnomes.

My independent stance did not go down very well with some of the Yes-men at Head Office, and our relationship was always a rather uneasy one.   Within months of our removal, Steel House was closed down and Coles were moved to the Acrow Depot at Harefield.   I personally settled in very well at South Wharf and enjoyed the buzz of a central London office location.

Priestman Export Sales Team in 1975.
Rodney Akester, Ray Miller, Dick Lloyd, Peter Purves, John Davies, Richard Aldersley, Trevor Midgley.

Priestman

Despite being based in London, close liaison with Hull was essential, mainly through Ray Dalton, who had been Stuart Anderson's first boss. He was the liaison man with the Works and he was always most helpful and realistic about such important matters as deliveries, always adding a few weeks to the promises which he received from production. Another stalwart was the Publicity Manager, Bill Bromwich, who had been released from his incarceration in Sunderland during the Steel Group era, when all publicity was centralised. Acrow had their own Press and Publicity Dept at South Wharf, who printed the Acrow Review on a regular basis, but they left us alone to produce our own leaflets and Bill, a true artist, turned out excellent full colour sales brochures, as he had done for years before. I also had a great respect for the Design Team, originally headed up by Bert Richardson, who was poached by Hymac not long after I joined Priestman. I desperately tried to stop him leaving - he had been there for 30 years - but he had a very highly qualified team beneath him and he certainly must have contributed to the increased reliability of the Hymac.

The Service and Demonstration Teams also provided tremendous support to our export efforts. Service was headed by Norman Taylor, another very long-served Priestman man, who had travelled the world for the company, and his product knowledge knew no depths. We did a number of trips together, and, apart from my deep respect for his technical abilities, we became firm friends. During the Steel Group period, he had been obliged to operate from Sunderland and accept the overlordship of a Coles Service Manager, but this individual was as long in the tooth and as wise Norman himself and they got on well, but, back in Hull, he deservedly got the top job. He was another who had had to get used to long absences from home in the earlier days of his time with the Company when he was Chief Overseas Service Engineer. European visits had an average duration of six to eight weeks, and overseas trips three months, which was certainly far more arduous than what I had to put up with, but Norman's longest stint was for no less than nine months in Canada (followed by another of three months) when Priestman were setting up their subsidiary company there in 1958/9. Admittedly the carrot dangled in front of him was that the initial assignment could lead to his appointment as Service Manager for the Canadian subsidiary, and take his wife and family over there, but Priestman Canada was not destined to last more than a few years, and when Norman returned home after that mammoth trip and was met by his wife, Pat, and two sons at the airport, the youngest boy just burst into tears and asked his Mum who this strange man was!

Norman recounted to me recently how, immediately after his first arrival in Toronto in February 1958, following a 14 hour flight in a Super Constellation, he was despatched 150 miles north to attend to a problem with the hoist drum of a Cub.

The customer greeted him with sarcastic comments about the quality of "Limey Equipment", but Norman worked through the night to solve the problem, and the user was so pleased that he subsequently purchased a couple of Tigers. However this piece of customer satisfaction was not brought about without some personal cost to Norman himself. Used to driving about in a Commer van in the UK, loaded down with tools and equipment, he found himself at the wheel of a hired 400 BHP Pontiac Chieftain Ranch Waggon, on a deserted highway, but which had a speed limit of 60 mph. Norman could not resist the urge to power this vehicle along at its maximum speed and was soon hitting 90 to 100 mph, until he was suddenly brought down to earth by the wail of police sirens behind him, a sound which he had only hitherto heard on the TV at home. He was pulled over and stopped and asked, in descriptive language, whether he was blind and had not observed the 60 mph limit signs. When he produced his UK Driving Licence, he was asked what sort of a Mickey Mouse Document did he think it was, made to lock up his vehicle, was carted off to the police station some three miles away, fined $35 on the spot plus three penalty points and told that he would have to take a driving test! You would have thought that the least that Priestmans could do would be to pay the fine (a lot of money for him at the time), but they refused. However he had an understanding immediate boss, who saw to it that he was not out of pocket. He never seemed to have luck with speeding fines, being, as I recall, stopped twice in one day during the 1982 Miners Strike for exceeding the 40 mph limit on the Hedon Road which runs past the Works. When asked for his name the second time, he was so cross that he replied: "Arthur Scargill to you", which was not a very diplomatic remark at that period to make to any police officer involved in that scenario!

Despite the tremendous Company Loyalty which existed throughout Priestman, as with nearly every other British manufacturer of that era, problems with Unions existed. Hull was in the same "Shipyard Worker" catchment area as Sunderland, where the memories of the depression in the 1930s were still not forgotten. There were no less than seven different Shop Floor Unions and two Office Worker Unions. But Priestman generally had a good record in industrial relations, with only a few one - day stoppages up to the mid 1950s, and thereafter no more than three longer strikes, but even so for no more than a week each.   Charlie Hamshaw told me that one local Union official's opinion were that Priestman were the most forward looking company in the area, publicised by the advertisement on the railway bridge about a mile before the Marfleet Works on the Hedon Road: "PRIESTMAN IS A MILE AHEAD".

Open Days were held, when employees invited friends and families to visit the Works, which they were proud to show off.   I do know that Union demarcation cost the Company much more than it should have done every time that a new machine was installed on the customer's site in the UK.   This was the job of a demonstrator, of which there were three, and they belonged to the TGWU.   As such, they were strictly forbidden to make any kind of minor adjustment or repair, which was the prerogative of the Service Engineer, who was a member of the AEUW.   So, if the demonstrator found that there was an hydraulic hose which needed tightening up, then he had to send for a Service Engineer to do this.   One of the best demonstrators was Pete Dean, whose bulk contrasted with the small stature of his colleague, Ted Neylon, so that they were known as "Little and Large".   Pete was also a "Mr. Fix-it", and, when he was travelling with me overseas, he worked all hours, and would do anything to promote the Company's interests.   In the late 70s, we were carrying trials with the M120 of weed-cutting buckets to clear irrigation ditches of bamboo in Iraq, and Peter personally monitored the progress of the machine allocated for this task, and told his mates on the assembly line: "This machine is for my colleague, Dick Lloyd - it has got to be right".   And it was, because Peter had another side to him - he was a Union militant, and, I suppose, was popular thereby on the Shop Floor.   Back in the UK, he would be the first to call out the Service Engineer to tighten up the hydraulic hose, which he was more than capable of doing himself!   But, when we were travelling, Peter, Ted and I were mates - I had the same relationship with them that I had had with Dickie Bird at Hymac.   Most of my co-Directors were less democratic, but I suppose that I also could be a bit dictatorial when not travelling.   I recall being pulled up by one of my colleagues in the office, when I had summoned him to mine for a discussion on some matter, when he said: "Why do we always have to talk in your office - it would be nice if you occasionally came into mine".   I took the point.

Having failed to broaden the base of Priestman sales in Europe, I turned my sights overseas, and concentrated on small markets where the Priestman name

was good and of long-standing.   Trinidad, Guyana and Surinam in the
Carribean were three of these, where the only competition was JCB and
Hymac.   One of our most colourful customers in that region was Motilal
Moonan, an Indian contractor in Trinidad whose motto was "Moonan Moves
Mountains", and on one occasion he invited Norman Taylor and me to a meal
at his house, which was palatial, but decked out in the most jangling vulgar
taste imaginable, and eating the curry involved having to pick rather tough
meat with our fingers off small bones - I do not even recall what sort of meat
it was supposed to be.

In Guyana we dealt mainly with the Government and the Sugar Estates, and
in Surinam I travelled miles through the tropical jungle on mud roads, crossing rivers by ferry - there were no bridges - and then finally travelling by
boat up a crocodile infested river to reach my customer and his Mustang 120.
What I loved about the Carribean was the relaxed, laid back way of doing
business, the sound of the slow local drawl, the steel bands and the rum and
coke beach parties on a Sunday.   It was also perhaps my first in-depth experience of truly multi-racial societies, where black, white, coffee-coloured,
Chinese-featured and people of Indian descent all mixed together, and it did
not matter a damn what anybody's skin colour or facial features were.
Paramaribo is the prettiest capital city, with its wooden houses on stilts, which
I ever saw, and in Georgetown the largest wooden cathedral in the world,
with no glass in the windows, always fascinated me.   One of the main attrac-
tions of Trinidad was the "upside-down" Hilton, where the Reception was at
the top of the building to which one drove up a steep hill, and the rest of the
hotel tumbled down the hillside, so that the 6th floor was at the bottom.

The biggest population of Priestman machines in Latin America was in
Uruguay, where probably Priestman out-numbered all other makes of excavator in the country at that time.   Until I fully retired I still got enquiries for
parts for Priestman Mustangs from the dealer, Maquinas y Materiales
(although they never become orders!).   In Uruguay, machines have to last a
long time, as evidenced by the 50 year old cars still being driven around the
streets in the 1970s.   M y M was owned at that time by a character called
Emilio Zapata, a warm-hearted giant of a man whom it would probably have
been unwise to cross. His secretary, Lucy, completed the employee count, and
old Zapata's knowledge and enthusiasm for Priestman was boundless, and
he was never tired of extolling the merits of "el Tigre" or "el Panther".
Another Latin American character was Don Andres Navas Serrano, who rep-

Priestman

resented us in Colombia. His success for Priestman was considerably less, due to relative market conditions, but his enthusiasm for the company was unequalled, and he hosted the one Latin American Dealer Conference which I held in 1977.   He was a total Anglophile, and in his office hung Shakespeare's famous poem   "This royal throne of kings, this sceptred isle". He was a true caballero in every sense of the word, with an old-fashioned courtly bearing, combined with exquisite manners, but he would not be pushed, and on one occasion, when I was pressing him for a new stock order, I over-stepped the mark and he started lecturing me that Señor Philip Priestman had never, ever tried to push him in that way.   I had to eat humble pie very rapidly, and I did get my order in the end.   Don Andres used to drive his large and rather ancient American sedan very slowly in the middle of the road, quite oblivious to the hootings and impatience of other motorists. His son, Mauricio, who still runs the business after his father's death, preferred a heavily plated Jeep.   The last time that I saw Mauricio was in 1998, when he turned up unexpectedly in London, still representing Parker Plant with success, and it was then that he told me that he never now drives outside Bogota, so dangerous has it become, and has given instructions to his family that, if he be kidnapped, on no account are they to pay any ransom. "It is better to be killed than be ransomed" he said, "because paying a ransom bankrupts the whole family, and then the ransomed person has to live with the resentment of those nearest and dearest to him."

When my star was very much in the ascendant with Bill de Vigier, I boldly sought his permission to allow Audrey to accompany me on a Latin American trip, since the dealers were always asking when I would bring her, and in 1979 she took time off work and my sister and an old friend shared the care of our children.   The trip began in Caracas, with Bogota as the next stop, where we launched a new Mustang, for which Don Andres organized a suitable gathering of potential customers.

Audrey was quite shocked when the old gentleman ignored a human body lying in the road by just driving round it, but I am sure that he made the right decision.

The hospitality which we received was overwhelming, and the trip cost the company less than if I had been on my own, because everywhere we were royally entertained and sometimes even our hotel bill was met.   In Quito we had a fascinating experience which only could have happened because she was accompanying me.   The wife of the local Acrow agent, Patricio Teran, whose main business was selling bridges for Thos. Storey, was an important official in the local Tourist Board and she arranged for us to visit a Carmelite Nunnery dating from the 15th Century, where men were strictly forbidden to enter, and food was passed through a secret hatch whereby the lady nun who received it remained invisible to the person who placed it on a revolving tray especially built in to the wall for the purpose.   I posed as an expert on wood-worm, and so was admitted on this totally false pretext.   Our visit was clear-ly an exceptional event for the nuns, who showed us round with great pride. There were numerous gaudily painted wooden carved figures of no great artistic merit, which they spent their days meticulously cleaning, and which I pretended to examine closely for signs of infestation.   Their numbers were dwindling and most were elderly, since this sequestered life clearly no longer appealed to the younger generation.

Quito is probably the finest architectural example of a truly Spanish colonial city in Latin America.   I never sold a machine there, but always enjoyed my visits.

We also managed to squeeze in what was for me my second visit to Macchu Picchu, so my memories of Latin America, despite my nasty experience of being mugged in Bogota, remain dear.   I did take on three guys in succes-sion to help me out on that territory, but only one proved a success, the other two upsetting dealers by their arrogant attitude.   One was a man whom I was pressurized to employ against my better judgement, and the other was a proud Ecuadorian, who refused to deal with anyone in the office except for me, which did not endear him to his colleagues. In fact, his knowledge of English was not all that good, so I always addressed him in Spanish to ensure that there was no misunderstanding about my instructions.

I always found that taking on experienced sales executives was a risky busi-ness, and where I was most successful was in employing young people and training them, and I ended up with a young Oxford graduate, who had stud-ied Spanish.

I was less personally involved in the African Continent.   My one and only visit to South Africa took place in 1974, which was right in the middle of the Apartheid Era and I must say that I was shocked by what I saw.   On arrival at the Airport in Johannesburg, I stood in the queue to have my passport stamped, just behind a young girl from Swaziland, who was clearly petrified by the towering figure of the Afrikaner Immigration Officer, whose desk was probably purposefully placed on a plinth to increase the degree of intimidation.   On my first day, walking in the street, I nearly inadvertently broke the law by entering a public toilet which, as I only noticed at the last moment, bore the title: "Niet-Blankes".   We had an excellent Grab Dealer there at the time, of Irish extraction, who was very hospitable to me, but, despite being a relatively liberal-minded, he could not agree with my British viewpoint and said that I made him "talk like a Nat", by which I suppose that he meant an Afrikaner Right-Winger.   My mission was to look for a dealer for our excavators and cranes, and I had positive discussions with the South African subsidiary of Compair, the compressor manufacturer, who had a manufacturing subsidiary in Johannesburg.   The English manager showed me around the small works with its own machine shop, and I remember that all black workers had a steel barrier around the machine tool which they were operating, which was a relic from the past when slave workers had literally been chained up whilst they operated their machines.   The manager told me that the Afrikaner Unions were very strong and that this gave him a real problem, in that he was not free always to employ intelligent black South Africans, but had to fulfil his quota of thick Afrikaners.   I do not think that my discussions with Compair had any positive result, and I spent most of my time on Grab business which was flourishing.

Business apart, my trip had one big personal bonus in that I met up again with my first girlfriend, with whom I had fallen madly in love when I was doing my National Service in Port Said.   Suzanne was the daughter of a French Suez Canal Club Executive, and I had met her at a dance at the Maltese Club on New Years Eve in 1953.   Fraternatisation between even European locals and British officers was frowned upon at that time, and our meetings had to be held clandestinely in the Maltese Club in the European Quarter. We were only allowed in to Port Said in pairs, and my fellow officer, Jim Smith, who used to accompany me, would take himself off to the cinema, whilst Suzanne and I held hands - it was a very proper relationship.   Apart from the moral codes of the time, it never had any opportunity of being other. On one occasion, she invited me back to the family flat, and brought a beret so that I could disguise myself as a Frenchman.   We did not leave the Club together, but separately at intervals.   Jim had been appraised of the possibility and a coded message left for him with the bar-man.   I reached the flat safely, but in some trepidation as it was totally against the rules in the Canal Zone at that time, and it was clear that Suzanne's mother was really frightened.   When the doorbell rang, I was bundled into a wardrobe, in case it should be the police, but fortunately it was only Jim. That was the first and last time that I attempted what was probably a very foolhardy visit, and indeed I learned later from the British Security Liaison Officer that I had been watched by the Egyptian police, who knew all about my escapade.

Suzanne had eventually left Port Said, first for Australia, and then she settled in Johannesburg, and had married an Austrian. I rang her number during my 1974 visit with some hesitancy, and a voice answered in a strong Germanic accent. When I explained who I was, he replied: "I zink zat I haf heard of you", and called Suzanne with the announcement of a surprise. He was a delightful man, sadly since deceased, and our re-union was quite memorable, and definitely the highlight of my only visit to South Africa.

I also went back to Egypt in 1976, and was received at Cairo Airport with a warm welcome. "Is this your first visit to Egypt?" Embarassed silence on my part, followed by a hesitant reply: "Well, not exactly. You see, I was in the British Army of Occupation here in the early 1950s". To my intense surprise, and indeed relief, my Egyptian hosts smiled, and asked me whether I would like to re-trace my steps on the banks of the Suez Canal, because they could include this in the itinerary, if I so wished. Most certainly did I so wish and so a trip down Memory Lane, starting at Ismailia, where the old British barracks of Moascar (to which I had been posted prior to my assignment at Port Said) were now occupied by the Egyptian Army, was duly organized. We travelled up the Canal Road, where I had frequently ridden my 350 cc Matchless motor cycle, until the practice of stretching wires across the road by the "terrorists" to de-capitate unsuspecting British Army Despatch Riders caused me to travel in a 15 cwt truck with an armed escort. Finally to Port Said, which was a sad return, because it had, at that time, been badly damaged in the Six Day Arab-Israeli War. Nevertheless, I was able to see where the Old Cold Store had stood and I think that I identified the street where Suzanne and her mother had lived. Part of my job in Port Said, apart from acting as Liaison Officer to the Maltese Garrison Engineer, which brought me into contact with Frenchmen and Italians and kindled my interest in speaking languages, was to supervise the welfare of the sappers who operated the antiquated diesel engines in the Cold Storage Plant, which housed rations for the whole of the Middle East Land Forces. The engines had been converted from steam, and had to be hand-lubricated on a 24 hour basis. Each giant piston had its own oil-bath, which had to be be filled with oil every ten minutes, the "oiler" having to hold the oil-can over the bath with

Suez Canal Company Building, Port Said.

Canal Road

The old cold store, Port Said

Sue

EGYPT: FLASHBACK TO 1954

both hands, at the same time synchronizing his arm movements with the revolutions of the piston.

One night I had decided to discard my Second Lieutenant's uniform and become a sapper grease monkey, and I was able to find out exactly what it was like being a slave to those demanding diesel engines. It was not a premeditated action, to prove to my men that I could do their job as well as they, but it arose out of a small crisis. My job was to see to the welfare of the sappers - my sergeant was very capable of supervising all the technical work. The Cold Stores themselves were operated by the RASC, over whom presided a bullying Sgt. Major, WOII Lord, who was constantly trying to further his zone of influence to include the sappers. Because of the all-night shift work, we did not have parades and I did not believe in Spit and Polish, but the RASC Sgt. Major clearly did. One evening I received a call in the Officers Mess from Sgt. Major Lord, informing me in strident tones that all my men were drunk and dis-orderly and that I had better do something about it. So I donned my uniform, leapt on to my motor-cycle and went down to the Cold Store to investigate. I knew that the men were having a party, to which I had given my full assent, and indeed I had created a kind of "NAAFI" for them in a part of the Cold Store. After consultation with my Sapper Sgt, we decide to beard Warrant Officer Lord in his lair. He had, by this time, retired to his bunk, and it was clear to me that it was he who was drunk, not the sappers. He was quite abusive to me, and I made sure that my Sgt. witnessed it, and it was then that I decided to strip off and spend the night in the Engine Room.

It was a wise decision, because, within the hour, Lord appeared, dressed in his full regalia and flanked by two of his senior NCOs. He demanded to see the Sapper Sgt, but instead he met the Sapper 2nd Lieut, dressed only in a pair of shorts and covered in sweat and oil. I ordered him to leave, and, after the third repetition of my command, he obeyed, but I put in a full report to the Garrison Commander, and he was charged, found guilty of using insulting language to an officer, reduced to his substantive rank of Sgt, and soon afterwards, posted. Farewell to a Big Bully.

It was perhaps not surprising that I wanted to stay on in the Sappers rather than become an Oxford student, and it was probably only due to strong paternal influence that I did not make the mistake of throwing over my University career.

But back to West Africa, I only did one or two trips myself, because I had found just the right guy to back me up. This was not before I had rejected another seemingly very well qualified man for the post of Regional Manager. He was Rhodesian and had worked there with the Caterpillar Dealer, so he appeared to have the right experience, but I threw him a trick question at the interview and he fell into the trap. I asked him how he got on with black Africans, and he answered in his clipped Rhodesian accent that he considered that he had a "very good relationship with the black man". "Well", I continued, "suppose that you are in Nigeria and you have made an appointment to see a very important Nigerian Chief, who heads up a large construction company. Your appointment is at 10 o'clock in the morning and you arrive promptly and you wait. How long do you wait?" His reply was that if he was kept waiting more than an hour, he would, very politely, leave his card asking for another appointment at a more convenient time. That was the end of the interview, from my side, but I couldn't tell him that he might have to wait all day and that time to the African was relative.

The man I chose was very different. He had no experience of selling construction equipment, but he certainly knew Africa. Ed Farmer was an unusual man, not only because he had been married to five different wives in his time, but also because he was an honorary member of a Nigerian tribe, and he had a lot of useful contacts throughout West Africa. He used to tell the story of how, in the utter chaos of the Lagos traffic, a policeman on point duty asked him for his licence. Ed's reply was that he did not have it on him, but it was in his flat, just nearby, and if the policeman cared to follow him, he would be very pleased to show it to him. The officer duly agreed and, arrived at the flat, Ed offered him a beer, which he gratefully accepted and delayed the production of his licence for as long as possible. Finally, after a good half hour, he suggested to the policeman that it might be a good idea if he returned to his point duty, by which time, of course, there was utter chaos at the intersection where he was supposed to be directing the traffic.

This reminds me of another anecdote involving a Nigerian policeman, recounted to me by a British consular official who was posted there. His wife was once stopped by a very tall constable, also engaged in directing traffic, because she failed to understand his signal. He came up to the car and thumped on the roof with the words: "Silly little white lady, what colour am I?", to which she did not dare to reply that he was black, in case it caused offence, so she compromised by saying that he was a very attractive tanned colour. The policeman smiled, and holding his hand up, he replied: "Silly little white lady, when I am like this, I am red", and then, turning slightly round, "and when I am like this, I am green". I think that this is a very good example of Nigerian humour, although I cannot say that I very much enjoyed my stay in Lagos in 1978, with its over-crowded streets, dirt and smell. The hotel which Ed had chosen for me was economy-class, where the air-conditioner's continual buzzing made sleep difficult, and the service in the dining room was painfully slow. A Nigerian at the next table to mine started complaining in a loud voice about this, but, as timid as the "silly little white lady" in the anecdote, I did not dare say a word!

My next port of call on that trip was Côte d'Ivoire, and what a contrast. Clean, tidy, still totally French, it was a relief to be there for a weekend after Lagos. In the hotel a theatre group straight from Paris put on a show, and I could easily imagine myself to be in a part of metropolitan France. Every potential dealer which I visited was headed up by a Frenchman and the one organization who showed real interest told me that the final decision on whether to take our franchise depended on the sanction of the Head Office in Paris. (Current events tell me that now the picture has changed somewhat). Therefore I routed my way home via Paris, but not before spending a few days in Liberia, where the US $ was still the common currency at that time. I did not find the place any more attractive than Lagos.

Arrived in Paris, I was kindly met by someone from Coles France, who had booked me at the splendiferous Georges V Hotel in Montmartre. I woke up in the morning not feeling very well and struggled on to the Metro to keep my appointment with the Head Office of the Ivorian company who had expressed interest in the Priestman franchise.

Whilst I was waiting for the meeting, I felt worse and worse and staggered to the toilet to try to be sick. The result of the meeting was totally negative - they were not the least interested in taking on a small British crane and excavator manufacturer in Abidjan, but by that time I really did not care and I just wanted to get back to the hotel and collapse into bed. At midday I cancelled my return flight to London and summoned a doctor, who immediately asked me to show him my tongue, and then said: " Voilà, c'est jaune", and I looked in the mirror and saw that it had turned bright yellow. He informed me that my problem was due to "les microbes Africaines", prescribed medicine, and forbade me to eat for 24 hours. He wisely re-emphasised this instruction by placing a notice written in a clear bold hand by my bedside:

"Ne Rien Manger pour 24 heures" (*"Eat nothing for 24 hours"*), because, by the evening I was not only feeling a lot better, but hungry and just fancying a potage de legumes - there is nothing to beat a good French vegetable soup. But, as I reached for the telephone to place my order, my glance fell on the notice and I replaced the receiver, and, following the doctor's instructions I starved myself until lunch the next day and then tucked in to an unappetising meal of plain boiled meat and steamed rice, specially prepared for me by the chef de cuisine.   What a way to lunch at the Georges V!

Tony Bodimeade, who had spent time in Liberia asked me whether I had cleaned my teeth with tap water, which I had, and he then assured me that that was the cause of my problem - he said that he always used to clean his in whisky.   I suppose that I had had a mild dose of hepatitis.   Bill de Vigier later advised me to follow his example and only eat bananas whilst travelling in West Africa or India.   He recounted how he had advised his wife not to take ice with her whisky on one occasion, "But, Lloyd," he added, "you know vot vimmen are - zay never listen to advice", and she suffered accordingly.   She was a most charming and delightful lady, who suffered badly in the last years of her life from cancer.

My most successful overseas sales trips were to the Far East.   Priestman's reputation in Malaysia dated back to 1930, when Philip Priestman first flew out there to appoint James Whyte as the dealer.   The journey took him 10 days, and numerous Tigers, Wolves and Panthers were supplied to the rubber estates.   When I first arrived on the scene in 1974, these were being replaced by the Mustang 120, and the local offices were still manned by hollow-legged Scotsmen.   The regular invitations to supper parties which I enjoyed in Kuala Lumpur started with drinks sessions lasting at least two or three hours, so that it was usually about 10 pm before delicious local dishes appeared on the table.   The only time that I ever attended a St. Andrews' Night was in KL, being specially requested to pack my dinner jacket for the occasion.   Another guest was a visiting fireman from Australia, who was obliged to have his made on the spot for the purpose - one could have a suit made to measure within about 24 hours by a local tailor.   He chose to have his in scarlet colours, which fitted his personality, since he was one of the most unpleasant loud-mouthed Pommie-Bashers whom I ever had the misfortune to meet.   My good friend, Sandy Taylor, who was responsible for the Priestman franchise, was quite amazed by my apparent patience in putting up with his constant stream of anti-British jokes, that the next morning he asked me how I had refrained from planting my fist in his face!

Quite different from KL was the J. Whyte office in Singapore, presided over by another Scot, Mac Sutherland, with whom I used to do battle on the squash court (I think that he always beat me), before plunging in to the refreshing pool at the club where we played.   Mac, having lived in the South of England for most of his life, had lost his Scottish brogue, and the wild parties of KL were not repeated in what was a more reserved ambience.   However I liked the extreme cleanliness and order of Lee Kuan Yew's Singapore - when one is travelling alone on business, it is quite a different experience from going as a tourist.   Homesickness definitely creeps in, however seasoned a traveller one has become and to be welcomed into an ex-pat circle, and to meet people again who have become friends through business, was one of the enduring pleasures of my travels in both Malaysia and Singapore.   It was Mac's wife, Fay, who taught me how to fold a suit properly so that it did not crease in the wrong places in the suitcase.

Thailand was another market in which we had some success, this time with Lion Draglines rather than Mustangs, where we managed to win a tender for five machines from Weserhuette, who had dominated the market for some years.   Admittedly Bangkok was a more interesting place from a sight-seeing viewpoint, and I had my fill of Buddhist temples and Thai boxing, where both hands and feet are used in an incredibly acrobatic display.   I was also rash enough to eat raw fish on one occasion, persuaded thereto by my Thai hosts, washed down by some very fiery local spirit. 24 hours later I was extremely ill with severe food poisoning, so I never repeated the experience.

But Indonesia was where I achieved the best results, and it was undoubtedly the most interesting of all the South-East Asian countries from my personal viewpoint, where I was able to gain an insight into local culture.   As in Malaysia, we were represented by an old-fashioned trading company, but this time a Dutch organization called Ruhaak.   Fortunately they decided to sell out to a local firm, and with the name PT New Ruhaak (Indonesia), the business was put into the hands of a Chinaman rejoicing in the name of Bing Tampi.   Mr Bing, as he was known, had a large family of six sons and two very pretty daughters, and many were the visits which I made to his home for a large Chinese dinner, followed by a musical evening when one of the daughters played the piano and we all sang.   I even remember the words of an Indonesian song about a Cockatoo "Bu-rung Kakatua", which became our theme song.   Always of the party was Bert Anthonio, born in Indonesia, but a Dutch citizen who had worked with the old trading company. Bert was the go-between, who liaised with me and did the groundwork sales promotion. In 1974, I made one of my early visits to Indonesia in the midst of a Round the World trip taking me on to Australia and New Zealand and back via Canada. We started negotiations for a large number of hydraulic excavators for the Ministry of Water Resources, which was to be funded by a UK Line of Credit. Two sizes of machine were required, the smaller being centred on the Hymac 580, for which we had, at that time, no equivalent. So we concentrated on the larger unit, and, at the end of my visit to New Zealand, after a month of continuous travel, I received a message to go back to Jakarta for further talks. It is a long way to fly back, but I did it, and then had to get back on track for Vancouver, which gave me my only visit to Japan (a one-night stop!). Brock had an old friend in Vancouver who actually bought a Priestman Mustang, but he never did anything with it and it certainly did not re-establish us in the Canadian market, where Priestman had had a subsidiary company before my time, but it did give me the chance of a conducted tour around what I believe to be the largest Caterpillar Dealership in the world, Finning, which seemed to dwarf the whole of Priestman in size. Arrived there, I had another message to visit Guyana before heading for home, and again I did it and prolonged my whole trip by two more weeks. I was completely jet-lagged by the time I reached London, living on sleeping tablets, but this was one of the penalties of attempting to sell world-wide from such a small base.

The Tender for the 31 excavators closed at the end of March, 1975, and I was in Jakarta putting in our final bid. Bing and Bert's contacts in the Ministry were exceptionally good and we soon had accurate information on the competition, which was, in our case, from JCB. Our price level was too high, so I put a call in to Hull to speak to Brock. I waited five hours in my hotel room for the call to come through and when it did , it was about 1.15 pm UK time. "Oh, I am very sorry, Mr. Lloyd", said the Priestman switchboard operator, "but Mr. Brocklebank's just gone to lunch. Could you ring back in an hour?" "Put me through to the Directors' Dining-Room", I screamed down the phone, "It's taken me hours to get through". Old Brock gave me his rock-bottom price, no doubt taking his slide-rule out of his pocket to do so, but it was not enough. Our bid went in, and Bing got hold of the prices. We were higher than JCB.

And that would have been that, had it not been for Alan Cooper. Alan had been a Senior Executive at JCB for many years involved in manufacturing, but following a personal disagreement with Joe Bamford himself, he had left a couple of years earlier, and had tried, not very successfully, to run his own business   There are many mentions of him in the JCB 50 Year Book published in 1995 - he really had been one of the original close team around the Great Man.   Bill de Vigier brought him in to Priestman as Deputy Managing Director.   I am not sure that old Brock was too pleased about this at the time, but it was certainly the right decision for Priestman and in fact they got along and worked very well together, Alan eventually taking over when Brock semi-retired in 1977 at the age of 67.   In April 1975, just after his initial appoint-ment, Alan came down to London to meet me immediately after my return from Jakarta.   "What do we have to do to get this order away from JCB?" was his first question.   I reached into my briefcase and pulled out a copy of a very confidential internal document from the Ministry of Water Resources, which showed clearly all the prices and technical spec comparisons. Technically the M120 was preferred - a number had been sold previously by Ruhaak and the machine had a good reputation, but on price we would lose out.   Alan went back to Hull and with his JCB experience he revised the pric-ing and convinced Brock that it would still be very profitable for such a large number of machines.   Back I went to Jakarta, not once, not twice, but about six times in so many months.   The revised Priestman bid was finally accept-ed, even though the Tender was officially closed, and on the evening of the day on which we finally signed the contract for 31 Mustang 120s, I got so drunk on Scotch that I was still intoxicated when I boarded the plane for London several hours later. I treated myself to a First Class seat, but it was wasted.   I could not resist having a few glasses of free wine on board, pre-ceded by sherry, and consequently spent most of the flight throwing up in the toilet.....

The noise, dust and heat of Jakarta, crowded with humans and crammed with cars is an unfading memory.   When one got out into the country, it was very different.   I do not think that I have ever seen such fertile land, where one could almost see the tea plants visibly growing, so that the peasants, existing on a wage level of about 10 pence per day, were not starving, but, nonethe-less, the contrast between their life-style and that of the rich was very marked. Bing's house was not in the least ostentatious, but he had a very high level contact with a Government minister, whose name was Sudwikatmono, known to Bert as "Mr. Dwi".   This gentleman's mansion had a tropical fish tank of immense proportions under the floor, which was transparent.

Priestman

We would sit on luxurious low chairs around an equally low long table sipping sweet tea and exchanging polite conversation with Mr. Dwi, who exuded charm and courtesy. Business was never discussed. One just visited, but the visits were without doubt very significant. Bing and I also occasionally visited the home of the man who made the decision, Mr. Moebagio, (apart from official visits to his office), but these visits were rather different. They usually took place late in the evening, and I would stay in the car outside in the road, whilst Bing investigated as to whether or not it would be propitious for me to appear - it usually was.....

Bing had other business than acting as a selling agent for foreign manufacturers - he was a manufacturer in his own right, making motorized "bechas" under licence from an Indian company. The becha is an Indonesian trishaw, and Bing's production facility was housed under a corrugated iron roof, open on all sides, with minimum attention to safety concerns. After JCB, Alan Cooper was wide-eyed with amazement following his conducted tour around the "factory". The cost of labour was certainly very low and overheads reduced to a bare minimum, and bechas came off the "production line" in astounding quantities.

The low cost of labour in Indonesia was brought home to me by another incident. Just around the corner from the hotel where I used to stay was an "English pub" called the George and Dragon, which I used to frequent to have a change from Chinese and Indonesian food, which I love, but not day after day. In fact one could eat far better Indonesian food in Amsterdam than in Jakarta. One evening, as I came out of the hotel, there was a young boy holding a beautiful model three-masted sailing barque, made out of balsa wood, crafted to the last detail with sails, rigging, ropes etc.

He wanted me to buy it for the equivalent of £10. I really did not want it, as I had no means of taking it home, so I offered him £2, just to get rid of him. By the time that I had reached the pub, he had reduced the price to £6, but I still said "£2 maximum" and went in to dinner. I emerged, one and a half hours later, full of steak and chips, and he was still there and accepted my offer. I just had to buy it, and I managed to get it home un-damaged by putting it on the open luggage rack above my seat, which would not have been possible on today's modern aircraft. It sat in my study for many years, but when we finally moved from Uxbridge, it went, dusty and somewhat damaged, to a Charity Shop.

There was one occasion when I was invited to spend a Sunday on the beach with Bing and his family. The sand was a dirty mud colour and the sea was stagnant and lukewarm, and I got stung by a jellyfish whilst swimming. It did sting too and my arm soon came up in a nasty red rash. Bing just laughed and told me to rub sand on the wound, and then, just to demonstrate that there was nothing to be concerned about, he picked up a jellyfish in his bare hands and rubbed it all over his leathery chest!

One of Priestman's most successful markets in the 1970s was New Zealand, where we had been represented by an old-established trading company, Richardson McCabe, since the early part of the century, and in fact I made my first visit there in 1970 with the specific object of thwarting a move by Hymac, who had an assembly operation in the country, to stop imports of the Mustang 120 as being directly competitive with the Hymac 580 which was "manufactured in New Zealand". This I succeeded in doing and we re-named the M120 the M140, to take it out of the 12 ton weight class! McCabe were an old-fashioned organization, but in 1973 they engaged the services of a new Sales Director, who blew a fresh wind through the company. Bob Youngman was a large ex Rugby player, very down to earth, even by Kiwi standards, and he organized demonstrations and open days for customers up and down the country, so that my visits were made very worth while. The customers would be given free rein to drive the machines themselves, so that the whole performance was rather like a Rodeo in a Western movie, and, in fact, he launched one new Mustang model by hiring a well-known New Zealand jockey and painted the machine in his colours. At the end of one riotous party which normally followed these events, I was ticked off by a straight-laced Priestman owner who disapproved of one of my salacious stories. I was really quite taken aback by this and mentioned it to Bob the next morning, to which Bob replied, having been given the name of the particular individual: "Oh, don't worry about him, he's just a bloody Pom...." Bob took me fishing on Lake Taupo, the only time that I ever indulged in the sport in my life, but it was trawling with an imitation fish on the end of a hook, so not very sporting I think, and there was a limit on the size of the trout which one was allowed to keep, probably at least one foot in length. At one point we were approached by another boat, which Bob felt might contain Rangers bent on inspecting our catch, so he threw a completely dead fish back into the water which might have been considered as under-sized, and then, when the danger had passed, it not being a Ranger after all, he turned the boat about and scooped the fish out of the water again. Those trout cooked over an open fire on the shore that evening was one of the most delicious fish dishes I ever tasted, which included, of course, the one which I had caught myself.

In 1982 Bob suffered a horrendous accident, which would have finished off a lesser man.   He was being driven to the airport by a colleague to catch an early flight, when he stopped to buy a newspaper, and, in crossing the very busy highway, he looked the wrong way and stepped right into the path of an oncoming vehicle which knocked him for six.   He was unconscious for several days and suffered innumerable broken bones, ribs etc, not to mention a cracked skull, to deal with which the surgeons had to lift a part of the skull-bone off his brain with a suction pad.   According to his own testimony: "When I was lying there in the road, a joker came along and prodded me with his foot, saying 'He's gorn', but I hadn't , yer know...."

By this time Richardson McCabe had gone to the wall, and Bob had started his own company with Tim Richardson, the great nephew of the founder, and wisely built up the business selling Japanese machinery.   I visited Youngman Richardson early in 2003 and found them to be one of New Zealand's leading dealers in Construction Plant.   Bob was supposedly retired, but he still had a desk in the office, so that he could still poke his nose into the smoothly running operation now totally controlled by Tim, who would, I am sure, agree that without the Youngman drive and charisma, it would never have reached its present day success.

Australia was a different scene.   Apart from the successful establishment of the manufacture of grabs, Priestman were not in the market.   But Bill de Vigier was determined that they should be, like Acrow and Coles, both involved in local manufacture.   So he found what he thought was a high-flyer, a Swede called Mark Lindberg, to head up the whole Acrow operation in Australia and to be responsible for sales in South East Asia as well.   Rodney Akester had joined my export team to remove himself from the dubious pleasure of reporting to Brian Wildsmith, and he was offered the position of Sales Manager for Priestman in the region, based in Sydney.   Lindberg offered him attractive terms and so he transported himself lock stock and barrel to the sub-continent, and worked himself into a standstill travelling the length and breath of Australia to sell Mustang excavators.   Lindberg threw Acrow money about without stinting, and salesmen were recruited and presented with company cars painted in Priestman orange.   In 1977 I sensed that not all was going very well and flew out to see for myself.   I did my usual couple of weeks in SE Asia on the way and arrived in Sydney on a

Saturday morning on a night flight from KL looking forward to a weekend of rest before entering the fray once again.   Rodney greeted me at the airport with the information that Lindberg was insisting that I join him that evening at the Scandinavian Businessmen's Dinner, at which event I had apparently made a hit on a prior visit.   It was the last thing which I wanted to do, but I decided that politically it would be wise and tried to get my head down for some rest in the afternoon.   I did in fact survive that experience, despite having had some pretty straight talking with Lindberg based upon the verbal report that Rodney had given me.   Rodney and I spent all day Sunday in discussions, in which his charming wife Christine participated, and on the Monday we flew to Melbourne to have a meeting with the new salesmen, who kicked off with the question: "See here, you Poms, what are you going to do to back us?"   It was a tough session, but I think that we came out on top, and in the evening we had a tremendous piss-up in which the Aussies tried to drink the Poms under the table, but ended up first under the table themselves.

However, on the next day I regretted our victory in the drinking stakes, because I was unwise enough, with a heavy hangover, to play squash with one of our Aussie colleagues who was far better at the game than I was, and after about 20 minutes of being beaten around the court, I suddenly felt sick and nauseous and stopped immediately.   Convinced that I was having a heart attack, I went back into the changing room and sat down for some time before I could even face getting in to the shower.   Meanwhile the Aussies were in the bar, exchanging jokes about the Pom who couldn't take the booze, and Rodney cancelled all our forward travel plans and got me back to bed in the hotel asap.   The doctor just pronounced me as being over-tired, and after a good night's sleep I sat up in bed and fancied a light breakfast of scrambled egg.   In Australia this is impossible and at the sight of the tray groaning with scrambled eggs, sausages, bacon, fried potatoes and mushrooms, I felt physically sick again and phoned again for the doctor.   Rodney paced up and down the room saying: "Tin soldiers, plastic people - that's what we are" and he was right.   Several days of rest, followed by an extensive heart check on an exercise bike ended with the verdict that "I was fitter than normal for a man of my age", but it was a warning, which I heeded   -   I think.

Mark Lindberg, who was up to more tricks than I even knew about, was finally sacked by Bill de Vigier himself, after embarassing me considerably in Indonesia, where he tried to take kudos from our big sale of Mustangs.   He was introduced to our influential contact man, Mr. Dwi, in his mansion built over the tropical fish pond.

After the formal introductions were completed, Lindberg spun his visit card across the long low table to Mr. Dwi. Bert Anthonio, shock paling his dark skin, jumped up from his seat, retrieved the spinning card, and presented it ceremoniously with a bow to Mr. Dwi. I think that the effect was totally lost on Lindberg and I was not sorry to see the back of him....

I have commented earlier on the difficulties which I found in finding good travelling staff, and that my best successes were in taking on young people and training them.

In 1975 I recruited a young man of 19 with long hair to replace a secretary, as an export trainee. His name was Richard Aldersley, and he had been invalided out of Sandhurst because he suffered from hayfever, and had been working as a clerk in a shipping agency for about three months. I offered him the prospect of joining an export sales team, with the possibility eventually of travelling and I was extremely disappointed when he turned the opportunity down, because I had really taken to him and had seen that he had excellent potential. I decided that perhaps, as an ex-Sandhurst officer cadet, he felt that a job initially based in an office was beneath him, but I decided to give him another chance, and, this time, opening the door to possible travel sooner rather than later, he accepted. Subsequently he told me that it was his father, who warned him about changing jobs too soon, who was behind his initial refusal. After about six months of training, I set him an exam, which he passed with flying colours and then I seconded him to Rodney Akester to learn about selling.

It was not long before he was handling the Irish market on his own. Even the North was treated as export, because it was a dealer territory, where we were represented on both sides of the border by a small, but highly professional company in the North, and an even smaller, but extremely unprofessional company in the South. Nevertheless, in the Republic connections were more important than professionalism, and evidence of the strength of their connections in the South had gained for Priestman the order for 16 Mustangs for the Office of Public Works in Dublin in 1970, just before I came on the scene. Whilst the owner of the company, who had a long association with Priestman, was a somewhat feckless, if charming individual, the groundwork was done by one Alf Duggan, who knew and was known by everyone who mattered.   He pulled in orders for the Grab Division regularly, as well as for Lions and Mustangs, but inevitably the Northerner lobbied me for the Southern franchise as well, where they certainly sold more machines than he did.

Strangfords were run in Belfast by Harold McCollum, and his Sales Director was Derek Hamilton.   They were very effective in the North, and a great pleasure to deal with, both with a keen sense of humour.   Derek would ring up and say: "You are looking well this morning" when I answered the phone. Harold and his wife were our guests of honour during the Queen's Silver Jubilee celebrations in London and we took them to see a riotous comedy where the curtain fell upon a group of "nuns" who turned their backs to the audience and revealed bare bottoms because their "habits" only reached halfway round their bodies.   The raucous laughter from the audience at this finale was increased in our row by Harold's dry comment: "Good God, we don't have nuns like that in Ireland".   But their attitude to the Republic, which Derek always referred to as the "Free State" was tinged with a degree of superiority.

On a visit to the Dublin Show, Harold had parked his car in a side street, and, when we returned to it in the late afternoon, he opened the boot and threw a whole lot of rubbish on to the pavement.   "You litter lout, Harold, you would-n't do that in Belfast!" I remonstrated.   "'Tis only Dublin" he retorted, but I made him pick up all the litter and put it back in the car boot.

However, finally Harold prevailed on me, but my condition was that he would engage Alf Duggan as his Dublin manager.   He agreed willingly, but Alf did not, and went independent, taking the grab franchise with him, and a Northerner who had lived many years in the South took the position and did an excellent job.   But the difference in the character between the North and South of Ireland has never ceased to intrigue me.

Strangfords were eventually taken over by T.B.F.Thompson of Garvagh, who was the JCB Dealer.   Alan Cooper's old connections here were extremely valuable, and TBF, as the owner of the company was known, decided to put more money into the Priestman franchise and thus offended JCB, who fired him.   TBF was an extreme Protestant with almost Calvinistic tendencies, who had "seen the light" at the age of about 50, and no alcohol was ever served at his table, nor was any permitted in the entertainment of customers by his sales staff, although I am sure that they found ways round this rule.....   We used to be entertained to sumptuous luncheons at his home, just near to the offices, waited on by local country girls dressed as maids-in-waiting, washed down by Estate-Bottled Grape Juice. The house was like a museum, crammed with antiques and relics - I recall that the TV was housed in a French eighteenth century mahogany cabinet, and, each guest, before he left, would be presented with a pile of simplistic religious tracts by TBF, who was wont to declare that he would rather have written them himself than gone into business, a statement which I found hard to swallow. But there is no doubt whatsoever that T.B.F. Thompson certainly boosted the sales of Mustangs, with the money and power which they were able to put behind the franchise. In 1978/9, they ordered and sold more than 60 units, and rightly gained the Dealer Award. At the Acrow World Convention in 1978, Richard Aldersley and I organized a special dinner for about 30 customers from both sides of the border in a private room at the ancient Rules Restaurant in London. The Northerners sat at one end of the table drinking orange juice, whilst the Southerners were tucking into whisky and wine at the other end, with Richard and me occupying the middle ground between the two parties. They did not mix with one another at all, until, right at the end of the meal, the singing started, and Irish tunes of all political persuasions rang out into the night from the joint "choirs".

Richard eventually graduated from Ireland to parts of the Middle East, where I had had an old trooper as Regional Manager, until I realised that his reports rarely materialised into orders and he had a drink problem. I then decided that I must also conquer my own reluctance to visit a part of the world which I did not fancy, probably coloured by my National Service in Egypt. Soon after my unforgettable return to that country in 1976, I ventured over the border to Libya. This was on the back of Coles success, where a Frenchman born in Pondicherry and brought up in Yorkshire, Richard Gledhill, had astonishing success in a market which was closed, of course, to our main competitor, Grove, because of the ban on the sale of US products there. All business in the Jamahiriya was conducted through a general importer known to us at Genco, and one of the keys to the success of Coles was a Pakistani, Saleem Bukhari, who spoke fluent Arabic, and who had not a very high, but an extremely influential function in oiling the bureaucratic wheels in this import organization. I eventually hired this guy directly as the Priestman man on the spot, having some problems in dealing with the Home Office bureaucrats for a Work Permit - where on earth, I fumed, would I find a Brit fluent in Arabic ready to live and work in Libya?

I must say that I never took to Libya. Obtaining a visa necessitated first of all having one's passport translated into Arabic, and, having got over that hurdle, on arrival at the airport, one's bag would be emptied on to the floor by insolent Customs' officials, and anything considered as subversive material (such a copy of that day's Observer newspaper), promptly confiscated. Departing from the airport was even worse. Colonel Gadaffi refused to have any signs in English, only in Arabic, and this included the exit card which one had to complete, and which, if not specifically requested by the departing passenger at the check-in desk (reached only after a "queue" resembling a rugby scrum), was not forthcoming and the unfortunate individual would not be allowed to board his plane. One needed the assistance of an Arabic speaker to complete the form (they did accept English at least for that), and then one joined the queue for Immigration. My Coles colleague and I were fortunately advised on one very hot June afternoon when we were leaving together, to get in the "queue" next to the wall. There were only three windows behind each of which sat an officer checking passports, and each examination took five minutes at least. One then had to fight one's way back down the queue to the departure lounge. With three flights leaving consecutively, the room became more and more crowded as passengers crammed in, and, being against the wall, I was able to fend off the mass of humanity in the Black Hole so that I could breathe. My colleague was carried further forward than I, so he passed his briefcase over the heads of the crowd to me, and I did the same with my passport, so that he could present both at once. Streaming with sweat, I fought my way out to an open space away from the "queueing area", and was just wiping my brow, when a Libyan came barging through and nearly knocked a young baby out of the arms of its mother, who was sitting next to me. I was so furious that I grabbed the man by his coat lapels and shook him, abusing him roundly at the same time, completely disregarding the possibility that he might have run me through with a knife or something similar, but, in the event, he was so taken aback that he did nothing!

As a result of that unforgettable experience, I caught a bad chill as soon as I got home. Even with the aid of Saleem, we never had any great success in Libya - although I had the doubtful pleasure of entertaining the senior executives of Genco at my home in 1982, when they treated my daughters who waited on them at table like servants.....

In February 1979 made my first trip to Saudi Arabia, and fortunately I kept

Entertaining Libyans at my home with Saleem Bukhari

an account of my experiences.   Getting in and out of the country was easy compared to Libya, and I could probably have smuggled in a bottle of whisky, so cursory was the Customs inspection.   Ed Farmer accompanied me in the search for a new dealer, the existing one, Ali Al-Gilani, a charming man, having run into some considerable financial problems apart from not selling very much for Priestman.   Ed had not been in Jeddah for three or four years and could not recognize anywhere because building was going ahead at an enormous pace.   We hired a car with a driver, who proved to have a wooden head, because he could not locate any place at all.   There were few street names, only POB nos., and in the areas where development was going on, no streets.   We had to ask someone who spoke English to explain to our driver in Arabic exactly where we wanted to go, and every time he floundered and we had to stop time and again to ask once more.   His response to my impatience was to put his foot down and drive like a maniac.   On the second day we got a brighter lad, but, even so, it took us three separate attempts to find an office and showroom described as being "at the 14th kilometre on the Medina Road".   We did find it eventually, down a dusty track behind a whole lot more half-completed new buildings, and, once inside, there was the contrast of smooth executive offices, occupied by ex-pat Europeans and their Saudi partners.   It was not necessary to worry about making appointments to see people in Saudi Arabia, and you could be received by an ex-pat or Saudi without ceremony.   In that respect, it reminded me of Venezuela, with large open-plan offices, and a lack of formality.

Quoting from my journal: 'Discussions with Ali would take place in an office full of people, with whom he would carry on several discussions at once, switching from one topic to another and being constantly interrupted by the telephone, of which there were three on his desk, the other two being used simultaneously by his colleagues.   The whole office is a hubbub of excited conversation.   As visiting English businessmen, we have to be very patient, and constantly press our point: "Now what about these overdue Bills, Ali, when do you think that you can pay?"   "I will write a new Agreement to pay you £10,000 per month from next April, even if the customer does not pay me".   So I disappear into another office and draft out an Agreement which the boy typist eventually types out and back I go with it for Ali to sign. But by this time it is one o'clock and he is thinking of his lunch, and he still has an office full of people, so he suggests that we come back at 5 pm to discuss it. "But there is nothing to discuss, Ali, it is just as you agreed".   Finally, saying good-humouredly that I am a very aggressive and demanding person, he reads it and signs it.

All the time that this is going on, there is a constant stream of other callers on Ali, what Ed calls the extended family. He is very good-natured and cannot refuse anything to anyone. One man comes in and asks if the regular gift of 50 riyals per month can be increased to 60 on account of inflation, to which he receives a very dusty answer, but the petitioners continue to come in an unending flow. Another of Ali's favourite subjects are the Koreans, the new invaders of Saudi Arabia who are gobbling up all the big construction projects with their low rates of labour, and who buy earthmoving equipment in vast quantities. Ali is busy cultivating them, for the commission he hopes to make on these contracts by introducing the Koreans to the right people. He waves signed documents at us to prove his point, documents written on paper headed with names like "JUNG WOO DEVELOPMENT CORPN" But he admits that he has been caught out in the past, and now he will demand his commission in advance "I learn, you see", he says, "I learn from experience." One wonders.

The operations of the Korean Contractors are fascinating to see. We visit one of them, DONG AH, (who, incidentally, eventually bought Priestman wheeled Mustangs, and described them as the "Priestman Poclains"). The offices are laid out in the usual open-plan fashion, and all employees are dressed in a grey uniform. The managers have desks raised only slightly above those of the others. Few of them speak any English, and it is clear that they import their own world with them. Cartoons appear on the walls telling jokes which may be hilarious to the Koreans, but are totally incomprehensible to us. There are announcements of a Korean musical evening with dancing girls in local costume. We are told that they even import all their own food, but no alcohol, of course. Which reminds me that it is now 6 pm and could I do with a drink, but no chance. It will have to be tomato juice, or a thin gassy non-alcoholic beer, or an apple juice to remind me of all that cider stored in the garden shed back home. The disadvantage in Jeddah is that there is a complete lack of entertainment in the evening, not even a cinema. I am told that they all buy Video Tapes and watch them on their TV screens. This afternoon, Thursday (Saturday to you), we sat by the hotel swimming pool, drinking "beer" and swatting away the flies which crawled over the bottles and fell into the glasses, and being deafened by the blaring pop music which was played non-stop. Not very romantic. Now at dusk the wailing sound of prayer is coming from the mosque. I can see that this is a country which can fascinate, but it is not really my cup of tea.

But back to Ali. As I got up to leave his office today after we had finished our business discussions, he made me sit down and said: "You are not leaving?" "But, Ali, we have finished our talks and I want to get out of your way"."Stay", he replied, "I like to see you", and proceeded to ask my age, which was 45. He expressed great surprise that I was older than he, and had no gray hair.

"But," he continued, "it was always gray, and I am very strong, very impulsive - you know why? Because my father made me eat raw the balls of the.....how do you say the male of the hen - the cock, yes, the balls of the cock, quite raw without anything else. You see, he was doing me a favour...." But Ali's amusing attempt to delve into his youth do not conceal the fact that his ways of business are not what we are looking for. We have to look for a more modern company to represent our interests, and they exist, where the Saudi masters simply hold on to the purse strings and leave the running of their businesses to Europeans.

But it is not so easy to terminate an Agreement in Saudi Arabia. One has not to forget that "loss of face" means much and anyone can appeal to the King in person.

"Loss of face" was amply illustrated to me by a contretemps with a taxi driver in Riyadh. I had agreed with him, through the hotel receptionist, a fare of 40 riyals to a certain address. We had the usual problem of finding it, because he did not know exactly where it was, and hence some delays en route. Finally arrived, I proffered him the agreed 40 riyals which he angrily refused. Not wanting to have a prolonged argument, I increased it to 50, expecting immediate assent, but again he refused and followed me into the offices. I explained to the Filipino Receptionist what had occurred and that no way would I pay more than 50 riyals. The taxi driver flatly refused to accept it and demanded the number of my room at the hotel, which I gave him readily because I had already checked out, and I got my taxi ride for nothing, but he had not given in and lost face.'

Business-wise I was, finally, lucky. An old colleague of mine from Hymac was holding a senior position in Kanoo, the powerful family-backed dealer who had, and still has the Grove franchise. He readily agreed to take the Priestman excavator franchise on, and placed a stock order for 10 Mustangs, but they had much greater difficulty in selling them than they had anticipated, and never bought any more. Most of them ended up with Dong Ah.

However, this contact put me in touch with the ex-pat community and life on visits became more tolerable, although I never really took to the place. Wild parties took place in the compounds inhabited by the ex-pats, where one knocked back quantities of home-brewed beer and siddiqui, a dangerously potent colourless spirit which was usually mixed with tonic. At one such party, presided over by a Devonian banjo-player, who held court every Thursday evening (just before the Day of Prayer on Friday) at what he described as the "The Pheasant-Pluckers Inn", I surprised everyone by drinking siddiqui neat. They all watched for the moment when I would fall down in a drunken stupour, but I had had plenty of training in Polish vodka and I was very parsimonious with my sips. Nevertheless the alcohol did eventually have its effect, and I suddenly burst into raucous song for the remainder of the evening. Years later I ran into one of the guys who attended that party in the UK - he recognised me, but not I him!

However, at least I did not have the experience of witnessing a public execution, which was the fate of one other businessman whom I met. It was a Friday morning and he was in a taxi, which was suddenly stopped by the police in the middle of the main square in Riyadh. A space was cleared by the police in front of his taxi, into which a black van was driven, an unfortunate convicted prisoner hauled out and beheaded on the spot. The chap who related this incident said that he was physically sick, and I am not surprised. It is no wonder that, once, in a restaurant, when I carefully put my wallet, containing passport, tickets and money, on the table in front of me, the waiter removed it to a vacant chair. He indicated that there was no possibility whatsoever that it would be stolen, since thieves had their right hands amputated under Islamic law.

The Gulf was certainly a pleasanter place in which to travel, particularly since there was no ban on consumption of alcohol, but I did not find it particularly interesting either from a cultural viewpoint.

Only a month after that first visit to Saudi Arabia, in my capacity as Chairman of the Export Committee of the FMCEC (The Federation of Manufacturers of Construction Equipment and Cranes), I led a Trade Mission to Korea, with the objective of promoting the sale of British Construction Equipment to the Korean Contractors.

We had numerous meetings in high rise buildings, and visits to factories

where activity could only be described as frenetic, but extremely well organized, and the total discipline of the South Korean nation was completely impressed upon me by the Air Raid Practice, which occurred regularly in Seoul.   A notice in the hotel room advised each guest that this would take place at 11 am on a particular morning and that we should not be alarmed. We were in an office on the 20th floor of a very tall building at the time, and a huge siren sounded the alarm all over the city.

We watched, fascinated, from our grandstand seats, as the bustling city ground immediately to a halt.   Buses and cars stopped in their tracks in the streets, and all the passengers got out of their vehicles and disappeared rapidly into underground shelters. In seconds, the whole city had come to a halt and the silence was deafening. Ten minutes later the all clear sounded and the ants returned from their burrows and the city sprang into life once again. I have never witnessed such a mass acceptance of law and order in my life.

Iraq was another interesting Muslim country where we managed to do some business, and it had the big advantage in that the consumption of alcohol was permitted.

We decided to base Richard Aldersley in Iraq in the early 1980s, where there was good potential, particularly for Mustangs working on irrigation projects. We participated in the Baghdad Fair in 1982, alongside Coles, who were also very active in the market. Richard had virtually pre-sold four Mustangs to a Jordanian Contractor, and at a Board Meeting in Hull, I was asked for assurances that they would be sold, which I was able to give.   "Is there no potential for a Lion Crane?" was the next question.

I answered in the negative and so it was decided that we would confine our exhibit to the four Mustangs.   Within the next few minutes, Alan Cooper was called out of the meeting to take a call from the Chairman, Bill de Vigier himself.   He returned to the room with the announcement that we would be taking a Lion crane to the Fair.

To spec a mechanical crawler crane for an unknown use was complicated and expensive, since one did not know whether it would be required for use as a grabcrane, a dragline or a liftcrane, so the combined animal was a highly expensive one.

We tried to cut costs by appointing a cheap Turkish transport contractor, which meant that the crane finally arrived in the middle of the exhibition only just still attached to the decrepit bald-tyred low-loader on which it had been transported. However we learned that there was a Coles user who was looking for a crawler crane, an Indian contractor, Bandhari Builders. We prepared an offer and visited them, to be informed that the decision for purchase could only be made by Mr. Amrik Singh Bandari himself, who would be arriving within a few days for a short visit.

An appointment was duly made and Richard and I were ushered into the great man's presence, sitting behind a palatial raised desk, his turban making him seem like some Eastern potentate, in whose presence we felt quite small. "I like your crane", he announced in a positive voice, "and I know that it is of good quality, but the price is much too high. I can buy a Japanese crane in the Gulf for half the price of yours." I replied that I was sure that he would be willing to pay some more for a quality product. "Some more, yes" he replied, "but not what you have quoted me". When he named his figure, my heart sank, and, after a few rapid calculations, I said that we would exceptionally agree the price, FOB UK Port, with cost of freight in addition. His reply nearly knocked me sideways, as he rose to his full height and roared at me from behind his desk: **"Take it or leave it! I do not bargain!"** Richard and I exchanged a few words sotto voce. We took it, and sold the crane. The next day, Alan Cooper arrived at the Fair, and threw a wobbler, saying that it would be better to take the machine back. I did not agree with him, pointing out forcefully that the crane had been brought to the Fair against my wishes, and that we were committed. In fact the written contract had an error in it, in that the price was stated to be FOB Baghdad, instead of CIF Baghdad and I tried to argue that the freight should still be paid in addition. However the Company lawyer back in London told me that, unless I was prepared to swear in court that that had been agreed verbally, (which I certainly was not), the verbal contract must stand. Payment was made very promptly, and a lucrative parts order followed, and after installation, we never heard another word. I think that I had made the right decision.

We stayed in Baghdad in the Orient Palace Hotel, the most mis-named hostelry which I have ever experienced. Breakfast was put out at 6 am, including a huge urn of tea, and the inevitable semi-warm hard-boiled eggs and stale rolls. The tea urn was never replenished nor refreshed, so that latecomers had to drink stewed very lukewarm tea. On one occasion, at dinner, the waiter succeeded in breaking the top of the bottle whilst uncorking the wine and splinters appeared in the bottom of my wine-glass. When I drew his attention to this, enquiring if he was trying to kill me, he replied, quite upset, "I no kill you - you my friend". It was always a problem getting the bill accepted and signed, and, on one occasion, Ken Turner, a Coles Service Engineer from Bristol, having waited a quarter of an hour to get his breakfast bill signed and accepted, announced: "I be goin' to sign this 'Mickey Mouse'," which caused the worried waiter to appear a few minutes later at the Reception enquiring anxiously for the Room No. of "Meestair Mo-uss" Ken had the doubtful pleasure of being sent to Casualty at the local hospital, following the laceration of one of his legs when an Iraqi labourer assisting him in the erection of a crane failed to hold on to the end of the steel wire rope which then came snaking down the boom at breakneck speed and Ken could not get out of the way in time. He gave a vivid description of how a surgeon proposed to bleed him "to let the bad blood out", after wiping the scalpel, which he had taken out of his pocket, on his filthy blood-stained apron. "No, you bloody aren't!", shouted Ken as he withdrew his leg rapidly from the stool on which it was resting and hobbled as fast as he could out of the hospital, wisely preferring no treatment at all to the certain risk of blood poisoning.

Priestman also ventured into the markets of Turkey, Syria and Jordan, all three of which countries I visited at various times. The Jordanians always struck me as being the gentlemen of the Arab World, and from the numbers of Palestinians whom I met there arose a strong support and understanding of their cause. Israel I have never visited, nor had any desire to do so - I suppose that my experience in the 1960s with the Roumanian Jew, Martin Kiczales, coloured my attitude to that country, but, in my personal view, Israeli polticians have turned the oppressed of the Second World War into the Middle Eastern aggressors of today, although I am sure that there are nonetheless many ordinary Israeli citizens who would agree with me.

Most fascinating of all were my visits in the Middle East were to Iran, which came right at the end of my career at Priestman, but this is a story for a later chapter.

"Little and Large" - my two stalwart colleagues from Hull, Pete Dean and Ted Neylon, who formed the backbone of the demonstration team and accompanied me all over the world to sell Priestman, pictured here in 1979 in Malaysia, where Pete had served as a National Serviceman. Without first class demonstrators, one could not sell excavators in the 1970s.

The dedicated Latin-American Priestman enthusiast, Emilio Zapata, with Mr. and Mrs. de Vigier at a convention.

Uruguay. The 1950 vintage Tiger and the 1980 Mustang.

Priestman Lion III face shovel in operation in 1980 in a quarry in Uruguay.

Don Andres Navas and Dona Beatriz in Bogota in 1979, and his son Mauricio in London in 1998.
Don Andres was a true caballero of the old school and a great anglophile.

Priestman

Fifteenth century Carmelite nunnery in Quito, entry to which was strictly forbidden to men. Food was passed through a secret hatch to avoid the possiility of prying eyes.

Priestman in Malaya, 1930s. The drainage channels in the palm estates could not be easily cleaned from the banks due to density of the plantation. Priestman devised a grab crane with an automatic counterweight, behind the machine, which counterbalanced the loaded grab when the crane slewed to discharge.

INDONESIA.
Sightseeing in Surabaya with Bert
Anthonio (seated in Becha) and
convivial evenings in Jakarta with
Bing Tampi and his family

Celebration of the order for 31 x M120 FOR THE MINISTRY OF WATER RESOURCES, INDONESIA. Left to right: Alan Cooper, Hans Tampi, Dick Lloyd, Bing Tampi, Norman Brocklebank and Bert Anthonio

I am presented with a set of silver wine goblets by the Chairman in recognition of the Indonesian order at the 1978 Acrow convention.

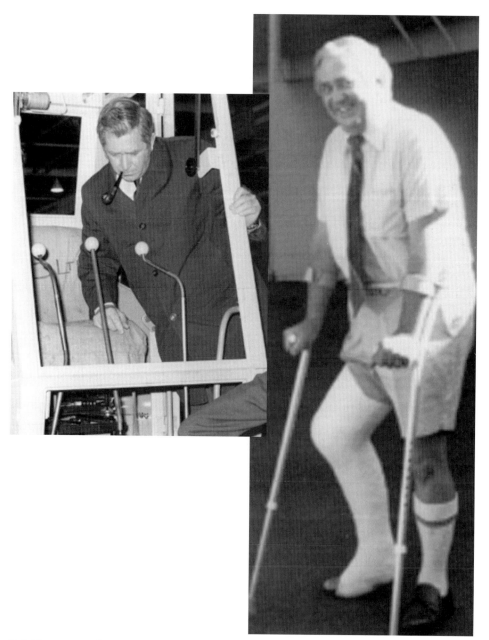

Bob Youngman, the top Kiwi salesman examining the controls of a M120 in the mid-1970s, and after his horrendous accident in 1982.

Launch of the M108S in Invercargill, New Zealand, February 1979, rodeo-style with a barbecue, Bob Youngman and Alan Cooper in attendance

Derek Hamilton of Strangfords, Belfast receives the 1975 Distributor Award from Richard Aldersley. Inset: Harold McCollum

Priestman

The old and the new - a 60 year gap. The 1921 ditcher and the 1981 Bogmaster outside the Hull works

Mustang 108S Bogmaster in operation in the peat bogs of Ireland

Ali Al-Gilani of Saudi Arabia with Norman Brocklebank.

Ed Farmer in 2003, married for the sixth time and living in Thailand.

CHAPTER FIVE - PRODUCT DEVELOPMENT AND POLITICS AT PRIESTMAN

In 1976 Brian Wildsmith decided that Priestman was no longer for him and he departed from the Home Sales scene. Alan Cooper consulted me on his replacement, making it quite clear that he had no intention of offering me the top sales job, but clearly wanting to make sure that his appointee was a man with whom I could work alongside, and he told me that he was going to go for the best man he could find at Hymac. They still dominated the UK market scene with the Hymac 580 in terms of volumes of sales, and Alan also intended to produce a Mustang to compete directly with it. Two or three names were floated, and I recommended Bob Sheavyn, with whom I had always got along very well in my Hymac days, although, after his appointment, I certainly got to know him a great deal better. For me, after Wildsmith, he was like a breath of fresh air. We drank beer and played squash together, visited each others' homes, and on one occasion he invited Audrey and me to join him at the Lighthouse Club Ball on St. George's Day, where Bob had arranged a large party for customers. For Bob was a showman, rather than a salesman. Maybe he was rather flamboyant and not too careful about expense, but he certainly could put on an excellent display in launching a new product and this is exactly what he did when Priestman came out with the Mustang 108S to take market share from the Hymac 580.

Initially, it was proposed to call it the Mustang 580S, but Hymac rightly protested at this on legal grounds and won the day. It was an excellent 12 tonne excavator, incorporating many of the features of the well-tried Mustang 120 and it won the Silver medal at SED in April 1978. It certainly made some impact on the sales in the UK and Ireland of the Hymac 580. In the Republic of Ireland, the Bogmaster version, which was built with special lightweight steel box section track pads 1575 mm wide, and incorporating the well-tried Priestman long reach front end equipment reaching out to over 11 metres, displaced the 580 fitted with wooden swamp pads for operation in the peat bogs. But, apart from the Mustang 220, development of middle weight Mustangs was not so successful. The Mustang 160 was a smaller version of the M220, with variable displacement high pressure hydraulics, but it proved too expensive and not reliable, so it was replaced by the simpler Mustang 168S, with gear-driven hydraulics, but no greater reliability. We gained what was probably the biggest single order for this model of eight units for a large pipeline contractor in Trinidad. taken against fierce competition from Caterpillar. Every machine overheated and we had a service engineer living in Trinidad for months carrying out modifications.

Bob brought in other experienced men from Hymac, including the used equipment wheeler-dealer, John Wishart, mentioned earlier in these writings, but he failed to maintain the right profile with his co-Directors in Hull, in particular the Managing Director, Alan Cooper. Alan and I had our ups and downs, and occasionally these reached fever-pitch, when one of us would slam the phone down on the other after an altercation over the tie-line which linked Hull to the Export Office in London.

Minutes later he would call again: "Have you cooled down? Now let us discuss the problem rationally...." We never lost our personal contact, however, and often he would say: "Well, its your decision, but you'll find you are wrong". We travelled the Far East together and got along very well. One of the biggest differences which we had was over Zeevenhooven, our best and most loyal distributor, in whom Priestman had a 10% stake-holding. Finding it harder and harder to compete in the hydraulic excavator business with the limited range provided by Priestman, apart from the quality problems with the middle-weight excavators already mentioned above (Holland was never a market for the M108S), they decided to take the franchise for the Japanese Mitsubishi in 1980. I could understand and appreciate the commercial nature of their decision, and was satisfied that they would continue to sell Lion cranes, but the rest of the Board were outraged and furious, as if Zeevenhooven had stabbed us in the back.

I was directed to investigate setting up a Direct Sales Organization in Holland for Priestman. I totally disagreed with this, but I had no choice but to carry it out.

At that time, Acrow had appointed the MD of Thos Storey, a retired Army Major, as a non-executive director on our Board, and he had a successful subsidiary in Holland whom I was told to approach. The Dutchman who ran this company said to me: "But I cannot possibly offer spares and service facilities - you need to talk to someone like Zeevenhooven". He did not need to tell me that - I was already decided to do it. I could not possibly muddy the waters by openly discussing the Priestman franchise in such a small market, where the word that Priestman were looking for a new sales outlet would spread like wildfire and affect our whole market position. Kees agreed with me that their decision to take Mitsubishi should have been first discussed with Priestman and he felt a bit bad about it, so I suggested that, with the 10% holding in their company, we could set up a separate sales organization to sell Mustangs direct, in competition with Mitsubishi, but still with the assurance of their after-sales parts and service. He agreed. The Priestman Board did not, accusing me of disobeying orders, if you like, by even talking to Zeevenhooven, and that, in any case, I had burned my boats.... So I had, but nothing ever was done about it and Zeevenhooven continued to sell Lions and Mitsubishi excavators, but the atmosphere between Hull and Rotterdam became very frosty. Six months elapsed and Kees then proposed that he make a special visit to Hull to lay the ghost and re-establish personal relations with the remainder of the Priestman Board. We met with Alan Cooper for dinner at the Royal Station Hotel, and, over pre-dinner drinks, Alan opened the discussions: "Kees" he said, "When you took the Mistsubishi franchise without consulting us, we were very angry. The whole Board was against you, except for Dick Lloyd, who stood up for you without wavering. Kees, I have to say to you now that Dick was right and we were wrong". I nearly fell off my chair with surprise and my respect for Alan Cooper shot up from that moment.

But Bob Sheavyn rode his horse differently, and, as it proved, disastrously.

He would often say to me that he hardly ever had anything to do with Alan, to which I would reply, trying to warn him: "Well, he is the MD, Bob", but my hints seem to fall on deaf ears. In March 1982 I was making what proved to be my last visit to New Zealand for Priestman, when Alan Cooper started to phone me up and ask when I was coming back, because he needed to talk to me urgently, but he would not say over the phone what the subject was likely to be. I countered that I could not just abandon a planned trip with customer visits, and refused to cut it short, but as soon as I had landed back on a Saturday evening, he was in my office in London as early as possible on the Monday morning, not even giving me the chance of a proper weekend to recover from the trip. "What do you think of Bob Sheavyn?" he demanded. I was taken aback, and replied, cautiously, that generally speaking I got along with him very well, but occasionally had to tread on his toes when he ventured outside his UK sales orbit. "Well, the rest of the Board have decided that he has to go, and we want your support." I replied immediately: "Leave me out it - I will have nothing to do with it. We do have our ups and downs, but Bob is a mate of mine and I will take no part in his being sacked." I think it was Alan who was now taken aback, and he made me promise that I would not divulge any part of the conversation to Bob, which promise I kept, even if my hints became broader. Alan chose a day when I was due to be in Hull to fire the bullets, and gave me this information as soon as I arrived at the Works.

Fortunately I had arranged to have a working lunch with some of the technical boys to discuss a problem, so I was able to dodge Bob's invitation to lunch in the pub.

At about 4 pm two things happened simultaneously: A call from Bob on his car phone as he drove out of the Works having been given his marching orders, and a summons to a distraught Managing Director's office saying that Bob had refused to resign and accept the package offered to him, and what could I do now to help. They clearly did not want to fire him because of his reputation in the market-place.

The situation was so comical that I wanted to laugh, but decided that it would not be very diplomatic. The upshot was that I had dinner with Bob that night and acted as the go-between all next day, at the end of which time he finally agreed to resign.

He bought a pub in a nearby village and we used to visit him there, but I don't think that he was very happy, and it only lasted a year or two, and he went off to start a new life in the Canary Islands, so far as I am aware. He was replaced by a man called John Coates, who came from somewhere else in the Group, and reminded me of Dennis Mattingley. I did not have much to do with him, fortunately, until right at the end of my career with the company, and then only for a short period.

The most exciting excavator ever developed by Priestman, for me, at least, was the VC 15. I claim some influence on the decision to produce this remarkable machine with a variable counter-balance enabling it to reach, first to 15 metres and then to 20 meters, and finally to 30 metres. I am well aware that today, long -reach excavator front ends have been developed by Kocurek in the UK, by Liebherr in Germany and Caterpillar in the USA, without using a variable counterweight system, but I still find this principle very interesting in the design of both cranes and excavators.

Variable counterweights have been used before, but a small company in Belgium, Sobemai, under the ingenuity of its owner, Edelhart de Lille, produced a scrap-handling crane for the local market with a variable counter-balance in 1980. Sobemai had represented Priestman for many years. De Lille was not perhaps the most popular visitor to Hull, because he was constantly critical of Priestman's design. He modified Priestman machines to meet individual customer specs - he produced the only M220 ever on a wheeled undercarriage, and he designed and built a very special hydraulic piling rig for the Lion. He bought up, at keen prices, the one-offs which Priestman had developed, like the Rhino, and I think that all four of the Mustang 320s ever produced ended up in his yard. Mustang 90s became reliable machines after he had modified the transmissions.

The Rhino was a 1960s development, and the earliest attempt by Priestman to build a larger crawler crane, based on the success of the Lion, which featured totally enclosed gearing with pumped lubrication. The idea was to offer this

Priestman

proven mechanical drive for crane and dragline duties, which could also be used alternatively to drive two hydraulic pumps for a shovel.   To power this highly innovative combination, a 185 HP GM Engine was selected, but it needed to be run at very high speed (2600 rpm) to give the required power and this gave the designers some headaches.   Furthermore the GM Engine was not very well known as a Prime Mover in Construction Equipment, and it was felt that it would be difficult to market, and so the project was abandoned.   It remained a typical example of the inventiveness of the Priestman Design Team.

De Lille was a brilliant, if somewhat eccentric engineer, and apart from cranes, he used to buy up old steam locomotives and renovate them in his "museum".   As soon as I saw the first E-Crane that he produced, I told Brock and Chief Engineer Ken Deighton that they must go and have a look at it, and I believe that it was from this that the VC was born, with the simple change of substituting the rod which connected the variable counter-balance to the arm by a rope, to avoid infringement of patent, although Edelhart told me that he was rather sore about being copied.   Apart from its appeal to the UK Drainage Boards, the most loyal group of Priestman users in the country, it caught the eye of an American entrepreneur, Leo Gerbus, who sold the largest number of export machines, mainly for clearing fly ash, the waste from Power Stations, and we scattered quite a number of units around Europe and the Far East.   The very last VC machine which I myself sold was a long time after the collapse of Acrow, to a user in New Zealand, who had also taken one of the last VC15s shipped out of Hull in July 1984, and was so delighted with it that I sold him a used VC20 ten years later.

But the most interesting negotiation on the VC15 which I had was in Iran.   Richard Aldersley got involved in pioneering the project, and I joined him there at the end of 1983.   We used the Coles Agent, who were middle class educated Iranians, and it always used to amuse me that, although they wore suits, they omitted to put on ties, in order not to offend the fundamentalist clerics.   Ties were considered to be extremely bourgeois.   When we were invited to their home, it was like being in another world, the ladies abandoning their Islamic head-dress and putting on their finery, and excellent vodka was served with the food.   Even in the hotel, one could drink very tolerable non-alcoholic locally brewed beer, which came from a traditional brewery.   One of my fellow guests, an Iranian living in the USA, to whom I got chatting in the hotel lobby, whispered that he had some whisky in his room and would I like to join him in a glass or two.   I prudently declined, not only because I did not trust him, but I felt, in the strongly religious atmosphere that pervaded the place, that I would be acting inhospitably if I did.

Our discussions were held with the Jihad y Sazandegi, which translates into the

"Peoples' Revolutionary Reconstruction Crusade", and they showed great interest in the VC concept. Discussions were held in a small place north west from Tehran, and all manner of courteous preliminaries had to be undergone before one sat down to discuss any business. All wearing beards and clad in traditional Islamic dress, the brothers, as I shall describe them, showed us with great, but sincere pride their workshops where they were hand crafting arte-facts for the promotion of the Islamic faith, like a simple but rather crude wood-en stand on which to put one's copy of the Koran. In contrast to my feelings in Saudi Arabia, I respected and felt somehow in tune with these very devout Muslims. Discussions, often preceded by hours of waiting for the Haji, as the religious leader of the community was called, were held squatting on the floor, shoeless, because it was a holy place. The upshot of these deliberations was that they could be interested in purchasing not one, but several machines, per-haps as many as twenty, but first of all one had to be donated to the cause of the Revolution.

It was at this stage, when we were working towards getting some kind of docu-ment signed which would be the equivalent of a "Letter of Intent to Purchase" that political events, totally outside our control, nearly scuppered the whole deal and destroyed the carefully constructed atmosphere of mutual trust which we had built up between ourselves and our potential business partners. It was early in 1984, when I set off on a six week trip to promote the VC, first of all car-rying out demonstrations in Spain, then in Pakistan and Thailand, with one of the Hull lads in each location to carry out the practical work. My trip was to end in Iran, and whilst still in Bangkok, I read with horror in the newspaper that Britain had been accused of supplying chemical weapons to Iraq. I immedi-ately contacted Acrow HQ in London asking them to put pressure on the UK Govt authorities to issue an official denial (as it was clearly a put-up job). I received assurances that all possible would be done, and, as soon as I had arrived in Tehran and met up with Richard, we went to the Swedish Chargé d'Affaires who was looking after British interests, since we did not have our own Embassy in Iran at the time. He gave us a copy of an official denial from the UK Govt, and assured us that it was a rumour deliberately put out by the Iranians, in order to put pressure on the UK to supply them with arms in the war against Iraq. When we arrived late that same evening at our destination, we were immediately ushered into the presence of the brothers, all sitting cross-legged on the floor and subjected to a long tirade against the British, with refer-ences as how they were suffering in the war against Iraq. One man, who only had one arm, was illustrated as a war casualty, who, I happened to know, had lost his arm in an accident whilst using a circular saw. The only way to counter the tirade was to make an impassioned speech about how we had outlawed the use of gas after the First World War, during which I was able to say that all four of my uncles had fought and been wounded, and that my wife's uncle had been killed in the trenches. This was all pure theatre, of course, but it seemed to have the desired effect, and the Haji finally intervened and said that, whatever, we personally could not be held at all responsible, and that we were welcome, as friends and brothers, as before. The whole procedure went on for some hours and it was after midnight when we escaped to bed, and, having travelled all the way from Bangkok on the same day, I was out for the count!

When one of the brothers, who had been absent the previous evening, raised the matter again the next day, the Haji brought him sharply to order, by saying firmly that the matter had already been discussed and was closed, much to my relief. We did not come away from that visit empty-handed. Some days later, also late into the night after endless talks, we signed a document headed, as they always were "In the Name of God", whereby, subject to the approval of the Priestman Board of Directors (which I was not too sure about at all), we would supply a VC15 on a trial basis, as a gift to the Revolution, and that, if it operated satisfactorily, they would be ready to place an order for up to 20 units, subject to agreement on price and conditions.

This document had some far-reaching consequences, as I shall relate later, but, as events proved, it was to be my last throw of the dice.

The Priestman Rhino crowd shovel.

Priestman

The Priestman VC15 long reach machine which introduced the sliding counterweight, at the rear of the boom, to automatically keep the excavator in balance, as the bucket moved through its full cycle. By eliminating weight from the equipment, and using only one small bucket ram, the VC15 had a reach of 15 metres, ideal for long reach drainage work.

The VC15 clearing fly ash from a power station in the USA.

The Priestman VC15 at BAUMA in 1983.

CHAPTER SIX - THE WORLD OF ACROW, POLITICS AND THE END OF THE ROAD

As I hope that I have made clear in these writings, I was never one for politics, but, inevitably, I got sucked in. My main problem was that I got on very well with Bill de Vigier. It was totally due to him that I was able to take Audrey to South America. At the famous Acrow Conventions, which took place every three years, I was soon regularly masterminding the demonstration of machines, which was intended to give the customers and dealers who poured into London from all over the world for these events, the impression of a large Construction Site employing only equipment supplied by the manufacturers in the Acrow Group. Originally the Conventions had involved delegates being transported by bus and train round all of the manufacturing plants, but although one-day Works visits were still on the menu, the 1978 Convention was centred at Kempton Park Race-course, where Seminars were held, Static Exhibitions of products were organized, a Grand Parade of machines took place and, every day, the Demonstration. The overseas delegates, of whom there were more than 1000, together with their wives, spent two whole weeks in the UK, and for the UK and European customers, who were flown in from all parts, the Programme was repeated on four consecutive days. Ladies Programmes, with sightseeing visits etc were also laid on, but Mr. de Vigier always insisted that the ladies must also make the Works visits, whether they liked it or not. The scale of the organization required was staggering, and it was all carried out by Acrow men.

This meant that senior executives like myself had to abandon running their departments, take off their selling boots and concentrate on the build-up to the Convention, which took place in September. In fact, the pre-organization and rehearsals took up the whole of August, so that it was perhaps the family holiday which suffered more than absence from the business scene. Sandwiched between the Parades, Exhibitions and Demonstrations were conference sessions held by each individual company with their own dealers, involving the preparation of papers on subjects such as "The case for capital investment in Priestman cranes and excavators" and "Coles World Market Perspective", so that for an Acrow Group Export Director or Manager it was a very busy time indeed, each one having to take his turn also as Officer of the Day. Lesser fry were found employment as Coach Marshals, or piloting the ladies around historic houses - everyone was involved. The Convention started with a visit to a London Theatre, and ended with a Grand Ball at Grosvenor House, where the Chairman handed out cups for achievement to successful salesmen and others. Then, for the elite, was a splendiferous evening at Bill de Vigier's mansion in

Mill Hill, when a marquee took in part of the garden and the swimming pool.

The final Acrow Convention took place in September 1982 at Thorpe Park, where, in addition to all the foregoing, a water-borne procession on rafts built by Thos Storey of all Group Products replaced the terrestrial Grand Parade, and an army tank gave a very impressive demonstration by travelling at high speed across a Thos. Storey floating bridge.   According to the Acrow Review, this Convention was hailed as "the best ever in terms of attendance, presentation and immediate financial return", but the City did not share this view and the Acrow shares took a plunge immediately after it.

After the record profit year of 1979, which was the crowning glory of a continuous succession of increased profits of Acrow from the very beginning, Acrow had started to lose money. On the wall behind the Chairman's desk was a chart depicting these year-on-year successes, but, as one commentator rather acidly put it, after 1979, Bill de Vigier strangely "ran out of wall".   Within the Group, with belt tightening going on all around and a worsening economic outlook for Acrow, there were many who thought that the £2 million spent on it could have been put to better use, but Mr. de Vigier was not to be gainsaid and it went ahead.   As we danced together at Tinkers Lodge on the last evening, amid all the glitter, I said to Audrey;   "Let us really enjoy ourselves tonight, since this will never happen again", and I was to be proved right.

But Group events were not confined to the UK Conventions. Sometimes a Joint Exhibition of all products was decided for some international fair in a developing market.   The most unforgettable to these was the British Exhibition in Beijing in the golden year of 1979.   The Managing and the Export Sales Directors of almost all companies in the Group were bidden to attend this event and show their products.   Coles had already sold successfully to China over a period of about 20 years, but for the rest of us it was a leap into the dark from a commercial viewpoint, and not a successful one. However it provided me with one of the most interesting overseas visits of my entire career, coming, as it did, just after the end of the disastrous "Cultural Revolution".

We lodged at the "Friendship Hotel", which was very clean and comfortable, but there was no air-conditioning and it was extremely hot at night, being in mid June.   Service in the hotel was excellent, each floor having its own Reception Desk manned by several grinning boys, who roared with laughter at my attempts to speak pidgin Mandarin Chinese.   However, if one ordered a beer, it was immediately brought to the room, and there was no need to make up a laundry list, but simply put all one's dirty linen into the Laundry Bag provided and leave it in the room in the morning. Upon return in the evening, there it would be all beautifully clean and pressed, although possibly a little smaller than before! It was against the law to tip, which actually made life very easy. Another nice touch was the provision of a thermos flask of hot water and jasmine tea in each room. The food in the restaurant was good, and very cheap - the first night I was too late for the main meal in the restaurant, but was served with a soup, omelette, salad and a beer for the equivalent of £1.00. I talked to a Chinese engineer, who earned £19.00 per month, but the rent of a three-roomed flat for himself, his wife and daughter, was £1.50 per month and his midday meal in the Works canteen cost 15 pence.

At that time in China, everyone was dressed exactly alike in white shirts and blue baggy trousers, and it was difficult to tell men from women, the latter all being fairly flat chested and having their hair cut short like the men. Traffic consisted almost entirely of bicycles, of which there were thousands, and privately owned cars were non-existent. Trucks, buses and a few official cars, like the one which picked us up from the hotel in the morning to take us to the Exhibition, which were all made in the Soviet Union, made up all the motorised transport. Our driver used to shoot out of the hotel courtyard into the street, with his hand on the horn, without giving way to any of the numerous cyclists, who seemed adept at weaving their way in between the sparse but extremely ill-disciplined motor traffic. I never saw a road accident, nor did I see a cat, nor a dog, nor a bird during the whole time that I was in Beijing. The streets were immaculately clean and constantly being swept with besoms made out of brushwood, and there was also a complete absence of mosquitoes, which was pleasant.

The British Exhibition, which lasted two weeks, was open in the morning and afternoons to selected visitors by invitation only. Long before the doors opened, orderly queues of ticket holders formed outside the main entrance, and it was just as well that numbers were limited, because otherwise we would have been swamped.

Really we were just objects of incredulous wonder to most of the visitors, none of whom could speak English, and who had no power to purchase anything at all. They just came and stared at us, and Norma Trickey, our one secretary who acted for all of us, and who sat at her typewriter in a small office at the rear of our Stand, had to put up with the incessant gaze of as many faces as could peer at her at any one time through the office window.   Bill de Vigier kept having high level meetings with various top-ranking Chinese officials and then holding meetings with us to communicate the names of this or that "verr' verr' important man", and demanding special packs of literature to be prepared for them.   On one occasion, he insisted on Company Profiles being written for some particularly important personage, so I sat down frivolously at the type

Priestman

writer to compose in a loud voice: "Priestman has been in business for over 100 years...... The Managing Director of Priestman is a small, gray-haired little bastard", which caused much hilarity amongst all my colleagues, and Alan Cooper, the object of my wit, took it in very good part.

De Vigier made some critical comment on a Coles leaflet which he had been given to present to some high-ranking official, out of which I made much capital with David Steel, who promptly retaliated by saying that my blue safari suit (of which I was quite proud) made me look like a retired Wing Commander, and so it went on.....

This was one of the great benefits of all of us being together in close proximity - there was great camaraderie, because we were all like fish out of our usual waters. In fact, at the time, the Chairman was seriously considering making an offer for Aveling Barford, and wanted Alan Cooper to be MD, but the latter was not at all keen on the idea. I certainly had never been in close proximity to so many senior Acrow executives at any one time.

The other recurring feature of our attendance at this exhibition were the banquets. I still have the text of the speech of Vice Premier Wang Zhen at the first official banquet hosted by the Chinese for Duke of Kent, who was the chief British guest in his capacity of Chairman of the British Overseas Trade Board. Unforgettable were the opening words of the girl who was acting as interpreter:

"Your Loyal Highness, the Duke of Kent, Fliends and Comlades". The speech went back in time to the first trade contacts between Britain and China in the reign of Henry VIII, when John Cabot was commissioned to explore a direct sea route between the two countries. The speeches at these banquets always followed the same pattern.

Shortly after the meal had begun the Chief Host would stand up and make a speech of welcome to the Chief Guest. Then soon after that the Chief Guest would reply, and then at each table anyone seemed to get up and make a speech welcoming anyone from the other side. There was a strict protocol on these occasions. The Chief Guest sat next to the Chief Host, who had to feed him with his own chopsticks as a start to the feast, and the same procedure was followed by all the hosts to all the guests.

The food at these banquets was nothing like as good as what had in the Friendship Hotel, being mostly cold and clammy - I had my first taste of 100 year eggs, an experience which I did not want to repeat too often. Drink was plentiful and the waiters kept filling up the beer glasses, after each "Gan Bei!" ("Cheers"), following every speech, washed down by Mao-Tei, a fiery spirit of which I still keep a bottle just to sniff at to remind me what it was like. Someone said that it would make good paint stripper. The official banquets were followed by each and every company in the Group giving their own private banquets, so that in the end the whole procedure became exceedingly boring, especially since usually only one Chinese in each party spoke any English. Alan Cooper once asked one lady interpreter, just to try to make conversation, what she did for her holidays. Her answer was quite simple: "We don't have any holidays". I have to say that, after years of travelling in Eastern Europe and witnessing the inequalities of the Communist system, where Party members enjoyed a lifestyle and privileges much removed from the ordinary people, I got the impression that Chinese Communism was much more even handed, and that, for such a huge population, it was probably a more equitable system than Capitalism. Clearly Beijing was a showpiece, and I am sure that conditions elsewhere were much worse, and probably what we were shown was very selective. Be that as it may, a visit to a People's Commune was, for me, an unforgettable experience. It had a population of about 20,000, and consisted of agriculture (mostly pig farms) and factories. It had its own hospitals and clinics, but 90% of the population owned their own houses, which might only have one room, with a communal kitchen for all.

Official sightseeing visits apart, one or two of us were very fortunate to tour Beijing privately on bicycles. This was arranged by a young English girl who was a student at the University and who was earning some pocket money at the Exhibition as an interpreter. She borrowed some bikes from her student friends on a Sunday and not only did we visit the Forbidden City and other places of interest, but also the University, where the spartan living conditions (especially in winter) were most apparent. Cycling around Beijing along streets deserted of motor cars, and along roads running alongside lotus ponds was a lovely way to visit the great city.

As far as Priestman were concerned, this costly exhibition in Beijing brought no commercial benefit whatsoever. Ted Neylon flew out to demonstrate the Mustang 108S excavator which we had on the Stand, which the Chinese certainly would have purchased, but only to take it to pieces and copy it, and so we declined to sell it. Maybe we should have sold it to defray some of the expenses of the Exhibition.

I cannot think that a Chinese copy would have prejudiced many sales from our own production. But I had as little involvement in the decision not to sell it as I had had in the decision to participate in the show at all. Ted and I flew out on China Airlines to Canton, where we over-nighted before taking the train to Hong Kong and on to Malaysia. Here again, on this overnight stop we were treated like royals, being met at the airport, accompanied to our hotel and escorted to dinner in the old quarter in a restaurant recommended by our guides. It had three floors. On the ground floor the local Chinese were eating, on the first floor the overseas Chinese, but the top floor was reserved for non-Chinese visitors like ourselves, and Ted and I had what was virtually a private room to ourselves, where we were served the most delicious Cantonese food. The two boys who were guiding us kept popping up to see if everything was alright, but very discreetly, and refusing to eat or drink with us. The next day they accompanied us to the station to take the train to Hong Kong and when we got back into the World of Capitalism, battling to get a taxi and fighting our way through the crowds at the airport, it was a considerable cultural shock!

Bill de Vigier created a Group HQ structure at Paddington by bringing in a Group Managing Director and then two Deputy MDs. I personally only rated one of these individuals, and that was Ian Green, a straight speaking Lancastrian with a great sense of humour who tried hard to co-ordinate the export activities of the diverse companies in the Group and get the stronger to assist the weaker. In the latter days of the Callaghan Labour Government, there was a Day of Action orchestrated by the TUC to bring London to a grinding halt, and Acrow actually held a special Board Meeting to organize transport so that everyone could get in to the office. I had an Office Manager and a team of about 10 people at the time, but I was busy flying about in various directions and I decided that I was going to work from home on that day, with John Davies, on the composition of the Priestman News, which we could better concentrate on away from telephones and interference. On the day before the Big Strike, I was in Hull and received a warning from Acrow HQ that "The Chairman" was definitely expecting everyone to be in the office the next day. I was damned if I was going to comply with such a stupid instruction and waste hours sitting in a car, but I realised that I was heading for clash with the Old Man himself and sent him a telex, couched in as diplomatic terms as I could muster, saying that I was sure that he would agree with me that my time would be better spent working from home than sitting in a car, but I also made sure that all my other staff would be there. The fun started when my Office Manager refused the lift arranged for him, chanced the train and was lucky, which upset the Gnomes. When they found that I was not there, the shit hit the fan, and I received an angry phone call from Alan Cooper: "Why aren't you in the office? The Chairman is furious." I had to sit down and write a defence of my insubordinate action, and I was ready to throw in the towel, so angry was I at being treated in such a childish way. But I had my Friend at Court, Ian Green, who disliked the Gnomes as much as I, and he told de Vigier: "You have upset one of my best Sales Directors". "Ach, you mean Lloyd" was the cryptic reply, but the threats to make us clock in and out and toe the line never came to anything.

Priestman

Mr. de Vigier went off on an overseas trip the very next day, and, as soon as he returned, he was in my office, telling me all about it and how there was tremendous potential for Priestman in the countries he had just visited. I knew that this was his way of saying that the Day of Action incident was over, and I suspect that he smiled to himself over it.

Bill de Vigier had hoped that one of the three would be capable of taking over from him "so that he could retire" (his words), but finally in 1981 he picked a man of a different calibre, Norman Cunningham. I found out that Cunningham had known de Vigier since he was a young man, since he had been a sub-contractor to Acrow making props in the early 1950s, before Acrow opened their own factory in Saffron Walden, and apparently at that time de V said that Cunningham should work for him "one day".

Thirty years later he was head-hunted for the position of Acrow Group MD, and, as he told me recently, he really thought that he could pull the Group round, which was in great debt to the Consortium of banks, headed by Barclays, which supported it.

He certainly tried very hard, reducing the workforce from 6000 when he joined to 3500 at the time of the collapse. The fact that de Vigier kept the majority of voting shares in his own hands and that of his family, the employees and the public only being able to purchase non-voting "A" shares discouraged, according to some financial analysts, outside investors who might have seen the Group through its difficult times, but clearly the Chairman, having built up the Group with his own entrepreneurial skills found it very hard to let go, and felt that it would be possible to sell ourselves out of the recession which hit Acrow after the record year of 1979.

Norman Cunningham was a tough Glaswegian Scot, and he did not make himself very popular. That was not his style. He clashed with the Old Man and they did not get on, and this meant that he had no time for those whom he probably regarded as the Old Man's favourites. I found myself in a nutcracker position. In 1982, The Group won the Queens Award to Industry (not for the first time - Coles notched up no less than five between 1966 and 1982), and it was decided to hold the presentation at Priestmans in Hull, to give them a morale booster. The day selected chanced to be Old Man's 70th Birthday, so he invited all the Priestman directors and their wives to dinner to celebrate it. Norman Cunningham was furious, because he was spending his evening talking to the bankers. When he heard that I had asked Audrey especially to come to Hull for the dinner, he exploded and I think that this was the beginning of his vendetta against me, telling Alan Cooper that he should get rid of me.

Priestman

Well I nearly left Priestman, but certainly not because of Cunningham. Early in 1983 I was myself head-hunted, and by no lesser a company than JCB. I told Alan Cooper immediately and that I had been invited to Rocester to meet Dick Ryland, MD of JCB Sales. "Ooh", said Alan, "be careful", and he told me something about Ryland to prepare me for my visit, but he encouraged me to go for the interview.

As an old JCB hand, he was intrigued. The Personnel Manager showed me round the JCB Plant, and, of course, I was highly impressed. It was a tremendous contrast to anything in the Acrow Group, stream-lined and up-to-date to a degree. However, I had been invited to go to JCB, and I was a Priestman man, and when I was shown into the great man's office, he asked me why I wanted to leave. My reply shocked him. "I don't", I said. "Then what are you doing here?" he demanded, "Are you not absolutely convinced that you want to work for JCB?". The Personnel Manager hurriedly explained that I had been head-hunted (it appears that Ryland did not like head-hunters). I rose from my chair and walked to the door, briefcase in hand. "Mr. Ryland", I said, "I do not wish to waste your time. I came here because I was invited, and I wish to see for myself whether JCB could offer me a better future than Priestman. But, I am not yet convinced that I want to work for you, and so I will leave now." I did not leave because he immediately invited me to sit down.

"I want to talk to you, because you speak languages". After a couple of hours, during which, whenever I mentioned the word "Priestman", he interposed with "JCB", he had offered me the position of European Sales Manager, but on certain conditions:

1.   I must decide that I would leave Priestman immediately.

2.   I must move my home and family immediately from Uxbridge to Rocester.

I left, very excited, to think about it. Audrey was prepared to support me absolutely. She relished the prospect of living further north, not far from her native Yorkshire, and felt that it was time for us to have a change. Our daughters, brought up in Uxbridge, were less enthusiastic, and so was I.

Shortly after this, I left to Iran, and I discussed the whole project with Richard Aldersley. "Go for it, Dick", he said. "You deserve it". Still I hesitated, and at the end of this trip, I came back with the Letter of Intent for up to 20 VC15 excavators. I arrived in Hull for a Board Meeting on the very next day. Alan Cooper was delighted. He walked into the Board Room to be greeted by Norman Cunningham with the question as to whether he had got rid of Dick Lloyd yet, since he was useless. "Yes", replied Alan, "absolutely useless - that is all that he can do" and put the paper in front of Cunningham. The change was dramatic. I was called in and congratulated, and it was I who had to warn him that it was not yet an order, and not to get too euphoric about it.

The Board endorsed the sending of a VC15 on a trial basis to Iran, and I told JCB that I would only accept their offer if I could remain in Uxbridge for at least 12 months, to find out whether they liked me and I liked working for them. They refused.

When Acrow collapsed only a few months later, I regretted my decision, but, with hindsight, I do not. I was much too independent to accept the military discipline which working for JCB would have entailed, even though I was to be propositioned once again by JCB a year or two later. I have always held them in the highest respect, and admired them as the greatest British success story in the manufacture of Construction Equipment, but working for them would not have been for me.

However, it was only shortly afterwards that Alan Cooper rang me to stun me with the news that he was going back to JCB. This was, undoubtedly, a terrible blow for Priestman. Alan had served them very well, bringing in new ideas, cutting through the bureaucracy, and driving us all along. I think that everyone regretted his departure. Back at JCB, he was behind the decision for them to go for a Joint Venture with the Japanese in the production of 360 degree hydraulic excavators, and I am sure that he brought with him valuable experience gained in Hull. Sadly, just as he decided to retire in his early 60s, he was diagnosed with a serious brain tumour.

Typically and courageously, he opted for an experimental treatment in the USA, whereby the tumour was deadened by the implantation of an atomic seed, but it left him with terrible side effects, a sick man. The last time on which I saw him, some 10 years after the collapse of Acrow, he could only talk about JCB - his time at Priestman seemed to have disappeared from his memory, which was interesting.

I never saw him again, but I kept in touch with him by phone until his death in February 2003. He was a man whom I liked and respected enormously.

After Alan's departure, Priestman were under the microscope. Duncan Wordsworth, whom Cunningham had brought to manage the Coles manufacturing plants, was given the job of deciding whether we should be closed down. Coles had already closed Glazebury and Darlington, leaving only Sunderland and Grantham to carry on producing cranes, but the latter was also under close scrutiny and eventually suffered the same fate. Wordsworth was not someone who appealed to me personally for a number of reasons. He was a tough man of business, and I was a salesman whose job depended upon getting on with all types of people. But, in the event, we established quite a reasonable working rapport, which came about like this:

He interviewed each of the Priestman directors individually in turn, and I was grilled on my abilities and likely future performance. I was trying to convince him that the Iranian business would certainly materialise into an order, because my experience and gut feeling told me so. The document signed by the bearded brothers "In the Name of God" bound them ethically and morally, and to renege on it would be to offend the cardinal principles of Islam. But how to convince a man like Wordsworth, a calculating businessman, who was primarily concerned with material facts and figures, was a major task. He kept peppering me with questions, until I finally told him, when he actually paused to assess my reaction to the grilling, that I felt like the pilot of an Boeing airliner who was being buzzed by MIG fighters, at which point he seemed to feel that he had pushed me as far as he could and he released me from his office.

At the time I had a visitor in Hull from Germany. He was an old colleague and friend from my Hymac days, one of the salesmen whom I had taken on for Hymac Baumaschinen, Juergend Teltz. He had built up a successful little business selling used hydraulic excavators, and now he was making a concerted effort to introduce the VC15 in to the German market, which was a great challenge for both of us.

All the time that I should have been having discussions with him, he was kicking his heels in my office whilst I was being pinned down by Wordsworth, and when I finally emerged, late in the evening, he rightly blew his top and said that my behaviour was "unverschaemt", which amounts to being impertinent, insolent and ungentlemanly to a degree. All I could do was to apologise profusely and promise that on the next day when his first potential customer was arriving, I would be with him all the time, since I had warned Wordsworth to that effect. Imagine my fury when, halfway through the Works tour with the German buyer I was summoned to Wordsworth's presence once again. I entered his office fuming. "Dick" he said, and he actually apologised for calling me in, "I want your co-operation". "Duncan", I replied, "Am I or I am not being co-operative?" Well what he wanted me to do was to resign my directorship! Really I did not care, and having established that I would not lose out financially, and that I could keep my title, I agreed, even though it meant that I would have to report to John Coates. In fact, Coates left me alone, and when Duncan Wordsworth rang me up a few months later to ask me how I was getting on with him, I said that I had no complaint.

Priestman was not closed down, but more severe cuts were made in the workforce - in fact it was halved from 600 to 300. Charlie Hamshaw had brought in Tim Dillon as his deputy and Tim got rid of demarcation practices within the unions and made those that remained realise that unless there was full co-operation, there would be no jobs. My export department had virtually disappeared, even old stalwarts such as Richard Aldersley and John Davies seeing the writing on the wall. Richard joined Coles for a time and then went off to the USA to seek his fortune. As for John, our paths were to cross again. I was moved from Acrow HQ to the Coles Office in Harefield, which suited me in personal terms, being very near my home, and I did everything for myself, including my own typing. It was a marvellous preparation for the difficult times ahead. But I am not going to pretend that I foresaw the collapse of Acrow.

After all we had made big cuts and sacrifices and had slimmed down to a degree. The VC Range was very exciting, and I had no thought but that my future was secure.

On September 1st, 1984, I returned to the office after my summer vacation, and, three days later, I entered hospital for a hernia operation, which I had deliberately planned to be done under the Company BUPA Scheme at that time. As I waited in my gown to be taken down to the operating theatre, a man selling newspapers came past the ward and I opened the Guardian to read the dramatic headlines:

"Acrow in Receivership"

I really did not know quite what it would mean for me, but I soon found out what it was like trying to continue to work under Cork Gully. One had to ask permission for every action and every letter and telex had to go out signed "On behalf of Manager and Receiver". The Hull Directors were involved in trying to find a buyer for the company, and I felt that the best that I could do was to maintain the morale of the dealers and keep the network in place so that we could continue to sell after we had been bought. I did get involved in one attempt to save the company, which came from James Priestman, and I thought "Well, he does hold the Priestman name, and he may have influence in the City", so against the wishes of John Coates and Tony Bodimeade in Hull, I supported it, but it came to nothing. I lasted until the end of November, and when the axe finally fell on me, it came as a relief. One of the most unforgettable memories of the Receivership period was the complete lack of ethics displayed by the Receivers. A few days after September 4th, we received a telex from Iran confirming that they were ready to place an order for up to 20 VC15s, and inviting me for final talks, but I was not allowed to go. However, we had already sold three Lion cranes in Iran, through a private "agent". All authorized dealers had, of course, been formally informed of the Receivership, but he was not one, being not officially allowed to carry on an agency business in Iran. So when he rang up to say that the cranes had arrived and could we supply the name of the installation engineer, so that he could support his visa application, I had to say, guardedly, "Hussein, you know that we have some problems". "Yes," he replied, "I did hear. What about the technical problem of the differential?" This was the codeword for commission, which was being held by us for disposal at his instructions. I knew that he would not get a penny of it, but I simply replied that we would have to discuss that when I would see him next. I never did, but I explained the matter of our obligation to send an installation engineer to the Receiver, and he sanctioned the visit, after I had given him an estimate of the cost. It took two months for the man to get his visa, and when I applied again for the funds, the Receiver answered: "There is no point in sending him now, since there is no Buyer for the business." I was shocked and flabbergasted, and I protested to him that it was he who had sanctioned the visit, not something which had been promised prior to Receivership. "I've changed my mind" he replied coolly, and nothing I could do would persuade him that he had a moral and ethical obligation to stick to his word. I have never quite got over breaking my word to that Iranian, but there was nothing which I could do about it.

The week after I had been made redundant, I went up to Birmingham to the International Construction Equipment at the NEC, and there I met Norman Cunningham, who asked me what I proposed to do. "Find a job asap" I replied. "Would you like a reference?" he offered, and he gave me a glowing written reference, which certainly helped me. Life is full of surprises. That was the most practical and thoughtful help that I had from anyone in the Acrow Group, on being made redundant.

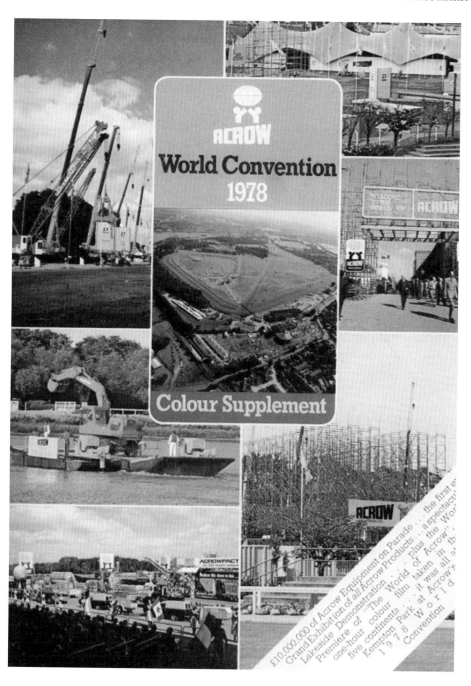

British Exhibition in Beijing, June 1979, opened by "His Loyal Highness, The Duke of Kent," pictured with Li Qiang, Cinese minister for trade.

Sightseeing on the Great Wall of China.

£12,000,000 worth of A
water in a unique 'float p

With special commentary by
well-known broadcaster Raymond Baxter
Thos. Storey Uniflote pontoon ferries display
the many diverse products of Acrow

1. Acrow's Managing Director and Chief Executive, Norman Cunningham, making a welcoming speech to all visitors.
2. Interlude music during each day's events was ably provided by the Regimental Band of the Grenadier Guards.
3. One of Thos. Storey's new Motorflotes which were used for the first time at Thorpe Park to propel the six Uniflote ferries.
4. The entrance to 'Acrowland' at Thorpe Park, flanked for the occasion by Coles cranes.
5. The 'Acrow Girls' display flags of different nations to represent the numerous Acrow Overseas companies, while the Bentall Simplex ferry passes by in the background.

6. Three divisions of Acrow-Adamson Containers, Adamson & Hatchett, and ACV Valves – shared this ferry which is seen getting under way for the water-borne parade.

28

Acrow equipment takes to the past'

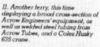

11. Another ferry, this time displaying a broad cross-section of Acrow Engineers' equipment, as well as welded steel tubing from Acrow Tubes, and a Coles Husky 635 crane.

12. In addition to several hundred Acrow delegates from more than 90 countries, thousands of UK and European buyers and decision-makers were at Thorpe Park to see the 1982 show.

13. The exciting climax of the 'float-past' – a Chieftain tank races across Thos. Storey's 280ft floating causeway, which carries the 55 ton weight with ease.

14. The new Priestman VC15 demonstrates its tremendous outreach on a special float.

15. The six Uniflote ferries passing by in convoy after the 'float-past'.

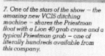

7. One of the stars of the show – the amazing new VC15 ditching machine – shares the Priestman float with a Lion 40 grab crane and a typical Priestman grab – one of literally hundreds available from this company.

8. Thos. Storey's 280ft long floating causeway is manoeuvred into position to act as a bridge for the climax of the water-borne show.

9. Acrow Automation, Crawley Refrigeration and Steels Engineering show off their diverse product ranges on yet another ferry.

10. The massive Coles Octag 8130, with its revolutionary boom, the design of which won a Queen's Award for Technological Achievement, leads the parade.

1982 World Convention Special Report

Priestman

ACROW REVIEW

JANUARY 1983 Vol 9 No 2

The latest news from the Acrow construction equipment and material handling companies

1982 Acrow World Convention earns Multi-Million Pound Orders – see our Special Report inside

Bill de Vigier at the age of 87 at his London office being interviewed for these memoirs in May 1999, and his very long served secretary, Lorna Powell.

AFTER ACROW
PRIESTMAN AND COLES AFTER ACROW AND THE FINAL YEARS OF BILL DE VIGIER

At the beginning of 1985, Priestman was finally acquired by Sanderson, the Rough Terrain Fork Lift Truck manufacturer from Lincolnshire.   Roy Sanderson and I had a lengthy telephone conversation on one occasion, but it was clear that he was only picking my brains as to whom I thought he should retain on the senior management side.   In effect, he made two very good choices in Tim Dillon to run the Works and Ken Deighton the Design Office.   Sales of VC long reach excavators expanded under Sanderson and the VC 20 competed with the traditional dragline on sand and gravel applications.   Following my own success in introducing the VC15 into Pakistan, through a very powerful dealer, more than 20 VC20s were despatched to that country for military use on the Pakistan/Indian border, but there were problems with maintenance and constant visits by service engineers.   But the other core businesses of Sanderson were not in a very healthy financial situation and, not only was he unable to invest in Priestman, but he tried, and failed, to prop up his other businesses with the Hull company.   In 1990 he sold the rights to design and manufacture of the VC Range and the Grabs to RB Lincoln, and that spelled the end of the road for Priestman as an excavator manufacturer.

Ken Deighton joined RB as Chief Engineer to ensure continuance of the production of the VC Range, and, in my view, they improved the product considerably.   Not only that, but they landed the largest and most prestigious order for 25 units of VC20 in May 1991 just after the end of the Gulf War.   The machine was the ideal tool for capping the oil wells which had been destroyed by Saddam Hussein.   Ken Deighton takes up the story: "The machines were required with great urgency and because of the low overall transit height which had been built in to the design concept to make the machine easily transportable on a low-loader, they were able to be despatched to Kuwait on massive Russian transport planes, three units at a time, and 'they hit the ground running'.   They were dispersed around Kuwait to the US Fire Fighting Teams, and by October 1991 they finally succeeded in extinguishing the last of 640 well head fires. Their role had been to rip away the hot oil/charcoal deposits from around the well head fires and let the fire-fighting teams get close enough to extinguish and cap the well heads.   A US oilman involved said that he would like to shake the hands of those at RB who had produced this remarkable machine, but really the whole venture was a tribute to Priestman."

Back in Hull, Tim Dillon rescued the rump of the company and set up Priestman Equipment Ltd in the old Spares Dept in Marfleet Works. Using the ideas and experience of a long served Priestman design engineer, Gordon Scott, who had already designed a small access platform which could be towed behind a Land Rover, he built up a complete range of very specialist access platforms, acquiring further designs through acquisitions. He occupied the whole of the old Spares Department in the Marfleet Works, which had been turned into a Business Park, so the Priestman flag flew on Hedon Road for a bit longer. However Tim eventually sold the company to a firm in Bradford called Syltone, who continue to produce the Priestman range, so that the name still has not totally disappeared from the construction equipment scene, but I think that after he had sold out the drive to keep the name in front of the public tailed off.

The story of Coles after the collapse of Acrow is very different. David Steel and Duncan Wordsworth immediately set about trying to organize a Management Buyout, and they soon obtained the support of the 1000 strong workforce (who were to be offered shares in the company) and the Tyne & Wear County Council, and other local financial institutions. Government was also backing this deal after lobbying by the local MPs. But Cork Gully, the Receivers, hesitated, whilst they investigated a potential bid for the whole of the Acrow Group from an Arab source. Then Grove came into the ring, through their US Parent the Kidde Group, and during October 1984 the battle between the two contenders raged. It was alleged that, if Grove bought Coles, it would create a monopoly, one being at the time the largest US manufacturer and the other the largest European, and attempts to refer the matter to the Monopolies Commission were made, but failed. In the end Grove pipped the Management Buyout at the post by increasing their bid at the last moment, but then came impasse. The workforce, who had backed the Steel/Wordsworth bid, refused to co-operate with Grove. Martin Benchoff, the President of Grove, decided that co-operation with the old Coles management would be the wisest course of action to maintain continuity, and the upshot was that, with their co-operation, a company called Grove-Coles Ltd. was born. Duncan Wordsworth continued to run the Sunderland Works (Grantham had already been closed by the Receiver) and David Steel emerged as MD of Sales of all Grove and Grove-Coles Cranes for Europe, Africa and the Middle East. It was a considerable coup for the defeated organizers of the Management Buyout, because it meant that not much changed, apart from the grafting of the name of Grove on to Coles. It also proved lucky for me in personal terms, but not immediately.

After Acrow

Bill de Vigier continued to be active with the Acrow Overseas companies for another 15 years. Directing the operation from "Acrow S.A.", a Swiss-registered company with a suite of executive offices in the West End, he purchased the Acrow PLC minority shareholdings in the overseas companies and took complete control of them himself. Then, one by one, he sold them off to local managements, gradually divesting himself of further involvement. In his final years, one of his main activities was to establish a foundation in Switzerland to provide funds for would-be young entrepreneurs like he had been to get started.

He remained fit and active right up to the end of his long life. "I vill never retire", he often said, and he never did. Had it not been for a bad fall which he had in the middle of the night in December 2003, he might well still be carrying on, but he had no desire to drag out his life as an invalid and told his family, as they flew him back to his beloved Switzerland to die, that he had had a wonderful life and was content to go.

He hosted a party at Tinkers Lodge in June 2001 for COBBLERS (Coles Old Boys Been Left and Early Retired Society), and he clearly thoroughly enjoyed this re-creation of the past. My lasting final memory of him was when he had a long personal discussion with me in May 1999 after which he invited me to a slap-up lunch at the RAC Club in Pall Mall. The waiter ushered us ceremoniously to a table and he asked me what I would have. I explained that, since my wife is vegetarian, when I go out, I like to eat meat. "Zen" he said, "You vill have a steak". I demurred and asked for the menu and said that I would prefer calves liver and bacon. "Vaiter", he commanded "zis gentleman vill have calves liver and bacon to start with, and zen he vill have a steak". This, for me, epitomised his hospitality and his dominant character

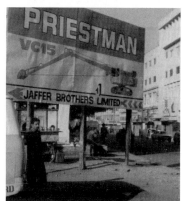

The launch of the VC15 in Pakistan in 1984.

After Acrow

VC15 manufactured by RB Lincoln fighting oil fires in Kuwait in 1991, and Ken Deighton, the Chief Engineer of Priestman, who joined RB to continue making the VC range.

The Priestman name goes on ...

GRABCRANEX

CHAPTER ONE - UNEMPLOYMENT AND SENNEBOGEN

Although it was a relief to be rid of the Receivers, unemployment was a depressing business.   To have to go and queue at the Dole Office to receive the pittance of £27 per week on which one was expected to live was degrading.   I did receive the grandiose sum of £1740 from the Receivers in July 1985, followed by £387 in August 1989, but I just had to dip into my capital in December 1984, when we were paying for our two elder daughters at Haberdashers, as well as a hefty mortgage on the house.

I was very grateful indeed to have a wife who was still earning. Fortunately the Acrow Pension Scheme was protected, but the Receivers, Cork Gully, even tried to claim a substantial share of that.   There had originally been independent Pension Schemes for Coles, Priestman and Acrow (the latter only having been in existence since the Takeover of the Steel Group in 1972), and in all of these schemes a clause stating that the Employers had no right to return of their contributions had been inserted.   Only a few months before the Group collapsed, all three individual schemes were amalgamated into one single Acrow Group Pension Scheme, and this vital clause was omitted.   Whilst basic Pension rights, arising from their own contributions, were secured for those who reached retiring age, the Receivers laid claim to a substantial amount of the pension created by the Employers' contributions, which was therefore withheld, and some unfortunates died before the matter was resolved.

The battle raged in the High Court for years, reminiscent of the case of "Jarndyce vs Jarndyce " in Dickens' novel "Bleak House", and was only resolved in the mid 90s.   Fortunately the monies were wisely invested, and the total fund had, by that time, risen to £13,000,000.   As a former Priestman director, I was eventually involved in legal discussions on the issue of suing the pension advisers for neglect.   Although we apparently had a good case, by this time all the beneficiaries were fed up with the whole business and opted to settle out of Court with the Receivers for a £1,000,000 cut out of the total fund, without trying to get these monies back from the advisers, so that the Scheme could be wound up and everyone paid out.

In most European countries, the State guarantees a very high percentage of the annual salary of any employee of a company which has gone bankrupt, but in the UK it is merely a flat rate for all.   I was determined to get back into employment within two months' maximum - by the end of January 1985.   Nobody was interested in discussing employment over the Christmas Holiday.   Promises to "get in touch" from my colleagues on the FMCEC Council (to which, I had, by that time, been elevated) came to nothing.   Only one true friend offered practical help (and excellent help it proved to be) - Kees Zeevenhooven, the Priestman dealer in Holland, already well recorded in these writings. He recommended that I should get in touch with the Bavarian crane and excavator manufacturer, Sennebogen. I had never heard of them, but I recalled that I had, in fact, made a tour of German crane and excavator manufacturers some time in the late 1970s, on behalf of Taperex, trying to interest them in slewing rings, and probably had, at that time, visited Sennebogen.

I met Erich Sennebogen Jnr at the International Construction Equipment Exhibition in Birmingham in November 1984 in the week following my being made redundant.

My plan was, in fact, to look for a manufacturer to take on the production of the VC long-reach excavator, and sell myself with the product. Erich Sennebogen did not show much interest in the VC excavator, but he certainly did in me, which was much more important. I spoke pretty good German (he spoke very little English at that time, and our discussions were all auf deutsch), and I knew the crane and excavator business, so he asked me if I would like to work with them. "Of course", I answered, "I need employment". "Then you must come to Straubing to meet my father" to which I replied that he would have to pay my airfare, as I had very little to live on. It was agreed. Early in December I flew to Nuremburg, and Sennebogen hired me a self-drive car to go to Straubing. Before I left UK, I had to go to the Dole Office and explain that I would be unable to report that particular week (one had to "sign on" regularly ever week). "No", I said firmly, in response to the question from the goon behind the desk, "I am not going on holiday, I am looking for a job". It was beyond the scope of his experience.....

My first impression of Sennebogen was its similarity to Priestman, or what Priestman might have been if it had remained a family business. The product mix was very much the same - hydraulic excavators and crawler and wheeled lattice boom cranes up to about 30 tonnes in weight. I found that Erich Sennebogen Snr lived in a flat above the offices in the central tower block which dominates the Straubing Works. He still does. Recently he told me the story of how he started the Company in 1952.

As a boy, before the Second World War, young Erich Sennebogen had helped his father, a farmer, mend agricultural implements, thus showing an early interest in engineering. His father died in 1942 - "There was no penicillin" was the laconic comment which I received from him on the cause of his father's early death, which left the young man to stand on his own feet. His grandfather owned a saddlery, and even as a boy during the War, he learned the basis of production and selling. He fashioned money purses from the offcuts in the saddlery to earn a few pfennigs.   Shortly after the end of the War he also soled shoes - in fact he was ready to produce anything for which there was a need - like sparrow-traps, which he manufactured on a series-production basis.

Immediately after the end of the War, he obtained a three year apprenticeship as an engine fitter.   This was just up his street.   It was a very thorough training - there were no text books, but, in his own words, it taught him to think and fend for himself.

In 1948 came the currency reform, and the birth of the Deutschmark which gave a fresh start to entrepreneurs, and Erich Sennebogen started producing a braking mechanism for farm trailers, and a remote control system for ploughs in his grandfather's saddlery in 1950/51.   Lack of workshop space meant that production had to be carried out in the open air.

But Erich Sennebogen was not just an entrepreneurial engineer - he was also a salesman, who carried out his own marketing.   He toured Bavaria on his motor cycle to find out what the farmers needed to mechanize their farms.   In 1951 he engaged his first employee, and kept a regular job himself so that he could earn money to pay this individual.   He put in long hours himself in the evenings and at weekends.

No one supported him financially.   One of his first products was a manure loader, based upon his assessment of local market needs, and this was followed by a farm trailer.   In 1954 he built his own workshop at Piling, where he started to manufacture excavators with backhoe and front shovel with used machine tools.   It was very difficult in immediate post-War Germany to obtain tools and equipment, as there were a number of restrictions imposed on them by the Allies, as for instance that they were apparently not allowed to instal hydraulic systems, which I can only presume was to prevent any kind of re-armament programme being clandestinely undertaken.

Despite all such privations, Erich Sennebogen continued to expand his business by selling his excavators not only in Bavaria, but also in North and West Germany. By 1958 he had 120 employees and the original Works in Piling was already too small. There was a large area adjacent to the Railway Station in Straubing which had been destroyed by bombing in the War.   This was an ideal site for the new Works, enabling finished product to be loaded directly on to rail-wagons for transport.   The first production machine rolled off the line in Straubing in 1960.   By the time of my first visit in 1985, six excavators per day were being produced.

By the end of my first visit to Straubing, the interest that Sennebogen had in me was made clear.   It was to broaden the scope of their sales in the UK.   Up to then it had been confined to Scrap Handling Machines, and they wanted to break in to the Construction and Earthmoving market. The fact that I had no knowledge of the UK Market, having in mind that I had spent almost all of my career in Export, seems not to have affected their desire to enter in to some kind of agreement with me. I had a lot of experience in the industry and I spoke German. Few people in the Company spoke English at that time. Their bread and butter business was the manufacture of excavators for the German market, and sale through the big CAT dealer, Zeppelin Metalwerke, who badged them with their own name and marketed them alongside the larger excavators made by CATERPILLAR themselves. Any exports were then generally confined to the neighbouring German speaking countries of Austria and Switzerland, Holland and Scandinavia where German was understood.

A knowledge of English and sales brochures in the English language were not necessary. Perhaps my appointment was the beginning of a widening of their export sales, because in fact I made initial sallies for them into France and Spain, and I know that I produced the first Operator Instruction Manual for a Sennebogen excavator in the English language.

Sennebogen asked me to work on a commission only basis. I refused point-blank. I knew that it would be an extremely uphill task to introduce an unknown excavator in to the very competitive UK market, and I certainly was not willing to risk my own limited capital in so doing. But I suppose that it was hard for Erich Sennebogen Snr, having in mind his own background, not to expect that I would be prepared to do something similar. However I was not 21 years old and single. I was 51, with a mortgage on my house and daughters at a private school. I had, also, an alternative.

I had been head-hunted by the same organization who had put me up to JCB, for the position of Sales Director, mainly export, with a textile machinery manufacturer in Halifax. I had liked the MD very much and the Company had been through the fire of cutting back and slimming down and was ready for re-expansion. It was an exciting prospect, with no condition that I should move to Halifax. The fact that I knew nothing about textile machinery did not concern them, since the MD had already decided that he must seek a suitable candidate outside the textile machinery industry.

I would fit the bill, he had told me in early December, but he had other candidates to see before he could make a final decision, and he would re-contact me in the New Year. All this I related to Erich Sennebogen Snr. "Aber, Sie sind ein Baumaschinen Man, Herr Lloyd", he said (*You are a Construction Equipment man*). "Yes", I replied, "but I have to earn my living", so he asked me to put forward a proposal for operating for Sennebogen and how much it would cost.

Grabcranex

This I duly did, proposing to work from home, where there was room to make an office, and "my" own car, which was, in fact, Audrey's Metro. I asked for a reasonable amount to cover expenses and a remuneration equivalent to what I had been earning at Priestman, based upon a 12 month contract. Christmas came and went and, on New Year's Day, 1985, after a riotous party with our local friends at the Uxbridge Cricket Club on the previous evening, it suddenly hit me that I was facing the New Year without a job, and severe depression overcame me. Five months earlier I had had what I thought was a secure job, with self-respect. Now I was nobody.

I even suggested to Audrey that we could convert our spacious home in Uxbridge into a Bed and Breakfast business, if all else failed. Her refusal even to entertain such an idea was uncompromising.

Finally in mid- January, 1985, I was invited to re-visit Straubing for further discussions. The upshot of this was that I accepted a six month engagement, with option, if initially successful, to extend for a further six months. The agreement had to be confirmed by the owner of the UK Distributor for Sennebogen, Saville Gordon Machinery. Here Norman Cunningham's glowing reference certainly impressed John Saville, the wealthy Birmingham businessman who was Chairman of the Saville Gordon Group.

The day after I returned from Straubing came a telephone call from Halifax inviting me for a final interview. "Sorry", I said, "you are just too late. I am staying in the Construction Equipment business." It was a defining moment. My association with Sennebogen was to last for many years, from 1984 until I retired from full-time selling in 1998, and up to the present day on a personal basis.

Herr Erich Sennebogen Snr was chatting to an old customer at BAUMA in 1995, when he noticed my approaching him and remarked to his old friend: "Herr Dick Lloyd, der alter Kaempfer! Sollche Leute kann man heute nich mehr finden". It was one of the finest compliments which I had ever received...... ("The Old Fighter. You don't find guys like him any more").

Graham Pearson, who was the director of Saville Gordon Machinery, gave me a cautious welcome. He was already doing an excellent job selling Sennebogen in to the scrap market, and I think that he was probably rather sceptical about the realistic chances of broadening the basis of Sennebogen sales into the earthmoving market. I do not think that he had been privy to the first discussions with me, but he gave me every support and left me alone to get on with the job.

I contacted my old colleague, Arthur Arundel, one of Priestman's longest serving UK salesmen, who had taken over the Southern Area from Rodney Akester.

Arthur himself had got a job with Atlas Weyhausen, so there was another experienced salesman who had sold British all his life forced by circumstances to sell German equipment instead.

Arthur recommended me to a small local dealership quite near to Uxbridge, who were in Plant Hire, had a contracting business, and had a sub-dealership for Japanese Mini-Excavators. It seemed to be an ideal point from which to start, particularly in view of the fact that they were located just down the road.

After a visit to Straubing, they agreed to take on the franchise and order a 16 Tonne excavator, the Sennebogen 216, for stock and demonstration purposes. Then together we organized a visit from the UK Technical Press to Straubing, and representatives from Construction News, Plant Managers Journal, Contract Journal and one or two others flew with me to Straubing. This gave me an initial contact with the industry's Press, which I have maintained and broadened, and I am hoping that these will help publicize these writings!

Then came SED 1985, then held at Whipsnade, where I decided that we must put some colour in to the Show, and I donned a Bavarian jacket and hat for the occasion, whilst my youngest daughter, Fay, served drinks clad in a dirndl. We imported several casks of Straubinger Pilsner, but I grossly over-estimated the quantity of this excellent beer which would be consumed. I do not think that my 1960s experience of the Poznan Fair in Poland was a good yardstick in this respect for SED in the 1980s.

The result was that there were several casks left unopened, which were consumed at home by members of the staff, and in fact we held a special party in July in our garden to empty the one which fell to my portion, which happened to take place on the same day as Boris Becker won the Wimbledon Tennis Final for the first time, making it truly an all-German occasion. The problem of returning the empty casks to Straubing caused ES Jnr some headaches.....

Despite all my efforts, competition in the hydraulic excavator market was such that our success in actual sales was very limited indeed. I therefore decided that we must also tackle the scrap-handling market in the South of England, the actual sales of Sennebogen machines being, at that time, mainly confined to the Midlands and the North. Saville Gordon themselves owned a number of scrapyards where clearly only Sennebogen would be sold. Graham Pearson and his Service Chief, Neil Redfern, operating from a base near Doncaster, obviously concentrated on the North.

I went for a Big Fish, Coopers Metals, one of the largest scrap metal merchants in the country. Graham was sceptical - he knew much better than I what they were like. "You don't make money from sales to Coopers Metals" he told me, and he proved to be right.   I regarded myself as appointed to prove myself by effecting sales - Graham had to show good profits to keep his job, and I have to pay great tribute to his business acumen - in 1989 he and Neil bought Saville Gordon Machinery themselves and expanded and developed the business.   So I turned to Northern Ireland where I knew the scene better than on mainland UK.   The Kobelco dealer was looking for an alternative supplier because of the penalties for dumping then being imposed on Japanese excavator manufacturers.   They ordered six machines, but complained that they lacked digging power when fitted with long arms and became disillusioned.

I did have one personal success story with a company in Essex called Cory Sand and Gravel, but it was one of the toughest sales of an individual machine which I ever had to make, and I think that it illustrates very clearly the magnitude of the task which I was facing.   They were the users of an old Priestman Lion Dragline, and they needed to replace it.   By that time Priestman had ceased to produce Lions and RB and NCK were in disarray, so here was a golden opportunity to introduce a Sennebogen hydraulic dragline.   I took the Plant Manager to Straubing and he was impressed.

Then he delivered me a bombshell: "I am sorry, but we have decided to replace the old dragline with an hydraulic excavator".   "So what", I countered, "we quoted you for that as well."   But here was competition, unlike for the dragline, Akerman, Liebherr, O&K and Atlas - he was honest enough to tell whom I was up against, and none of them were Japanese.

PRICE: I dropped to the lowest level and matched my rivals.

BACK-UP SERVICE: I brought in my local dealer to re-assure him.

Still he hesitated.   Having spent the Company's money taking this customer all the way to Straubing, I just could not face ES Jnr without an order.   I presented my case to John Saville.   He backed me to the hilt.   "Offer him a three month trial", he said, "We will support you".   It worked, the indecisive Plant Manager admitting that I had boxed him in to corner, but he still insisted on a Perkins Engine instead of the standard Deutz, and ES Jnr agreed and engineered it in especially.   I think that this story certainly illustrates to me why Sennebogen are still in business and expanding in today's difficult market - for them the individual customer's needs are paramount.

My efforts earned me a further six months' extension to my contract.   I had by now a potential network of dealers throughout the UK, and in September I organized a small dealer meeting which Erich Sennebogen Jnr. attended personally.   But, inevitably, I could see the writing on the wall, and I began to anticipate that by the end of January 1986 I would again be out of a job.   Towards the end of 1985 matters came to a head.   My local dealer had had no success what-ever in making any sales, but I am sure that they had certainly amortized the cost of the stock machine by using it in their own contracting business and hir-ing it out.   They had some very minor technical problems which they made a big fuss about.   I sent a long telex in German to ES Jnr explaining the urgency of sorting these problems out asap and it was done rapidly by the visit of a Service Engineer.   I had also been to great lengths to cultivate good personal relations with this company, entertaining the owners of the business at my home for dinner with their wives.   They were, clearly, unhappy at their lack of Sennebogen sales success, but this was not for want of effort on my part.   Just before Christmas, I went specially to their offices with small gifts for the staff, who had been most helpful to me.   To my intense shock and surprise, I was ver-bally attacked by the owners.   They made what I regarded as totally unfound-ed accusations about my activities, and, when I tried to defend myself I was physically thrown out of the office.   Never, in my whole career and travel world-wide, had I been so treated.   I am not afraid to admit that I left the prem-ises in tears.   The Dole Queue loomed ahead of me once more....   But I survived and they did not - they went bust a few years later.....

Grabcranex

(above) Young Erich Sennebogen with his manure loader.
(below) The first excavator production in Pilling.

The early workforce.

John Saville, Chairman of Saville Gordon (left) with Graham Pearson and Erich Sennebogen Jnr. who allowed me to show him Oxford University (below) in April 1985.

Sennebogen 216 with hydraulically
articulating boom which I sold for
demonstration exhibited at SED in April
1985, and
(right) my youngest daughter, Fay,
dressed in a dirndl, who served drinks
on the stand.

David Steel's invitation to me to attend the retirement party for Vic Canham *(left)* rescued me from the threat of further unemployment.

CHAPTER TWO - GROVE COLES AND POLAND/DDR

In January 1986 my luck turned. I was invited by David Steel to Vic Canham's Retirement Party. David knew that I wanted to bid farewell to Vic, a true gentleman in every sense of the word, so off I went to the Reception at the Hyde Park Hotel ready to forget my recent troubles and enjoy myself. I succeeded. "Hallo, Dick, good to see you. I hear that you are doing really well" was the greeting which I received from old friends and colleagues. "You are mistaken", I replied, "I'm almost out of a job again". David Steel said: "Come and see me on Monday morning", and Duncan Wordsworth clearly endorsed the suggestion. I had known David long enough to know that it was an invitation with an intent behind it. I carefully up-dated my CV. "There's no director's job here at Grove Coles, Dick" was David's opening remark after briefly perusing the document which I put before him. My reply was succinct and to the point: "David, I need a job, any job within my capability and experience. Titles do not interest me." "Well", he replied, "we need a man of your experience in Eastern Europe, particularly in Poland". I countered that I had not been there for 15 years, except to look at Warynski excavators for Priestman. "You will find that nothing much has changed", he rejoined. In one sense he was totally right. The Communist System was still very much in place, and the methods of doing business unchanged since the 1960s, but the position of Coles (and indeed Grove) who had dominated the market between them for so many years was a thing of the past. This, however, I only found out later.

My appointment had to be vetted by the Sales Director, a Grove Oxford man called David Milne (now MD of Liebherr UK), but this was almost a formality, because my old friend and colleague, Terry Dracup, who had been battling against heavy odds to keep the Grove Coles name alive in Poland had just decided to give up the unequal struggle and resign, so there was a vacancy. I was immensely relieved and grateful to have a job again, but I was soon to find out that there was relief also in Grove Coles at my appointment.

Graham Pearson was, I think, pleased to learn that I had found alternative employment and would not be asking for a renewal of my contract and we parted very amicably, he thanking me for all my efforts under very difficult circumstances. It had been a hard twelve months, the toughest of my whole career, but it had taught me to stand on my own feet and it had given me a very important top level personal contact with Sennebogen, which was to bear fruit later. I was relieved to be receiving a regular income once again and to be part of an export sales team, but I decided that I would go out on my own as soon as circumstances permitted. I did not trust large conglomerates any more, and, in view of the changes which were to take place later in the Grove organization, I

Grabcranex

know that I made the right decision.

Both Grove and Coles had dominated the Polish Crane Market since my involvement in the early 1960s. Grove came on the scene in about 1970 and operated from Bietigheim-Bissingen where their German Sales Organization was located. Coles had entered into Co-operation Agreements and had purchased axles, slewing rings and even hydraulic components from Polish manufacturers. Centrozap in Katowice had long since ceded the crane importing responsibility, first to Polimex in Warsaw, out of which a special Foreign Trade Organization called Bumar had been established in the capital in 1970 to deal specifically with the import and export of Construction Machinery. Bumar employed specialists who understood the technicalities of the product, so that they now wielded much more power than Centrozap had done in the 1960s. There were many more end-users needing cranes which were less powerful than Mostostal, and they relied on Bumar, not only to get them the best commercial deal, but also to give them the best technical advice on what make to purchase. Coles had developed a very close relationship with Bumar and David Steel had had an exceptionally good personal rapport with the Directorate. In the 1970s Coles had literally poured cranes into Poland. In 1972 a special Parts & Service operation had been established in Warsaw as a branch of Mostostal Warszawa, where a large Consignment Stock of parts ensured immediate supply to the end-user. All the commercial transactions had, of course, to go through Bumar. Grove Deutschland had set up a similar arrangement with Mostostal Zabrze in Silesia, and so the two giants dominated the market. The two locations suited both suppliers very well, Warsaw being staffed by English-speaking executives and Zabrze by German-speaking. But temperaments were miles apart, and, following the acquisition of Coles by Grove, and the formation of Grove Coles, attempts to merge these two organizations were beset by difficulties and personal clashes.

At the time that I first arrived on the scene in March 1986, something had gone badly wrong. One would have thought that the coming together of what had been for years the two largest suppliers to the market would have strengthened their position. But the reverse had occurred. Grove Coles UK had taken away the right to sell Grove in Poland from Grove Deutschland and this caused deep resentment. During the period of martial law in Poland in the early 1980s, the man who controlled Grove sales into Poland, Hans-Dieter Schulert, had made substantial donations of food and medicine to Poland via Bumar and was highly regarded. To have put his nose out of joint had been a grave mistake. Twelve months before I joined, Grove Coles UK and Schulert had actually competed for a very large potential order for the Port of Gdansk, Schulert putting forward a "Grove" crane, manufactured by Locatelli in Italy, which was technically accepted by the customer, but Grove-Coles insisted that only the Sunderland-built product be officially offered. They were favoured, but there was indecision on the part of the Management, coupled with the fact that it was only just after the merger of the two companies. Liebherr, hitherto almost unknown in the Polish market stole the business from under their noses - a large order for 14 cranes.

I had walked in to a hornets' nest..... It did not bother me. I soon realised that Grove Coles had taken me on to sort out a mess and that they needed me as much as I needed them. I was in a much more secure position than I had been 12 months earlier. I had to report directly to a much younger man than I, Peter Cooper. A charming guy, he knew that I would be best left alone to do it in my own way and he left me totally to my own devices. For me, it was a challenge. Although I was nominally supposed to handle the whole of Eastern Europe (except Czechoslovakia already covered by a colleague), I decided to concentrate on Poland, so as to avoid dissipation of effort. There was a turnover of £1 million in parts, but the sales of new cranes had dried up. The Parts Manager, Steve Watson, proved to be a great friend and colleague in keeping that ticking over nicely, but he could not help me to revive the sale of cranes. My only other support was Jerzy Szulczewski, known to Coles men for years as "George", who had managed the Coles Mostostal Service since its inception. George had been a UDT* *(see page 355)* Inspector in his earlier days, and was a lifelong anti-Communist, who had refused to join the Communist Youth Organization in the Stalinist period of the late 1940s, which must have taken considerable courage.

I recall that when the Polish service engineers from Warsaw made their very first trip to Shady Grove for training in 1987, they had to fly via Moscow and George issued a strong instruction that on no account must they give any information on the purpose of their journey to the USA, as a result of which one unfortunate individual spent the whole of the transit time in Soviet police custody!

It took me quite a long time to find out just why we were not being taken seriously by Bumar. We issued dozens of quotations in response to the numerous enquiries which flowed in, and the Admin Staff at Harefield gave me superb back-up. I began to learn myself the useful art of word processing, but it was all wasted effort. David Steel and I met the top management of Bumar in March 1986 at the BAUMA and again at the Poznan Fair in June, but his high level personal connections were no longer there, and we were simply told that the end-users now preferred Liebherr and Demag, and that there was nothing which they could do about it.

Grabcranex

I bought a Polish Linguaphone Course and started to teach myself some rudimentary Polish. The annual Poznan International Fair was still, at that time, the major event in Poland, where, if you failed to participate, it was assumed that you had given up trying to sell in the market. I fired the Warsaw based "agent" whom I had inherited and opted for a policy of direct selling myself. I was already aware that this was partly the reason for Liebherr's success - their man on the ground, Hans Puvogel, who visited the market regularly, had an excellent reputation, and customers much preferred to deal with foreigners, who commanded a status to which no Pole could aspire.

However I needed a backstop, someone whom I could trust implicitly and who could make appointments for me and act as my interpreter. There was only one candidate for that position, my dear old friend Alfred Gorniok, who had continued to organize the Poznan Fair Stand for Coles since I had set him on in 1960, and who had Coles in his blood. He had just retired at the age of 60 and was very pleased to join me.

I have earlier mentioned that he was a superb "Mr. Fix-It" under the Communist regime and now he employed his talents and his contacts to his own advantage, as well as to mine. He had been very upset at the way in which Coles had lost the market after his long association and, on our first re-union, he uttered the greeting: "Thanks God you have come". He got himself engaged by the Poznan Technical Information Bureau as an official who would disseminate technical literature for us and arrange appointments for me for a fee of US$1600 per annum, out of which they gave him a pittance in złotych. Of course we topped this up by paying him illicitly what was for us peanuts, but, converted at the black market rate, a comparative fortune for him. One could still play tunes on illegal currency exchange, and, after I had paid my basic hotel bills in hard currency (all booked in London, and secured by vouchers), Alfred could supply me with złotych at a very good rate, for my other expenses. In this respect, nothing had changed since the 1960s.

To start with, I used to drive the company barouche, a roomy Ford Station Wagon all the way from the UK and do trips of 2 to 3 weeks at a time. My first such trip, in July 1986, was memorable. After the Poznan Fair in June, I left the barouche at Hannover Airport. Arrived back on a Monday afternoon, I spent the best part of an hour arranging all my belongings and papers for the trip. This involved such details as ensuring that my Duty Free bottle of sherry (purchased for my own consumption) was secreted in my suitcase, for sipping in my hotel room, and stocking up with beer and lemonade before crossing the West German border in to the DDR.

I had never relished the drive through the East German People's Republic and

Grabcranex

on the way back from the Poznan Fair, I had inadvertently strayed from the direct route from Frankfurt on Oder (in strict contravention to the conditions of the Transit Visa) and found myself in a line of Trabbies heading for Halle. "Trabbie" was the nickname for the Trabant, the East German People's car, small and squat like a toad, with a two-stroke engine which puffed out noxious fumes in thick clouds behind it. An old joke from the 1960s recounted how a Trabant met a Donkey on the road and the latter said: "Good morning, Motor-Car", to which the Trabant replied: "Good Morning to you, Donkey". The Donkey was most upset by this and rounded on the Trabant, telling him that if he was greeted so politely, he should have replied: "Good Morning Horse"! When one arrived at "Kontrollpunkt Marienborn", the East/West German bor-der crossing point just outside Helmstedt, after the usual stupid enquiry: "Haben Sie Funk, Waffen?" (Have you a radio, or arms?), they would demand that the bonnet and boot lid be opened, and they had a mirror at the end of a long pole on wheels which enabled them to see whether there was any fugitive hang-ing to the underside of the car. Their manner was always brusque, so that it was with a sigh of relief that one let the clutch in to carry one over to the bright lights of Helmstedt.

On this return journey I had planned to start my sales tour in Szczecin, so it was an unfamiliar route through the DDR. On the northern part of the Berliner Ring, I was unsure of which direction to take and I stopped very briefly on the hard shoulder to take a look at the map, carefully putting on my hazard warn-ing lights, although the autobahn was totally devoid of traffic. Two minutes later I was overtaken and pulled in by the Volkspolizei. I was sure that I had not been exceeding the 100 kph speed limit, so what could be my crime? It proved to be stopping on the autobahn not in a Parkplatz. Useless to explain that I was a complete stranger to the area and was only looking at the map. DM50 fine. My only satisfaction was that, while standing at the roadside checking my documents, both Vopos were attacked and bitten by ants, who crawled up their trouser legs. I managed not to laugh.... Ten minutes later, I was again flagged down by the Vopos. "Bloody hell, what next?" I cursed to myself, but it was only a document check. Small wonder that I was relieved to get over the Polish border. In the 1960s the Customs and Immigration offices used to be separate, but now they seemed to have merged, and on another occa-sion when I thought that I was over the Polish border and was accosted by an East German official, I said, innocently: "Bin ich noch in Deutschland?" ("Am I still in Germany?") to which he spat back at me: "Nein, Sie sind in der DDR!" (No, you are in the GDR!") "Not one moment longer than I need to be" was my unspoken reply.

I got lost finding the hotel in Szczecin and it was 10.30 pm before I reached it,

Grabcranex

thinking that there would be no hope of a much-needed hot meal at that hour, but was delighted to hear that the restaurant would be open until midnight, and I had an excellent steak, washed down by red wine and followed by coffee and brandy.   An extremely inebriated gentleman came and sat down at my table, but when I signalled to the waitress, she promptly ushered him firmly away. The next day I visited both Port and Shipyard.   Nobody from Grove nor Coles had visited for a very long time and my reception was extremely cordial, interpreters being found who could speak English or German.   The first courtesy prior to any meeting in Poland was the offer of Herbata (black tea from China), or Kawa (grainy coffee served in a tall glass), always served with great ceremony.   Old-fashioned courtesy lived on in Communist Poland.   What a contrast from dealing with scrap metal merchants in the East End of London!

From Szczecin I drove right across the north of Poland to Gdynia and Gdansk, travelling first on the old German autobahn, unrepaired since Hitler had built it. It was very important to fill one's tank with petrol before leaving any large town, since roadside petrol stations were few and far between, and, in fact, I always carried a couple of jerry-cans for safety.   Westerners could obtain petrol at West German prices by purchasing coupons in hard currency.   Locating petrol stations at night was particularly difficult, since they were usually ill-lit and set back from the road and one had to keep one's eyes peeled for the tiny pump sign at the roadside appearing in the glare of one's headlights.

The working hours were from 0800 to 1500, after which Poles went home to their main meal of the day, but they kept themselves going throughout the day with home-made sandwiches.   I used the afternoon for travelling between towns, and, since there was nowhere to eat outside the main Orbis (State Travel Bureau) hotels, I used to order extra rolls, cheese or ham with my breakfast and snack lunch en route, always making sure that I had a stock of beer in the boot of the car.   The other necessity which I carried was a camping gas stove, kettle and tea-bags.   Lloyd could not operate without his four o'clock cuppa and once when I had a German visitor with me, he watched, astounded, as I pulled in to a parking place and ignited my stove, and declared that when he related this to his family back home they would not believe him!

On another occasion, when I just pulled off the road, not in an official parking place, I was approached by the police and asked to show my passport, and then asked to move on as soon as possible.   I had inadvertently stopped near the barracks of the Secret Police!

On that first trip, I gave a lift to a family, a young couple with a small girl, all the way from Gdansk to Czestochowa in the South, a distance of some 500 km., which included an overnight stop and meeting in Torun.   I simply dropped them off in the evening at a boarding house and found them again on the roadside the next midday. They belonged to a hitch-hikers association, evidenced by a sign with a red circle which the girl had used to flag me down, and this covered them for insurance whilst accepting lifts. They were heading for Katowice for a few days' holiday in the mountains, and my kindness was re-paid in full because she spoke quite good English, and assisted me in finding the way. My meeting in Czestochowa was with a construction company definitely in the market for a new crane, who had visited us at the Poznan Fair. We were late, and first of all some of all the electrics on the car packed in and I found myself without fuel gauge and direction indicators, and then we ran out of petrol. I literally abandoned the car to the care of my hitch-hikers, and hastened on foot to keep my appointment, already after the appointed time. The director was about to leave, and was reluctant to meet me, but I persisted and he handed me over to some colleagues to complete the discussions and it was one of the first serious sales prospects which I had. When I got back to the car, the girl's husband had managed to fix the electrical problem, filled the tank from the jerrycan and re-started the engine! I dropped them off at the station in Katowice with a bottle of cheap brandy stuffed into one of their rucksacks. I was less lucky with my next hitch-hiker, a young lad who turned out to be as pissed as a rat, and kept chattering at me in Polish and offering me cigarettes which I certainly did not want, and then he kept tapping me on the shoulder until I realised that he was bursting for a pee! I was glad to be shot of him when I reached my destination, and firmly refused his pressing invitation for me to have a drink with him. I was rather more careful about picking up hitch-hikers after that experience.

Finding my way around Silesia on that first trip was far from easy. Certainly the hotel was a great deal more comfortable than the gloomy Hotel Monopol which I remembered from the 1960s. But the only maps which I could obtain were out-of-date old town plans obtained from second hand bookshops, which did not cover more than a part of the whole area where Katowice, Bytom, Ruda Słanska, Śląskie Piekary and Zabrze seemed to merge one in to another, and the only common link were the trams which weaved their way crazily along uneven tracks through the unending soot-covered urban sprawl and out in to the countryside. It is not surprising that I was an hour late for my first appointment. My direction finding started with a long dissertation with a friendly policeman, who invoked the aid of a roadmender to decide between them which was the best route to show me. Their advice proved not to be very good, so I stopped again to ask the way of two more roadmenders, one of whom was so delighted to learn that I spoke German that he danced up and down thumping his hands on the bonnet of the car and singing: "Ich bin von ober-Silesien", until I realised that he was as drunk as an owl (at 0830 in the morning). But everyone was extremely helpful and one citizen even rode with me in the car for a short distance to put me in the right direction. By the time that I reached the hospitable Gorniok flat in Poznan on Friday evening for the weekend, I was completely exhausted.

But it was not enough for me simply to enjoy the freedom of touring around Poland. I had to get a result and quickly. At the Poznan Fair I had hosted a large meeting of end-users at which various senior executives from the company spoke and I rounded it off with some words in pidgin Polish, which Alfred had translated for me and I wrote the pronunciation out phonetically. It got a round of applause and one delegate said that he felt that there was a wind of change blowing through the Grove Coles organization. One very important customer who attended that meeting was Petrobaltic of Gdansk. This was an Off-Shore Oil Company, jointly owned by three governments, Poland, DDR and the Soviet Union. They needed a large capacity self-propelled mobile crane for their wharf. For me there were three advantages:

1.   Liebherr could not meet the required spec.

2.   Bumar would not be involved, since the customer preferred to deal with Centromor, a very old-established FTO in Gdansk, very much involved in the local scene and suppliers of equipment to Ports and Shipyards in the area.

I went after this customer with a single-minded determination to get the business at whatever cost. I was lucky in that Grove had only one of a short series of 150 Tonne capacity RT cranes available, the largest Rough Terrain crane built at that time in the world, the RT1650, of which, coincidentally one was already in operation in Poland. The crane could pick and carry an amazing 90 Tonnes on the hook. Most had been sold to China and had been mis-used by being driven like trucks and had had major transmission problems, as had the one at the open cast coal mine at Turow in Southern Poland. The last unit was being used as a yard crane at the company's headquarters at Shady Grove in Pennsylvania, so that the list price of $1,000,000 was discounted by 50% and at a little under $500,000 I secured the order in October 1986 after a whole week of hard negotiations in Gdansk. I became frustrated at the slow decision-making process between the UK Sales HQ and Shady Grove and, poised finally to sign the contract I gave Peter Cooper an ultimatum that I would sign in any case by a certain time on a certain date if the OK had not been given. It was.....

In February 1987 I made my first visit to Shady Grove for the Takeover. I was very impressed. The Works seemed like a very well oiled machine. Everyone was very friendly - office doors all open, and a relatively modest entry hall - I

had expected something very ostentatious like JCB.   Everyone drove themselves around the vast Works in vehicles, except for me.   Lack of my usual exercise, coupled with too much to eat and drink induced me to walk from the
offices two or three times a day down to the Test Track where the crane was
being put through its paces.   I had a pair of suede boots to keep my feet warm
in the winter cold of Pennsylvania and, on one occasion, a fork truck driver
stopped to gawp at the eccentric Englishman striding down the length of one of
the shops with incredulity.   Finally he found words: "Say, those boots are sure
made for walkin'" and off he drove without waiting for a reply.

They loaned me a car to collect my first Polish Takeover Delegation from
Kennedy Airport in New York.   LOT, Polish Airlines, only flew to New York,
and Polish business travellers were not allowed to fly on any other airlines
(involving expenditure of precious hard currency) unless it could possibly be
avoided.   The Delegation consisted of the Centromor representative, Lech
Ptasinski, a cultured man with whom I established an excellent personal rapport, Werner Kaeppler from the DDR, a Polish Petrobaltic engineer, and the key
man, the UDT Inspector, Roman Albinski.

The Urząd Dozoru Technicznego, or Technical Supervision Authority, which
had existed since the 1930s, had started to inspect cranes the late 1960s.   They
would have ben horrified at our experience in erecting the Coles Endurance
Truck Crane at the 1960 Poznan Fair recorded earlier in these writings, for they
were a very strict and exacting body, and, if the crane did not pass the inspector's scrutiny, it could not be shipped, so it was also very important to keep on
the right side of this official.   George Szulczewski was himself, as already mentioned, an ex-UDT Inspector and he warned me (fortunately) that Albinski had
a drink problem.   Grove had provided a cottage on the estate known as the
Lodge, located in pleasant wooded country some distance from the Works,
where important customers were entertained and conferences held.   This was
the baby of the President Martin Benchoff, and it was a very splenditerous setup with a Cordon Bleu cuisine in the main complex.   When I became independent and was the Grove agent rather than employee, we had to arrange our
own accomodation, but the highlight of each trip was the night when Grove
hosted us at the Lodge.

On that first trip, we started off with a weekend of sightseeing in New York (an
essential part of every Takeover, as I was soon to learn), so that we arrived late
on the Sunday evening at the Lodge, I having lost the way several times.   There
was a well-stocked bar in the cottage, and plenty of alcoholic refreshment
always oiled the wheels of the Takeover, but on that first night Albinski got very
drunk indeed and my heart sank, because the Takeover was due to last some 10

days. What was worse was that he managed to lock himself out of his room and blamed me for his predicament.

I offered to let him sleep in my bed, but he declined and spent the night on the couch in the lounge. By the morning he had recovered, and after that I did my best to ensure that I restrained him as far as I could, suggesting that a cup of tea would be more appropriate than a beer when we got back to the cottage at 4 pm from the day's activities, and, to be fair, he took a grip on himself and there were no more problems.

A Polish Takeover was always an extremely boring business, with an infinite number of tests to be carried out on the crane and carefully recorded, a host of documentation to be completed in both languages, and, what was to become the bane of my life, the crane had to be festooned with Polish decals. The US Product Liability Regulations stipulated that every possible misuse of the crane or potential danger point had to be the subject of a warning sign."Nie Deptac̓ " - "No Step" still haunts my dreams of that period, but that was the simplest one, many times repeated. The more complicated were individual to each model, and some had to be produced on steel or aluminium plates. Even if one sold the same model a year or two later, often the old decal had been re-worded and the original Polish equivalent which we had in stock was not acceptable (it was only economic to produce them in batches of 10).

Grove Quality Dept insisted that every prescribed decal must be in place before they would allow the crane to leave the Works. The UDT Inspector insisted that every decal (even if not actually required by Polish Regulations) that was on the crane must be in Polish. It was a nightmare. When I retired in 1998, I had still a large stock of Polish decals, initially costing hundreds of £, which were quite worthless, apart from the £5 note which I got from a scrap metal merchant for the aluminium ones!

It was fortunate for me that the Head of Quality in Shady Grove at that time was a young man named Greg Davis, because it was their very first experience of a Polish delegation, which helped me in later years when he had transferred to Sunderland, due to the excellent personal rapport which we had established. The crane finally passed its rigorous inspection, but not before several adjustments had to be made to the internal stabilizers before it could achieve its maximum "Pick & Carry" duty of 90 Tonnes on the hook and this caused problems later. The conclusion of successful tests at the Works was not the end of the story - the crane had to be re-tested on site after arrival in the presence of another UDT Inspector, always the local man, whose nose had probably been put out of joint because it was not he, but a senior inspector from Head Office in Warsaw (like Albinski) who had had the privilege of a trip abroad. All delegates travelling overseas were paid "Daily Allowances" in hard currency by the manufacturers whom they visited, supposedly for out of pocket expenses like meals and drinks.   But Grove then (and Grabcranex later as the agent), like all other companies, always paid for everything, so that in fact going on an overseas delegation was the only means for a Pole to get his hands on highly prized foreign currency in the days of Communism.

So when the crane arrived on site the problem with the internal stabilizers reappeared and I did not make myself very popular with Grove Coles Service in Sunderland by insisting aggressively that it be put right asap.   It took several months for a design modification to be worked out - the fact that it was the last of the line sold at a knock-down price did not help my cause.   That I had relieved the company of a used white elephant was quickly forgotten.   Finally the customer lost patience and I was summoned to Gdansk in October 1987 to face his wrath.   Alfred came with me as interpreter, but his presence proved unnecessary.   The Soviet Managing Director presided over the discussions, which were conducted in Russian, and translated directly into English by their own interpreter.   I attempted to communicate in German directly with Werner Kaeppler and was firmly put in my place by the Russian.   Alfred, as a patriotic Pole, was incensed beyond words by the use of the Russian language in the Polish city of Gdansk.   Fortunately I had come to the meeting well prepared, since we had the technical solution by then, the parts required and the Polish service engineer standing by to carry out the work.   I took the wind out of their sails by eating humble pie on behalf of Grove for the problem, and I agreed to extend the warranty by a further six months.   I had no authority to do this, but, as Grove were to discover later on, I sometimes took decisions on their behalf, if I felt that the customer had a justifiable case, and there was little that they could do about it, apart from curse me.

12 months' later when I re-visited Petrobaltic, I received the warmest of welcomes from Werner Kaeppler, for standing up for them.   They were very satisfied with the crane's performance, and I was presented with a jug and set of beer mugs.   The crane is still working very well as I write these lines more than 15 years later and I believe that it is the only RT1650 in the world still in operation.

The visit to Shady Grove was, for me, the first of many, and one of the things my American colleagues had to get used to was understanding my strange use of the English tongue, which caused quite a lot of merriment.   But then I had to accustom myself to the equally strange (for me) way of making a cup of tea. There were any amount of coffee machines in the Works, but not a single kettle, and the only way was to put a cup of water in the Microwave and then, when it was hot, stick a tea-bag in it.

Grabcranex

Once, having just arrived from the UK, I was speaking to Sunderland and complaining that I was "knackered", and had to explain to the girl overhearing my conversation what it meant, and, more difficult, how it came to have the meaning of being completely exhausted. On the last day of the RT1650 Takeover we awoke to find ourselves completely snowed in, the cottage being surrounded by a metre's depth. Time was tight and arriving late at the Plant not an option, so at 6 am I started to dig my way out to the car with a saucepan from the kitchen, and ably assisted by the efficiency of the local authority who arrived with a snow-plough not much later, we were there on time. My answer to questions as to how we had achieved such a feat was incomprehensible. "A saucepan", I repeated, "a cooking pot, if you will". "Oh, you mean a pa-a-an" the girls all screamed in mirth. I think that they regarded me definitely as something from another planet, but their genuinely warm courtesy towards me is a strong memory.

But the RT1650 success had no influence on my efforts to crack the anti Grove Coles attitude within Bumar. My discussions there always took place with a bearded young man named Paweł Kędzierski, who spoke excellent English, and, as Technical Adviser, clearly knew much more about hydraulic tele-boom cranes than I did. He was usually accompanied by his older German-speaking colleague, Marian Kukawka, and whilst they were both always extremely courteous, I had the feeling that our discussions were, for them, nothing more than a polite formality. I was up against a further disadvantage. Every contract had a Compensation Trading Clause in it, in which one had to agree to purchase Polish engineering products up to a value of 20% of the value of the contract for the crane, or face a penalty amounting to 3% of the Contract price.

Building this extra 3% in to the price make-up effectively killed our competitiveness.

Our German competitors got round it because the groups to which they belonged did in fact purchase from Poland, but attempts to induce Grove Purchasing to invest in Polish made axles or slewing rings, as had been done in the old days of Coles, were a complete waste of effort.

I followed up the sales prospect in Czestochowa vigorously, and matters came to a head in January 1987 when I arrived at Warsaw Airport on a freezing Sunday afternoon for a meeting with them the next morning. I set off as it fell dusk in a hired Polonez of Polish manufacture, and the roads were so icy that 40 kph was the maximum speed at which I could drive with safety. The heater was so inefficient that I was obliged to stop every hour and get out of the car and jump up and down, cabby's flipping my frozen hands at the same time, to restore my circulation. The warmth and cheerfulness of the modest but com-

Kontrollpunkt Marienborn, no longer in use but I feel guilty taking these photographs, expecting the ghost of a Vopo to challenge me.

Grabcranex

Hitch-hikers who helped me on my way.

Polish National Day, 1986.
Back on the road in Poland after a gap of almost 20 years.

The Takeover at Shady Grove of the RT1650 February 1987. Werner Kaeppler (DDR) is on my right in the centre, Lech Ptasinski and UDT inspector, Roman Albinski on the right.

Grabcranex

The RT 1650 on test.

February 1987. The Lodge at Shady Grove.   I dig my way to the car with a "saucepan".

fortable hotel which I reached at about 10 pm were unforgettable, especially as the Christmas decorations were still up, by tradition until the end of the month. After my meeting I drove on to Krakow. I had attempted to fill up with petrol, but the lock on the tank was completely frozen, so after my next meeting I went to the car hire depot to complain that it was broken.   The guy came out with some newspaper and a box of matches, which he proceeded to light and then hold up against the petrol tank for about five minutes, whilst I stood back at a safe distance anticipating the explosion which miraculously never came.   It did the trick and I was able to re-fuel; but the next day the windscreen shattered and with that I had had more than enough of driving in those conditions and I handed the car in at the Katowice Depot and returned to Warsaw by train.   But the week was crowned with "success" by the signature of a contract for the crane for Czestochowa at Bumar.   Kędzierski and Kukawka had wry smiles on their faces, for they knew that it was very unlikely that the customer would be able to raise the foreign currency to finalise the purchase the crane.   It was built and brought to the 1987 Poznan Fair, and then had to be returned to Germany.

Paweł Kędzierski had joined Bumar in 1973 with a university degree in engineering. By 1981 he had graduated to the position of Technical Adviser. A man of independent spirit, he had managed in 1979 to organize a "sabbatical" trip lasting over twelve months, touring all round Africa, and keep his job on his return. He had managed to accrue quite a long leave entitlement, but he craftily extended it by sending cables from obscure places informing his bosses that due to unforseen circumstances he would have to postpone the date of his return, always making sure that he moved on before they had any chance to reply.   He still had his job waiting for him on his return, which was a tribute to his value.   He commented on the reluctance of any so-called manager to make any decision in those days, with pieces of paper requiring an authorized signatory being passed from hand to hand!

Paweł was unimpressed by the deteriorating quality of Coles cranes in the early 1980s, and, in defiance of the wishes of his pro-Coles directors, he started advising end-users to consider Liebherr and Demag, and he and Hans Puvogel formed a close personal relationship.   Matters came to a crunch in 1983 when two Coles RT cranes purchased by the huge open-cast coalmine, Kopalnia Bełchatow, failed to pass the UDT Inspector's test in Sunderland.   The Inspector who accompanied Paweł on that particular trip, Iwo Jakubowski, later became the President of that august organization. The problem had to do with the internal stabilizers and attempts were made to pull the wool over the eyes of the Polish delegates by over-inflating the tyres on one side of the crane. They were rightly incensed at this ruse and decided to leave, which would mean that their return visit would have to be additionally paid for by Coles.

Grabcranex

The Works Management refused to offer them transport from the Works unless they signed the Protocol of Acceptance, so they departed by taxi infuriated at the rude treatment which they had received. Paweł Kędzierski was absolutely anti-Coles from that moment on and this was the problem which faced me in trying to revive their sales, but it was only some years' later that I found all this out.

I had not been with Grove Coles many months when I took my first steps towards independence. I suggested to David Steel that I solve the Compensation Trading problem myself by promoting the sale of Warynski hydraulic excavators in the UK. They were ruggedly constructed and had already sold in some quantities in the Republic of Ireland and Holland, but these sales had been made in the 70s. Kees Zeevenhooven and I had attempted to persuade Norman Brocklebank to badge their small wheelmount as a Priestman in the early 70s, but after trials in the UK old Brock had turned it down, probably wisely. I also had knowledge of Warynski from my Hymac days when I had negotiated the licence deal which was never ratified.

So I was genuinely optimistic that something could be done. I found an ex-Coles/Priestman service engineer, now running his own business, to undertake the after-sales service. David Steel agreed to this arrangement provided that Grove Coles would not be involved in any financial risk. I agreed, and the already formed Grabcranex could now be made public. We exhibited the Polish version of the Priestman Cub Dragline (there had still been limited demand for Cubs in my latter days at Priestman, but no-one was interested in a Polish Cub!), and a 16 tonne hydraulic excavator at the Haydock Show in the Spring of 1987. An Irish contractor bought the excavator off the Stand at a price about 40% below that of the equivalent JCB.

It broke down on the first day of operation. Swarf was found in the hydraulic system, which had to be totally cleaned out and the pump replaced. The customer was very satisfied with the digging performance of the machine, but the reliability was appalling and all the purchase moneys disappeared rapidly in settling warranty claims. Bumar were most embarassed. I believe that the machine had been deliberately sabotaged in the Works. The shop floor were very used to turning out shoddy machines (I am sure that the quality had deteriorated since the 70s) and despatching them to the Soviet Union from where no complaints were ever issued, that the last thing they wanted was to have to improve quality for the UK market. But all this helped me to my first contract with Bumar for Grove Coles. The two Ks decided to give me a break - they felt that Liebherr and Demag were becoming too complacent, and we had an end-user who was still pro-Coles, so that in December 1987 I came home with a contract for three Sunderland built 60 Tonne AT865 cranes with the Compensation Trading Clause waived by the Management.   It had taken me 18 months to break back in.

I realised now that I had to broaden the base of the local representation.   Alfred Gorniok's son-in-law, Jerzy Tracz, had just returned in 1987 from a year in the USA, where he had gone, illegally according to Polish regulations, to learn English.

He had worked in a Chinese Restaurant in New York, and had trained as a draughtsman prior to his departure.   I had, of course, known his wife, Ewa, since she was a little girl of 5.   Here, clearly, was a young man of talent and enterprise whom I could trust implicitly.   I think that Alfred was a little jealous of his son-in-law coming on board, so it was agreed that we would let him loose on customers in the southern part of Poland, whilst Alfred retained contact with Ports and Shipyards in the North.

The Takeover of the three AT865s in mid-1988 just had to go well, so I left Jerzy Tracz to concentrate on establishing a good personal rapport with Paweł Kędzierski, who was leading his first delegation to Sunderland since the 1983 debacle. Fortunately it all went quite smoothly, since, at the first sign of any hiccup, I bearded whoever was in charge aggressively to put the matter right.

In the Spring of 1987 Grove Coles found a permanent car for me in the form of a well-used Ford Taunus Estate Car with a left-hand drive which had done much duty in Yugoslavia.   It was left for me to pick up at Munich Airport, and after a week or two in Poland I left it at Grove Deutschland's new HQ at Recklinghausen to be properly serviced, only to learn that I had been driving it around Poland in a pretty dangerous condition.   But thereafter all I had to do was to fly into Germany and collect the car, but it was still involved an overnight stop at Helmstedt and an effective two day trip from the UK into Poland.   On one occasion I had driven through the DDR all the way to Katowice on the second day and, extremely tired, I missed a bend and drove off the road, fortunately with no serious result.   So I decided to see if I could do something in the East German People's Republic en route, despite my antipathy to the country.

Dia-Maschinen-Export was located in East Berlin, but, rather than tackle them direct, I engaged the services of a go-between in West Berlin, Deutsche Handels-Gesellschaft West-Ost, who travelled through Checkpoint Charlie every day to talk to the FTOs of the DDR.   Most businessmen stayed in West Berlin and simply walked through the checkpoint for the day, which was relatively simple and required no visa.   I found that the hotels in East Berlin were less expensive and more comfortable (one still had to pay in Deutschmark), and that I preferred the rather old-fashioned pre-War atmosphere on the eastern side of the border to the brash modernity of West Berlin. So crossing through Checkpoint Charlie became second nature to me. On one occasion I was carrying a book which I was reading entitled: "The Best Years of their Lives", a very entertaining account of the two years of National Service which all young Brits of my post-War generation had to experience, and the pictures of uniformed soldiers on the cover led the frontier guard to suspect that it was a subversive military manual, and I had difficulty in preventing him from confiscating it!

On another occasion, just in front of me an elderly Mercedes, driven by a middle-aged West Berlin lady, broke down in front of the East Berlin checkpoint. As I sat in the Taunus, patiently waiting for the problem to be resolved, the Vopo came up and appealed for my assistance in pushing the old car back over the border in to West Berlin. The driver steered whilst the two of us pushed and eventually gained enough momentum to get the heavy old car rolling, when he suddenly threw up his hands and shouted at me: "Ich darf nicht weiter gehen!" ("I dare not go any further"), anticipating, probably with good reason, that he might be shot in the back by one of his Kamaraden, as a potential escapee.... So Lloyd ended up by pushing the West Berlin lady safely back into her home city, and was rewarded by an extremely short and cursory formality to complete his entry into the Haupstadt der DDR.

My sole business success in the DDR was to sell some parts for some ancient Coles diesel electric truck cranes sold in the 1960s by my old rival, Stephen Grey, but we did exhibit once at the Leipzig Trade Fair with an information stand, in March 1988, and this was another unforgettable DDR experience. Peter Cooper came with me and we turned up without an hotel booking. When we arrived at the Auslander Treffpunkt (Reception Centre for Foreigners) we found that there was a room for one night only at the Hotel Deutschland. I assured Peter that once you had a hotel room in Eastern Europe it was always possible to hang on to it, and off we went in the morning to the Messe, but returning in the evening we faced the wrath of the Receptionist: "Wir haben Ihnen gesagt nuer fuer eine Nacht!" ("We told you for one night only!") he said aggressively, and we had to clear out quick, but when we came to pay the bill they refused to accept the Ostmark which we had been obliged to change at the border in order to obtain a visa, and this time it was my turn to become aggressive: "Und wass soll ich mit diesen verdamften Papier-Geld machen?" ("And what shall I do with this cursed paper money?"), but it was like water off a duck's back - they just shrugged their shoulders and insisted on a D-Mark payment.

So we found some lodgings with a charming family (who, of course, were only allowed to accept Ostmark).   The standard of living in East Germany was always relatively high compared to the rest of Communist Europe, but it was like walking into a Time-Warp, since one might have been entering a house in the 1930s.   We were warmly greeted and introduced to all members of the family, including Grandma, who sat in imperious and stately isolation at the head of the table.   The old lady was clearly as deaf as a post, since her son went right up to her and bellowed in her ear: "Sie haben Messe-Gaeste!" *(You have guests from the Fair!")*, which she still had not heard correctly and so he turned to us and uttered a masterpiece of understatement: "Die Omar hoert nicht so gut" *("Grandma is rather hard of hearing").*

Some years later, long after the Berlin Wall had come down, Audrey and I travelled to the Poznan Fair via a ferry-boat to Denmark and we journeyed through the hinterland of East Germany, passing through quite poor villages with old-fashioned cobbled streets which played havoc with the car's suspension. However I never felt like stopping overnight anywhere - it was too much of a hang-up from the past.   Of course many Polish villages were similar, but there was always a feeling of comparative freedom or relaxation in Poland.   The Polish police were just as keen on fining motorists as the Vopos, but, not only were the fines much less onerous, but one could always discuss and even joke with a Polish policeman.   For exceeding the 100 kph speed limit on the DDR Autobahn, one was fined DM 100.   If one could not pay on the spot, a stamp in the passport was enough persuasion that one might not get another entry visa if one attempted to dodge payment.   The normal fine in Poland, at that time, was zł. 2000, which was about $2 at the Black Market rate of exchange.   On one occasion, after being stopped, I pretended not to understand any Polish, nor any German, until the policeman finally pronounced the magic word: "Mandat!" *(Fine).*   I then took refuge in histrionics and protested in pidgin Polish that I was very tired and that zł. 2000 was a great deal of money for my offence, and I offered to compromise at zł. 1000, to which, to my surprise, he agreed with a huge grin on his face.   I am sure that my reduced fine never reached the police coffers.   On another occasion, I was travelling with a Polish colleague, and I said to him: "Hell, Wojciech, this is the third time I have been stopped and fined this week".   "Leave it to me" he replied and for about five minutes he had a heated discussion with the police officer, who finally handed me my passport back and let me go free.   "Whatever did you say to him, Wojciech?" I asked.   " I told him that you were a very important foreign businessman, travelling a great deal, and that you had the firm impression that all Polish policemen were very unfriendly towards foreigners".   This touched a patriot chord with the officer, who protested that he was certainly not unfriendly to foreigners, and so I got was let off!   If I tried that tack with a Vopo, I would probably have been arrested.

Some of the most important potential customers at the time were the Polish Ports, Szczecin, Gdansk and Gdynia. The first two of these were very long established and had been German before the Second World War, and Gdynia had been built from scratch in the 1930s as the only commercial outlet to the sea which existed in pre-War Poland. I decided on a series of seminars, in November 1987, and I set out on a cold snowy Monday afternoon in the Taunus (which, by this time I had obtained a special permission to keep in Warsaw). It soon fell dark, but traffic was fortunately light, and seeing an unlighted ox-cart ahead of me, I braked and the car spun round 180 degrees and landed me at the roadside facing the direction from which I had come. I then proceeded more cautiously, and stopped to brew a cup of tea in an inhospitable totally unlit parking shelter, shortly after which I was nearly involved in what could have been a serious accident. Another car overtook me, travelling much too fast for the conditions, and then, just as he had got past me he went into a long skid. I braked intuitively and my car did the same. By some miracle we both missed colliding into each other. He did not attempt to overtake me again. On another occasion, also not far from Gdansk I came on the most horrendous head on smash between two trucks, with bodies hanging out of the cabs. There was really nothing which I could do and I just drove on, quite shaken, and it was several kilometres further on before I passed an ambulance on the way to the scene. Driving late at night in the winter in Poland was a hazardous business, especially in foggy weather. A further nerve-wracking experience was in thick fog, driving in a queue of traffic, when a loud horn sounded out of the darkness, apparently from nowhere, and suddenly a train crossed right in front of me. It was a gate-less level crossing on which the lights had failed. Seconds later and I would have been mincemeat.

So I reached Gdansk for my first seminar at about 2 a.m. Alfred had been waiting anxiously for my arrival. Really, since it was now a Liebherr stronghold, it was largely a waste of time, but I had to keep trying, and they certainly tucked in well to the eats and drinks which we provided. There was a German-speaking engineer there, who used to ask such interminable technical questions that Hans Puvogel once asked him if he was trying to re-design the crane. He never made any decisions about anything however, except once when, after I had given him all the information on a Priestman serrated seal grab in which he was interested, he went and placed the order directly with RB Lincoln without reference to me at all. They must have thought that it fell out of the sky! Strangely enough the frostiest reception which we had on that occasion was in Gdynia. This had always been the stronghold of Jones mechanical cranes back in the 1960s and 1970s and Coles had never succeeded in breaking in. We

Grabcranex

arrived a few minutes' late to find a room full of delegates, and an irate director, who berated us for being behind the appointed hour and then promptly left the meeting. But we had more genuine interest in our presentation than anywhere else. We were not permitted to offer any refreshments there, and I responded to the director's rudeness by dropping a bottle of good cognac in his office, and the next time which I met him, he could not have been more cordial, and it was the one port in which we eventually succeeded in doing some useful business.

Peter Cooper was supposed to have been joining me for these Seminars, but was prevented from doing so at the last minute, much to my relief, since he would have found out too much about my side activities. As it turned out, I think that he would have cast a blind eye on them, but I did not know that then. I had already started to promote Sennebogen amongst the scrap metal organizations. The Austrian Fuchs dealer was already actively selling in Poland, and on my very first trip to Poland I had met him by chance in a Warsaw hotel (he was also the former Priestman dealer), and he had spilled all the beans to me on his activities, unaware that I had any connection with Sennebogen. ES Jnr agreed to my activities, but barred me from one important customer, since they were already confident of selling him a pedestal mounted scrap handling crane. The most important scrap metal organizations in Communist Poland were the Centrozłoms, who were the Mostostals of the scrap business, with branches all over the country. The Sennebogen customer was Centrozłom Katowice, so, barred from offering Sennebogen, I offered him the Sobemai Equilibrated Crane in competition.

The old Priestman dealer in Belgium, Edelhart de Lille, had, by this time, developed a range of E-Cranes, mostly rail-mounted on huge gantries, but also on crawlers and even on wheels, with the possibility of producing cranes up to capacities of 35 tonnes at 45 metres radius, and he was only too willing to co-operate with me in the Polish market. It was easy for me to stop over in Belgium on my way back to the UK, and indeed, when it suited me I started to leave the Ford Taunus at his Works at Maldegem, not far from Bruges. The Warynski venture had cost me quite a lot of money, and had been a significant factor in my breaking back in to the market for Grove Coles, so I had no compunction about trying to re-coup my investment by promoting the sale of another product. It also strengthened my hand when Grove Coles decided to move their Sales HQ from Harefield to Bicester in September 1987. David Steel knew that I would not move house to be near to the new offices, but he offered me monetary compensation for the additional cost of travel to the office, and I think that he was rather surprised when I turned this offer down and proposed, instead, to work from home. "Suppose that we do not accept" he said, to which I replied that I would have to take my chance on that, but I hoped that he would.

Grabcranex

I really was throwing my hat in to the ring, but, pragmatic as ever, he agreed to compromise, stipulating that, when not travelling, I must spend at least two days per week in the office. In practice, I managed to get away with only one and my independence increased.

1988 was a year of drama. Jerzy Tracz was really starting to push the boat out with his energy and enthusiasm in making customer contacts, and it was clear that he would soon replace his father-in-law, but I had to handle this delicately since I owed a great deal to my old friend, Alfred, and, without him, I could not have started. In May 1987 my efforts in promoting Sobemai to Centrozłom in Katowice (I even took some working shots of cranes with my 8mm cine camera and projected them on the wall in their offices) finally bore fruit and the FTO involved (my old partner, Centrozap) agreed to send a commercial/technical delegation to Belgium as well as to Sennebogen.

Fortunately for me the particular model which Sennebogen was putting forward was a lattice boom pedestal mounted crane of which they only had a few in service and, instead of going to Straubing, which would have impressed them, they went to visit a customer in Switzerland. The owner of the crane was highly suspicious of "Communists who might be spying on his business" and the reception was not very cordial. In contrast, Edelhart de Lille laid out the red carpet for the visitors and I took a few days of "holiday" to join the delegation. Several very satisfied owners of equilibrated cranes were visited, and also the new Works in Tournai in the Walloon part of Belgium. This had formerly been a Poclain subsidiary, and all the workers there spoke only French, whereas the management were Flemish from Maldegem.

The connection with Sobemai gave me a fascinating insight into this nation split so definitely into two different cultures and languages. It is only near the unmarked border between them that signposts were bi-lingual. Heading for the first time towards the famous city of Mons, I looked in vain for mention of it, not realising that the Flemish name for Mons is Bergen.

The contract for the SOBEMAI crane, mounted on a rail gantry and having a capacity of 6 tonnes at 20 metres was finally signed in April 1987 but we had to wait until the end of the year for the finance to be approved, and when it was, manufacture of the crane and the Takeover followed quite quickly. So whistle-blowing time for Lloyd was rapidly approaching - I really could not get involved in a Takeover Delegation for SOBEMAI as a full-time employee of Grove-Coles. Peter Cooper had started to express concerns about what the Warynski debacle was costing me, so I spilt the beans to him, and, to my surprise, he seemed almost relieved and agreed to keep the matter to himself. I soon found out why - he also had his own embryo side-show going in hiring out a mini excavator, and when I really had to declare my hand in May 1988, he had already left the company to concentrate full-time on his own business. David Milne was totally surprised and taken aback when I proposed to go totally independent with my then basic salary of £18,000 p.a. being paid to me as a Consultancy Fee, all travelling expenses to my account and a commission on sales. David Steel was not taken by surprise, however, and he agreed to the proposal, and asked me to continue as a full-time employee until the end of the financial year in October. The move to Bicester had had a very unsettling effect on many long-served employeess and several notices were handed in. At least I was staying . . . That apart, I had initiated discussions on a possible Co-operation Agreement with Bumar-Łabędy in Silesia, and this interested him., and he accompanied me to Poland in October for preliminary discussions.

This huge engineering works had originally been the Hermann-Goering Maschinen-Werke during the Second World War, turning out tanks and armaments for the Nazi war effort. Its role as an armaments producer had continued under Communism, working this time for the Warsaw Pact, with a pay-role of some 10,000 workers. But they were now forced to diversify and were building truck cranes of their own design and were also building crane carriers for Krupp, where by this time Hans Puvogel was employed. Hans had left Liebherr after a difference of opinion with his boss, and it was a godsend for me to have this powerful adversary removed from the scene, since his departure was definitely counter-productive ionsofar as Liebherr were concerned. Due to their wartime activity, the Krupp name was not very popular in Poland and Hans struggled hard to get the Krupp crane accepted. Bumar-Łabędy would prove an excellent partner for Grove since the quality of their fabrication and welding was as good, even if not better. An AT crane built in Poland and available to the local market in złotych would prove a winner, but the problem was that purchase of components and technical know-how had to be financed by counterpurchascs, and here lay the big challenge, which I personally was ready to take up. But it was not to be.

Major political changes, of which I was totally unaware, were taking place within the Grove organization. The fact was that, with the exception of Coles France, most of the Grove dealers in Europe had taken on the combined franchise of Shady Grove and Sunderland built cranes, and were not at all satisfied with the quality of the UK built product. Added to that, Kidde had sold out to Hanson Industries in 1987, and they had removed the President, Martin Benchoff, who had been a keen supporter of Grove Coles. The sudden action which took place in November 1988 was later described as the moving in of the "Seventh Cavalry". A new "cut and thrust" executive, Don Zorn, was hired in to carry out the transformation. In order to avoid suspicions of the changes leaking out in Sunderland, a request was made for an hotel booking for one visitor from the Head Office in Shady Grove, and for the exact name, address etc of the hotel to be communicated. Reservations for another six senior men from Shady Grove were made directly from the USA, without anyone in Sunderland being made aware of this. One of these was Greg Davis, the Quality Chief who had been involved with me in the Takeover of the RT1650, and he was the only one to stay on permanently, and he became, for me, a valuable ally later on. Duncan Wordsworth must have got wind of what was about to happen and he cleared his desk in preparation for the arrival of the US troops. David Steel was also toppled and suddenly the newly independent Consultant Lloyd found himself without any high level friends at court in the Grove Organization, the Coles name immediately being dropped, and the hybrid company, Grove-Coles Ltd., was reduced to a paper legality.

Concerned with the future of our embryo Co-operation Deal, I wrote to Zorn requesting a meeting to discuss it, and I was immediately summoned to Sunderland.

"These guys are really on the ball", I thought innocently, but soon after I entered the Boardroom, I soon realised that Zorn, and his co-Director, Larry Boyd, were not in the least interested in the potential of the Polish market or the Co-operation Deal, but only in what kind of a deal I personally had negotiated with the Company. Suddenly I appreciated the precariousness of my position. Upon my explanation that I had exchanged my employee status for a Consultancy arrangement, the answer was succinct: "We don't have Consultants in Grove", they drawled, "you are either an employee or an independent agent". I replied politely, but firmly, that mine was a rather unusual, but essentially different position. "You don't have any Contract with Grove" came the answer. "No, gentlemen" I countered, "but I do have a letter signed by the former Managing Director which would, I think, stand up in a Court of Law".

They were clearly taken aback, and asked for a copy of the letter, which, when produced, changed the atmosphere radically. "See here, Dick" said Zorn, "we will have to discuss this", and when we met a bit later in Bicester, he agreed to continue the arrangement on the basis of a 20% reduction in the regular payment, but a doubling of the commission rate from 1% to 2%. Even though his main function was Director of Purchasing, Larry Boyd was given the responsibility of overseeing my operation.

The arrival of the new Top Management from the USA also spelled the end of the short career of Bicester as a Sales Office, which was soon moved up to the Works in Sunderland. Resignations followed fast and furiously and the Grove-Coles Export team effectively broke up. Had it not been for one ex Coles employee, Marie-Helène Lopez, a key member of the Export Admin Department, who agreed to move with the office, the whole system would have broken down, in my view. Born in France in Tarbes, not far from the Spanish border, of mixed French/Spanish parentage, Marie-Helène had joined Coles in 1981, after 8 years of experience with another UK producer of handling equipment, making her a very valuable member of the team due to her tri-lingual abilities, and she was an excellent administrator. I found that once I had something agreed with her, even if she did not have the authority to confirm it without consultation higher up the tree, in practice she knew what was possible and whatever she agreed to was rubber-stamped from above. Her support was of great assistance to me in building up my business - it has always been my contention that good administrative back-up is equally as important as effective salesmanship in the field.

Just before Christmas 1988 I had another approach from JCB, and, once again I was invited to Rocester. This time the reception was very different, with a cordial welcome by Dick Ryland and an immediate introduction to Gilbert Johnson, and to Sir Anthony Bamford, who politely claimed to have met me before. I had certainly met his father, Mr. JCB himself at a European exhibition, but I did not recall ever meeting Sir Anthony and said so. "Well, I certainly know you by reputation" he replied and I glowed with pride at the unexpected compliment. It seemed that they had decided to appoint a senior contact man in London to liaise with leading Civil Engineering Contractors and cultivate top level connections within Government to assist with business within the EEC. I had no aspirations whatever to political influence. About the nearest connection which I had was to have been at Oxford at the same time as Michael Heseltine, when he was President of the Oxford Union, but he certainly did not know me. However the fact is that I was always a great admirer of his style and am convinced that if he had followed Margaret Thatcher as Prime Minister, matters would have gone much better for the Tory Party. The fact that he did not get the top job called to mind a debate in the Union in the mid 1950s when his opponent was Palme Dutt, a very sincere and earnest Communist. Heseltine opened his scintillating address by stating that he had looked up his opponent in "Who's Who" to find out more about him, but his name did not appear there. He then looked him up in "Who Was Who", and "Who Will Be Who" with the same result. "Finally" he went on, "I found him - in "Who Might Have Been Whom". In the light of future events this remark was rather interesting, but my knowledge of this was not likely to be of much help in this new job opportunity with JCB! Dick Ryland told me that I was the "mucky-boots" man favoured by him for the position, but there was another candidate who had the political connections, but lacked the experience of the industry.

Grabcranex

With the uncertainty of my situation with Grove, I might well have gone for this opportunity had it been formalised, but JCB prevaricated.   In the meantime time I landed another franchise for Grabcranex in Poland, Altas Weyhausen, only due to the fact that Bumar came up with a firm enquiry for some Atlas pedestal-mounted truck-loaders for timber handling from an existing satisfied user.   So I decided to keep my independence, and my letter to JCB crossed with theirs turning me down.   I never discovered who my rival was, but the job finally went to David Steel and I was glad that I had not been selected, because the position was wound up within a year or two, and, despite the ups and downs in my career which followed, I believe that I had again chosen the right path.

George Szulczewski, the King of Coles service since 1992 is attended on by Alfred's wife, Renia.

Starting to revive the fortunes of Grove Coles in Poland, I took on my old and trusted friend Alfred Gorniok ("Alfski") pictured here with his two daughters, Ewa (left) and Basia. Soon Ewa's husband, Jerzy Tracz (top), demonstrating his talents as a waiter, joined the team.

Grabcranex

Paweł Kędzierski.

UDT President Iwo Jakubowski *(left)* on a tour of inspection of Shady Grove in February 1992.

Flashback to 1962. "Checkpoint Charlie", East Berlin and Polish border at Frankfurt on Oder.

Grabcranex

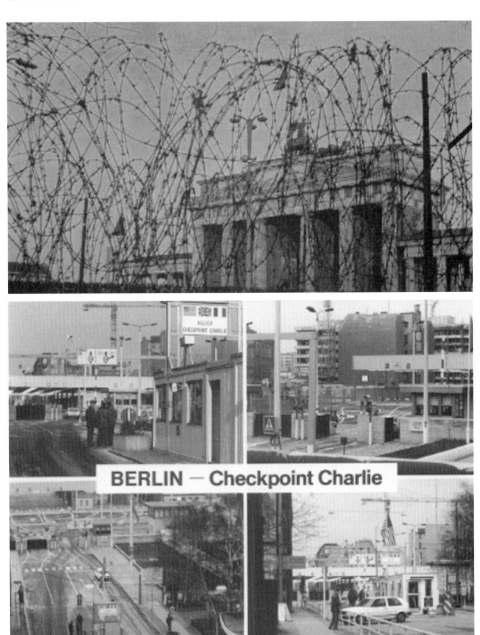

As it was in the 1980s.

Grabcranex

1992 Brandenburg Gate no longer obscured by barbed wire.

Sale of DDR memorabilia in Berlin.

Grabcranex

SOBEMAI

Crane tested at Tournai.   Edelhart de Lille with Bill Bromwich.

The first step towards an independent existence - the sale of a large Sobemai equilibrated crane to Centrozłom Katowice.

Edelhart de Lille displays his talents as a chef and cooks moûles for the Polish visitors . . .

. . . well appreciated by Dyrektor Henryk Sleziona.

Grabcranex

Marie-Helène Lopez

Grove Coles moves from Harefield to Bicester.

Left to right: Balcer, Szulczewski, Steve Watson, Heidrich, Pietrzak.
This visit aimed to reconcile the Grove service from Zabrze with Coles from Warszawa.

In September 1988, just before the seventh cavalry moved in to erase the name of Coles, Karol Heidrich, MD of Mostostal Warszawa, led a delegation to Sunderland of Polish service chiefs. Soon the Coles steam crane, manufactured in 1879, was to bear a Grove label.

CHAPTER THREE - GRABCRANEX

From the beginning of 1989, Grabcranex was floating on its own, tied for two more years to the Grove Wharf by an umbilical cord in the form of a constant payment of the regular monthly consultancy fee. I was closely watched over by Larry Boyd. How he should have been the one chosen to oversee a sales operation was a mystery to me, but I had no choice but to accept it. He clearly did not trust me very much. He would examine my agreed expenses (costs of Takeover of each crane sold, built in to the price) with a fine toothcomb. Battling hard for every potential order, mostly from production at Shady Grove rather than Sunderland, I secured an order for two RT cranes from a long established customer in Silesia and the deal went through Centrozap. I had quoted keenly and then made an error of calculation in the price build-up. I had not yet got fully used to US crane technical terminology and the way the price list was made up. So when it came to the final negotiation, knowing that the end-user's decision for Grove was already firmly taken, I refused to give any discount at all to Centrozap, and almost felt sorry for the members of the purchasing department when I saw the crestfallen look on their faces, but they had no choice but to accept. After the contract had been signed, the Centrozap director asked me a favour - could I possibly obtain some ribbons for them for an electronic typewriter which were unobtainable in Poland. "Of course" I replied, feeling very charitable, and requested the exact name, model no. etc of the typewriter to be telexed through to me. The £150 which I expended on the ribbons went down on my expenses as "Gift to Customer" upon signature of a contract for over $500,000, with all supporting documentation including the telex from Centrozap. Larry Boyd refused to pass my expense claim for the Takeover Costs. "Do you doubt my word that I actually spent that sum in the Company's interest?" I asked rather aggressively. "No", he replied, "but I cannot accept that wording". To my further question as to exactly what wording he would accept, he replied laconically: "Office Supplies". The Americans were paranoic about anything which remotely smacked of bribery.

Larry Boyd and I eventually established a good working relationship and his suspicions of me subsided, although he would often say, half in jest, as I entered his office: "Watch your pockets, boys". I even persuaded him to make a trip to Poland to look at the possibilities of component purchase, and he actually placed an order for a trial slew ring, but it did not stand up to rigorous testing and nothing came of it. His visit coincided with an acute petrol shortage and he could not believe his eyes when he saw the long queues at the pumps.   I think it opened his eyes to see how the other half lived.

I had some more success with Sobemai, and, following a Seminar which I held in Katowice upon delivery of the first crane, which Edelhart himself attended, I sold another rail-mounted equilibrated crane to Centrozłom Warszawa, with a capacity of 6 Tonnes at nearly 25 metres radius in September 1989.   This time the purchasing organization was by no means a specialist in cranes, dealing mainly with motor vehicles, but they involved a delightful character who resembled a ballet dancer more than Chief of an Import Dept, whom I shall call "Mr. I", because he always referred to the other characters who made up the various components of the technical and commercial entourage by the initials of their names only.   In fact they included a rather sinister and aggressive middleman whose name also began with "I", who spoke a crude form of German and was always tackling me with the words: "Herr Lloyd, ist dass moeglich........" (Mr. Lloyd, that can be").   I was forced to involve him, because he did have some influence, but he remained a shadowy figure in the background and was not invited to any of the official meetings.

Edelhart de Lille was always extremely hospitable to his business guests, and often used to cook moûles (mussels) for them in his own home.   On this occasion, the Polish director of the scrapyard refused to eat them, so Edelhart gamely turned round and cooked him a steak, and the "ballet dancer" Mr "I", who shared my embarassment at this situation, felt obliged to eat more moûles than he really could manage.   The next morning he reported that the moûles had been going for walks all night all round his stomach, and he had felt the necessity of walking with them, so he had little time for sleep!

Edelhart decided to hand over the running of the business to his youngest son, Kilian, in 1990, but it ran into financial difficulties, and a finance company from Brussels became involved. This split the company into two camps, with Kilian continuing to operate at Sobemai from Maldegem, the Flemish home of the family, whilst the finance company formed a new enterprise called Sobecon, who claimed that they now had the legal rights to manufacture and sell the E-Cranes, but at the end of 1991 Kilian won the battle over them in the courts and regained control.

I had a meeting with him at the end of that year and managed to get the balance of commisions owed me in cash, fearing that the business was unlikely to continue much longer. Manufacture in Belgium did, in fact, cease, partly due also

Grabcranex

to environmental problems, but Kilian established a design office to continue the production of equilibrated cranes elsewhere, finally having them built in Poland. This is an ironic turn of events for me, having sold two cranes built in Belgium to that country during the Communist era. Edelhart found that retirement was not for him and rejoined his son, and in 2003 he sent me information on what is probably the very largest Equilibrated Crane (supplied to a Belgian Steelworks), with a capacity of 55 tonnes at 44 metres radius, clearly illustrating the huge possibilities of this unique type of design (see photograph). Edelhart de Lille has now been in the crane business for over half a century, having started in 1952 by representing the US manufacturer, Quick-Way, who disappeared in 1968. He commented to me recently on the immense technological changes, especially in control design, going from mechanical levers to joysticks and now, according to him, the latest Sobemai product is controlled by a computer mouse, thereby also permitting remote control. At the age of 77, he must be one of the oldest soldiers in the crane manufacturing business.

Probably the largest equilibrated crane ever produced, this superb crane from Sobemai has a capacity of 55 tonnes at 44 metres radius, and was for a Belgian steelworks.

Grabcranex

In December 1989, Jerzy Tracz and I travelled to Shady Grove to prepare for first Takeover since the sale of the RT1650 in 1987. Three cranes were to be taken over - the two RTs which I had sold via Centrozap and Tracz's "first blood" - a small mobile for a textile factory sold through Bumar. All three cranes were on a 9/10 month delivery lead-time, and when we informed Shady Grove of all the tests which would have to be carried out as well as the extensive documentation prepared, the attitude was: "Why bother? We can sell these cranes several times over in the US without all this fuss". But contracts had been signed and there was (fortunately for Grabcranex) no get-out. I appealed to Greg Davis and he sent a sharp message across the Atlantic to the effect that if they did not comply with the regulations, they would not get paid. Jerzy Tracz and I took the precaution of visiting the Works prior to the arrival of the customers, and we then established a very good rapport with one man in the Quality Dept, Leroy Myers, who became quite a friend, and did an excellent job with Polish Takeovers from that time on. The two delegations (comprising at least half a dozen people each) arrived on different days in New York, and on the first occasion we met them at Kennedy Airport with a mini-bus and a car, and, arrived at the hotel, we found that the UDT Inspector was missing! He had stopped to chat with friends who had also been there to meet him, and had not been counted. Fortunately he turned up again the next day when the second party arrived, but we had quite a lot to do to smooth his ruffled feathers. In fact it was the other UDT Inspector who became really angry on this occasion, because two of the Directors from the Silesian customer did not even bother to attend the testing of their cranes, but preferred to spend a lazy day in the Motel or doing some local sightseeing, just turning up for the signature of the Protocol, having left him to do all the work. We ensured that the evenings were very convivial, and we found an inexpensive Chinese restaurant, without an alcohol licence, who were quite happy for us to bring in quantities of booze purchased in the local liquor store. The problems began when the Polish directors insisted on our going back to their rooms to drink vodka after dinner! This was how it was in the days of Communism, but not for much longer....

Jerzy Tracz, now known to me by his Polish nickname, Jurek, had formed a very good personal rapport with Paweł Kędzierski, who was leading the Bumar delegation, and tipped me off that Paweł was thinking seriously of finding another job, knowing that there would be major changes following the collapse of Communism, and rightly drew my attention to his value if he could be persuaded to join Grabcranex. I heartily agreed and tapped on his hotel room door

Grabcranex

late on the last evening before they flew back to Poland. He was already in touch with our German crane competitors, but was looking for a guaranteed remuneration on a scale which it was impossible for me to offer him. All I could do was to offer to split my monthly Retainer fee between him and Jurek plus commission on sales, and fortunately for me he accepted and by Poznan Fair 1990 he was on board the Grabcranex train, and together we three welded ourselves into a partnership. Paweł had all the customer contacts in Poland, and he knew more about telescopic boom cranes than I did. Jurek had the entrepereneurial spirit and bonhomie essential for a good salesman, and I could provide the financial backing, the experience and the technical know-how on lattice boom cranes and excavators. It proved to be a recipe for a successful enterprise, but it took time to come to fruition.

By this time Audrey had also joined us as a partner in the business, her own career as a peripatetic teacher of French in primary schools having been terminated by a change in policy by the local Education Authority. This was a sad blow for her and her colleagues, after putting years of effort in to this very worthwhile project, involving taking of children of all ages across the Channel to show them a totally different culture, not just another language, and thereby most usefully broadening their outlook. It was indeed fortunate that this had not happened during the period of my redundancy. So she became my helpmate at the Poznan Fair, assisting me with the long two day drive from Uxbridge, the car laden to the gunwales with goodies from Sainsburys to enable us to offer hospitality on the Stand, not to mention other essentials like decent toilet paper, the Polish variety of that period having some affinity with sandpaper. As the cost of booze in Poland increased rapidly, the custom of handing out bottles of brandy to every Tom, Dick and Harry who came on the Stand had to be abandoned, but it was hard to carry out this change in a time-honoured practice without causing offence. We loaded up with cheap wine from French supermarkets, and weinbrand in Germany on our way through instead. After the first year in a noisy and none too comfortable hotel, we took to hiring a lakeside chalet, where we could set up a small home, and I could take a morning dip in the lake.

It also enabled us to accomodate visiting firemen from our principals, or journalists from the technical press inexpensively, although not all of them responded to my invitation to join me in the lake of a morning! Audrey's other very valuable contribution to Grabcranex was her Amstrad word processor for turning out quotations, before we could afford to invest in computers. I know that she found it very boring sitting on the Stand churning out quotations, but it was the beginning of making our little enterprise more professional.

Our relationship with Atlas Weyhausen, whose franchise had been the final convincing reason for me to keep my new-found independence, did not last very long.   There were design faults with the pedestal-mounted cranes which we had supplied (cracks in the welding around the base of the columns), and the Atlas rep put the blame on the lack of our back-up service!   I had a furious row with him on our Stand at the Poznan Fair, and he dodged facing the customer when he turned up.   The final straw which broke the back of the camel was when he reneged by telex on an agreement on pricing made verbally at the Fair on a particular enquiry, but this proved to be a blessing in disguise.   We found a much better principal, as a result.

During the 1990 Poznan Fair we received our first enquiry for lattice boom cranes, and so Audrey and I routed ourselves back via Straubing.   The welcome which we received from Erich Sennebogen Jnr and Karl Klein, the old soldier of Sennebogen, was extremely warm.   I was careful to bring along a copy of the Grabcranex Polish news sheet highlighting the sale of the Sobemai E-Crane to Centrozłom in Katowice and Erich wagged his finger at me as if I had been a very Naughty Boy to have stolen the business from him.   But I am sure that it helped me to convince him to let us have the Sennebogen franchise for Poland, and this was a most important step forward for us.

In fact, as it proved, our first success was not with cranes, but excavators. Gazobudowa, a large potential customer involved in gas pipeline construction, was interested in hydraulic excavators from a West European manufacturer, having little faith in the home-produced Warynski, and after my experience try-ing to promote this product in the UK, I could well understand why.   The Director of this enterprise, Jan Lewiniec, had been born and brought up in France.   Just after the end of the Second World War, at the age of 17, he had decided to make a visit to what was his true native country.   It proved to be a disastrous error of judgement on the part of the young man.   He was told that he must hand over his French passport for immigration purposes, which he duly did.   It was never returned to him.   He was forced into accepting Polish citizenship, and he was not allowed to return to his beloved France.

He attempted to escape illegally, but he was caught and imprisoned, and so he resigned himself to his fate, but he never lost his command of the French lan-guage, and when I turned up and addressed him in French, a smile of pure

Grabcranex

delight appeared on his lips.

Long before there was any prospect of their having money for purchasing new equipment, we promised to invite a delegate from his organization to visit Atlas Weyhausen, and this visit was scheduled for July 1990. Paweł was to drive him there, but the visit was marred by the row which I had had with the Atlas rep at the Poznan Fair in June, and I asked Paweł to continue his journey down to Straubing, where I met him in person. The reception there cemented the connection, and by June 1991 we had secured an order for a trial machine. The terms and conditions of the contract were discussed between me and Lewiniec without either of my Polish colleagues (or any of his) being invited to attend, and there were many written communications between us in French, and, not only that but the first multiple order which followed in December of the same year was typed out by me in French in the Gazobudowa office. It then had to be translated by me into English, so that Paweł could prepare a Polish version and then by me into German so that it could be understood by Sennebogen, as Karl Klein knew not a word of English!

It was a bizarre situation, but we secured the deal against Caterpillar, which was some achievement, since they used all Caterpillar tractors for their sidebooms. (For the uninitiated, a sideboom is a short jib attachment mounted on to a crawler tractor, which is especially designed to handle pipe in a continuous pipelaying sequence).

It was so important to gain the first order with a Polish customer, since, if the first machine operated satisfactorily, a policy of standardization on the same product was sure to follow, which was logical because it would be much easier to train service engineers and stock parts for the same type of equipment. Trying to break in against established competition was, as I had learned to my cost, like climbing a brick wall in bedroom slippers.

The key to our success was Gazobudowa's involvement in a very important contract for a huge gas pipeline, which was the supply of natural gas from Russia to Poland and through to Germany, a massive improvement scheme which was known as GAS 2000.

Gazobudowa was one of three contractors who obtained the pipelaying contract for the first sections on the Polish side of the border from Frankfurt on Oder to Włocławek. The size of the pipe was huge with a diameter of 1400 mm. The terrain through which the pipeline was being constructed lay mostly through pine forests, and a great swathe had to be cut through the forest prior to laying the pipe on the surface ready for welding. The one particularly tricky problem which the pipeliners had to overcome was to avoid cutting down any trees in a conservation area, a small hill right in the path of the pipeline to be preserved as an area of natural beauty. The only solution was to tunnel under the hill, but no special tunnelling machine was available in Poland, and the pipeliners had to come up with another means of solving the problem. This they did by digging an horizontal "mineshaft" through the hill, shoring it up and roofing it over with wooden pitprops in the old-fashioned manner. Two or three men with picks and shovels dug out the face, and the spoil was carried back on a conveyor. It was like something out of Snow White and the Seven Dwarfs.

After the order for the trial machine, we supplied a total of 16 Sennebogen excavators and a crawler crane for this project, the excavators all fitted with trapezoidal buckets of differing shapes and sizes, and, since the manufacture of such special attachments was of no interest to Sennebogen, I found a UK supplier, Allied Construction Equipment, to do this, the great advantage being that I could drive over to Billericay in Essex from Uxbridge to discuss all technical details.

Many visits were made to Gazobudowa and we were even able to make use of their private workers' accomodation, known to us as the "Gazobudowa Hotel". This extremely inexpensive hostelry consisted of a number of dormitories rather like a Youth Hostel, with none too clean communal showers and toilets, which reminded me of my days as a National Service recruit, except that standards of hygiene in the British Army were certainly a lot higher. But fortunately the hostel boasted one private apartment with two separate bedrooms and a bathroom, and it was here that we usually slept, and met with our "friend at court" who would give us the lowdown on the situation in the evening prior to formal discussions with the directorate. Jan Lewiniec eventually retired and his replacement was a Pole born in Poland, so that the importance of the French connection disappeared. But, by that time, we were established.

Grabcranex was a lean organization. We could not afford to be other. The economic bonanza which was predicted after the collapse of Communism just did not materialise. When Grove cut the umbilical cord of a regular monthly payment at the end of 1990, and substituted it by tripling the commission on all outstanding orders, we had sufficient cash coming in to cause us no great worry, but then the Order Book dried up. Large State Organizations, like Ports and Shipyards, cut their links with the Foreign Trade Organizations, and established their own Purchasing Departments, often staffed by experienced persons from the FTOs. Bumar's influence and power dwindled rapidly, and Paweł had certainly made the right decision to jump ship before it hit the rocks.

Gdynia Shipyard had purchased a large Grove Manlift Access Platform from us in 1989 through Centromor, which had to be adapted for use on board ship by being fitted with an electric motor as an alternative prime mover to the diesel engine.

The machine had been shipped from Shady Grove to Bicester, and the mods were knife and forked in the workshops there. When an enquiry came for a second unit to the same spec, we decided to to the knifing and forking in Poland. The deal was structured on the basis of a three year credit, with Bills of Exchange being guaranteed by the Polish State Bank, Bank Handlowy. Grabcranex purchased all the components for the special modifications in the UK, a Takeover was held in Shady Grove at our cost, with a particularly pernickety technician from the Shipyard, who drove Leroy Myers and his colleagues to distraction. The machine was ready for shipment, when Bank Handlowy declined to endorse the Bills of Exchange accepted by the Shipyard.

The whole deal collapsed like a pack of cards. The shipyard, perhaps the largest in Poland, had never imagined that they would not receive the Bank Guarantee, nor had we. Grove stripped off the lovingly and expensively prepared Polish decals, painted the machine and sold it elsewhere, not forgetting to invoice Grabcranex with all the costs, plus an additional bill for loss of interest. I was forced to settle the accounts of the local UK suppliers of the parts required for the special modifications, and I faced a total loss, without any sale, of £10,000. I harried the customer to meet his contractual obligations, knowing that to take it to a Court of Law would be a complete waste of time. We had received no down-payment, a major error on our part, from which we quickly learned. The responsible executive in the shipyard acted with complete honour. He never tried to deny that they had an obligation to us, and made strenuous but unavailing efforts to find the money to complete the purchase.

After two years they found enough funds to meet my claim for losses and accept shipment of the components, for which they found some other use. It was a hard lesson learned in the changing situation from Communism to Capitalism.

This kind of experience, plus the lack of orders, obliged us to operate as inexpensively as possible. The Ford Taunus "tank" was handed over to my Polish colleagues and registered in Poland. However the poor old beast came to a sticky end in November 1990. The three of us were returning late one evening to Warsaw after a few days in Gdynia and Gdansk. We were beginning to make significant progress in the Port of Gdynia, where the first hydraulic cranes to be purchased to replace the ageing Jones mechanical cranes supplied in the 60s and 70s by Walther Husser, were two Sunderland built Coles-designed Grove RTs. Paweł was driving as we entered Warsaw via a long dual carriageway running alongside the River Vistula on that wet November evening, when suddenly an idiot drove right across the highway through red traffic lights, and escaped scot free as the line of traffic proceeding along it braked sharply and one vehicle after another collided in to the back of the next, in an effort to avoid hitting the miscreant broadside.   I was thrown forward from the rear seat, but fortunately none of us was injured.   The old car, however, bashed front and rear, was a write-off.   We had to wait for at least two hours in the shivering cold, for the police to complete their report, which was my worst memory of the incident, but fortunately the car was insured, and the insurance company paid us the equivalent of £1500.   Armed with this sum, I located a second-hand left-hand drive Audi 80 from a dealer in the UK specializing in cars obtained from Englishmen returning from working in Europe, for £1100, and had it thoroughly checked and serviced.   I then drove it to Poland and it served us for 12 months.   When a part was required, I would purchase it from the local dealer in Uxbridge and carry it out to Poland on my next trip.   At the end of that period, when it was about to give up the ghost, I accepted that, despite the lack of income, we just had to have a new and reliable vehicle in Poland and I obtained a Bank Loan and bought a new Toyota just before prices and taxes shot up in that country.

There was no more living it up in the Novotel at Grove's expense for Lloyd on his trips to Warsaw. Paweł had rented an apartment on a busy thoroughfare as his office and here I slept on a makeshift couch.   To darken the windows at night, I brought over some old curtains from home, but sleep after 5 am was impossible once the trams started to clang past in the street.   In Poznan I was more fortunate, occupying the spare room in Jurek's new house which he had built during the time that hard currency had yielded a small fortune in Polish złotych. The Polish authorities adopted a very pragmatic approach to the problem of "black market" złotych. The visiting businessman still had to pay for his hotel at the artificial "official rate", but then he could purchase as much as he liked at the so-called "free market" rate, which was the equivalent of the "black market" rate, which latter then effectively disappeared.

In time the "official rate" became the same as the "free market" rate.   In the meantime, to accelerate all this, they decided to introduce a new złoty, which was the equivalent of 1000 old złotych. It reminded me of what had happened in France in the late 1940s after the end of the war, and how many older people still continued to calculate in "anciens francs". In Poland in the early 1990s, scruffy notes with innumerable "0"s circulated alongside tiny coins worth the same, and to a pidgin-Polish speaker like myself, coping with this problem in the vegetable market was a nightmare. For these changes came about when Audrey and I literally lived in Warsaw for periods of a month, involved in a project quite extraneous to the Grabcranex business, which put bread into our mouths just when it was most needed.

Another change for us as a result of the collapse of Communism was the potential demise of the Grove Coles Mostostal Service Organization. This would have been a disaster, since the organization provided the essential service back up for every crane which we sold, and still gave us an edge over our competitors, who serviced their cranes directly from Germany. Robert Brouwer, an old Coles Sales Executive who had followed my initial efforts in the late 1960s and sold a lot of Coles Cranes into Poland, had also been in on the setting up of this organization in 1970, but he left Coles in 1974 to found his own sales company specialising in selling to the USSR and Eastern Europe, Arcon Machinery. When I had first joined Grove Coles in 1986, I made my one and only trip to Moscow in the company of Robert's charming business and lifelong lady partner, Ingrid Hoffman, in an unsuccessful attempt to sell a crane there, and I had had the experience of walking out of my hotel into Red Square late at night without any fear of being mugged or robbed, which I think might be difficult today. At Poznan Fair 1990, Robert approached me and said that he would like to privatise the service organization and would I like to come in with him. Although I really did not know from where I was going to find the cash, I immediately agreed, since I wanted to be able to ensure that the new organization would still provide the service back-up which we needed. The new company, with the grandiose title of Industrial Service Corporation, was to be headed up by George Szulczewski.

I was very lucky in that my initial investment of £25,000 in ISC, could partially be spread. Grove had inherited from Coles a large amount of vehicles, tools and equipment located in Poland, and I "purchased" these as part of my investment.

Steve Watson, and his boss, David Fenner, the only surviving Coles director on the board of Grove UK, offered me "credit" in meeting my debt by asking me to fund capital purchases for the Sunderland Spares Department, as and when they were required for which they could not obtain approval through the official channels.

When David Fenner retired and Greg Davis took over, the latter raised his eyebrows when he learned about this arrangment, but I was able to show that it was all totally above board and documented. Steve Watson still operated the Consignment Stock, which was gradually run down. ISC did not prosper immediately and Robert Brouwer had to invest a lot more money in the company to keep it afloat, but I just could not afford to do this, although I remained the largest shareholder after him, the balance being divided amongst the Polish employees, as well as Paweł and Jurek.

During the Poznan Fair in 1991 we struck our biggest blow against Liebherr. The big opencast coalmine, KWB Bełchatow (one of the largest in Europe) had had some problems with the Liebherr RT cranes which had replaced the very unsatisfactory Coles, which was what had turned Paweł, then at Bumar, totally against Coles, and one had even gone on fire. This is where Paweł's personal connection really came to the fore, and a high level shopping delegation arrived on our Stand, headed by the dynamic Managing Director, Inz. Jerzy Wagenkneckt. I found myself back in my old role of selling Hymacs to the Ministry of Agriculture in Roumania in the late 1960s, namely that I was dealing direct with the man who made the decisions and had the power to do so, in his native language. Wagenkneckt, despite his German name, spoke only Polish, and he carried out the price negotiations in person, leaving his Purchasing Manager simply to rubber-stamp what he had agreed. "Troche lubrikacji, *(A little lubrication)* Panie Lloyd" he would say as he squeezed the pips dry after two hours of hard bargaining, at the same time re-charging my glass with vodka, but finally we shook hands on the deal and the Letter of Intent was typed out by me and signed on our Stand at half-past 8 in the evening. The delegation had already visited the Liebherr Stand, where their visit had been regarded simply as a preliminary prior to serious discussions at the coalmine. Had Hans Puvogel still been working for Liebherr, I doubt if we would have got away with it. So we broke back in to the most important customer in Poland at that time with two Grove 80 Tonne capacity RT990s, and in September the Contract was extended to include a 50 Tonne RT760.

But by the end of the following year we were desperate for business. My bank overdraft was creeping up, and I was really beginning to worry about it. Theoretically we were making a profit, averaging at £12,000 to £14,000 p.a.,

Grabcranex

which was certainly not enough for us to live on, so we were effectively living off our capital.

In December 1992 I went to Poland to negotiate another potential sale to a large opencast coalmine, Kopalnia Konin, again by a direct negotiation between me and the Managing Director, Bogdan Boronski.   The night before the crucial meeting I sat up for hours carefully going over the figures of what we needed to do to secure the business.   Liebherr were expecting that the decision would be made in January, but we offered such a good deal on a 100 Ton AT crane that he accepted our offer a month earlier.   We were lucky, in that it was the last of a series to be produced in Sunderland and so Grove were prepared to discount heavily on the price.   However, when the current Supremo in Sunderland queried the amount of commission we earned on the deal, I was furious.   He was OK with his regular salary paid monthly in to the Bank - we had had not an order for six months.....   Flushed with our success in Konin, we journeyed on to Bełchatow, and not to be out-done, Wagenkneckt gave us a repeat order.   But he wanted the same price as before, emphasising the advantage of his 100% pre-payment policy (to convert the złotych into dollars before the former de-valued, which meant that the business was golden for Grove).   Grove had put their prices up by 10%, taking the value of each crane from $390,000 to well over $400,000.   Finally Wagenkneckt agreed to some increase, but, he said, the first figure must remain the same, and he left the room for us to consider.   A phone call to my "friend at court" in Sunderland, Marie-Helène Lopez, conducted in Spanish so that no-one in the room could understand me, enabled me to propose to Dyrektor Wagenkneckt a final price of $399,999.   "So many "9"s in a row is unlucky", he replied and we settled at $399,998, and were entertained to a slap-up lunch to celebrate.   He did not lack a sense of humour, but he was also basically very different from most Polish directors of the time, who liked their little jaunt to the USA or the UK for the Takeover.   Wagenkneckt would not participate himself nor allow any of his staff this privilege - he sent the UDT Inspector on his own.   Boronski was much less cautious - not only did he accompany the large delegation which visited Sunderland for the Takeover - he also brought along his wife.   It was a big mistake - the powerful Trades Unions indicted him on his return and he was sacked.   Wagenkneckt also had his problems with the Unions.   Like the coalminers in the days of Arthur Scargill in the UK, the Polish Unions were very powerful.   In the days of Communism they even had access to special shops and other privileges, and as Poland moved into the capitalistic world, Dyrektor Wagenkneckt had to face some massive strikes due to his refusal to give in to unreasonable wage increase demands.   Finally, in February 1997, the Unions won and he was forced to resign. It was a big shock, reported in the National Press, and stupid that such a competent individual should have been ousted by Union Power.

Wagenkneckt considered investing in an RT1650, at the same time as the Port of Szczecin were thinking the same way, but the machine would have to be especially built to order, so in May 1993, I found myself taking one of his engineers to Shady Grove to meet up with Jurek and Paweł already involved with the Port delegation. The guy spoke nothing other than Polish and was a somewhat unattractive character. It was my first experience of hiring and driving a car in the USA, and after the technical discussions, which came to nothing, we all ended up in Baltimore for a sight seeing tour. I left it a bit late to drive back to Washington to catch the late afternoon plane back to London, losing a valuable half hour trying to locate the hired car in the multi-storey carpark having been obliged to re-enter by a different door from where I had exited. The getting out of Baltimore was like a nightmare with continual stops to ask directions ("Take a right, take a left, then straight on, then again a right and left.....). As we neared Washington I thankfully picked up the Airport signs, and drove in to the Car Hire Depot about 75 minutes before Take-Off time. It looked unfamiliar, but I hoped for the best. Shock and disbelief followed, when, enquiring which was the right terminal for BA to London, the reply came: "British Airways don't fly from this airport". I was in the local domestic airport instead of Dulles International. Attempts to retrieve the hired car, as advised, were met with instructions to "Stand in line and wait your turn", so I found a co-operative Pakistani taxi driver, who drove like a madman to Dulles and we just got the very last seats at the back of the plane. And all this effort and expense for no result whatsoever.....

But this was part and parcel of selling in Poland.

One of the things at which I excelled was upsetting the hierarchy in Grove which, I must admit, I rather enjoyed doing. As an independent agent one could get away with saying and doing things which no employee would dare to do. Early in 1992 we sold a 50 Tonne AT crane to a Polish customer who had a contract on which he needed to use it in Finland. It was a tight deal and we had to pay a 5% service commission to the Finnish dealer, who complained that it was not enough, but, not only that, after the Polish Takeover at the Works in Shady Grove, it had also to be accepted by the Finnish Technical Supervision Authority before being released to the customer, and their regulations were different from those applying in Poland. We had undertaken that the crane would be in operation on Monday, April 6th, and it arrived in Helsinki about one week earlier. I went over there to ensure that there would be no hitches, and by Friday morning, everything was approved, with one exception. The Finnish inspector wanted an official statement in writing as to the exact weight reduction when the "swingaway" (or lattice extension to the telescopic boom) was removed. Marie Lopez contacted the technical department, who replied that this would require weeks of investigation. This was a pure piece of pedantic bureaucracy, but without this declaration the crane would not be allowed to operate and Grabcranex would have to start paying a penalty out of our meagre profit. I always had a stock of Grove Headed Paper (my title was "Authorized Representative for Poland"), so I simply typed a letter out with the required information, signed it and handed it to the Inspector. I faxed a copy to Sunderland and boarded my plane for London. Screaming faxes repudiating the validity of what I had done appeared in my home office and in that of the Finnish dealer, which I simply ignored until I reached the Grove Stand at the BAUMA in Munich on the following Monday morning. The first person I met was Greg Davis. "Hi Greg" I greeted him, "I gather that I am in some trouble". "Falsifying documents is a capital offence at Grove" he grinned back and I was summoned to explain my action to a large group of serious-minded Americans. After much discussion and explanation, they fortunately saw my point and agreed to accept my action - really they had no choice! I think that they realised that my success in sales in a very small market was more important.

In April 1994 we did sell another large Grove RT to Poland, the equivalent to the RT990, but a newer version named RT9100 for the Port of Swinoujscie. It was the first time that I left Jurek and Paweł to sign the contract without me - they had done all the basic work, but they were quite taken aback when I told them that I was not going to travel to Poland simply for a signature. "You sign and I will endorse your signature" I said. It was a valuable order, but it was the first and only time when we had problems with a Shady Grove product. The crane was delayed in shipment, which upset the customer to start with, and then, when it finally arrived on site, cracks in the welds in the outrigger housings were discovered and the UDT Inspector refused permission for the crane to be put into operation. George Szulczewski and his engineers rushed to the scene, made a complete report with photographs, which were then hand-carried to the Service Division in Sunderland. Days elapsed with no sign of a reaction from Grove. It was a Tuesday evening, when returning to my home office after my mid-week squash and a few pints with my mates, I heard the fax line crackling, and through came a fax from the Finance Dept at Shady Grove asking why the final 10% payment due on the installation of the crane had not been received.

I sent a furious message back asking whether the Left Hand in Grove knew what the Right Hand was doing, repeated the saga of the technical problems with the crane, and the empty promises for action on their part and then I concluded: "In crude Limey Language, FUCK ALL HAS HAPPENED, and so are you surprised that your invoice has not been paid?" My fax reverberated around the halls at Shady Grove, and the hierarchy came down like a ton of bricks on Wayne Lawson, who had taken over from Mike Lamb as the UK based Sales Supremo. He was most upset that I had not consulted him before reacting, but when I got a call from Leroy Myers the next afternoon (who had been responsible for the Taakeover), asking what it was all about, I felt totally vindicated in raising the whirlwind and it certainly produced some action to rectify the problem.The next time that I showed up in Sunderland, I had to throw my hat in through the door of Wayne's office before entering, but he gradually calmed down, and eventually gave us some spare parts foc, which was only in part compensation for the cash settlement which we had to make out for our commission to mollify the customer and ensure that he did make the final payment. Grabcranex paid for Grove's errors.

Grabcranex

The second Sobemai crane for Poland, sold to Centrozłom Warszawa in 1991.

Transported by rail from Belgium.

Reception committee, headed by Dyrektor Malczewski, later tragically killed in a road accident. He invited me to dinner in his Warsaw apartment. Standing next to him is Audrey, now a partner in Grabcranex.

Grabcranex

The Atlas timber handlers which had cracks in the welding on the pedestal. The attitude of their rep cost them the franchise.

The first MZ 90 platform for Gdynia shipyard. The frustrated sale of the second unit cost us dearly, but we learned from the experience.

Alfski retired from the service of Coles, now envelopped by Grove, in 1991, after over 30 years of loyal service. He died in May 2004.

Robert Brouwer and Audrey drink his health.

Grabcranex

Sennebogen crawler excavators at work
on the "Gas 2000" pipeline.

And the "mining shaft" is dug out to take the pipeline under the hill.

Grabcranex

Poznan Fair 1996. Dyrektor Połubok of Gazobudowa (who succeded Lewiniec) proudly takes over a Sennebogen crawler crane.

1992. 20 years of Coles service in Poland . . . and Hello to Industrial Service Corporation.

Grabcranex

Cranes to Poland

One of the world's largest single coalpits has bought Grove mobile cranes to service its enormous bucket wheel excavators and walking draglines. Three cranes were delivered earlier this year following initial discussions on the joint Grove/Grabcranex stand at the 1991 Poznan Fair.

First to arrive were two RT 990s and these were swiftly followed by an additional order for an RT 760. All were delivered from Grove's US facility at Shady Grove where they were first inspected by a crane inspector from the Urzad Dozoru Technicznego, the official Polish Testing Authority.

Jerzy Wagenkneckt, managing director of the Kopalnia Beychalow mine, says he is pleased with the cranes and adds that whenever the mine is next in the market for mobile cranes, Grove will be a strong contender.

Grove at BAUMA 1992, where I was "hauled over the coals" for "falsifying documents."

The RT 9100 for the Port of Swinoujscie which cost us some money in 1994.

Grabcranex

Audrey and I find the perfect place to live during the Poznan Fair and visiting firemen are encouraged to join in the morning dip.

To cap the story of Grabcranex in Poland, I come to the last of the companies whom we represented, the French forklift truck manufacturer, Manitou. To those in the industry, the name needs no introduction, but in the hope that these writings may appeal to a few readers outside, a few words about Manitou will not come amiss. Like Sennebogen, Grove and JCB, this is a company which arose out of the ashes of the Second World War, founded by Monsieur Marcel Braud in 1945, and starting with the production of small concrete mixers. The first rough terrain forklift truck, the product which has made the company famous, was produced in 1957, coincidentally the same year in which I entered the crane world. This new product was named "Manitou" in a decision taken by the family. I can only suppose that "Manier Tout" *(Handling Everything)* was what decided the family to adopt this catchy abbreviation, which would be recognisable in all languages. Be that as it may, by the time that I made my first contact with Manitou, it was a name just as well known as JCB, and already established in the UK with its own subsidiary for almost 20 years.

Our contact with Manitou derived from an enquiry from the Polish State Timber Industry for a number of Rough Terrain Forklift Trucks in January 1991. I got in touch with the MD of Manitou Sitelift who had strong connections with Monsieur Braud, and he asked me if I could prepare some information on our activity in Poland. "Shall I write it in French?" I asked, and he assured me that this would secure immediate attention. Audrey's written command of the language being far better than mine, she prepared the document on her Amstrad and in April we found ourselves in Ancenis in the office of the newly appointed Export Manager, François Piffard. He was somewhat sceptical, but when Monsieur Braud, son of the founder of the company, entered the room, the atmosphere changed rather dramatically, due, purely, I believe, to the fact that we both spoke French, and that Poland was not a market which they had even considered up to that point.

I have to admit that I was rather proud, as a Brit, in securing the agency for a renowned French manufacturer for a third market, but it was to be rather short-lived. The large enquiry for the Timber Industry melted away with the onset of privatisation.

We exhibited Manitou for three years running at the Poznan Fair and we sold a few machines with a considerable amount of effort and expense, which was not justified by the results. The market was difficult and Piffard was seduced by an offer to take on the whole of Eastern Europe by a German firm, promising much business, but, in the event, not producing much more than we did in the

Grabcranex

Polish market.   However the whole experience was to have much greater influence on our personal lives than any other of our business associations, and, despite my lack of sales success, I have always found a warm welcome at International Exhibitions waiting for me on the Manitou Stand.

The most important order which we secured for Manitou was the sale of a Telescopic Handler to the Port of Gdynia in 1992.   The deal was for three units, reduced to one, and still projected to lead to many more machines, but it did not. The machine was rated by the Poles as a crane, requiring all the paraphernalia of Technical Takeover which has already been well documented in these pages. The UDT Ports Inspector was known to us as a good friend, a huge man with a large appetite named Kazimierz Schott.   In addition to the Delegation from the Port, I had service personnel for training from ISC, and two additional UDT Inspectors from Poznan whom I had invited in order to try and obtain a General Certificate of Approval for Manitou, to avoid the expense and tedium of individual takeovers.   This was a mistake, compounded by the fact that I decided to lead the whole delegation myself without either Paweł or Jurek, in an attempt to save costs.   In total, at the end of June I met 12 Poles at Charles de Gaulle Airport on a Saturday and spent Sunday showing them around Paris, constantly counting them up so as to ensure that none had failed to get in or out of the Metro at the appropriate station.   In the late afternoon we boarded the TGV for Ancenis.   The hotel was fortunately situated immediately opposite the railway station and we dined at a nearby restaurant.   I was completely exhausted and, after probably an excessive intake of vin rouge, I collapsed into bed in my room without bothering to do more than strip my clothes off.   In the middle of the night, I woke up badly needing a pee, and stumbled out of bed looking for the door to the bathroom.   Instead I landed, still befuddled, in the corridor outside the room and then opened another door and retreated hastily after seeing a distinctly hair-less leg sticking out of a bed.   I then realised where I was, but, to my horror, the door of my room had clanged shut behind me and there I was, completely naked, in the passageway.

I just had to get to the toilet, so I walked to the lift, descended to the ground floor and relieved myself in the Gents.   All the lights were on, but there was no sign of any Night Porter, to my intense relief.   I covered my nakedness with newspaper and searched for a spare key to my room.   Finding none, I selected another key at random, and carefully opening the door of the room, discovered it to be unoccupied and went to bed.   In the morning, I rang down to Reception to explain my predicament, to which Madame exclaimed: "Ooh la la!", delivered me a spare key to my own room and declined my offer to pay for the extra room which I had occupied. At breakfast I noted that the only other guests in the hotel on that Sunday night apart from our all-male contingent, were female......

This was just the beginning of a difficult few days, as the two UDT Inspectors whom I had invited for the General Certificate insisted that they should have stayed a full week (whereas I had programmed three full days only with fixed price flights), and refused to accept the self-certification welding procedures current in the factory. They wanted crane norms. Mr. Schott was much more co-operative, but the Technical Documentation was not totally acceptable and we had to re-schedule the whole Takeover for a month later. All this for one single machine!

However, when we came back again in July, only with the trio from Gdynia Port, it went smoothly, and Lloyd, with a commission in French francs burning a hole in his pocket, went out and bought a cottage. It is true that Audrey and I, fran-cophiles to a degree, had always had a dream about having "une petite maison en France", after innumerable very enjoyable holidays in the land of Molière, but my decision was impetuous to a degree. I saw an advertisement in the win-dow of the local Notaire for a "Maison à Restorer" for FFR 60,000 (c.£6,000) in a small village on the north side of the Loire. It certainly needed restoring. No window at all on the roadside, one large front room, a "kitchen" behind and a ladder up to a loft. There were outbuildings and a garden behind. However I was excited about its possibilities and offered FFR50,000 and it was accepted, and I put down FFR10,000 there and then, with formalities to be completed in October. One of the guys at Manitou assisting with the delegation laughed outright when he heard what I had done. "Mon Dieu! Vous avez acheté une maison sans consulter votre femme" - it seems that he had once bought a prop-erty without discussing it first with his wife, and she had refused to have any-thing to do with it, so that finally he was forced to sell it. His words proved to be somewhat prophetic.

Came October and one wet and windy Saturday evening Audrey and I arrived in Ancenis, and the next day we went to view the cottage. Although Audrey had been caught up to some extent in my excitement, when she saw the place, she was not very impressed, and I also began to have misgivings. Then we met the next-door neighbour to tell him that we had just bought the cottage. This was the coûp de grace. "Bonjour, monsieur", I said cheerfully, "Nous venons d'acheter cette maison". "Vous avez acheté cette maison - il y a beaucoup de problêmes - l'eau coule dans la maison du jardin pendant l'hiver", and with these welcoming remarks he turned his back on us, whilst his dog snarled furiously at us through his garden fence.   What he had just told us about the risk of water flooding in through the back of the house from the sloping garden appeared to be quite possible when we investigated further, which I had had no time to do when I bought it.   But it was his attitude which really put us off, apart from the slummy mess in his garden, which again I had not previously noticed.

We drove, rather low in spirits, to the next village and over a snack lunch in a café, I asked Audrey if she thought that I had made a mistake.   "Definitely" was her succinct reply, so I said that we would back out of it, however difficult.

On the Monday morning we visited the Notaire's office, where we were due the next day to finalise the contract.   When we expressed some doubts, the Notaire's assistant with whom I had done the deal was furious, and threatened fire and brimstone if we attempted to withdraw, because in France, unlike in the UK, once you have agreed to purchase, there is a contract.   We decided that further discussion with this gentleman was of no avail and went to Manitou, where help was immediately at hand.

"You must consult a lawyer" said Guy Alligand, then Chief of Administration at Manitou and my main point of contact, and gave us the name of their Notaire, the rival in the town of the one we were dealing with.   We explained to him that we were quite ready to forfeit 10% of the value, plus expenses, but that we were determined not to proceed.   He replied that we were legally bound to finalise the matter and could be dragged in front of a Tribunal, but, in view of the fact that we were English and that there had been misunderstandings, he believed that we could back out.   He offered to be present the next day at the final meeting. It was like being in Court.   The Notaire himself, a bouncy dapper little man seated himself in a high desk in the centre of the room, flanked by his assistant and the three ladies to whom the property belonged - it was a "succession", an inheritance.

We had prepared a carefully crafted address in French to explain the reasons why we did not want to proceed, adding in some minor details about which I had not been informed to add weight, but emphasising the hostile attitude of the neighbour as the nub of the matter.   Our Notaire attempted first to speak on our behalf, but was shouted down by his short-statured rival, who declared: "J'applique le loi francais - on vous amène à un Tribunal!" ("*I will apply the Law of France and you will be taken before a Tribunal!*")   At this point I stood up and firmly put our points without giving him a chance to stop me, and ending with the assurance that we would forfeit 10% of the agreed price and pay all costs. The little man then did a complete volte-face, repeating almost word for word what our Notaire had said to us on the previous day, and advising the three ladies to accept my offer, which he agreed was "Très raisonable", at the same time rapidly totting up his costs in the matter, which amounted to another 10% of the agreed price. We shook hands cordially with the three ladies, who agreed that the neighbour was very difficult, and in fact wanted the place for himself but did not have the money to buy it. The Notaire's assistant walked out of the room in high dudgeon without even saying "Au Revoir", and £1000 lighter in pocket, we were relieved to leave ourselves.

Now you would think that, after this experience, we would have had the sense to say "Enough in Enough", but, over lunch, Guy Alligand asked us if we were really serious about purchasing a house in the area. I certainly was, thinking that it would help to cement our relationship with Manitou and give us a base from which we could entertain Polish visitors, apart from being a holiday home, and Audrey, swept along behind me, did not disagree. Guy then said that he had a property to sell, which had belonged to his late grandmother, and was jointly owned by himself and his brother. So that afternoon we crossed the Loire to the south bank and drove up to La Chapelle St. Florent, a large and prosperous village set high above the Loire, surrounded by vineyards with a magnificent view over the whole valley. In the middle of the main street, Rue Bonchamps, named after a celebrated Vendéen Royalist General, was a solidly constructed terraced house dating from before the Revolution, clearly in much better condition than the cottage, and with certainly much more character. The large Salle de Séjour and one of the first floor rooms had beamed ceilings and quarry tiles on the floor, giving the bedroom a delightfully uneven crazy appearance, and the oak staircase was classic. Two good lean-to outhouses, and a small vegetable garden, detached from the property and forming part of a large area of jardins potagers completed the property. The tiled roof had caved in, but, that apart, the place seemed to be in good order. "How much are you asking for it?" I said to Guy. "FFR 40,000", he replied. "It's a deal" we replied, and I think that Audrey was by then also totally convinced. He said that surely we wanted to reflect, but I replied that we wanted to settle as soon as possible and get on with the renovation.

Madame Alligand Senior, a highly respected lady, had lived in the house in to her early 90s, with no bathroom, no toilet and only a sink with a cold water tap in the corner of the Salle de Séjour, but then she had had to go into an Old

People's Home, and the house had been empty for some years. It seems to me that the French do not like restoring old properties - this is a hobby of the Brits, and the co-operation which we received from the Mairie in clearing the place out was clear evidence that there was a sense of relief that the mad English had decided to rectify what was becoming rather an embarassment in the centre of the village. Guy introduced us to his aunt who lived next door, and what a charming contrast she was from the hostile neighbour at the cottage. She became one of our closest friends in the village. Guy organized immediately for the roof to be renewed, which cost us almost as much again as we had paid for the house, but, because they cut off the old roof trusses and positioned the new ones on top, it gave us a huge attic room with a wonderful view over the valley. Guy recommended all the other artisans, carpenter, mason and plumber/electrician and they all worked together very well to effect a complete renovation of the house, apart from the cleaning and re-decoration. This we did ourselves, and it cost poor Audrey the following August a detached retina in the eye, which was fortunately promptly and efficiently dealt with by her flying home and going straight to Moorfields Eye Hospital. We exerted more personal "sweat, toil, blood and tears" on that house than on any other we have ever possessed.

There was on rather nasty fly, however, who buzzed in and out of the ointment. He was the peasant who cultivated all the vegetable gardens, a strange rather wild-looking individual known to all as "Jo-Jo", who did not live in the village, but whose family owned the other neighbouring property, which they let out. We did not really want the garden at all, so we invited him to go on growing his vegetables in it, but he abandoned it, so we had to cultivate it ourselves. He then proceeded to vandalise our work, pulling up the plants which we had lovingly put in, and completely wrecking a tubular steel arbour which we purchased. He even broke in to one of the outhouses and stole the motor out of a second-hand fridge which our electrician had donated us and later he punctured some cans of English beer which I left in there. We had no absolute proof that it was he, but he displayed open hostility whenever we met, refusing to give me the time of day, and he made it clear that he objected very much to the presence of English foreigners in the village. I had a word with the local gendarmerie about it, without trying to make too much fuss, but in the end we were obliged to get the mason to build a wall around our little garden and I put double locks on the door of the outhouse. We then employed a professional gardener to put plants and a tree in to the garden which would suit the local climate, and all of our new-found friends in the immediate neighbourhood made it clear to "Jo-Jo" that they were on our side and not his, although it took a little time for us to convince them that it really was he who was doing the damage. I think that he made a conscious attempt to drive us away, but he did not succeed, and now, whilst my professional connection with Manitou has long receded in to the past, the legacy of a pied-à -terre in the lovely Loire Valley, with easy access to quantities of Muscadet and Gamay (vin rosé) has added a second dimension to retirement without which we would be the poorer. "Jo-Jo" just ignores us and we ignore him......

Before we parted company with Manitou, in October 1994 I entertained one Polish delegation to dinner in the house, from the Port of Szczecin. Some 10 or 12 delegates came over, and signed an order for a large Telehandler, but when they got home they found that they had no funds to purchase it. It was the old Polish story: "Przepraszam, alé niemąpieniądze" ("I am so sorry, but we don't have any money")....

Even if Gdynia Port only purchased one Manitou, they followed on their first purchase of Grove hydraulic cranes with Sennebogen, reverting again to Lattice Boom rather than Tele-Boom cranes for cycling work in a stockyard. The old soldier, Karl Klein, was starting to move towards retirement, and a young man, an engineering officer straight out of the Bundeswehr, whose commercial knowledge when he joined Sennebogen was limited, took over. He arrived just at the time that we had landed this important order. Every technical detail had been agreed with old Karl verbally, but carefully confirmed by me in writing, and I think that young Stefan Proetzel was somewhat taken aback when he first met the wily old English fox who could speak German and had much experience in dealing with his principals and fighting his corner.

He says now that I taught him a lot, but, however that may be, we became good friends and played squash together whenever I came to Straubing. He used to enjoy his visits to the Poznan Fair, where in the evening I would regale him with the tunes of old German songs on my mouth organ, and my memory of him swimming in the lake with his Sennebogen hat on, looking like a Polish kaczka (duck) is still with me.

1994 was probably the year when the Sennebogen franchise overtook Grove in importance for Grabcranex. It was quite normal for me to find myself sitting in the Sales Office in the Sennebogen Works, driving away at the computer like any other employee of the company, and this was unusual, because mostly all visitors were confined to the special receptions rooms allocated for them. I was more like one of the family. These were before the days of cheap airfares, but my youngest daughter, Fay, was then employed by BA, so I could travel to Munich for £50 return, which was only 20% of the standard fare, and then I would simply hop on the train to Straubing. When she left BA, I even did one trip all the way by train, which took me all day with a lovely ride along the banks of the Rhine, and left me a very clear impression of the punctuality and smooth efficiency of the the State-owned Continental railways compared to the expected delays of the privatised and fragmented UK network.

Lack of any other business forced us to earn a few crusts by buying up old Coles and Grove cranes in Poland from companies who could no longer afford to keep them, and re-selling them in Western Europe, which was where my old friend, Bill Murray, a specialist in second-hand cranes, came in very useful with his contacts. One deal involved me in an unpleasant contretemps with the VAT authorities. Two old Coles cranes were purchased in Poland and transported to Hull Docks, where we sold them to second-hand dealer for re-furbishment and re-export, for £20,000 apiece. "No", he said, in answer to my query about charging him VAT in addition, "I will pay the VAT on the landed value at the Docks, and I can only re-claim it once". A phone call to my local VAT office appeared to confirm what he said, but I made a mistake - I did not get it in writing. Some weeks later I had a VAT Inspection. Normally I had no problem with these, and in fact one VAT Inspector actually complimented me on the tidiness of my book-keeping, having accepted an invitation to lunch and asking if he could watch some of the Test Match on the TV. This Inspector was the opposite, and he sat all day in my dining room like a nasty spider weaving its web unseen around me, refusing any kind of refreshment, and finally coming up with some critical comments. He averred that I was wrong to claim VAT deduction on all of my Accountant's fees, because part of the fees were payable for work done on my personal taxation. I never received any official demand on this matter, but only on the invoices for the two used cranes, which the Inspector had not even mentioned in his criticsms. So the demand for several thousand pounds of unpaid VAT came like a bombshell through the letter-box and was not read by me until late on a Friday evening after returning from a week in Poland. It cost me a great deal of emotional upset, and money, to sort it out. It seems that I should have charged VAT to the UK importer of the cranes, and did eventually did so, but, until his VAT office in the North-East had agreed that he could re-claim the VAT a second time on the same deal, he would not pay me, and his VAT Office were tardy in their agreement to this. The whole matter was a bureaucratic "wash-through" situation with a double payment and double reclamation of VAT, but I had to pay interest on the monies until it had been sort-ed out, and fees to my accountant to help me resolve the matter. When I retired, tearing up my VAT file was one of the most satisfying pieces of destruction which I ever indulged in.

In 1995, we had a much-needed piece of luck, and again through the good offices of David Steel, who rang me to give me the sad news of his father's death, and, at the same time to put me in touch with a firm of Consultants involved in an EEC-funded project to try to introduce the manufacturing companies in the BUMAR Group to marketing and selling techniques in the West. He himself had been offered the assignment, but was unable to undertake it having by that time regained full employment once more. It certainly was a project for which I had the knowledge and experience, but it was a mammoth task which really could only be nibbled at in the time which we had at our disposal. Audrey joined me, as her teaching and understanding skills would certainly be of benefit but we found ourselves in strong disagreement with the norms laid down by the supposedly experienced consultants, whose objectives appeared to us to avoid committing themselves to anything which might possibly redound on them personally, preferring rather to pontificate, write copious reports, take their fees and disappear. All the companies whom we saw were very co-operative, with up and coming young managers eager to learn, but there was one notable exception - Warynski excavators, the manufacturer whom I certainly knew best out of all the companies which I visited. The Director reacted in a hostile manner to my probings on the company setup, and, when we returned for the second meeting to give them some training, we found that the Sales Manager (clearly the key figure) had been despatched somewhere abroad, and we were ushered into a conference room where half a dozen motley individuals were assembled, some clad in jackets and trousers, but some in overalls, without any idea what their functions in the company were. The Director, after I had started my usual tack of going over some points from the first meeting to ensure that I had the facts straight, rudely interrupted and said: "Mr Lloyd, your job is not to ask questions, but to train these people. Train them!", and he left the room, never to re-appear. I was angry, and felt like getting up and walking out, but here Audrey really came to the rescue and we started a dialogue with these people which ended up by our acquiring a lot of knowledge of their problems, and being able to make some positive recommendations, which I then put into a report and handed it to them. It never reached the hands of the absent Sales Manager, as we found out on the third visit, and we had to do it all over again for his benefit, but at least he listened.

Grabcranex

As a complete contrast to this, another company, the manufacturer of an agricultural attachment for a farm tractor produced an excellent sales brochure exactly as I had recommended, which we had translated into French and German for them by native speakers, and they clearly had a high quality product since they were selling it successfully in Norway and Sweden, but they had no idea about (nor the money to invest in) proper sales and marketing, and there were only two persons in the factory with any command of English, and that limited. Discussions were half in Polish and half in English. I actually undertook some serious market research for them in the UK, but they were unable to adapt to the specific technical requirements needed and it came to nothing. Part of our task was also to visit Trade Associations in Western Europe and obtain lists of potential sales outlets, which was a complete waste of time, but still earned us fees, so we did it! All in all the assignment was an interesting diversion from my normal intense pursuit of sales.

We stayed very reasonably in Warsaw in the "UDT Hotel", courtesy of Iwo Jakubowski. This establishment was normally only for the use of employees of UDT, and for us it was a very special and much appreciated privilege and enabled us to save some money out of the allotted daily expenses for the Consultancy, which only covered me in any case. We had our own room with shower and toilet and access to the communal kitchen, where we could cook for ourselves, which is how I came to be battling with the new/old currency mix in the local market. We have always been good at "setting up house" on our travels, preferring that to long stays in hotels.

I had got to know Iwo Jakubowski when I had taken him on my own to Shady Grove in February 1992 in order to obtain a General Certificate of Approval for all Grove cranes and platforms and avoid the expensive cost of individual Takeovers. His father had been one of the Polish officers who had risen up against the Soviet Regime during the War, and he was dragged off to Siberia in 1945 and put to work in a salt mine. He was physically a very strong man, but he knew that, if he remained there it would be a living death, and he decided that he just had to escape, whatever the risks.

He rode in freight trains right across the Soviet Union, sometimes having to hang underneath the rail wagons. At one point, when he was resting up in a station siding, he was spotted by a Russian guard, who raised his rifle to shoot, but then suddenly decided to show compassion, and deliberately turned his back on and ignored his potential victim. Eventually he made it all the way back to his family in Warsaw, but his clandestine return was kept a close secret for fear that he would be discovered and re-arrested. Only his mother was privy to the secret, and Iwo himself only learnt about his father's escapade long after the death of Stalin, when the risk of re-arrest had receded.

The memories of the Stalinistic period lingered on in Poland long after those of the Nazi atrocities. A quiet unassuming man, who lasted much longer in the Bumar Import Dept than anyone else whom I knew, had spent his childhood in Warsaw during the Nazi occupation, and I commented to him that it must have been a terrible experience. "The Soviet dictatorship was much worse", he replied, and in answer to my request for an explanation he went on to say that under the German Occupation, if people were taken away from their families upon suspicion of being anti-Nazi saboteurs, and subsequently executed, their families would be informed, and at least there was certainty as to the individual's fate, which, after a period of mourning, could be accepted. Under the Russians, people just disappeared mysteriously, and enquiries made by friends or relatives through the official channels would reveal nothing, thus producing a great deal of angst and worry because of the uncertainty. The Nazi Regime was also relatively short-lived in comparison, since even after the death of Stalin almost eight years after the end of the War, it took much longer for the Soviet political influence to thaw.

By the mid-1990s ordinary life in Poland was vastly different from when I had started with Grove-Coles in 1986. Little cafés and restaurants sprang up along the main highways, offering good food at (for foreigners) very reasonable prices accompanied by excellent service. Petrol stations grew like mushrooms, and Motels offering good accomodation made it much easier for the traveller. It was also hard for older people, brought up under Communism, to adapt. Alfred Gorniok complained to me that different shops were selling bread at varying prices and it completely confused him. But Capitalism also brought in its problems. Crime increased enormously, and, for a time, there was a lack of trust by the ordinary people of the police, who had been regarded as the "enemy" - the tools of the Communist Regime. But at least Poland did not have the problems on the scale of the new countries emerging from the collapse of the Soviet Union, with businesses having to be protected by Mafia-style "heavies".

1996 witnessed a big reversal in our financial problems when Robert Brouwer very kindly offered to buy me out of Industrial Service Corporation. Clearly he had his own motives for so doing, in order to gain complete control, but, after a firm but very friendly haggle, he paid me a very fair price for my shares and, accompanied by our cashing in some investments, we were enabled to wipe off the whole of our Bank Overdraft.   This also enabled me to make my plans to retire at the age of 65.

Paweł and Jurek were against the idea, and, whenever in meetings with Principals I would mention my intention, they would tick me off in private about it.   But I could see that I was just becoming an interlocutor and administrator between them and our Principals, all business deals being effectively negotiated by them with the customers without my participation, and therefore, no longer being at the cutting edge, I started also to lose interest.   With the collapse of Communism and the privatisation of businesses, the necessity for the role of the foreign direct representative of the manufacturer declined, and, in any case the acquisition by Grove of Krupp Cranes of Wilhelmshaven in 1995, brought Hans Puvogel on to our side, with a knowledge of the latest Deutsche Grove product which I could never hope to emulate, and, with his groundwork for Krupp we benefited with the sale of three Wilhelmshaven built cranes to Mostostal Gdansk.   In the very last year of my involvement, with hardly any participation on my part, the boys also landed a very important order for a 180 Tonne Sennebogen crane for use by a Polish Contractor in Libya, which also, because the specification was such that it eliminated most of our competitors on technical grounds, we were able to obtain a very profitable price, in which, of course, I shared.   People asked me if I intended to sell my interest in Grabcranex Poland.   "No way", I would reply, "I am now getting much more out of the business than I am putting in, and that is my due reward."

So, when I was invited to the 50th Anniversary Dealer Convention of Grove in May 1997, I raised the subject with Wayne Lawson, wanting to be sure that Grove would appoint Grabcranex as an official dealer in Poland after my retirement.   "You have to control the service as well as the sales" was the condition he laid down.   ISC had lost a few of their very good service engineers who had set up independently, and Jurek and Paweł wanted to cut their monopolistic control of the After-Sales Service, but before we invited Greg Davis to Poland to see what alternatives we proposed, I decided that it would only be fair to George Szulcewski to appraise him first of the situation.   When he was in the UK I invited him to my home and, over dinner, I delivered the bombshell, which was perhaps rather inhospitable, but the most straight-forward way which I could think of.   He was most upset, and vowed to fight his corner, but he was unable to impress the American with his presentation of the Glorious Past, and Greg fully endorsed the new arrangements of utilizing independent regional-based service engineers or companies.   He stipulated that a man should be engaged to oversee and co-ordinate the operation, and Jurek's cousin, a technician just out of the Polish Merchant Navy, provided the right answer.   This Grabcranex Trio still exists today, and my decision to leave the scene was endorsed as the market for cranes shrivelled up.

My career in Poland had a rather sour ending in some ways.   In addition to reviving the market for Grove, I also introduced the access platform side in to the market, Manlift.   One of the first units which I purchased for stock took two years to sell, and then at cost price on totally unsecured credit terms (which were met without problems), and then we gradually built up a good population of some 30 to 40 units.

In 1998 a new Sales Manager was appointed, an inflexible Swiss with no knowledge whatever of Poland, who insisted on the production of a future Marketing Plan, and how sales would be financed etc etc.   All this was provided and discussed at the Poznan Fair, but he would make no decision then and there.   We soon found out why.   Without any further consultation or warning, a week or two later Grove Manlift appointed their powerful Dutch dealer instead, simply upon the promise that this company would open up the market by hiring machines out.   Our track record was totally ignored, and when I visited the Dutch company, they alleged that they had never heard of us or our activity and assumed that they were taking on a new and un-touched market.   The upshot was was Manlift lost the market totally to their competitors, and, as I write, I am not in the least surprised to learn that Grove have now sold the whole of the Manlift business.   It also clearly demonstrates the vulnerability of a small private enterprise being in danger of having their birthright removed at the stroke of a pen by a large conglomerate with no knowledge of the situation on the ground.

I really enjoyed the 1997 Grove Conference.   It was the swansong of the Lodge where customers had been so hospitably entertained for years.   Much was made of the "Role of Grove in the Hanson Corporation", the senior executives being clearly quite unaware that, six months later, Hanson would put Grove up for sale.

True to form I left my personal mark on the event.   After the final dinner and speeches, Wayne invited all the delegates to the bar for a drink.   Before he could stop me, I had leapt to podium to deliver my own "Old Campaigner's Speech" ostensibly to thank Grove on behalf of all the delegates for the excellent hospitality (which, of course, I did), but really to deliver some anecdotes about my 40 years in the crane business and to make the delegates laugh, in which I was definitely successful.

The serious-minded American top brass gaped with astonishment at this Old Upstart daring to usurp the rostrum for his own personal delight, but they just could not prevent it!

The following year saw the closure of Crown Works in Sunderland by Grove, which was probably inevitable after they had acquired Krupp, bringing the manufacture in the UK of wheeled mobile cranes to an end. Little could I have forseen this when I first stepped across the threshold of that proud and important establishment in 1957, and for me it was a very sad event.

Manitou at Poznan Fair 1992 with Francois Piffard.

Grabcranex

July 1992. A delegation of 12 Poles for the sale of one Maniscopic to Gdynia Port. My night adventure in the hotel is *not* an camera.

August 1992. "Maison à restaurer" impetuously bought by Lloyd without consulting his wife . . .

Grabcranex

November 1992. Guy Alligand's grandmother's house which we did buy for Ffr 40,000. It was a bargain.

The cold-water sink in the corner was the sole sanitary convenience in the house.

Grabcranex

November 1994. Better luck with the Gdynia Port - an order for four lattice boom cranes. Kazimierz Schott inspects whilst Sennebogen engineer Otto Herrnberger carries out tests.

1997 Grabcranex stand at Poznan Fair shows how far we have come.

1998, my last appearance, relaxing with a "Piwo"*(beer)* whilst Hans Puvogel and Stefan Proetzel use their mobile phones.

Winds of change in Poland.

. . . and scratch a Polish communist, and you will find underneath an nationalist.

Rural scenes in Poland in the early 1990s.

Grabcranex

Storks' nest in Southern Poland and seaside swans in the North.

Snack bars spring up along Polish highways.

The Germans have not
forgotten that Silesia used
to be theirs.

Grabcranex

Crown works, Sunderland, the home of Coles Cranes which saw the expansion of the Company and its product range to worldwide success.

EPILOGUE

My 40 year career in the sale of cranes and excavators had an unusual conclusion. In June 1997 I received a telephone call out of the blue from a Ports Development Consultant named Anthony Bellew, who informed me that Grove had recommended me to him, and that he was looking for a crawler crane to handle 30 Tonne Containers at 10/12 metres radius, for the remote island of St. Helena in the mid-Atlantic, famous for its being the exiled home of the Emperor Napoleon. I immediately informed him that this duty would require a 100 Tonne capacity crane, and since the machine would have to be broken down for shipment, my first suggestion was the only crawler which Grove ever built, the HL150C, a crane which had fascinated me because it was the first time I had come across a machine which could build up, not only its own boom unaided, but also the crawler tracks. This was achieved by shipping the machine with the basic superstructure and carbody supporting itself on outrigger jacks, from which it could operate as a fixed base crane and build in the crawler side-frames. Grove agreed that I could offer it, but then informed me that production was about to be terminated and that there were only two units left to sell, which were already practically spoken for. So I turned to Sennebogen. Stefan Proetzel and I discussed the specification at the Poznan Fair, and, before the end of the month our offer for a 100 Tonne Model 6100 Superlifter, able to be broken down into individual weights not exceeding 25 Tonnes, was in the hands of Anthony Bellew and on its way to St. Helena. Our offer was accepted technically by the Port Authority, but it had then to go to Public Tender and be handled through the Crown Agents, since payment was to be made from UK Aid Funds.

Having obtained the Tender Documents, I went to Straubing and spent two full days discussing and drawing up our bid. We had to quote CIF Cardiff, because the only way of shipping the crane was on the RMS St. Helena, a combined passenger and freight vessel which leaves Cardiff once every three months for St. Helena, calling at Ascension Island en route, and then going on to Capetown. The boat spends several weeks to-ing and fro-ing in between Capetown, St. Helena and Ascension, with the occasional visit to Tristan da Cunha, and then back to Cardiff for the next run.

Finding a transport company to haul the crane from Straubing to Cardiff was not easy, but I finally located one very near to the old Priestman Works in Hull, which was rather ironic.

Much of the autumn was spent in technical discussions with Crown Agents' officials whose knowledge of cranes was non-existent. Everything was conducted by phone calls and by fax - they refused to meet me in person, which would have enabled me to make my technical explanations much more easily, since they were, of course, trying to shoot down the Sennebogen offer in favour of less expensive alternatives which could not meet the required spec. But, fortunately, we had the support of the Port engineers on St. Helena, who knew what they wanted and had accepted the Sennebogen even before the Tender was opened.

In January 1998, with still no decision having been taken, and noises being made about the need to have the crane on site and working by the end of September, the shipping line decided that the 25 Tonne limit on the maximum individual weight around which the whole Tender had been drawn up, was acceptable for handling by the ship's gear in calm weather, but not if there were storms, a likely occurrence in mid-Atlantic. So Crown Agents asked if we could reduce the weight still further to 22 Tonnes.

Here I lost patience, and pointed out to them that we had met all the conditions of the Tender, that even to investigate this would cost time and money, probably involving removal of the hoist drums, and I refused even to ask Sennebogen without being able to give them an assurance that we would get the business. "Oh, no, we cannot possibly make any commitment on that, but we can confirm that our clients are quite interested in the crane, provided that you can confirm this point". My telephone call to Erich Sennebogen Jnr and his reply ("Wir werden es tun - *We will do it*") was reminiscent of that call to the Managing Director of Coles in 1960 from Warsaw, prior to my very first crane sale in Poland, asking for an especially longer boom on the Coles Endurance Truck: "Tell them that we will do it, Dick, get the order, lad". Here was proved to me beyond all doubt the value of working with a manufacturer still privately owned and where important decisions could be made immediately. I was careful to point out to Crown Agents that extra cost would be involved, and I made sure that this extra cost was only passed on after a very decent profit for myself had been added. I felt that I had earned it! Stefan Proetzel made his first visit to London on February 26th to sign the contract, and my very last crane sale was made.

At the beginning of July the crane was ready for inspection by TUV (the German Technical Inspection Authority), and then stripped down and loaded on to nine trailers for the journey to Cardiff. I was responsible for checking the shipping spec at the Docks, about which I was quite nervous because there was only so much which I could check. If a vital component were missing, there was no possibility of sending it out by airfreight unless it could be dropped by parachute, since the only connection to St. Helena is by sea. On August 24th, accompanied by Ulli Dirrigl, the young Sennebogen service engineer, Audrey and I flew with the RAF to Ascension Island, accompanied by large numbers of squaddies on their way to garrison the Falklands Islands. The flight was none too comfortable, and the long evening wait in the RAF Barracks brought back memories of the smoky interior of a NAAFI Canteen during National Service. The "Airport" on Ascension consisted of a landing strip and a few scruffy huts, where we deposited our luggage whilst waiting to be taken out by launch to the RMS St. Helena, anchored out in the bay. Once on board, installed in a comfortable cabin for the two day trip, we could relax, but getting in and out of the launch which carried us out to the ship required some athleticsm, since the swell was rising and falling by about a metre, and one had to choose the right moment to jump as the gunwale of the boat came level with the quay. Busy with my video camera I nearly missed my footing and received a good soaking. On the return trip we had to spend a couple of days on Ascension, a vast military establishment built on solid rock, the only bit of green being a peak in the centre of the island up a steep road which our clapped-out hired car failed to climb.

The RMS St. Helena spends two or three days off the island, which rises steeply out of the sea and is intensely beautiful. Passengers and freight are all unloaded on to boats and lighters, which are towed in to the quayside, often in heavy swell. The same method was used for the crane, superstructure, undercarriage, crawlers, counterweight and boom sections, all travelling on separate pontoons, not to mention four containers filled with counterweight, hookblock. auxiliary hoist drum and parts. An old 25 Tonne Butters derrick, known locally as "The Thompson's Crane" after the old hand-operated derrick which it replaced, was the only means of unloading the pontoons, and, as soon as the undercarriage was landed on the quay, the hydraulic jacks were positioned, ready to receive the superstructure. Fitting these together was the most critical operation, and it was fortunate that we had such a cool-headed and experienced engineer as Ulli Dirrigl in charge, ably assisted by a team from the PWD. Had we not reduced the individual weight of each component to 22 Tonnes, I do not think that the operation would have been successfully achieved. Two old 16 Tonne capacity Jones cranes assisted the derrick to lift the superstructure, which was much heavier at one end than at the other, and, in order to centralise the super over the chassis, two lifts had to be made, with the super being lowered to rest partly on the undercarriage whilst the Butters hung on to one side of it, during which the two old mobiles were re-positioned. All three cranes

Epilogue

were straining away at maximum capacity in this most delicate operation, where one false move would have spelled disaster.   Watching, helplessly, with my video-camera, my heart was beating at twice its usual rate, but Ulli remained as cool as a cucumber and absolutely in control.   Fourteen days had been allowed for erecting the crane.   It was completed in three.

This enabled us to explore the island.   Until the ship returned from Capetown, we were marooned.   All the normal tourists just stay for the two or three days when the RMS is in port.   St. Helena is a Time-Warp, a colony still totally dependent on UK Aid.   We learned that it costs the UK Tax-payer £9,000,000 per annum, of which only one third gets through to the island.   The rest is spent on bureaucracy, because there is a Governor with a cocked hat and all the trappings of a bygone age, a splendid residence to go with it, where we were regally entertained to tea and cakes and then there are all the people employed in the administration of the colony.   One leading "Saint" (as the islanders dub themselves) said to me: "Half a dozen people could run this island and make a profit".   Its importance as a watering-hole for sailing ships after rounding the Horn of Africa en route for Europe has long disappeared. The only legacy from those far-off days are the ruined forts which bedeck the island, from which no one shot was ever fired in anger.

In the 19th Century the island had a contract with the UK Post Office for mail-bags.   The Tenders were in fact closed since they stipulated that the mail-bags should be made of St.Helena flax.   For this purpose New Zealand flax was introduced to the island, but, when the Post Office changed to bags made of plastic, the business collapsed, and now the flax has spread like a cancer all over the island and is threatening the natural flora and fauna.   One of the mills is still there, preserved as so-called tourist attraction, and we saw that it was in a very run-down condition, accessed only by a muddy path on foot.   We found the people, all colours from white to coal black, to be extremely friendly, speaking with a local accent which was a mixture of Cockney and Kiwi.   Everyone waved at us as we drove up and down the steep, winding mountain roads in a hired car which had always to be parked on a hill in case it would not re-start, but they had not learned about litter, and rusty tin-cans and empty beer bottles desecrated many of the beauty spots.   One of my favourite walks was round the headland from Jamestown to the next bay on a path cut out of the cliff side, and each time I picked up several beer bottles and deposited them in the hotel dustbin.   The hotel was colonial in style, with a courtyard in the middle and a long gallery over it leading from the guest-rooms to the dining-room and kitchen, where at first tinned peas and sweetcorn were the only vegetables which we were given to eat.   We dined out at one of the few other eating places in Jamestown one night, Anne's Cafe, where we had to order our meal in advance and were the only diners.   We found Anne to be an interesting and communicative lady.   One of a family of 10, all but one had left the island to find work and earn money, mainly on Ascension Island or in the Falklands on military installations.   At that time the islanders did not have full UK citizenship and were restricted as to where they could go to find employment.   Her 17 year old son was about to leave to the UK to join the Royal Navy, finding life at home too tedious.   "I have to let him go" she said philosophically.   She served us delicious Tuna Fishcakes with fresh carrots and cabbage.   This may sound an odd combination, but the local Tuna tastes more like meat than fish.   We made the hotel proprietors aware of this meal and immediately our diet was changed and became much better.   In fact, as we were the only guests until the ship returned from Capetown, we ordered in advance each day whatever we wanted, and they provided excellent packed lunches for our forays into the interior.   The only locally grown fruit is a stubby, but very tasty banana, and once the boat had departed all other imported fruit rapidly disappeared from the market stalls. We never saw an apple nor an orange the whole time of our stay.

There was no Bank on the island, and Credit Cards were not accepted.   We prepaid the hotel from England and, because we decided to throw a party for the staff of the PWD (Public Works Dept) after the crane had been handed over, I had to arrange for more cash to be transferred from the UK to the hotel account. The PWD Offices reminded me of the RE Admin Offices in Moascar in the Suez Canal Zone in the early 1950s, with their wide outside wooden staircases, ceiling fans and shuttered windows.

During our stay it rained a great deal and swirls of cloud would descend on the peaks blotting our everything and then suddenly clearing and revealing the most stunning views.   We could well imagine how depressed Napoleon became, incarcerated as he was at Longwood House, a rather gloomy building situated in a part of the island which seemed to be shrouded in perpetual mist, because he was never allowed out to wander around and see some of the beautiful scenery.   One certainly had a feeling of being cut off from the world, with the only newspaper being the St. Helena News, a brief broadsheet published locally every week, and without anything on TV, except video tapes.   There are those who go back regularly to St. Helena, and because of its old-fashioned charm and isolation, this is not surprising.   But we also found that there was something rather depressing about the place, and could equally understand the desires of the younger generation to escape.   There is talk of providing the island with an airport to encourage tourism, but it would probably turn it into a kind of Madeira, highly commercialised.   There are certainly similarities in the terrain, but that is where it ends.

This visit, perhaps the most unusual of my whole career, was a fitting end to 40 Years of world-wide sales.   Looking back, it was undoubtedly the prospect of overseas travel which attracted me to my chosen career in exporting.   I had never thought consciously of becoming a salesman, given the old idea of the archetypal commercial traveller, the guy peddling vacuum-cleaners door to door, and wedging his foot in the jamb before the housewife could shut him out. But become one I did, and enjoyed the excitement of personal encounter which selling entails, and the tremendous thrill of pulling off a deal.   Today "marketing" is the catchphrase, particularly in the consumer industry, but, if one goes in to a store to buy something, how much is one influenced by the attitude and personality of the sales assistant.   The marketing may have been done, but the man or woman who serves you in the shop can still has an influence on the sale, in my opinion.   When we were first married, we were attracted by the marketing of a washing machine called Rolls, which offered lower prices by direct sales to the householder.   We asked for a demonstration and it was a cold foggy November evening when the salesman knocked at our door.   After the demonstration, we said that we were well impressed, but that we would have to think about it.   His face fell a mile: "I thought that you were buyers" he said.   I replied that we might well be, but that it still represented a fairly large investment for us and we would need time to think about it.   A few days later I rang him up and said that we would order the washer, but that I wanted a discount for cash.   He replied brusquely that the prices were rock bottom and absolutely non-negotiable and I just hung up on him.   I had been quite ready to pay the full price, and was just trying it on, and all that he had had to do was to explain politely but firmly that he would very much like to take the order, but regretted that the company policy was "No discount", and he would have made the sale. Selling is a science in personal relationships.   It may be that the salesman or woman has to risk the chance that he or she will lose the deal, but it should always be done with a smile on the face.

What motivated me?   Was it an urge to prove my late father wrong?   He used to say that "all jobs are damn dull, boy, and you just have to put up with it".   A dental surgeon, who enjoyed the technical side of his job, he undoubtedly became frustrated with standing on his feet day in and day out in the same room, looking into the mouths of his patients. He had also reacted against his father, a stern Victorian village schoolmaster who was always known as "Pater". My father was one of a family of five boys and three girls and Pater told him that he was no good and would never get anywhere. So while some of his brothers had the benefit of some higher education, he was put in to the bank as a trainee clerk at the age of 16. Then came the First World War, and my father was commissioned in to the Welsh Horse, and, when that was disbanded in 1916, he trained as a pilot in the RFC, as I have already recorded. He used his gratuity after the war to become a dental student, and I have to admire the way in which he made his own way up in the world.

Was it that, having married young (at 25), I managed still to retain my bachelor freedom, and escape from the ties of family life in travel? In fact my father was definitely opposed to the idea of my marrying early upon the grounds that I was too young to know my own mind. Also, in bettering himself in the world, he had acquired a streak of snobbishness, and I believe that he also did not consider that the daughter of a Yorkshire carpenter was sufficiently high up the social scale as a suitable wife for his son entering upon a business career, even though he wrote me at the time that he would welcome any decent honest girl in to the family. Fortunately my mother took to Audrey immediately and he had to accept the fait accompli.

When I proposed to Audrey, her first condition of acceptance was that she should keep her job, with which I totally acquiesced, as I intended to keep mine. Neither of us, in tying the knot, had any idea what the stresses and strains of my chosen career, with long absences, one from another, would mean. But she always supported me, and when we had a row over this problem, and I would threaten to give up the job, she would retort: "No, you won't, you will never throw that in my face, but one day when you come home, I will not be here..." Of course she always was, and the welcome which I would get from the children, scrambling to see what I had brought them home as presents, would take the wind out of her justifiably angry sails.

The girls also suffered from my absences, and the fact that she was always there was the only reason why my job did not a greater toll on their childhood. I can say that I honestly tried to compensate to some extent by sharing more of the domestic duties than most men of my generation would undertake, when I was at home. Fortunately my mother had taught me to cook as a boy during the school holidays, by giving me detailed instructions on how to prepare the evening meal when she was not well, which started by having to light the fire to heat the Triplex oven..... The important thing was that our marriage survived, because we never got bored with each other, but it is certainly true that, on one occasion, I told her that my job was more important than my marriage and I have never been allowed to forget this!

My other main reflection is that I was of a lucky generation, too young to fight in the Second World War, but also too old to suffer the uncertainties and stresses of modern business life, with its lack of job security, high pressure demands for results, the curse of the E-Mail box, and the constant intrusion of the mobile phone. I did suffer with being sent away to boarding school at the age of seven to escape the London Blitz. My father was an extreme patriot, who refused to leave London because it would be "running away". He turned down the chance of a job as a school dentist in Cornwall, where we all could have been together. After all, he had more than done his bit for his country in the First World War, but he still would not leave the capital in the Second. My mother definitely suffered from not having my sister and me at home, and I was often homesick at school, and, as a result, never even thought of sending our daughters to boarding school, with which Audrey totally agreed. But it was a tough preparation for my future career, and even if my childhood was not golden, my life from the moment that I started my National Service was a very happy one.

The collapse of Acrow was a terrible shock, and the succeeding year very difficult, but the final chapter of my career was just as exciting and fulfilling as the earlier ones.

One Editor to whom I submitted a draft of these writings, commented that I had certainly led a full life in what most outsiders would regard as an unglamourous industry and then he added: "Your memoirs should be recommended reading for any A level student pondering their future career and heading aimlessly to their nearest bank, solicitors or accountancy firm". I think that he might be right. Whatever motivated me, I've had an exceptionally satisfying and enjoyable working life.

Ascension Island.

A Coles diesel-electric
S710 still in service on
the island after over 40
years.

Epilogue

The RMS St. Helena approaches the island.

The arrival of the boat is an exciting event for the local populace.

Jamestown, the island's capital.

With its main street.

Epilogue

The interior.

The coast path leading to one of the old 17th Century forts.

Epilogue

A flax mill still in operation as a "tourist attraction".

The flax gone wild which has ramped across the island.

The crane superstructure is floated in from the RMS St. Helena.

Epilogue

The "Thompson Crane" goes into action.

One of the crawler side frames arrives.

The carbody is unloaded.

The process of fitting the superstructure on to the carbody commences.

Epilogue

The cranes could not reach far enough to marry the two on the first lift. The super-structure was lowered and the mobiles re-positioned.

A critical three-crane lift.

Success at last but it was a very delicate operation.

Epilogue

Torquing down the retaining bolts.

Fitting the crawlers.

The auxiliary hoist drum goes in.

The assembly of the basic crane is complete.

Overload test.

Epilogue

The crane goes to work.

POSTSCRIPT

A MOST ENTHUSIASTIC CHARACTER

I first got to know Dick Lloyd on a press trip that he organised to the Bavarian factory of Sennebogen in the Summer of 1985. And I quickly discovered that he is one of the plant industry's characters - a most knowledgeable man with an obvious interest in construction machinery and an infectious enthusiasm for the products with which he has been involved.

What I found fascinating was how circumstances had dictated a dramatic change in his allegiance. For here was a crane and excavator salesman who had spent two thirds of his career waving the Union Jack to sell British products and then had been forced by circumstances beyond his control to make a switch to selling German machines from Bavaria.

As someone with a particular interest in historic cranes and plant, I have always enjoyed meeting up with Dick Lloyd and hearing more about his often exciting adventures whilst working for Coles, Hymac and Priestman. Now this book has thankfully recorded all of his most notable exploits for posterity.

This publication provides a unique insight into the management and sales practices of some of the former household names in the constuction equipment business. It "spills the beans" on some of the inventive ploys used to sell machinery overseas back in the sixties and seventies and it helps to explain the demise of a large chunk of Britain's crane and excavator manufacturing industry. Hopefully it will help others not to make the same mistakes.

The picture on this page provides a graphic image of the memorable personality that is Dick Lloyd. Which other Englishman would dress up in Bavarian costume to visit the Bauma show in Munich?

Wearing Bavarian attire so publicly reveals how Sennebogen had got into Dick Lloyd's blood - just as Coles, Hymac and Priestman had done in their turn in the past. How many machinery salesmen today can display his obvious allegiance to employer and product?

Nick Johnson

Editor, PHE - Plant Hire Executive, July 2005